GOODHEART-WILLCOX'S

painting and decorating encyclopedia

A complete library of professional know-how
on painting, decorating and wood finishing
in one easy-to-use volume

Edited by

William Brushwell
American Paint Journal
Staff Writer

South Holland, Ill.

THE GOODHEART-WILLCOX CO., Inc.
Publishers

INTRODUCTION

Painting and Decorating is a time-honored and highly developed art. Thus, the printed word can only be a beginning and a guide. Practice under actual working conditions with study and intelligent observation are required to convert a student into a skilled painter.

This Encyclopedia is a storehouse of practical knowledge on Painting and Decorating. It will serve as a valuable guide and reference work for the Painter, the Architect, the Builder, the Engineer and the Building Manager as well as for many others interested in paint.

This Encyclopedia includes, too, information on the all-important subjects of How to Use and Sell Color and on the Power of Paint.

Constant study and training will enable today's Painter and Decorator to develop his skill fully and to establish recognized usefulness in the community and thus to build his security.

The Publishers

CONTENTS

Almost every house has some outside wood. Houses built completely from wood are highly regarded. Proper painting and finishing not only contributes in a major way to the beauty of the home but also preserves it. By keeping out moisture and protecting the wood from rot and rust, paint helps to prevent costly repairs.

Unit 1

HISTORICAL REVIEW

It would be gratifying to be able to report in detail the exact circumstances of the first use of a colorful coating material. Unfortunately, there are no records available to provide us with this information. The discovery and first use of paint is shrouded in the mist of distant yesterdays.

Earliest Record of Painting

Paintings that were made in prehistoric times have been located on the walls of sealed caves in Italy, France, and Spain. The cave dwellers of that period (about 20,000 years ago) used three colors; yellow, red and black.

Painting shows up in early Egyptian and Babylonian records. The Egyptian Pyramids, built around 3000 B.C., used yellow, red, black, blue, green and white colors. Many phases of the life of that day were illustrated on the walls of tombs. The Egyptians also decorated such objects as pottery and mummy cases, all of which may be seen in museums.

The early Greeks developed painting into an art form. They not only decorated flat surfaces, but painted human figures and illustrated legends on walls, wood panels and vases. Many vivid colors were used to decorate their temples and houses.

The ancient Romans used stencils to paint borders on wall surfaces. They also painted stone and plaster to resemble costly marble and granite. If color cards had been available in those days, they would have shown black, green, purple, white, red, and yellow.

Early Christians used color in religious symbols and pictures of saints and martyrs on dark walls of underground catacombs. Later, when permitted to worship openly, they created colorful mosaics and murals. The Bible, incidentally mentions two mineral colors - - brown and vermilion.

Lost in the Dark Ages

In spite of the early start made with color application, the craft of the painter sank to a low ebb during the dark ages, (400-800). People of that day were indifferent to decorative surroundings.

Medieval days which followed brought a slight revival of the arts. In England, people began using bright blues and greens. Walls of churches were painted with visions of hell's fire and heaven's angles, Fig. 1-1. Soon the desire for decoration led the rich to encase the inner walls of their homes with wainscoting to imitate woven hangings and to paint cloth to imitate fine tapestry. Like most of the craftsmen of medieval Europe, the painters had their own guild of masters, journeymen and apprentices.

Fig. 1-1. Walls of English churches in Medieval days were painted with visions of hell's fire and heaven's angels.

Renaissance Revival

History records that during the 15th and 16th centuries--a period known as the Renaissance--enthusiasm for new ideas revitalized the people of Italy, Austria, France, Germany and England; invigorating architecture, sculpture and the arts. It was during this time that painters such as Michelangelo, and Leonardo da Vinci painted.

Indians Used Paint

Columbus discovered America at the end of the 15th century and a new continent, America, was introduced to the Europeans.

By the time America was discovered, most of the Indian tribes of North America used dyes and pigments to paint their bodies and to color baskets and rugs.

In the early days of this country's history, paint was a symbol of social prestige. The homes of a town's leading citizens could be recognized by their gleaming paint.

Coal Tar Dyes

The first important contribution to painting in modern times came when Sir William Henry Perkins discovered in 1856 that mauve, the first of the aniline colors, could be produced from coal tar. This discovery brought about a revolution in the dyeing industry and in the manufacture of colors. Coal-tar dyes were made in Europe, mostly in Germany, prior to 1914 - - the beginning of World War One. The war cut off shipments of these dyes. The lack of adequate dyes in the U.S. gradually brought capitalists and chemists together, and factories for making the dyes were slowly organized.

Today many pigments are produced in the U.S. synthetically.

Varnish

When liquid varnish was first used is not known, but samples of varnish have been found when old prehistoric tombs of Egypt were opened. Mummy cases, probably 2500 or more years old, finished with a pale yellow varnish, were still in a good state of preservation and may be seen in many museums throughout the world.

Thus varnishes have been used through the ages - - from prehistoric times to the present day.

Lacquer

The word "lacquer" is derived from the Hindi, "lakh," meaning "one hundred thousand - - a reference to the thousands of insects which produce "lac" or shellac on certain trees in India and Indochina.

Lacquer, made from tree sap, was used in China about 400 B.C. Japan later surpassed China in quality of lacquer finishes. Until comparatively recent times, lacquer was associated with ornamental finishes on wood or porcelain objects of art.

The Japanese type of lacquer is entirely different from the modern lacquer with which we are familiar. The lacquer in common use today is a solution of synthetic resin, nitrocellulose, in a suitable solvent to which plasticizers, resins, and pigments may have been added.

Drying Oils

Many of the drying oils used in the paint industry today have been developed in comparatively recent years.

During the early Egyptian period the dry climate of that part of the world did not serve as a stimulus for the development of durable protective coatings. Flax was cultivated by the Egyptians for its fiber, but its oil was used very little, if any, in making paints. The early Greeks and Romans employed weak glues, egg albumen and honey as binders. Pitch was used for tarring ships, and pitch and wax for protective coverings on ship bottoms.

Starting about 1850 in the U.S., linseed oil from flax became the most important drying oil for paints. Over the years, its position has declined due to the influence of a variety of other oils including soybean oil. The most important cause for the decline of usage of linseed oil, however, has been the advent of water-based paints for both inside and outside use.

Color Systems

Many systems have been devised to identify and measure color. Sir Isaac Newton in 1666 passed a beam of sunlight through a prism of clear glass and demonstrated that light consists of seven spectrum colors - - red, orange, yellow, green, blue, indigo and violet.

Since Sir Isaac's time many color systems and color theories have been advanced. Creators of the two major color systems now generally recognized, were Albert H. Munsell (1858-1918) and Wilhelm Ostwald (1853-1932).

Information on the Munsell and Ostwald systems will be found in the Unit on Color and Color Harmony.

The Paint Industry Today

The paint industry sells approximately three billion dollars worth of merchandise per year.

The paint industry today produces almost 880 million gallons of protective coatings in approximately 1500 paint factories, employing almost 60,000 workers. Anyone whose employment is related to the protective coatings industry can be proud to be contributing not only to an important part of America's economy, but also to the protection of many of the country's vital industrial, military and civilian installations, while at the same time making the country a more pleasant place to live by helping the consumer to utilize the decorative aspects of protective coatings.

Vehicle Trends

Paint, practically since ancient times, has been based on vegetable oils such as linseed oil. Combinations of linseed oil with red lead have provided yeoman's service over the years. Advancing technology, however, has affected the protective coatings industry just as it has all other technically based businesses. Thus, linseed oil has largely been replaced by other vehicles; and today we find linseed oil only in some house paints and in putty and caulking compounds. Even here its usage is declining.

The alkyds have replaced linseed oil for maintenance and industrial painting. These are resin-containing materials which are produced today to the extent of approximately one-half billion pounds per year. It may truly be said that alkyds are the workhorse of the industry, but their growth, too, has been stopped by other advances. During World War II, latex paints were introduced and these have taken over a large portion of both the inside and outside paint markets. Latex paints also are produced to the extent of approximately one-half billion pounds per year. Latex or water-based paints are also important for industrial coatings - - the paints used to finish products in a factory.

But the industry did not stop with alkyds and water-based paints. The resins and plastics which the chemist has provided find many outlets in the coatings area. Most spectacular have been the epoxy resins with their unusual degree of adhesion and their excellent resistance to solvents, chemicals, alkalis and acids. Acrylic resins and urethane resins are also becoming popular in the paint chemist's "bag of tricks."

The urethane resins are establishing themselves as floor coatings because of their excellent abrasion resistance and in other areas of specialized maintenance usage.

Vinyls, because of their highly protective character and excellent resistance to the elements, are widely used in maintenance painting.

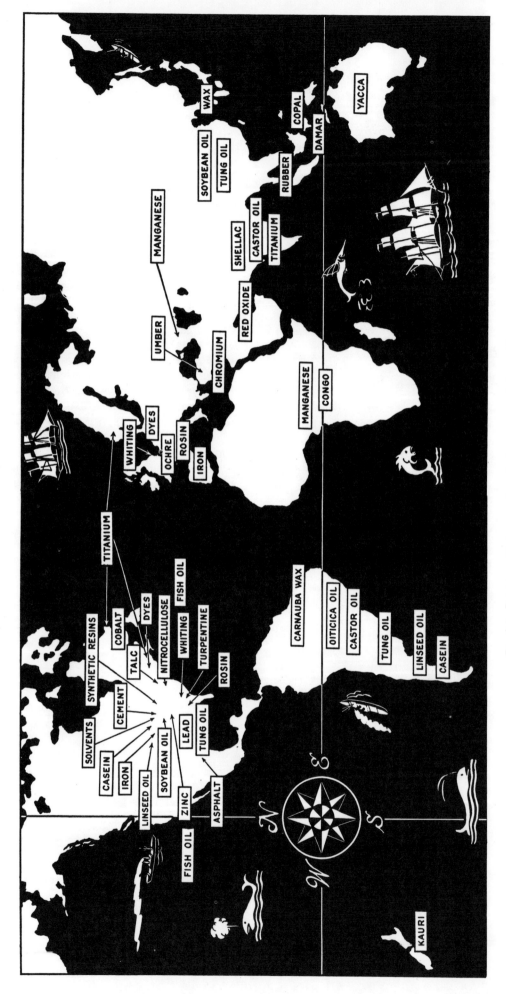

Fig. 2-1. Paint ingredients come from the four corners of the world.

Unit 2

MATERIALS USED IN PAINTING AND DECORATING

Broadly speaking, paint is an adhesive coating which is applied as a thin film to various surfaces for, among other reasons; protection, sanitation, decoration, as an aid to illumination, for the building of morale, for color coding for safety or as a fire retardant. When spread on a surface in a thin, liquid film, paint changes into a plastic solid which may be either dull or glossy.

The principal ingredients of paint are the pigments and the vehicle. The pigments may be either white or colored and of varying opacities from translucent to opaque. The vehicle is composed of a combination of binding oils or resins to which are added thinners, solvents and driers. The pigment is a powdery solid that does not dissolve in the vehicle. The binder portion is a solidifying oil or resin that causes the powdery particles to stick to each other and to the surface. Various solvents and thinners in paint make possible application by brush or spray. Driers are added to hasten the hardening of the film.

A knowledge of materials used in the paint trade is a basic requirement for the painter, who, armed with such information, is able to select and properly apply paints which most satisfactorily meet all the various needs. He will be able to follow specifications and to choose and discuss intelligently modern day paints and painting materials.

Obtaining Paint Materials

The materials from which the products of the paint industry are made come from many parts of the animal, mineral and vegetable kingdoms, Fig. 2-1. They come from every part of the globe and from every nook and cranny of the earth. Information on where and how paint products are obtained will be found in the sections of this book where these products are described in detail.

Pigments

An essential ingredient of an opaque coating is the pigment. Pigments consist of fine solid particles insoluble in the liquid portion of the paint. Pigments may be white or colored, opaque or translucent. Metallic pigments are a special type of opaque pigment consisting of metal in powder or flake form. Colored materials that dissolve in the liquid portion are considered dyes rather than pigments.

White pigments and colored pigments are used to provide opacity and color to the paint. Opacity is the property of a paint that determines its covering and hiding power. Translucent pigments are called extender or inert pigment. Generally, these pigments do not contribute appreciably to the opacity of the paint, but are used to contribute other properties. Thus, in primers, they provide "tooth" to help adhesion of subsequent coats; their addition also serves to control gloss or flatness of paints. In low quality paints, excessive amounts of inerts may be used to replace more expensive ingredients.

Pigments must be considered as materials with definite physical and chemical properties which define how they will perform. Thus, paint pigments are affected by the binder and solvent portions of the vehicle, by the reaction products of the drying process, by the surface painted, and by the exterior environment to which the paint film is subjected. Environmental factors include rain, dew and moisture of various types, heat and ultraviolet radiation from the sun and other sources, gases and fumes from industry and from decomposition of organic matter, and the effect of microorganisms on the paint itself.

Pigments range in composition from pure chemical elements to complicated organic and inorganic compounds. Metallic pigments are small particles or flakes of pure elements such as aluminum or zinc. Most pigments, however, are more complicated in structure, consisting of two or more elements combined to form a chemical compound. These compounds are roughly divided into two different classes - - organic and inorganic.

The inorganic pigments range from comparatively simple oxides of metals such as iron, zinc or chromium oxides to quite complex combinations of elements such as are found in ultramarine blue. All common white pigments and extenders are inorganic.

Organic pigments are generally much more complex chemically than the inorganic pigments. Their composition is based on the element carbon - - which by itself is our most important black pigment - - in combination with hydrogen, oxygen, sulfur and nitrogen. The raw materials for the organic pigments come mainly from coal tar and petroleum. The addition of metals to these organic compounds provides a broad spectrum of colors. For instance, copper phthalocyanine, a beautiful blue pigment owes its rich, wonderful color to one atom of copper. Lithol red is a pale orange red color with sodium, a rich red with barium, and a deep red with calcium.

A thorough knowledge of pigment chemistry is not necessary for the layman, the practitioner in the paint trade, the architect, or the specifier; but a few basic facts about these compounds may prove of practical use. Most of the organic pigments are not as permanent as the inorganic metallic salts. Being of very complicated structure they are more vulnerable to attack from ultraviolet rays of the sun and heat and from chemical attack from within or without the paint structure.

We are interested in the physical properties of paint pigments because these properties affect the structure of the paint, Fig. 2-2. There is an optimum range of sizes to which pigment particles should be ground to form mechanical bonds within the film. A study of a stone rubble wall will show why this is important. The wall may be made of large stones. In between, smaller stones are required to fill in spaces. This example is not completely adequate, however, for whereas the surface of the stone wall is rough, the pigment particles in the paint must contribute to a smooth surface and to the covering of the surface as completely as possible. This means that the pigment must be ground very fine. Pigments are ground finest for enamel, most coarsely for wall flats. The shape of the particles is interesting for the same reason. Each pigment differs in hardness which affects the final film. The specific gravity of a pigment is interesting to design engineers who are charged with the responsibility of specifying paint for large bridges or building structures where weight is a vital engineering factor.

Other properties of pigments important to the paint maker are wettability, oil absorption, and reactivity. The wettability of a pigment determines the ease with which it may be incorporated into a paint. The oil absorption is related to the amount of pigment that may be incorporated into a paint of normal consistency or viscosity. The reactivity is the tendency of the pigment to enter into a reaction with the vehicle components to form soaps which affect the film properties. The importance of brightness and opacity is obvious.

The painter is vitally interested in the various color pigments employed to mix with the basic whites to yield the myriads of tints required for various jobs. He is interested also in properties of permanence, tinting strength, cost, and ease of use.

Pigments will be discussed under the following headings:

    White pigments
    Extender or Inert pigments
    Color pigments
      Earth pigments
      Yellow pigments (includes orange)
      Blue pigments
      Red pigments (includes purple)
      Green pigments
      Black pigments
    Metal primers
    Metallic pigments

White Pigments

White is a widely used color and is the basis for the popular pastel colors. Thus, the white pigments are of great importance to the industry. In recent years, titanium dioxide has overshadowed all other white pigments in importance.

White pigments may be classified as reactive and nonreactive. In the nonreactive category are the rutile and anatase forms of titanium dioxide. Reactivity simply refers to whether the pigment can neutralize the acids which form in oil-containing films when these weather. Obviously, the nonreactive pigments do not do this.

The rutile form of titanium dioxide is nonchalking. Thus, this pigment is valuable for exterior paints where a high degree of weather

cate white lead which is probably the most widely used type of white lead pigment; basic carbonate white lead which is still used for outside paints but which chalks rather severely; basic sulfate white lead which is generally considered inferior to the basic carbonate because it increases film weathering; zinc oxide, particularly in the acicular form; and leaded zinc oxide which is a combination of basic sulfate white lead and zinc oxide and is a good, low-cost pigment.

	Sp. Gr.	Oil Absorp.*	Refract. Index	Particle Size	Hiding Power++	Tinting Power
Titanium Dioxide Anatase	3.9	21-27	2.55	0.3 micron	115	1200-1300
Titanium Dioxide Rutile	4.2	21-27	2.72	0.3 micron	appr.145 +	1500-1650
Titanium Calcium 30 Percent	3.25	21-23	1.98	- -	57	600
Titanium Calcium 50 Percent	3.47	20	- -	- -	82	880
Zinc Oxide	5.6	- -	2.08	0.2-0.3	20	210
35 Percent Leaded Zinc Oxide	5.85	- -	- -	- -	- -	- -
Zinc Sulphide	4.0	- -	2.37	0.2-0.3	58	640
Basic Carbonate of White Lead	6.7-6.8	8-15	1.94 to 2.09	0.9-2.3	15	120-160
Basic Silicate of White Lead	4.0	15	1.83	- -	12	80
Basic White Lead Sulphate	6.3-6.4	10-14	1.93 to 2.02	1.3-1.4	13-16	120-150
Lithopone	4.3	- -	1.84	- -	27	280
Antimony Trioxide	5.73	- -	2.20	- -	20	- -
Calcium Carbonate (Whiting)	2.71	15.75 (varies)	1.48 to 1.65	varies	- -	- -
Barium Sulphate (Barytes)	4.48	6.0	1.64	2.0	- -	- -
Barium Carbonate	4.29-4.35	- -	1.53 to 1.67	- -	- -	- -
Aluminum Silicate	2.60	36.0	1.56	0.2-.1	- -	- -
Magnesium Silicate	2.85	27.0	1.59	.5	- -	- -
Silica	2.6	25.0	1.55	.2-.5	- -	- -
Diatomaceous Earth	1.95-2.35	50-300	1.4-1.5	4.-.1	- -	- -
Mica	2.76-3.0	47.5	1.59	4.-.1	- -	- -
Calcium Sulphate	2.95	25.2 (50. for precipitates)	1.59	10.-.05	- -	- -
Aluminum Hydroxide	2.42	- -	1.5	- -	- -	- -

* Lbs. of oil per 100 lbs. of pigment.
** Sq. ft. over black per lb. of pigment with sufficient oil to make workable.

Fig. 2-2. Comparison of pigment properties.

resistance is required. The anatase form, on the other hand, does chalk and is utilized where controlled film chalking in exterior paints is desired to achieve a self-cleaning effect.

Zinc sulfide and lithopone are also nonreactive white pigments but are not as widely used because they are much less resistant to weathering and are lower in hiding power than titanium dioxide.

The reactive pigments, as indicated above, are those which react with the acids which form when oil-containing vehicles decompose during weathering. The neutralization of the acids extends the life of the paint film. The most important reactive white pigments are basic sili-

Basic silicate white lead may also be combined with the zinc oxide to obtain a pigment which neutralizes film acids and increases film toughness and hardness.

Finally, there are included in the category of white pigments the extender pigments which reduce cost and which contribute to other properties as well, as will be discussed in detail in other Units.

Titanium Dioxide (TiO₂)

Titanium dioxide, whose use in paints started at the end of World War I, is refined from ilmenite, a black mineral composed of titanium, iron and oxygen.

In the original process, the ore, ground to a fine powder and concentrated to remove sand and other impurities, is dissolved in sulfuric acid. Iron and other impurities are then removed from the solution, and the titanium dioxide is precipitated, filtered, washed to purify it, further dried, and calcined (heated to a red heat). It is then carefully ground to the proper fineness for use as a pigment.

There are other processes now used for the manufacture of titanium pigments, the most prominent of which is the "chloride" process. Essentially the same types of pigment result from both processes.

Titanium pigment is chemically inactive and is not affected by dilute acids, or by heat or light. It is used extensively in both interior and exterior finishes.

Titanium dioxide comes in two different crystalline forms, rutile, the newer form, and anatase, the older form. The rutile form has 25 to 30 percent greater hiding power than the anatase form, and is slightly heavier per gallon. It is by far the most widely used.

The anatase type of titanium dioxide comes in chalking and chalk resistant forms. In the chalking form it is used mostly in white house paints where it erodes slowly to provide a self-cleaning action. Only slight tinting of these paints is practical. Moderate to deep tones must not be made of the "self-cleaning" paint, because they would show streakiness on chalking. Paints of this type are usually labeled with a warning not to make deep tints from them.

Titanium dioxide is nonreactive with drying oils and thus it does not contribute to fast drying. Also, it imparts to paint a soft film, for which reason it is generally used with other pigments.

The titanium dioxide pigments are widely used in modern paints because of their great hiding power and tint strength. The rutile form is by far the more important but, as indicated above, the anatase form is useful where controlled chalking for self-cleaning paints is desirable. Chalking is, however, a disadvantage in dark colored paints because it leads to the appearance of fading and streaking. With whites or very light colored house paints, on the other hand, chalking provides a valuable means for providing a renewable surface.

The chemical inertness of the titanium dioxide pigments leads to paints which are quite stable on storage.

Titanium Calcium Pigments

The original titanium pigments for the manufacture of paints were the anatase type containing barium sulfate or calcium sulfate. Because its hiding power is twice as great, titanium-calcium soon replaced lithopone as the major pigment for interior paints. At that time titanium-barium was also used for exterior paints, but being more expensive, it was not popular for interior finishes. With the advent of the modern rutile type of titanium-calcium pigments, which have about 25 percent more hiding power than the corresponding anatase type, the latter eventually became obsolete.

At present, there are available titanium-calcium pigments in two strengths, the most common comprising 30 percent rutile titanium dioxide combined with 70 percent calcium sulfate. The other consists of 50 percent of each material. The use of other extenders for titanium dioxide has been abandoned. These pigments are used in most of the interior solvent type paints, along with other extender pigments, and are at times fortified with pure titanium dioxide. The price relationship of the extended pigment to the pure pigment is such that it is generally more economical to use the extended pigment where it is technically suitable.

Titanium-calcium pigments are now finding use in exterior house paints, porch and deck enamels and other exterior paints for which suitable formulas are being developed.

White Lead (Basic Lead Carbonate) $(2PbCO_3 \cdot Pb(OH)_2)$

White lead is one of the oldest known white pigments for there is mention of its use as early as 400 B.C.

It is made from metallic lead by several processes. In one of the most common methods, the metal is first cast into plates. These plates or "buckles," as they are called, are arranged in earthen jars containing a weak solution of acetic acid (vinegar). The jars are buried in spent tanbark which ferments, producing carbon dioxide and heat. Heat turns the acetic acid to vapor. The vapor and the carbon dioxide act on the lead, changing it into basic lead carbonate, a white powder. About three months time is required to complete this so-called Dutch process. There are many other processes for making white lead pigment.

The white powder is ground, and when mixed

with linseed oil forms the white lead used in the paint industry.

White lead is used by painters who formulate their own paints for commercial and industrial maintenance work. Because of the hazard of lead poisoning, lead paints for household use (those containing more than 0.5 percent lead after December 31, 1972, and 0.06 percent after December 31, 1973) are banned from interstate commerce. Some local restrictions have earlier deadlines and extend to commercial buildings easily accessible to children such as day care centers and schools. Some extensions include industrial product finishing of toys and furniture, and equipment exposed to children. White lead, as well as the lead pigments, Fig. 2-2, lead color pigments (i.e., yellow and orange chromates, and molybdate orange), and lead primer pigments (red lead oxide, lead suboxide, blue lead, basic lead silico chromate, calcium plumbate, and many others) are typical of the banned paints.

Basic Lead Silicate ($2PbO \cdot SO_3 + 2PbO \cdot SiO_2$)

Basic lead silicate which is also called basic silicate of white lead is a composite of monobasic lead sulfate and basic lead silicate, both of which are bonded to a silica core. The pigment is reactive with acids which form during weathering of an oil-based paint. It demonstrates good durability and has an economic advantage because of its low specific gravity and high bulking value. It is used largely in mixed pigment formulations where it contributes as much external durability as basic lead carbonate.

Basic Lead Sulphate ($2PbSO_4 \cdot PbO$)

Basic lead sulphate, also called "sublimated white lead," has approximately the same hiding power as basic lead carbonate, and in most cases it may be substituted for lead carbonate. Lead sulphate is usually considered slightly less durable than lead carbonate and is also less expensive. Most of it is used in conjunction with other pigments in formulating ready mixed paints for exteriors.

Zinc Oxide (ZnO)

Zinc, like many other metals, is mined as an ore, the most common of which is zinc blende, a form of zinc sulfide. Zinc is used in paint pigments in the form of the oxide, the sulfide and as zinc dust.

Zinc oxide is made by oxidizing zinc metal by heating in the presence of air (the French process) or directly from the ore by heating with coke with an excess of air (the American process).

Zinc oxide is the most important of the zinc pigments. It is nontoxic and nonirritant. Zinc oxide reacts with paint oils to form soaps that tend to make the paint film undesirably hard and inelastic. However, when used in proper amounts in combination with other pigments, such as white lead, titanium dioxide and extenders in exterior paints, zinc oxide performs several important functions. It controls chalking; promotes "self-cleaning" of paints through chalking and the washing action of rain; controls mildew, which is both unsightly and destructive to the paint film; promotes color retention in tinted paints; contributes to the hiding power of the paint; and, because it is relatively opaque to ultraviolet light, it protects the paint film from the destructive effects of radiation. Because of the water sensitivity of the zinc soaps, the presence of zinc oxide in exterior wood primers tends to promote blistering under conditions of high humidity. Primers that are "zinc free" should be used for exterior painting of wood.

Interestingly enough, however, modern formulation has made possible the incorporation of zinc oxide into latex paints where it contributes the same properties as it does in oil-based paints.

Zinc oxide was once an important pigment in interior enamels. Because of its limited hiding power and tendency to cause brittle paint films, it has largely been replaced by titanium dioxide. It is used in small amounts in modern alkyd resin enamels because it helps in the retention of whiteness. A special fine particle size material is used for this purpose.

Zinc oxide has other functional properties in paint. Its presence tends to impart a better drying quality and to eliminate surface tackiness. Because it tends to react with the vehicle, it can be used to impart a somewhat higher viscosity, a "puffy" body and better brushing to paints.

Zinc oxide is used in many paints because its basic nature enables it to neutralize acids, thus inhibiting corrosion. It is used with zinc dust in primers for water tanks and for other applications requiring maximum corrosion resistance.

Leaded Zinc Oxide (ZnO + PbSO$_4$ + PbO·PbSO$_4$)

Leaded zinc oxide is a combination of basic lead sulphate and zinc oxide. This pigment, made by co-fuming the two ores, is used in formulating present day exterior house paints. They are combined in proportions of 5 to 50 percent lead, 35 percent being most common.

Basic Lead Silicate

Basic lead silicate is available today as a composite of basic lead silicate and monobasic lead sulfate bonded to a silica core. It has the same paint-making characteristics as basic carbonate white lead and provides an economical means of attaining these desirable properties.

Zinc Sulfide (ZnS)

Zinc sulfide is a moderately high hiding pigment but is little used today. Zinc sulfide is the component of lithopone that accounts for the hiding power of that formerly used material.

Lithopone (ZnS + BaSO$_4$)

Lithopone is made by reacting zinc sulfate with barium sulfide in solution to precipitate zinc sulfide and barium sulfate, which is then dried and ground to pigment fineness. In co-precipitating these materials, better color and hiding power are obtained than would result if the dry materials were mixed in the same proportion. Prior to the common usage of titanium pigments, lithopone was the standard white pigment for most interior finishes. It also was useful in latex paints where it improved film characteristics and enhanced the washability of the paint. Lithopone, however, is practically a pigment of the past, having been replaced almost entirely in modern paints by titanium dioxide.

Antimony Oxide (Sb$_2$O$_3$)

Antimony Oxide is a nontoxic white pigment of about the same hiding power as lithopone. Its chief use in the coatings industry is in the manufacture of fire retardant paints where it is used in combination with chlorinated materials and calcium carbonate. The Navy uses paint of this type on interior surfaces of its ships.

Extender Pigments

Extender pigments--pigments which provide very little or no hiding power - - are used to stabilize pigment suspension, to improve leveling, control flow, build adequate film, lower gloss and influence opacity. They affect film properties such as cleanability, scrubability and appearance. A combination of several extender pigments may be used to obtain a combination of desirable properties.

The selection and addition of extender pigments is ordinarily handled by the paint manufacturer, but a general knowledge of the extenders will be helpful to the painter in intelligently selecting and using modern paint products. The words "extender" and "inert" are commonly used in the trade to label the white and colorless pigments of low refractive index, but these are misnomers because many of this group are chemically active in paint vehicles. This activity often contributes to their function in altering paint formulas.

All extender pigments have refractive indexes of 1.45 to 1.70, values which are near to the refractive indexes of oils and varnishes (opaque pigment refractive indexes range from 1.94 to 2.70).

Since the measure of opacity for a pigment is largely due to the difference between the refractive index of the vehicle and the refractive index of the pigment, even low refractive index pigments like whiting (R.I. = 1.60) will have opacity in glue or casein (R.I. = 1.3), but whiting in oil (R.I. = 1.5) is nearly colorless. This follows since subtraction of 1.3 from 1.6 gives .3, which is a measure of opacity for a typical calcimine. But 1.5 from 1.6 equals .1, a smaller number, indicating less opacity. Whiting in oil is a milky translucent yellowish color with no hiding power.

Calcium Carbonate (Ca CO$_3$)

Calcium carbonate or whiting is derived from both natural and synthetic sources. In nature, the material occurs as calcite, chalk, dolomite and other forms. The natural deposit is converted to pigment by crushing and grinding to pigment size. The grinding may be done dry or wet with water. The synthetic material is made by treating lime with either sodium carbonate or carbon dioxide. The precipitated calcium carbonate is washed, separated into desired sizes, and dried.

Whiting is quite low in price. It is available in many grades, suitable for a wide variety of paints. It is used to control gloss, to produce flat paints, to provide non-penetration in primers, and to control flow of paints. Calcium carbonate is used extensively in interior paints and, recently it has been found that the coarser grades of this pigment contribute to the durability and tint retention of exterior paints.

In addition to its use in paints, whiting has been used for many years in combination with linseed oil in the manufacture of putty.

Barium Sulphate (Barytes) (BaSO$_4$)

Barium is a chemical element of the alkaline-earth group. The pigment is made from the mineral barite by grinding it under water.

Barium sulphate is unaffected by acids and alkalies; it provides good durability and has minimum effect on paint viscosity. Two of its disadvantages are that it has a marked tendency to settle and it is high in cost in comparison with several other extenders.

Some manufacturers who feel that a good paint must be heavy, add barytes to the paint, in order to provide the necessary weight.

Blanc fixe is a precipitated barium sulphate of great fineness and has all the same properties with the exception of particle size. It is used to make titanium-barium pigments.

China Clay (Aluminum Silicate) (Kaolin) (A1$_2$O$_3$·2SiO$_2$·2H$_2$O)

This is a comparatively inert (chemically inactive) pigment which consists mostly of hydrated aluminum silicate. China clay has a tendency to impart to paint the quality of easy brushing. It is used to some extent in exterior finishes and in considerable quantities in water-thinned paints.

New, very finely manufactured kaolin is now being used to some extent in the manufacture of medium to high gloss enamels. The oil absorption rate varies according to the particle size. Because China clay is fairly inert it does not affect the vehicle. It does not change the composition of the paint chemically except to add a very fine soft textural condition, and it is also used to prevent settling of pigments in oil and varnish vehicles. It adds body because it is a very light, high bulking material. Its main use is in the manufacture of primers, undercoats and paints where a low pigment content is required but where the consistency of the material must be high for good brushing qualities. It has little or no opacity when used in oils or varnishes, but in water and emulsion type paints China clay offers good covering qualities and is used extensively with the latter.

Magnesium Silicate (Talc) H$_2$Mg$_3$(SiO$_3$)$_4$)

Talc is probably the most popular extender pigment for exterior paints. Usually in a fibrous form, it is also available in platy and nodular forms. This pigment combines good durability and low cost. It has excellent suspension properties tending to prevent caking and settling in paints. Because of this property and other desirable characteristics such as high bulking value, low cost, and low sheen, it is also a popular pigment in interior finishes. It finds considerable use in primers for metal where its fibrous form is of value in reinforcing the paint film. Originally a hard grinding pigment, it is now available in easy grinding forms.

Silica (SiO$_2$)

Silica, made from quartz rock is an inert transparent pigment, and is hard and highly resistant to acids, alkalies, heat and light. In the

When ladder is being used on uneven surface, the low leg should be blocked so both legs are level.

paint industry, it is used in two forms. In the crystalline form, it is comparatively low in cost, but settles badly. In the other form (diatomaceous) it is frequently used in coatings to lower the gloss. A type of flat varnish is made by adding silica to varnish to lower the sheen. It is also the basic pigment in fillers for open-pore hardwoods.

Silica is found in two basic forms. One form, which is very hard, comes from quartz. The other comes from the decomposition of chert, a flint-like rock, or from the decomposition of siliceous limestone. Various types of silica impart "tooth" to the finished film and, accordingly, are useful in undercoats and primers. They also improve brushing and help succesive coats to adhere. Tripoli is softer and finer than quartz.

There is a definite health hazard in the use of silica if its dust is inhaled over a long period of time.

The diatomaceous form of silica is the residual matter of skeletons of countless numbers of minute marine organisms. There are approximately ten thousand different main skeletal types of these organisms which make unusual and beautiful patterns when seen under the microscope. Because of the many different shapes of all of the particles involved, diatomaceous earth offers a fine "building" pigment. Just as sand and rock is mixed with cement to make good concrete, so many different shapes and sizes of pigment particles will add to the strength of the final paint film. Silica in this form is extremely porous and therefore contributes to a high oil absorption capacity. Because of its open skeletal structure it is approximately eighty-five percent open space by volume. As the paint is ground, these spaces are broken down and the oil absorption is lowered radically. When flatness or lack of gloss is desired, diatomaceous particles of silica are usually selected to add to the film. The tiny skeletal structures protrude from the surface sufficiently to scatter light rays, thereby diffusing light and cutting down gloss. Silica also contributes to a film porosity which allows water vapor to pass through a paint film creating resistance to blistering and preventing the loss of adhesion. This is particularly good for exterior masonry, porch and step and trim paints. It also has excellent filling and sanding properties.

Quite unlike the quartz and tripoli forms of silica, diatomaceous earth possesses very good suspension properties and for this reason is used even in fine enamels where gloss must be reduced. One of the most important uses for silica, as already indicated, is to furnish "tooth" to primers to help them bond to metal and to subsequent coats.

Mica ($K_2O_3 \cdot Al_2O_3 \cdot 6SiO_2 2H_2O$)

Mica is composed of silicates of aluminum and potassium. It occurs in nature in the form of stacks of very thin sheets or plates which are highly transparent and have been used for windows in stoves. When finely ground to pigment size, the thin sheet form is maintained and the pigment is composed of tiny platelets. It serves as a reinforcing pigment in exterior paints where it tends to reduce checking and cracking because of the strengthening effect of the overlapping plates. Mica is opaque to ultraviolet light and thus protects the binder from the destructive effects of ultraviolet radiation. It is chemically inert and heat resistant and is compatible with virtually all paint components.

The tendency to form an overlapping laminar structure aids in sealing porous surfaces for subsequent coats of paint. Mica is also a good pigment to use over paints that have a tendency to bleed. Bleeding is an undesirable situation which is caused because the color from the bleeding paint is soluble in dried paint vehicles and thus works its way up through the surface. Added to bronze and aluminum paints, mica contributes to brightness, good leafing and non-tarnishing. It has been found to be an excellent pigment for modern latex emulsion vehicles.

Calcium Sulfate ($CaSO_4 \cdot 2H_2O$)

Calcium sulfate is an inert pigment that occurs in nature as gypsum, alabaster or selenite. It contributes to sealing qualities and is used in sealers for porous surfaces.

If the original material, $CaSO_4 \cdot 2H_2O$, is heated under controlled conditions, it becomes $CaSO_4 \cdot 1/2H_2O$ which is plaster of Paris. Plaster of Paris, when in contact with water, rehydrates to the original gypsum composition and sets to a hard material. This property is used in making patching plasters and materials for molds useful to dentists. If completely dehydrated, the gypsum becomes $CaSO_4$ which is the "anhydrite" used in the manufacture of titanium-calcium pigments.

Materials

Magnesium Carbonate (Magnesite) (Mg CO₃)

Magnesium carbonate is not used extensively as an extender pigment. It does have the property of causing a paint to become somewhat "fluffy" when used in small amounts which improves application properties. Magnesite occurs in nature and is also manufactured.

Magnesium Oxide (MgO)

Magnesium oxide is not used as a paint pigment to any great extent. It is mentioned here mainly because freshly prepared magnesium oxide is the brightest, whitest material known and is used in the dry form as a standard of whiteness. It should be noted that there is little relationship between the dry whiteness or brightness of a pigment and its hiding value or opacity when mixed with a vehicle.

Aluminum Hydrate

Aluminum hydrate is used mainly as a base upon which to precipitate dyestuffs to convert them to pigments. Such precipitated pigments are termed "lakes" and are different from extended pigments in that the color is inseparable from the base.

Slate Flour

Slate flour is widely used as a filler in asphalt mixtures in roofing mastics and in some other types of paint. Slate is a dense, fine-grained rock, mostly mica and quartz, that splits easily into thin opaque layers.

Caution in Use of Extenders

Extender pigments are less costly than most hiding pigments and are sometimes used in excessive quantities in cheap paints. Too much chalking and poor durability can be expected from paints containing EXCESSIVE QUANTITIES OF and IMPROPERLY USED extenders. In states without pure paint laws, where the formula of a paint is unknown, the buyer must rely on the good name of the manufacturer.

Color Pigments

Colored pigments are those which are useful in the formulation of colored paints such as yellow, red, purple, blue and green formulations. Although they may be used alone, they normally are used in combination with white pigments. Colored pigments impart the appearance of color because they absorb a portion of light which falls upon them and reflect or return to the eye the remaining light waves of the spectrum. It is these light waves, in combination with the retina in the eye, which create what we normally term color.

So many color pigments are available and the field is so vast that it is necessary for us to limit our discussion here to the more important ones. They are usually grouped into 1-Earth colors, 2-Precipitated pigments, 3-Fire process pigments, and 4-Fume process pigments.

Earth Pigments

The earth pigments occur as natural deposits which are mined like other minerals. Thus they are frequently termed natural or mineral pigments or colors. Some examples of the earth pigments are the ochres, red iron oxides, siennas and umbers. These pigments are quite stable, being unaffected by alkalies, heat, moisture, and most vehicles.

Iron oxide is found widely distributed, usually in combination with alumina, silica, calcium compounds, magnesium compounds, manganese compounds and water. Iron pigments range from yellow through red, reddish brown, or brown to black, depending on the particular oxide composition.

A large proportion of the iron oxide pigments used today are made synthetically and are generally superior to the naturally occurring pigments. However, no synthetic replacement for the siennas or umbers, either raw or burnt, are available.

The brightest natural red iron oxide, a hematite ore, is found near the southern shores of the Caspian Sea, and the refined pigment made from this ore is known as Persian Gulf Oxide.

Deposits of iron manganese ores having a rich brownish green hue were discovered on the island of Cyprus and the product is marketed under the name of Turkey Umber. Siennas are named for the Italian town of Sienna where the bright yellow oxide is found.

The earth colors have long been used in the paint trade for tinting to pastel colors. Thus, yellow ochre or raw sienna imparts an ivory color. Burnt umber yields beige. Pinks result from red oxides, whereas burnt sienna provides a flesh color. When the earth colors are combined, still other tints result.

An interesting modern use for magnetic iron oxide pigment is in the manufacture of recording tape. The magnetic pigments are formulated into a special coating which is applied to a plastic ribbon. The key to the recording process is the magnetic nature of the pigment.

Precipitated Colors

Modern chemistry has developed a large number of pigments for use in paints, plastics and other materials. Because most of these pigments are precipitated from solution, they are sometimes termed precipitated colors to differentiate them from the natural or earth colors and the few colors that are made by fusion or fuming.

Precipitated colors may be organic or inorganic in nature. Chrome yellows and iron blue are examples of inorganic precipitated colors. Toluidine red and Phthalocyanine blue and green are examples of the many organic colors now available.

The lake pigments are a special type of precipitated color in which a normally soluble dye is precipitated on a base of aluminum hydrate or other suitable material.

Fire Process Colors

The fire process pigments are made by fusion or calcining in a furnace. Examples are ultramarine blue, chromium oxide, burnt umber and sienna, and animal or bone blacks.

Fume Process Colors

Pigments made by the fume process are lamp black and carbon black. Lamp black is mainly useful for its tinting quality and strength, while carbon black in its several forms is noted for its jet mass tone.

Yellow Ochre

Yellow ochre is an iron hydroxide which means that it is composed of iron (Fe) oxygen (O) and water (H_2O) = ($Fe_3 O_2 \cdot H_2O$) or ($Fe_3 O_2 \cdot 3H_2O$). There are many variations of these formulas. It is permanent to alkalies and mild acids and is

generally a pigment which, with oils, makes a soft film able to chalk rapidly. Yellow ochre provides a delightful cream tint and varies from semi-opaque with a calcium oxide base to semi-transparent with clay or silica bases.

Raw Sienna

Raw sienna is a form of ochre with an exceptionally transparent quality. It is yellow orange like yellow ochre but is grayer and redder.

When the ochres and siennas are calcined (heated above 350 deg. C) they lose their crystallized water molecules and become red ochre and burnt sienna. Red ochre is seldom used.

Burnt Sienna

Burnt sienna is a standard color pigment in the practical painter's pallette, because it is one of the very permanent low cost colors. It is a deep burnt orange capable of pale "apricot" tints, medium terra cotta tones, and rich grayed orange shades. It is very useful as an oil stain and glaze color, also, because of its transparency.

Raw Umber

Raw umber is an iron hydroxide with the addition of manganese oxide to its chemical structure. In mass tone it is near black and is a very good drier. Tints of raw umber are near gray with a definite yellow cast. It is more opaque than burnt umber.

Burnt Umber

Burnt umber is calcined or dehydrated raw umber. The dehydration has changed its ability to absorb light. Thus it becomes an orange color, losing some opacity and drying quality. Burnt umber tints white to the beiges and tans. It is an universally accepted pigment for brown oil stains.

Vandyke Brown

Vandyke brown is an organic composition found in earth deposits. It consists of decomposed vegetable matter that has almost reached the coal stage. Vandyke brown is weak in hiding power compared to umber and sienna and is transparent and fugitive. It is mainly useful as a stain and glaze.

Yellow Pigments

CHROME YELLOW: An important inorganic yellow pigment. The color may vary from a dark orange to a lemon yellow. This pigment provides good hiding power and is considered to be sufficiently permanent for most practical purposes. Chrome yellow is precipitated from solutions of lead acetate and potassium bichromate. All are strong driers and contribute softness to film structure. All but the very deep basic chrome orange darken on prolonged exposure to light. They will also turn grayish or brownish when sulphurous gases penetrate the film to the pigment.

Molybdate chrome orange is less grayed than basic lead chromates and is roughly five times as strong tinctorially.

The light, almost greenish shades of yellow contain sulphates and phosphates.

Zinc yellow is very similar to the light chrome yellows but has a complex and varying formula containing potassium, zinc, chromate, and sulphate. It is less opaque and weaker tinctorially.

CADMIUM YELLOW: This is a cadmium sulphide prepared by precipitation from an acid solution of a soluble cadmium salt with hydrogen sulphide gas. Cadmium yellow is fast to alkalies but not to acids.

Cadmium yellows are used mainly by artists for painted decorations, murals, and motifs of ornament. They are permanent to light and alkali but will dissolve to a colorless pigment if attacked by acids. Cadmium yellows vary in tone from a pale pure yellow to orange.

HANSA YELLOW: An organic yellow of the insoluble azo group. It is non-bleeding in oil and water but bleeds in coal tar solvents such as benzol, toluol and xylol. Hansa yellow pigment is alkali-resistant, making it particularly suitable for tinting casein and other water thinned paints where alkalies are present.

ZINC YELLOW: See also section on Metal Priming Pigments, page 25.

Blue Pigments

COBALT BLUE: Cobalt blue is a very stable greenish blue. It is insoluble in most acids and alkalies and is unaffected by sunlight. Cobalt blue is made by heating cobalt oxide and aluminum hydrate. Most "cobalt" sold to the paint trade is a light grayed ultramarine. True cobalt oxide costs many times the price of ultramarine.

ULTRAMARINE BLUE: A blue pigment which is absolutely alkali proof but may be affected by acids. It is made by heating in closed fire clay crucibles a mixture of China clay, sodium carbonate, sulphur and carbon. Although none of the materials is blue, the process yields a beautiful deep blue. It is not entirely permanent to light and has a purple blue cast in its deeper tones becoming more blue in lighter tints. This pigment is separated into many grades or qualities, the very deepest, bluest and finest particle size being the most desirable. Least desirable is the pale grayish coarse type.

Ultramarine has high oil absorption and low tinting strength. It exhibits a stringy viscous nature if stored too long and is difficult to disperse as tinting color until stirred and thinned.

IRON BLUE: The iron blues, variously known as Prussian, Chinese and milori blues are complex ferric ferrocyanides. Iron blues are sensitive to alkali and cannot be used where alkali resistance is a factor. They have excellent durability in full shade, but show a tendency to bronze on outdoor exposure. This tendency is greatest for the milori and Chinese blues and least for Prussian blue. Color retention is excellent in dark or medium shades but decreases markedly in light tints. All have good resistance to water, acid and organic media.

Chinese blue is characterized by its clean and jet mass tone and green tint. Milori blues are somewhat redder in tint and are favored because of their softer texture. Prussian blue is reddest in tint and finds its greatest use in the toning of black enamels.

The iron blues have the peculiar property of fading in color in the liquid paint due to chemical reduction of the iron by the paint vehicle. The reaction is reversed by the oxygen of the air when the paint is used and the color returns in a day or two.

PHTHALOCYANINE BLUE: A synthetic organic blue pigment which is insoluble in alkalies and in most acids as well as organic solvents. It is outstanding in fade resistance, making it ideal for use in exterior finishes and for tinting. Phthalocyanine blue is very strong color, having about twice the strength of Prussian blue and about twenty times the strength of ultramarine blue. It was commercially introduced in 1936 under a number of trade names. Almost all the yellow and red in the spectrum is absorbed leaving only blue and green bands reflected. It will therefore mix with yellows or reds to form ungrayed greens or purples.

Red Pigments

MERCADIUM RED: A combination of the sulphides of cadmium and the sulphides of mercury. Six basic reds, three quite clean and bright from red-orange through red and three black or maroon tones are available. These were developed to take the place of more expensive cadmium sulfo-selenide reds. Mercadium is less expensive, cleaner, and more brilliant than cadmiums. It is highly heat resistant, permanent, alkali resistant and nonbleeding.

TUSCAN RED: This pigment is an iron oxide brightened with one of the more permanent organic pigments. The result is a grayed purplish red. This "brightening" is accomplished by precipitating the organic lake red on the red oxide base, thereby mechanically linking the molecules of each, a process that cannot be duplicated by merely mixing the two together.

PARA RED: This is a brilliant red, which is opaque and nonfading in masstone. Its tints are not permanent and it bleeds or penetrates into coats applied over it. Para red is a coal tar product. It is used in masstone (unadulterated) for enamels, printing inks, and sign painters' colors.

TOLUIDINE RED: A brilliant nonbleeding red pigment made from coal tar products. It is used extensively in the automotive industry and in some of the better grades of exterior finishes. It is also the standard tinting pure red of the architectural paint trade and is known as Bulletin or Stayred. Its tints generally tend toward bluish pink, but the masstone of toluidine is pure red. It is oily, glossy, and a poor drier.

MADDER LAKE: A brilliant, transparent red pigment originally made by precipitating extract from madder root on a metallic salt base. It is now synthetically derived from coal tar. It is from the same group comprising alizarin red. The term "lake pigment" means a pigment made by precipitating an organic dye on a base of fine particles of inert pigment, usually a translucent clay base.

ALIZARIN: Also originally from madder root but now derived from coal tar. Characteristics of this pigment are about the same as those of Madder Lake. It is of the family of organic pigments known as Anthraquinones. It is a permanent type, bright red color with a blue undertone, made by a complicated chemical process. Madder and Alizarin react to form colorless compounds with strong alkalies and are not good

in mixtures with raw sienna, raw umber and yellow ochre. They are very compatible with the calcined or "burnt" earth pigments.

LITHOL RED: Lithol red is a complex organic lake pigment which provides good coverage. It is a bright red with a bluish cast. This pigment does not bleed in oils but tends to bleed when washed with soap and water. Lithol red is popular as a finish for toys and novelties. Because of its low cost, it is frequently used in inexpensive exterior trim paints. It is only permanent as a masstone; tints made from it fade. Lithol red and para red have no applications in the architectural paint field.

Green Pigments

CHROME GREEN: This is a compound of coprecipitated chrome yellow and Prussian blue. It is probably the paint industry's most important green pigment because of its moderate cost and because it contributes to a good paint film for exterior paints. Chrome green has good hiding power and is a fairly permanent color. Different shades of green are obtained by varying the proportions of the chrome yellow and the Prussian blue. Chrome greens have excellent lightfastness. They are used in both interior and exterior finishes. One of the main disadvantages is that they are not highly resistant to alkalies. The pigment contributes to good drying. Its tints have a tendency to become more blue in direct proportion to the addition of white.

PHTHALOCYANINE GREEN: This pigment, which is a complex copper compound with a bluish-green cast, is remarkable in many respects. It is nonbleeding in solvents and oils, is fast to alkalies and acids and is very lightfast in weak tints. In high concentration it has a strong bronze reflection, but even mild concentrations are apt to be a very rich, deep and concentrated green without surface bronze. Its use is limited somewhat by its high cost. Like its blue relative, it is very strong in tinting strength.

CHROMIUM OXIDE GREEN: Chromium oxide pigment is very permanent in color and has good resistance to both alkali and heat. It is well suited for use in limeproof, alkali resistant coatings. Chromium oxide pigment has a high infrared reflection making it well suited for use as a camouflage paint. The high cost of the pigment makes its usage in ordinary paints somewhat limited. It is olive green, very opaque, slow to dry and very weak in tinting strength.

CHROMIUM HYDROXIDE GREEN: Chromium Hydroxide, $(Cr_2O_3 \cdot 2H_2O)$, is more bluish, transparent, and considerably less grayed than chromium oxide. Otherwise it is very similar, being lightfast, alkali resistant, and in general one of the most stable of all the tinting colors. It is expensive, very weak in tinting strength and the tints become progressively bluer as they are made lighter. Many names are given this pigment such as "verte emeraude," "emerald," and transparent oxide of chromium.

Black Pigments

LAMPBLACK: A pigment made by burning coal tar distillates without sufficient air to produce dense black smoke containing particles of carbon about 99 percent pure. Lampblack is not quite true black, but is slightly gray in color. It makes good gray shades with a blue-purple cast, but is seldom used as a straight black pigment for making black paint. All the blacks are completely permanent both as tints and as masstones. Lampblack is light in weight and extremely fine. It seems to inhibit drying and has a tendency to "surface" or come to the free face of the paint film, an action known to the trade as "floating." This causes darkening when the color that "floats" is darker than the other pigments. Lampblack is grayer as it becomes more coarse and in the coarser particle condition floats less and exhibits a bluer undertone.

CARBON BLACK: Carbon black is widely used by paint manufacturers but is almost never purchased as such by painters in the architectural field except as prepared jet black enamels, lacquers, and stove paints. It is almost jet black, nonbleeding in oils and in solvents, is fast to acids, alkalies and heat and is lightfast. Its tinting strength exceeds all other blacks, but its very fine particle size makes the formulation of pleasing grays almost impossible. Carbon black is made by burning natural gas in an insufficient supply of air.

BONE BLACK (Ivory Black, Drop Black): Pigments made from calcined animal bones. They are as dark as fine carbon black in color but do not have strong tinting strength like lampblack. Because they have low oil absorption and low tinting strength, these blacks are useful to artists and decorators. They dry well, are as black as any obtainable, and are easier to juxtapose in the wet condition than the stronger tint-ing blacks. They are from 10 to 20 percent carbon and the balance is calcium phosphate.

GRAPHITE: Graphite is a gray pigment which consists mostly of crystallized carbon obtained from natural deposits produced from coke in an electric furnace. It is fast to light, heat, acids and alkalies but has poor tinting strength. It varies from medium to dark gray in color. It is an excellent roof paint pigment and is used for little else in architectural painting. Carbon crystallizes to a flake shape which gives it a slippery nature.

Metal Priming Pigments

Iron and steel rust in the presence of air (oxygen) and moisture. Rusting, or corroding, of iron may be explained very briefly as the reaction of the iron with oxygen in the presence of moisture to form various oxides of iron. Other metals also oxidize, but some, aluminum for example, form an adherent oxide film which tends to protect the metal from further corrosion. Iron or steel, on the other hand, form an oxide which is not in the form of a film nor is it adherent. Further, the presence of some oxide catalyzes or promotes more rapid additional corrosion.

A paint film may be used as a barrier to deter the moisture and oxygen from reaching the metal surface and thus prevent rusting. The paint vehicle should be chosen for excellent adherence, water resistance, and resistance to existing environmental conditions. The pigment can contribute greatly to the prevention of corrosion and is a major part of a corrosion resistant primer.

Under certain conditions, aluminum, magnesium and other relatively corrosion resistant metals require painting.

RED LEAD: Red lead is used extensively as an anti-corrosive pigment for iron and in priming coats for structural steel. When exposed to light and air, without a protective covering, red lead changes from red-orange to pink and eventually to white basic carbonate of lead.

Red lead is made by heating metallic lead or litharge in a special furnace to about 960 deg. C. The red lead varies in purity from 85 to 98 percent purity, the remainder being mostly litharge. For paints having storage stability, the 97 percent or better grades must be used, as the litharge causes progressive bodying of the paint. Litharge is sometimes added to red lead paint

This attractive bathroom has woodwork and ceiling painted with a moisture-resistant paint, perhaps an epoxy finish, which will not deteriorate in a steamy environment.

to promote harder drying, but these paints must be used within 40 hours.

Used with phenolic varnish, red lead is effective under severe exposure conditions.

CHROMATE OF LEAD: Chromate of lead, a very bright red orange, is too costly for industrial large scale use but is a superior metal priming pigment. In fact, all the chrome yellows have rust inhibitive qualities.

BLUE LEAD: This is a basic sulphate of lead containing small amounts of lead sulphide and carbon which impart a bluish-gray color. Blue lead is used principally in the fields of metal protection rather than for its color.

ZINC CHROMATE (ZINC YELLOW): Zinc chromate has rust-inhibitive properties which are important in preventing rust development beneath paint films and in preventing "rust creep" at areas where the film has been scratched or gouged through to the bare metal. It is one of the best of all metal primer pigments and is now used extensively for steel and aluminum. The oxides of lead, zinc, and chromium all seem to have metal priming qualities of merit. Zinc oxide white is a fair primer and white lead in all forms has mild rust inhibitive qualities not found in inert pigments.

IRON OXIDES: Red, maroon, and black iron oxides are good pigments for metal priming. They are low in cost and form hard films. For this reason they are quite useful in lacquers and hard drying synthetic enamels for automotive, appliance, and implement painting where hard scuff and abrasion resistant final coats are used.

Metallic Pigments

Metals which have value as paint pigments include: Aluminum, Bronze, Zinc, Lead and Gold.

ALUMINUM: Aluminum is the most important metallic pigment. Aluminum paint is a mixture of finely divided aluminum particles, in flake form, combined with a suitable vehicle.

Aluminum pigment is available in two principal types - - leafing and nonleafing. Leafing is the action where the fine aluminum flakes rise to the surface and "leaf," or form in parallel layers, the top layer being an almost continuous film of aluminum.

Nonleafing aluminum paint consists of aluminum ground to a powder and mixed with a vehicle to give a metallic-gray appearing finish.

About 1 1/2 to 2 lbs. of aluminum pigment per gallon of vehicle are required to provide good hiding power.

Aluminum paint is used to prevent bleeding, and is lightfast. Grades available are coarse, medium, fine, extra fine, and lining which is finest of all.

Paint made from flaked aluminum pigment is highly effective in deflecting sunlight, making it desirable as a finish coat for gasoline and oil storage tanks. It is also used in heat resistant paints for smoke stacks and fire walls.

Nonleafing aluminum is used in combination with suitable color pigments to make metallic lustre finishes of the type used on automobiles. It is also dyed various colors but this process used for either aluminum or bronze powders eliminates its leafing quality.

Aluminum paint has a limited use as a coating in house painting where it provides excellent sealing properties for use over knots, old gilsonite or creosote stains and similar difficult jobs. It is best used over a primer.

BRONZE: Bronze powders used as paint pigments are usually alloys of copper, zinc, tin, and antimony. Various shades are used in nitrocellulose lacquer and in specially formulated vehicles to make brass, bronze and imitation gold finishes.

Leafing paints containing bronze pigments do not have the hiding power of aluminum paint.

ZINC: Powdered zinc metal, either alone or combined with zinc oxide, is used in metal primers and is particularly suited for priming galvanized iron. The zinc dust is usually packed separately and added just before use because it will react with moisture in the paint to form gas.

LEAD: Lead flake is used to some extent in exterior primers. It provides good protection from rust and has excellent durability. However, it settles rapidly providing a problem to the painter.

GOLD: Gold is usually applied in the form of gold leaf. A small quantity is made into powder form for infrequent use. Gold powder and leaf application is usually limited to signs, book binding, picture frames, and ornaments and for decoration.

Pigment Usage

Years ago pigments were used almost entirely to impart color. Now they are recognized as influencing many other properties of paint as well. In modern paint making, pigments are seldom used singly. Selection and proportioning of pigments for achieving different colors is an important part of the paint formulator's job. When pigments are combined, consideration must be given to the effect of the combination on hiding power, settling, workability, stability after exposure and ability to protect organic vehicle binders from the damaging rays of sunlight. Costs have considerable bearing on which pigments are used.

Hiding power, or the ability of paint to obscure underlying color, varies greatly with the use of different pigments. Generally, dark pigments, being more opaque, are more effective than light pigments in this respect.

Pigment Particle Size

Another factor affecting the hiding power of paint is the particle size of the pigment. Within limits, the finer the pigment is ground the greater the hiding power of the paint in which it is used. Fine grinding also is necessary to provide smoothness in paint films, which is especially necessary in enamels and machinery paints. The particle size for most commercial paint pigments ranges in average diameter from 0.0001 to 0.006 millimeter.

The paint formulator is faced with the problem not only of producing desired colors, but of obtaining effective all-around performance, using materials that are economically acceptable.

Vehicles

Equally as important as the pigment in a paint is the vehicle or binder. The vehicle may be a liquid like linseed oil or it may be a solid resin like an epoxy resin made fluid with solvent. Even if the vehicle is liquid, there are usually solvents present since these contribute to the formation of good films. In addition to the pigment, binder and solvent, the paint may contain several small percentage additives including driers and a variety of surface active agents.

Thus, the vehicle generally contains both volatile (easily evaporated) and nonvolatile constituents. The volatile or solvent portion of the vehicle facilitates application and contributes, through evaporation, to the drying of the paint. It forms no permanent part of the paint film.

The nonvolatile portion is frequently referred to as the binder, since it remains as an integral part of the paint film to bind the pigment particles together. Adhesion of the film to the surface is an important function of the binder. It also is largely responsible for the protective qualities and durability of the paint.

Vehicle Classification

There are many ways to classify coatings, but one is on the basis of whether or not the vehicle contains oil. Vegetable oil coatings such as those based on linseed and tung oils obviously fall into this category. Alkyds are an example of oils combined with resins as are the epoxy

resin esters and the so-called urethane oils which have very recently been introduced. Accordingly, it is of interest to examine first of all the materials in oil-based coating vehicles. Oil-based vehicles, accordingly, may be simply vegetable oils such as linseed oil. Or they may be combinations of resins and oils, the resins contributing functional properties not available from the oil alone. The first resin-oil combinations were varnishes. Here the resin and the oil are simply combined and heated until a given set of properties are achieved.

In the next forward step, the resin and the oil were combined chemically. Alkyd resins are the best example. The advantage of chemical combination is that almost complete control can be achieved over the properties of the end product. Epoxy resin esters and urethane oils are the newest chemical combinations of oils and resins.

Some vehicles or binders consist only of resins without any oil at all. These will be discussed later. First of all, however, we will discuss the various oils which are used either as such or in combination with resins to provide paint vehicles.

Oils

Linseed Oil

The use of linseed oil, obtained from the seed of the flax plant, goes back to Biblical days. The seed contains from 32 to 43 percent oil, about 98 percent of which is recovered by modern solvent extraction methods. Less oil of poorer quality is obtained by pressing. The oil is either a golden yellow or greenish brown depending on the degree of refining.

Linseed oil is a drying oil - - that is, when it is exposed to the air in a thin film, it gradually thickens and eventually converts to a tough film. This action is accelerated and promoted by the presence of certain metallic compounds known as driers. Driers are compounds of cobalt, lead, calcium, manganese and other metals which are soluble in the oil. This type of hardening commonly called "drying" is the basis for the usefulness of the oil and alkyd-based paints.

Linseed oil may be modified in many ways for use in paints. Viscosity may be increased by heat bodying or by oxidation, or the oil may be chemically modified. The painter uses linseed oil in one of two forms; raw linseed oil or boiled linseed oil. The raw oil is a greenish brown oil, practically as it is recovered from the flaxseed with minimum refining. Boiled oil is raw oil that has been partially oxidized by blowing with air at about 200 deg. F. Thereafter driers are added. These oils are utilized in combination with paste paints that require additional oil before use.

Linseed oil yellows when used for interior finishes and thus is little used for light colors indoors. Outdoors, the yellowing is minimized by the bleaching action of the sun.

Soybean Oil

Soybean oil is made from the seed of the soybean, a leguminous plant, which is grown in many parts of the United States. Soybean oil is also an edible oil, and the food use, which is greater than the technical use, controls the price. It is classified as a semidrying oil and without modification does not dry adequately for paint use.

Alkyd resins made from soybean oil dry very well and permit the paint manufacturer to take advantage of excellent color retention of soybean oil. Alkyd resins based on soybean oil contain approximately 50 to 70 percent of the oil and can be used for interior paints and enamels, industrial enamels, and maintenance paints. Other chemical modifications of soybean oil are successfully used as replacements for linseed oils in outside house paints. Soybean oil is now a major raw material for the paint industry.

Tung Oil (Chinawood Oil)

Tung oil is obtained from seeds of the fruit of the tung tree, which is grown extensively in southern China and in southern part of the U. S.

Tung oil is pale amber in color. It must be cooked before being used, because the raw oil, on drying, forms a soft, white, opaque film. When heated, it provides a hard, tough, glossy film. This oil becomes extremely insoluble when dry, providing unusual resistance to water and alkali. This makes it ideal for use in exterior spar varnishes, concrete paints, marine finishes, porch and deck paints, and many other types of paint.

Tung oil, because of its quick-drying qualities, is used a great deal in quick-drying varnishes and for paints such as four-hour enamels.

In using tung oil care must be taken not to use too much drier for wrinkling may result.

Tung oil may be used for all interior and exterior finishes where fast drying and good durability are required.

Dehydrated Castor Oil

Castor oil used in the paint industry is obtained from oil found in the seeds of the castor bean plant. The plant grows three to fifteen feet high as an annual in cold regions and 30 to 40 feet as a quick-growing perennial shrub or small tree in tropical regions.

Castor oil in its natural state is a nondrying oil. It acquires its drying properties through a change in its structure. The oil is dehydrated, that is, water is removed. This change in its chemical structure changes it into a drying oil. Dehydrated castor oil dries faster than linseed oil but slower than tung oil. It imparts great toughness to varnishes and resins.

In appearance dehydrated castor oil is almost water white, making it suitable for use in many types of paint, even paint where an exceptionally white color is required.

Dehydrated castor oil has found wide usage in the same areas as tung and linseed oils. It is also being used in alkyd resin manufacture and in non-yellowing enamels and related products.

Perilla Oil

Perilla oil, which is golden yellow in color, is obtained from the seeds of a bush, called Perilla Ocymoide, grown largely in China and Japan.

The oil is quick drying. It would no doubt be used extensively in making paint products except for the fact that the United States government placed a prohibitive import tax on the oil, to protect American farmers who grow flax for linseed oil production. At the time the import tax was placed, perilla oil was fast replacing linseed oil for many interior uses. The paint film produced from perilla oil is usually considered to be too hard and too brittle for best exterior durability.

Fish Oil

Fish oil is the only animal oil used to any extent in the paint and varnish industries. It is extracted from fish such as the sardine and menhaden obtained on the Atlantic coast and the pilchard on the Pacific coast.

The oil when raw is dark and cloudy in color and has a bad odor, but when kettled and treated it is often difficult to recognize the oil by either a poor color or unpleasant odor.

Fish oil, because it is inexpensive, finds usage in many types of finishes. It is used to a considerable extent in stipple finishes, caulking compounds, and in some interior finishes where lack of running and easy brushing are desirable. It is slow drying with poor resistance to water,

acid and alkali. This oil should not be used alone in exterior coatings. It is frequently used to extend other more expensive oils.

Oiticica Oil

This oil, which is obtained from the nut of the oiticica tree, found mainly in Brazil, has properties somewhat similar to tung oil. Oiticica oil, has less resistance to water and alkali than tung oil, but has better resistance than linseed, soybean and fish oils.

Oiticica oil is generally considered as a satisfactory substitute for tung oil in such finishes as quick drying varnishes, enamels, and wrinkle finishes. It also has some importance as a paint oil where its properties such as good leveling and high gloss are desirable.

Safflower Oil

Safflower oil is obtained from the seed of a thistle-like plant grown originally in Egypt and India but now in the U.S. It has non-yellowing features similar to soybean oil but dries faster. Safflower oil is considered to be somewhere between soybean oil and linseed oil in good paint characteristics.

Varnishes and Varnish Resins

Varnishes are combinations of resins and oils in which the two components are heated to achieve a given set of properties. Any of the oils discussed above may comprise the oil component of the varnish. In addition, a resin is required. Certain resins useful for the manufacture of varnishes may also be used in the formulation of vehicles which are not strictly considered varnishes. For example, some of these resins may be added to lacquers to impart hardness.

Resins are useful in varnishes and other coatings not only to impart hardness but to increase mar resistance, decrease drying time, improve gloss and gloss retention, and to improve adhesion and chemical resistance.

The most important modern varnish is termed a phenolic. Although the discussion below will describe many of the resins which in the past have been useful in varnishes and, indeed, are still used to some extent today, the

varnish of greatest interest to the maintenance painter is one made by combining phenolic resins with tung oil or mixtures of tung and other oils.

Generally, phenolic varnishes or the paints made by pigmenting the varnishes have better chemical and water resistance than oil-base or alkyd paints. However, they tend to yellow or darken with age and they chalk more rapidly. Even so, they provide durable protection against atmospheric corrosion, particularly where protection is desired against moisture and corrosive fumes. The phenolic varnishes are widely used for marine applications.

In addition to phenolic resins, however, there are a number of other resins still used in varnishes. These may be classified as natural resins and synthetic resins. Natural resins are those which are formed by nature's chemical processes. These are imported from all parts of the world. There are many grades of the resins described below and this grade variation may actually change the properties of the resins.

Synthetic resins are manufactured resins. The manufactured resins have steadily grown in favor because of their generally superior properties.

The synthetic resins discussed below are those which are of interest primarily in varnishes or generally as additives to protective coatings. In addition, however, there are a large number of synthetic resins which are themselves film forming. These will be discussed later.

The chemistry of resins, natural and synthetic, and that of rubber compounds is probably one of the most involved in the chemical industry.

Natural Resins

Copal Resins

Copals are fossilized resins obtained from trees. They have good solubility in oil and are used in a wide range of products.

Dammar Resins

Dammar resins are imported from the East Indies. They are easily dissolved in oils and petroleum solvents and are used in such high grade products as non-yellowing enamels.

Manila Resins

Manila resins are obtained by tapping Agathis Alba trees. They are alcohol-soluble and are particularly useful for making shellac substitutes and spirit varnishes.

Rosin

Rosin is an important natural resin obtained from pine trees. There are two principal types - - gum rosin which is obtained by tapping live trees, and wood rosin which is obtained from tree stumps. The stumps are removed from the ground, cut to the desired size chips, and rosin, pine oil, turpentine and other ingredients are removed by distilling.

For most purposes either type of rosin can be used with very little noticeable difference.

Rosin produces a film that is tough, hard, glossy and dries well. It also has good initial color, but rather poor color retention, compared to several other resins. It has comparatively poor water and alkali resistance.

Rosin is normally used in finishes where price is a factor, including low-priced floor paints, interior enamels, gloss paint, and barn paint.

Rosin is also considered an important raw material for use in making synthetic resins.

Shellac

Shellac is an alcohol-soluble resin of great usefulness in the paint trade because it dries fast, sands well, is waxlike and abrasion-resistant and because it is not soluble in turpentine, pitch, and the ordinary thinners used in oil paints and synthetics. Shellac is dissolved, applied, and upon evaporation of the solvents, is again a hard waxy gum. It is useful for floor finishes, for sealing off bleeding dyes or stains, for pitch stains, and for many other uses. Shellac is soluble in alkaline aqueous solutions and water spots easily.

The "lac" comes mainly from India. It is obtainable in many grades and forms. Pale yellow unbleached shellac in flake form can be nearly as white as bleached shellac but is costly. Most of the natural product is red to red orange. "White" shellac is this naturally orange resin bleached to a milky liquid that is nearly colorless when applied.

Shellac is not used in varnish formulation. Rather, when cut with alcohol it provides a coating whose main use is as a sealer or prime coat on wood.

Synthetic Resins

Ester Gum

Ester gum is a resin produced synthetically by reacting rosin with glycerine. The chemical action yields a greatly improved water and alkali resistant resin. It is inexpensive and brittle but useful as a component of varnish and lacquers to which it imparts gloss and adhesion and a workable viscosity.

Copal Ester

This product is similar to ester gum but superior for use in spar varnishes, lacquers, and rubbing varnishes.

Pentaerythritol Resins

If instead of using glycerine, a higher alcohol, pentaerythritol, is used to react with rosin, a penta-type resin which in many respects is superior to ester gum, is obtained. Drying qualities and color retention are very good.

Gilsonite

Gilsonite is a black, coal-like substance obtained from mines, which is used as a resin in making black asphaltum varnishes.

Phenolic Resins

Pure phenolic resins are based essentially on the reaction between two chemicals, phenol and formaldehyde. They have excellent resistance to water, alkali and the many corrosive elements normally encountered. The fact that the phenolics are also coupled with good durability makes them well suited for use in high grade exterior spar and marine varnishes. Since they are resistant to alcohol, they are ideal for furniture and bar top varnishes. These resins, because of their extreme resistance, are useful as coatings for interiors of tanks and tank cars used for storing wine, beer, solvents and chemicals. The phenolics used for the lining of tanks and also, incidentally, for fruit can linings have a somewhat different chemical structure than the phenolic varnishes and must be cured by heat.

One shortcoming of the phenolic resins is that they tend to yellow, making them unsuited for use in high-quality white and light-shade finishes.

Where the extreme resistance and durability of pure phenolic resins is not required, modified phenolic resins are frequently used. As a matter of fact, the modified phenolics are the ones most widely used in varnishes because of their enhanced oil solubility. As indicated above,

phenolic varnishes are the most important of all types of varnishes available today.

Maleic Resins

The maleic resins are based on a reaction between maleic anhydride or maleic acid with glycerine and rosin.

An important property of maleic resins is fast solvent release or quick-drying. This is often quite important where a very heavy or thick coating is applied. An example of this type of coating is in quick-building gloss lacquers applied with great speed by spray on furniture assembly lines.

Maleic resins have good color retention and good sanding properties - - one of the few resins which possesses this property. Another important property is their compatibility with nitrocellulose. Maleic resins in lacquers can be used in high concentrations to provide good durability, light color and high gloss.

One of the disadvantages of maleic resins is that they tend to lose their fast drying qualities on prolonged storing.

Coumarone-Indene Resins

Coumarone-indene resins are derived as by-products in making coke from coal. In producing the coke, coal tar is produced. These resins are one of the important products obtained from the coal tar.

Coumarone-indene resins come in a variety of colors from water white to almost black. They are highly resistant to alkaline solutions making them ideal for such products as wall sealers and concrete paints where a high percentage of lime is present. They are also resistant to alcohol, dilute acids, and to heat. Many electrical insulating varnishes are based on the coumarone-indene resins. Coumarone-indene resins are used with heavy bodied linseed oil as the vehicle in aluminum paints.

Synthetic Oil-Containing Vehicles

As indicated above, important vehicles for paints are obtained by combining oils and resins, synthetically, in one molecule. Alkyd resins are the most important of these. Epoxy resin esters and urethane oils are alkyd-like compositions which have been devised recently to extend the functionality of oil-resin vehicles.

Alkyd Resins

Alkyd resins have won their place in the protective coatings industry because of their unexcelled gloss and gloss retention, the excellent whites that may be formulated from them, and because they are economical. These

Here's a pattern that owes its charm to delicate printing and subtle use of the pastel palette. Just the right background for furniture with a bit of French or Florentine elegance.

factors will help alkyds to maintain their position in the protective coatings industry for many years to come. However, it must be recognized that alkyds are deficient in the area of solvent and chemical resistance and corrosion resistance. It is largely for this reason that newer type vehicles, such as those discussed below, are making their mark.

Alkyd resins are chemical combinations of vegetable oils and resins. They are made by reacting materials which the chemist calls polybasic acids with polyhydric alcohols and with varying quantities of drying oils which impart flexibility and adhesion to the resin. The alkyds dry by reacting with oxygen in the air.

The greater the oil content of the resin, the more flexible the coating will be and the less resistant it will be to certain chemicals. On the other hand, longer oil content improves water resistance and weatherability. The oil-modified alkyds are described as short, medium or long, depending on the amount of oil present.

The alkyds dry faster than oil-base paints and the drying time depends on the amount of oil incorporated into the formulation, the shorter the oil length, the faster the dry. Short oil alkyds, for example, are commonly used as drum enamels, whereas the long oil alkyds are used where the utmost in color retention and weatherability is required. Medium oil alkyds frequently provide the basis for primers.

Thus, today the alkyd paints are more widely used on metal and wood products than any other single paint system, despite the advent of several more highly functional systems such as the epoxy and the vinyl resins. Major applications of the alkyd paints are in industrial plants for the protection of steel surfaces from atmospheric corrosion of moderate intensity and as an all-purpose paint for wood and metals where atmospheric exposure is involved. The alkyds are not suitable where immersion is anticipated or where corrosive conditions are severe. They are used widely for interior surfaces and can be made in the full range from high gloss to flat for architectural use. Alkyds are also the basis for industrial paints where they are combined with nitrogen-containing resins to provide compositions which must be cured by baking.

Alkyds may be modified by combining them with vinyls, chlorinated rubber and silicones to obtain higher functionality such as improved corrosion, chemical and solvent resistance. Also, the alkyd may be styrenated, by reaction with a chemical called styrene, to obtain faster drying, together with better moisture resistance, higher hardness and more oil resistance.

Interesting specialty products are the so-called thixotropic alkyds, the term thixotropic being applied to paints with a jelly-like consistency which can become fluid on stirring or brushing. The advantage of thixotropic paints is that the pigment does not settle in them and that they "stay put" when applied on a vertical surface or ceiling, thus eliminating dripping, sagging and "curtaining." Also, thicker coats may be applied in one pass.

Epoxy Resin Esters

Like alkyd resins, epoxy resin esters are a combination of resin and oil. Epoxy resin esters are manufactured by procedures similar to those used for alkyds and they demonstrate drying times like alkyds. Weathering resistance of epoxy resins, although good, is somewhat inferior to that of the very best alkyds from the point of view of gloss retention. Also, the epoxy resins tend to yellow more, and like alkyds, their resistance to acids is relatively poor. On the other hand, the epoxy resin esters are considerably more resistant to alkali than are alkyds and are somewhat more resistant to water. They are also more resistant to solvents than are the alkyd resins. Their primary virtue, however, over alkyds is their improved corrosion resistance. Thus, epoxy resin esters are used largely for maintenance applications where resistance to salty fumes and chemical atmospheres is required.

Urethane Oils

Urethane oils have virtues similar to those of the epoxy esters. They are the newest of the oil-based vehicles containing, in combination with the oil, a resin which the chemist calls a polyurethane. The urethane oils tend to dry somewhat faster than either the epoxy resin esters or the alkyds. Their weathering characteristics are on a par with those of the epoxy resin esters but somewhat inferior to those of the alkyds, particularly in the area of gloss retention where the alkyds reign supreme. The acid, alkali and solvent resistance of the urethane oils is generally better than can be found in alkyds and is on a par with these properties as exhibited by the epoxy resin esters.

Synthetic Resins

Resin-Based Finishes

Thus far we have discussed the newer types of paint vehicles in which resins are combined with oils. Paint vehicles also may be made from resins without any oil whatsoever. In this category are the vinyls, epoxy resins, urethanes, silicones and a variety of other materials, each with specialized uses. The virtues of these finishes may usually be found in the protective properties the resin demonstrates. Thus, resin-based finishes will provide much greater solvent and chemical resistance, much better acid and alkali resistance and much better corrosion resistance than will finishes based on oils alone or on oils combined with resins. In addition, the all-resin finishes will be harder and more abrasion resistant. On the other hand, they will not have the properties contributed by oil character which include a high degree of flexibility and extensibility and a high level of gloss retention. Good adhesion also characterizes oil-based finishes. However, this property may also be found in certain of the resin-based finishes -- primarily in the epoxy finishes.

The primary use of finishes based completely on resins is for maintenance and for industrial applications. They have not made headway to any great extent in the so-called "trade-sales" areas.

Resin-based finishes may be divided into three categories -- those which dry by solvent evaporation, those which depend on the interaction of two components to provide a resistant film, and mastic-like finishes which are characterized by the fact that they can be applied as very thick films.

The various oil-based finishes discussed above, dried or formed films because they combined with the oxygen of the air. Coatings which do not contain oil, dry either by solvent evaporation or by chemical reaction which takes place once the film has been laid down.

Vinyls, nitrocellulose and rubber-based resins provide coatings which dry by solvent evaporation. In order to make a paint from such a resin, it is necessary only to dissolve it in a solvent, pigment it properly and add whatever other small percentage ingredients are necessary to achieve proper performance. As soon as the solvent evaporates, a resistant film results. It is obvious that such coatings will be sensitive to the solvents in which they are soluble.

A second type of coating is exemplified by the two-component epoxy or urethane coatings. These must be mixed immediately prior to use. After mixing, they have pot lives which may vary from one hour to several days. They are, however, not stable indefinitely simply because the two components react to provide the high molecular weight cross-linked resin which is the basis for the film. Since these components frequently react at room temperature or even lower, the coatings are useful as maintenance paints. Because mixing of the components is required in the field, careful attention must be given to the directions provided by the supplier. The most popular cured coatings are those based on epoxy resins combined either with polyamines, amine adducts or polyamide resins. These are the so-called coreactants or curing agents. Normally, highly solvent and corrosion-resistant paints result from these cured coatings.

Still another type of curing results with certain types of urethanes which polymerize in the presence of moisture in the air. These so-called moisture-cured materials are particularly valuable as clears for floor coatings because of their high abrasion resistance.

Epoxy Resins

Epoxy resins, as already indicated, are one of the most important modern contributions which has helped to extend the painter's skills and capabilities. These resins have already been mentioned above as the basis for the epoxy resin esters which are oil-containing and which demonstrate better solvent and corrosion resistance than alkyds.

Of great interest to the painter are the two-component epoxies or so-called catalyzed epoxy coatings. These, as indicated above, are packaged in two separate containers and are mixed, following the directions of the supplier, immediately prior to use. The two materials start to react to produce hard, glossy, chemically resistant coatings which withstand oils and alkalis and are also resistant to acids and many solvents. There are basically two types of coreactants. The first are amines or amine adducts. These provide coatings with excellent solvent resistance. The second type of coreactant is a polyamide resin which provides somewhat less resistance to strong solvents but better water resistance. As a matter of fact, the polyamide-epoxy coatings are suitable for water immersion service. Also, they provide better adhesion and better corrosion resistance.

A catalyzed epoxy system is frequently used with a zinc chromate primer formulated also from the catalyzed epoxy vehicle. Red lead primers are also effective. Normally, two coats of primers are used, followed by two topcoats, particularly if the system is to be used in corrosive atmospheres or in areas where long-term water immersion is anticipated. The catalyzed epoxy resins dry almost twice as fast as alkyds. They chalk more readily but have excellent film integrity. Resistance to acids, alkalis and water is very good and solvent resistance is of an entirely different order of magnitude from that which can be obtained with alkyds. Probably the most important property of the catalyzed finishes, however, is their excellent corrosion resistance. This is particularly true of the epoxy-polyamide system.

One of the important virtues of the epoxy-polyamide system is that it may be applied to relatively poorly prepared surfaces. Indeed, it may even be brushed onto wet surfaces and to surfaces to which tightly bound rust adheres. Accordingly, this system is achieving great popularity in the maintenance paint area.

Chlorinated Rubber

Chlorinated rubber is an important resin for maintenance paints. The product results from the reaction of chlorine with natural rubber. This brittle resin, when properly plasticized, provides an elastic film. The formulations must include stabilizers since the resin is readily attacked by ultraviolet light. Chlorinated rubber paints fall into the category of those which dry completely by solvent evaporation. Depending on how they are formulated, they are useful on steel, concrete or wood, for exposure to the atmosphere and for water immersion. Indeed, they are frequently used on swimming pools. The most highly functional chlorinated rubber paints are those which contain at least fifty percent of the chlorinated rubber resin. These will also be fire-retardant because of the high chlorine content.

The chlorinated rubber paints normally do not have outstanding adhesion to steel for which reason rust-inhibiting primers are normally employed.

Another important area of use is for concrete where the chlorinated rubber paints are satisfactory because of their very high alkali resistance. Also, they may be used in direct contact with acids and corrosive fumes. In addition to swimming pools; floors, portable water tanks and chemical equipment may be coated with this material.

Good surface preparation and very dry surfaces prior to application of the coating are required for good service.

Vinyl Resins

Vinyl resins utilized by the paint industry are based on vinyl chloride copolymerized with small amounts of vinyl acetate. The paints based on these resins are used largely for maintenance. The most resistant coatings result when the vinyls are used as such. They may, however, be combined with alkyds to formulate less expensive paints.

Emulsions of vinyl resins, as will be indicated later, provide one of the important classes of water-based paints. Coatings containing vinyl resins have exceptional resistance to water, oils, alcohol, acid and alkali. They are, however, not resistant to the strong solvents such as ketones, alcohols and aromatic hydrocarbons which are used to formulate coatings from them. The vinyl resins, incidentally, are in the category of coatings which dry simply by solvent evaporation.

Vinyl coatings properly applied have a long life and a high degree of impermeability. Because they demonstrate relatively poor adhesion, very careful surface preparation is required and careful attention also must be given to dryness. Thus, a vinyl paint system will consist first of all of an etch primer which, as its name indicates, etches the surface because it contains acid. Thereafter, intermediate and topcoats may be sprayed on and as many as six coats may be utilized in order to obtain adequate film thickness for the type of protection required. There will result, however, a paint of unusually high tensile strength, flexibility and extensibility, excellent electrical properties, excellent weathering properties, very good acid and alkali resistance but, as indicated above, relatively poor resistance to strong solvents. Vinyl coatings find wide use in the marine area and for the protection of water tank interiors.

Acrylic resins may be added to the vinyls to improve brushing properties and gloss retention. However, chemical resistance is sacrificed.

Relatively new are the high-build or mastic-like vinyl coatings. These, unlike the traditional vinyl coatings, may be applied in thick films of up to five to six mils per coat. They tend, however, to be porous because they dry by solvent evaporation. Consequently, one or more seal coats must be applied over the mastics.

Silicone Resins

The silicones are expensive resins whose major contribution to a coating is heat resistance. When pigmented with aluminum, paints result which perform well at temperatures as high as 1000 deg. F. Thus, these are widely used on furnace stacks, mufflers, space heaters and other hot surfaces. The paints dry primarily by solvent evaporation but the heat encountered in usage tends to promote further curing. Their usefulness at very high temperatures depends on the fact that the silicone resin is actually carbonized at about 700 deg. F. with the net result that aluminum flakes are left adhering tenaciously to the surfaces. Best results are frequently obtained when two thin coats are applied with a heat cure after the first coat which frequently consists of a zinc silicate primer.

As indicated above, silicone-alkyd paints are available. These are useful where moderately hot surfaces of up to 500 deg. F. are encountered. Also, the silicone-alkyds demonstrate excellent weathering properties. Resistance to solvents, on the other hand, is relatively poor.

Catalyzed Phenolic Coatings

Phenolics have been mentioned above as the basis for the most important varnishes used today. A variation of these phenolic resins may be cured with catalysts such as polyamines. Two-component paints with short pot lives result. These phenolics may be combined with epoxy resins and oil-like materials may be included to improve film characteristics such as adhesion. The important virtue of these cured phenolic coatings is their solvent resistance. They are used where unusual resistance to acid, alkalis, solvents and chemicals is required. They are attacked by strong alkalis and by strong oxidizing acids. They will, however, withstand continuous immersion in hot water. They are useful as linings and patching coatings

for process equipment. Because they adhere to concrete, they are valuable as floor coatings in chemical and food plants. When used with metals, epoxy-phenolic primers are normally required to improve adhesion.

Urethane Coatings

The so-called urethane or polyurethane coatings come in several forms. Reference has already been made to oil-modified urethanes or urethane oils which resemble alkyds but have somewhat better solvent and corrosion resistance. Reference has also been made to the so-called moisture-cured urethanes. These are one-component systems which cure on interaction with the moisture of the air. Obviously, then, they cannot be used where humidity is very low. Normally, they are not pigmented and are useful for the coating of floors, particularly for gyms and bowling alleys.

The two-component polyurethane formulations are similar to the two-component epoxy coatings. Urethane films exhibit excellent resistance to water and to many chemicals and solvents. They have high abrasion resistance and retain their flexibility on weathering. However, they yellow and chalk in the presence of ultraviolet light. Adhesion must usually be facilitated by the choice of proper primers. These are frequently based on the catalyzed epoxy resins.

An important advantage of the urethanes is their ability to cure at temperatures below 45 to 50 deg. F. which is the threshold temperature for the curing of most epoxy compositions. Thus, they are useful when it is necessary to apply coatings to cold surfaces.

Lacquer Coatings

Traditionally, lacquers were based on nitrocellulose. More recently, acrylic resins have been made available for lacquers, also. Lacquers are normally nonpigmented although pigmentation is possible. They dry by solvent evaporation to provide tough films with high gloss. The nitrocellulose lacquers are used primarily for decorative coatings for metal products for indoor use. They are not widely used for maintenance because they are best applied with industrial spray equipment. The acrylic lacquers have found their largest application in the automotive industry. They have an advantage over the nitrocellulose lacquers because of their better color and color retention. They, too, however, are not widely used for maintenance applications.

Mastic-Like Coatings

Reference to mastic-like coatings based on vinyl resins has been made above. In addition, asphalt or coal tar may be cut back with solvents to provide mastic-like coatings which dry by solvent evaporation. Inert fillers are frequently incorporated. These coatings can be made thixotropic (paint which becomes fluid when shaken or disturbed, becoming rigid again when the mechanical disturbance stops) so that the viscosity can be reduced by stirring for proper application. Once applied, the coating sets up to a thick film which does not run or sag. These mastics are also available as water-base materials and as products which must be heated first to reduce viscosity for application.

Mastics based on coal tar or asphalt are low cost and are useful for protection against corrosion since they demonstrate excellent adhesion to both steel and concrete. Their water resistance is excellent as is their resistance to petroleum oils and weak acids and alkalis. They do not, however, resist most solvents or vegetable oils. They are widely used on submerged or buried steel and concrete surfaces.

Coal tar coatings may "alligator" or shrink and crack on exposure to sunlight. For this reason, a topcoat is frequently employed. This may be based on a water dispersion of an asphalt coating which, for some reason, does not demonstrate this property.

Gilsonite, a natural asphalt, may be added to asphalt coatings to upgrade them.

Another way to upgrade bituminous coatings is to include in them epoxy or urethane resins. This makes of them two-component coatings which, however, demonstrate much better adhesion and much better resistance to solvents. Epoxy resins are more widely used than urethanes for these types of coatings. As with the straight epoxies, the coreactants are either amines, amine adducts or polyamides. The latter produce more flexible coatings and make possible longer pot lives.

The bitumen-modified epoxy resins are intended for heavy-duty service. They usually are available at solids contents of 70 to 90 percent and two coats of eight to ten mils each are normally applied. Applications include dam gates, piers, barges, ship bottoms and many other types of surfaces which are to be exposed to or immersed in fresh or salt water. The coatings are applied by brushing, troweling or spraying.

Bitumen-base coatings require very little surface preparation and application cost is low. Curing of the epoxy-modified materials is rapid.

Related to the mastics are sand-filled coatings or sand or aggregate-filled coatings. These are formulated from as much as 90 percent sand or aggregate with 10 percent of a resinous material which usually is a catalyzed epoxy resin. The resinous components must not be mixed until immediately prior to use. The sand may be combined with one of the two components or it may be present as a third component. After curing, a cement-like substance results which is useful for flooring where unusually rugged service is anticipated. A major problem with these sand-filled materials is their poor trowel ability. They are, however, superb as patching compounds because they adhere well to old concrete. As might be expected, the resistance of these resin-based compositions to water, alkali, acid, solvents and corrosive elements is excellent.

Chlorosulfonated Polyethylene

Chlorosulfonated polyethylene has the trade name of Hypalon. The product is made by reacting polyethylene with chlorosulfonic acid. It is used as a two-component paint, the second component comprising a cross-linking agent. A rubbery coating results which is highly flexible and which demonstrates unusually good resistance to ozone and other highly corrosive elements. The coating will also resist hot water. It weathers well on exposure to ultraviolet rays and thus is useful in areas where severe corrosion is anticipated. The paints must be applied to clean sandblasted surfaces and chlorinated rubber primers are frequently utilized.

Polyesters

The polyester resins provide very hard, glossy coatings which are unusually attractive but which, unfortunately, are quite brittle. These materials, like the epoxies, certain urethanes and the Hypalon coatings, are two-component. Thus, cross-linking (method by which chemicals unite to form films) is effected by a catalyst which must be added immediately prior to use. The polyester coatings are frequently available at 100 percent solids. There resistance to

Materials

weathering is good. They have excellent acid and solvent resistance but poor resistance to alkalis. When applied at 100 percent solids, care must be taken to overcome the problems of poor adhesion and shrinkage on curing. One of the best ways to do this is to include reinforcing materials such as glass or asbestos fibers which are particularly suitable for use with polyesters. Specialized spray equipment is available for such compositions. Thus the paints formulated from these are useful where a high level of protection is required in a nonalkaline environment.

Water-Based Coatings

Shortly after World War II the protective coatings industry experienced a revolution which changed completely the use and marketing patterns in the trade sales area. The need to develop an acceptable synthetic rubber when World War II cut off supplies from southeastern Asia resulted in the development of inexpensive elastomers such as butadiene-styrene copolymers. These are actually manufactured as stable emulsions or latices with the ability to provide continuous films once the water evaporates. Thus, it did not take long for the imaginative paint chemist to visualize these latices as vehicles for paints.

Water-based paints were, of course, known prior to this time; but each of the materials available had defects which allowed it to achieve little more than specialty status. The butadiene-styrene based latex paints had numerous virtues and their acceptance for use inside of homes and buildings was a rapid one, especially for the painting of plaster and gypsum board. Latex paints eliminate, of course, the odor and danger associated with solvents. Brushes and spillage may easily be cleaned with water. The low odor and easy applicability of the paint provide additional plus factors. And once the paint film was applied and properly dried it could be washed readily.

Interest in latex paints has increased markedly in the last few years because of legislation aimed at smog and pollution control. It is generally recognized that solvents, particularly some of the stronger solvents used in paints, are undesirable in areas such as southern California where conditions conducive to smog formation exist. One important solution to the problem is to utilize paints which are based on water rather than solvents.

Soon the butadiene-styrene latices were joined by polyvinyl acetate and acrylic-based emulsions as well as by numerous copolymers formulated to achieve specific end results. Not only are these paints used as topcoats or finishing coats for plaster, masonry, wood and even metal surfaces, but they are also valuable for priming plaster and wallboard. The fact that latex paint can be used self-primed contributes markedly to the convenience factor. And, if the latex paint has sufficient alkali resistance, it may be used over relatively "hot" plaster or plaster which has not been allowed to cure for a very long period. This has facilitated markedly the decoration of newly-built homes.

For exterior masonry the latex must also have good alkali resistance. If this alkali resistance is adequate, however, as it is with the acrylic and polyvinyl acetate paints, usage is possible on new concrete and mortar. Because the latex paints have more permeability than oil paints, their use over masonry is possible with a minimum of blistering. Also, the quick dry of latex paints frequently permits application of two coats from one setting of a scaffold.

On the other hand, the latex paints do not adhere well to either chalky or glossy surfaces and this must be guarded against. Also, their high permeability, which is an advantage in the area of blistering, may lead to efflorescence (migration of salts to the surface) on monolithic concrete or concrete block.

When latex paints are used on cinder block, the surface must first be filled with a cement sand mix modified with some of the latex if a smooth surface is desired prior to painting.

Originally, the use of latex paints was limited almost entirely to inside wall decoration and to outside masonry, nor could the latex paints originally be used on metal surfaces. Great progress, however, has been made in the last fifteen years with the net result that today water-based coatings are available which are actually used as metal primers for important industrial items such as automobiles and home appliances.

Great progress has also been made in the area of water-based house paints. A material which is either water soluble or water dispersible could conceivably have many advantages as a house paint. If the vehicle "breathes," as might be expected from a water-based material, great headway will have been made in solving the blistering problem which plagues many homeowners. In addition, of course, are the advantages of easy clean-up and easy application as already mentioned.

Today water-based paints are available which do, indeed, function very well. The major problem thus far associated with their use is the need for an oil-based primer or a primer comprising a combination of oil and water. Recently, even this problem has been overcome, but even so the painter who utilizes water-based house paints should follow carefully the directions on the label relative to the use of primers.

Actually, if new wood is involved, it is frequently recommended that the latex paint be applied over a zinc-free oil primer of the conventional type. If a repaint job is involved, loose chalk may markedly affect adhesion. One may wash off all the loose chalk although this is expensive. A primer coat of a conventional oil paint is usually effective, but this in large measure cancels the advantages of the water-based system. A third approach is to modify the latex

paint by addition of some oil or alkyd solution. As previously indicated, however, the manufacturers' suggestions should be followed carefully.

To summarize, the water-based paints that exist today may be used on practically every surface found inside of a house or building including woodwork for which semi-gloss formulations are available. Excellent water-based paints are available for outside masonry surfaces and a very recent development is the availability of water-based paints recommended for outside wood surfaces. Water-based paints are not available in glossy finishes.

For outside use on metal, water-based primers with corrosion inhibiting pigments are available. Water-based topcoats are also said to provide excellent service on steel substrates in industrial atmospheres. There is no question but that the impact which water-based paints have made on the protective coatings industry will continue and that they will become more and more functional within the next few years.

Water-based paints may be applied by either roller, brush or spray. Roller coating is most common for inside application, whereas exterior surfaces are frequently sprayed although airless spray is not recommended.

Solvents and Thinners

Paint solvents and thinners are used to reduce the viscosity of paint products to a point where they may be readily applied. Solvents and thinners affect film formation, consistency, leveling, drying and even adhesion and durability. They must be carefully selected and blended as required for different types of coatings and different resins and drying oils. Thus, the painter

must follow carefully the directions of the manufacturer relative to thinning. Shellac, for example, must always be thinned with alcohol. Any other thinner would ruin it. Most oil-based finishes and many alkyds can be thinned with mineral spirits. The resin-based finishes, on the other hand, like the epoxies, must be thinned with so-called strong solvents such as aromatic

RIGHT   RIGHT   WRONG

Learn to climb properly. Place feet squarely on rungs, and grip ladder firmly with hands. Do not climb over top of ladder.

hydrocarbons (for example, xylene), ketones such as methyl isobutyl ketone, or alcohols such as amyl alcohol. Frequently, mixtures of these are used. The solvents used for thinning are also useful for cleanup.

Turpentine

This well known product is obtained from pine trees in the southern states. There are two principal types of turpentine, gum spirits of turpentine and steam distilled wood turpentine. In making gum spirits of turpentine the live pine tree trunks are tapped and a substance called oleo-resin, which oozes from the openings, is collected in pans. The oleo-resin is distilled providing liquid turpentine and residue or rosin.

Wood turpentine is made by steam distilling wood obtained from pine tree stumps.

A third type of turpentine, which is not considered of much importance in the paint industry, is sulphate wood turpentine. Sulphate wood turpentine is made from crude waste liquor obtained from paper mills which use pine pulpwood.

Turpentine is mostly a painter's solvent. Because of its cost, it is not used extensively by paint makers. It is a complex solvent containing many basic organic liquids and acts as a mild drier. It is also imparts a "short" quality to some paints because not as much volume of turpentine is required as other thinners. It is useful primarily with oil-based coatings and varnishes. It should never be used with the resin-based finishes such as the epoxies.

Dipentine

Dipentine is also obtained from the destructive distillation of pine stumps. It is stronger than ordinary turpentine and is used to some extent in organic coatings where a strong, slow solvent is desirable to improve brushing, cut down setting time, and improve leveling and flow. It is also used as an anti-skinning agent and as an ingredient of paint and varnish remover.

Pine Oil

Pine oil is similar to dipentine in its action. It is useful as an anti-skinning agent. It is also an effective disinfectant, and preservative for casein.

Petroleum Spirits

Petroleum spirits, the most popular group of solvents used by the coating industry, are obtained by distilling and refining crude petroleum oil. During the distillation, the petroleum fractions discussed below are drawn off at different temperatures.

Naphtha, V. M. and P. (Varnish Makers' and Painters' Naphtha)

This solvent has a distillation range of approximately 200 to 300 deg. F. It is used by painters as a thinning solvent.

Because of the fast evaporation rate, it reduces the setting time and tends to reduce the flow and leveling-out of paint films. Therefore care should be exercised in the quantity used.

Naphtha is not widely used by paint manufacturers because it evaporates too quickly for most finishes. Also called "benzine" this term is being dropped in favor of naphtha because it is too similar to "benzene," a toxic solvent.

Mineral Spirits

Mineral spirits with a distillation range of 300 to 400 deg. F., is commonly used as a turpentine substitute, as it has approximately the same evaporation rate as gum turpentine. For most purposes it can be used where turpentine is specified. Exceptions are some varnishes and enamels that may exhibit a lack of miscibility (capability of being mixed).

There are many different fractions of mineral spirits. The most volatile is generally most useful in cold weather and the least volatile best in the heat of summer.

Heavy Mineral Spirits

Heavy mineral spirits has a distillation range of 400 to 475 deg. F. This solvent, because it evaporates more slowly than mineral spirits, is well suited for use in flat finishes.

Kerosene

Kerosene, which has a distillation range of 350 to 525 deg. F., is the lowest cost solvent normally used in the coatings industry. It evaporates slowly and improves the brushing and leveling properties of a paint. In paint making kerosene is generally used with some other sol vent such as mineral spirits or naphtha. Kerosene, also called "coal oil", can be destructive to paint films that harden by oxidation before the thinner evaporates. Subsequent evaporation causes "pitting."

Ethyl Alcohol (Ethanol)

Ethyl or grain alcohol is manufactured in large volume from petroleum. Its greatest use in the paint industry is as a solvent and thinner for shellac. Ethyl alcohol for industrial use is made unfit to drink by denaturing with poisons or emetics. In the trade, ethyl alcohol is normally referred to simply as "alcohol."

Methyl Alcohol (Methanol)

Methyl alcohol is also made from petroleum sources. It is known as wood alcohol, because it was originally made by the destructive distillation of wood. It is quite poisonous, causing blindness when taken internally. Thus, its use in the paint industry is being discouraged.

The greatest use for methanol in the paint industry is in paint and varnish removers. It is also a denaturant for ethyl alcohol.

Airless spray equipment makes possible rapid and efficient painting of large commercial and industrial installations.

Lacquer Solvents and Diluents

Toluol (Toluene)

Toluol, which is obtained either from coal tar distillation or from petroleum sources, is one of the most popular lacquer diluents (a lacquer diluent lowers the viscosity of the lacquer but is not a nitrocellulose solvent), and serves as a solvent for the resin and plasticizer portion of the lacquer. A plasticizer is added to lacquer to increase the elasticity and flexibility of the dry film.

Xylol (Xylene)

Xylol is a coal tar distillate which evaporates more slowly than toluol. It also is available from petroleum sources. Xylol is frequently used in aluminum and bronzing liquids where it helps the leafing properties of these finishes. It is also useful in synthetic resin finishes like the epoxy resin paints.

Acetone

Acetone is a highly volatile liquid formerly obtained as a by-product in the fermentation process for butyl alcohol. It is now obtained from petroleum sources. It is completely soluble in water. A strong solvent for many paint and lacquer materials, it is used in some lacquer thinners where speed of evaporation is of importance. An important use has been in the manufacture of paint and varnish removers. It is highly inflammable and should be handled with caution. It is useful as a solvent for spirit soluble dyes.

Benzol (Benzene)

Benzol is also of either petroleum or coal tar origin. Its most common use is in paint and varnish removers. Since it is quite toxic, its use in the paint industry has been diminishing and is being discouraged by safety authorities.

Ethyl Acetate

Ethyl acetate is made from ethyl alcohol and calcium acetate or concentrated acetic acid. This is one of the most popular rapid evaporating solvents of the lacquer industry.

Amyl Acetate (Banana Oil)

Amyl acetate is formed by reacting acetic acid with amyl alcohol. It is a solvent for nitrocellulose and is used to some extent in making lacquers. It is often associated with its use as a bronzing liquid. These liquids, usually nitrocellulose dissolved with the very slow drying amyl acetate, provide a brushable lacquer.

Driers

Driers are catalysts or accelerators for the drying of oils, alkyds and varnishes - - that is, the paints based on vehicles which dry by oxidation. Driers are not used in resin-based paints such as the epoxies. Driers are metals which have been converted to what the chemist calls soaps or salts in order to make them soluble in the paint. Drier selection is critical for the proper driers must be used in the right amount if films are to be obtained which do not dry too fast or, correspondingly, too slow and which do not embrittle on aging. Driers are, of course, added by the paint manufacturer. The painter, himself, seldom has reason to add a drier. If he does, he should follow carefully the recommendation of the manufacturer.

Cobalt Driers

Cobalt drier, which is normally purple in color, is the most powerful drier used commercially in the paint industry. This drier is soluble in all drying oils, whether raw or processed.

Cobalt is what is known as a surface drier. If used in excessive quantities it tends to set up stresses on the surface which may result in wrinkling. This property is made use of in the production of the popular novelty wrinkle finishes. Such a film sprayed on as a thick film will, when baked, wrinkle and form a uniform product pleasing to the eye.

Manganese Driers

Compounds of manganese are lighter in color than cobalt. Manganese is intermediate between cobalt and lead in activity. It may be classified as a "through" drier for it acts on both the surface and the body of the film.

Manganese is used as the sole drier in certain types of coatings, but the combination of cobalt and lead is more popular than the use of manganese as a replacement for both.

Films based on manganese are not as flexible as films based on a lead-cobalt combination, becoming somewhat brittle and hard. Manganese has the disadvantage too, of having a brownish or pinkish cast which has considerable tinting strength.

Manganese is used to some extent in making wrinkle finishes and gives slightly more uniform wrinkles than cobalt.

Lead Driers

Lead driers are used in great quantity -- probably equal to all of the other driers put together. They are almost water-white in color and will not discolor any vehicle.

Lead dries beneath the surface of the film. Thus the use of lead in combination with cobalt results in a film which dries rapidly on the surface as well as throughout the depth of the film.

Various combinations of lead, cobalt and other metals are used in formulating modern finishes.

As with lead pigments, lead driers are restricted under the interstate orders, and state and city laws banning lead paint as outlined on page 15, paragraph 2.

Calcium Driers

Calcium does not function well as a drier when used alone but it is useful with other metals such as cobalt. In many vehicles the mixture displays desirable drying properties. It is also used as a substitute for lead where the presence of lead is undesirable, as in nontoxic enamels and fume-resisting enamels.

Iron Driers

The iron driers are dark brown in color and have high tinting strength which limits their use in colored finishes where the discoloration will not be noticed. These driers are used to some extent in iron oxide pigmented paints and certain other color finishes, especially industrial baking coatings. The iron driers are much more effective at high baking temperature than at room temperature.

Zinc Driers

Zinc, like calcium, will not function as a drier when used alone. It does, however, have many properties which are important and which tend to provide a film that is harder than the film would be without the zinc.

In some cases zinc also acts as a wetting agent to speed up the mixing of the pigment with the vehicle.

Japan Driers

Japan driers are essentially weak combination driers, usually manganese and lead. Sometimes cobalt, lead and manganese combinations are used along with some resin, like rosin. The resin lowers the cost of the drier and acts as a hardener for the final film.

Use Driers with Care

A small amount of drier is usually required when thinning or mixing paints with raw linseed oil.

In mixing paints and varnishes the manufacturer's instructions should be followed closely. Remember that excessive use of a drier may cause wrinkling and other defects in a finish.

Proper ventilation is essential to fast drying of all types of paints and varnishes. Heat and the movement of air increases drying. Oxidation and evaporation increase in proportion to the rise in temperature.

Some paints, particularly paints containing large amounts of carbon black, lampblack, titanium dioxide, Prussian blue, and some organic reds, tend to lose their drying properties on aging in the can. The addition of a small amount of Japan drier will restore the drying properties of the paint.

Fillers and Sealers

Fillers

Woods containing open pores such as oak, ash, walnut, chestnut, and mahogany, require an application of filler, after staining, to give a smooth base for additional coats. Filler is not required on close-grained woods such as birch, fir, hard maple, cherry, and yellow pine.

Paste filler is composed mostly of silex, a form of silica, linseed oil and Japan drier. It is supplied in several colors, including natural or transparent, and white.

Fillers may be colored with colors-in-oil or dry pigment color. Wood stain (dye) added to filler stains the wood that remains visible, i. e., the unfilled portion. This is sometimes done as an economy measure.

Sealers

A sealer, as used in wood finishing, is a material used as a first coat on close-grained wood, or over filler on open-grained wood. Its purpose is to seal the pores and also to provide a good solid foundation for succeeding coats.

Shellac, varnish, lacquer, and synthetic sealers are available. Sealers may be applied with a brush, or by spraying. Instructions supplied by the manufacturer should be followed.

Wall Sizes

A wall size is a solution of glue, starch, casein, shellac, or varnish, used to seal or fill the pores of a wall surface to stop suction, counteract chemicals or stains which may be present in the surface coating, and prepare the surface for paint, wallpaper or fabric.

On painted walls the size is usually applied after the priming coat and before applying the final coatings.

The practice of mixing sizes on the job, once common, has been largely supplanted by using water mix and other pre-prepared sizes.

Glue and casein sizes are mostly used to prepare walls for papering and for other wall coverings.

Varnish sizes are primarily used on plaster before calcimining so the old calcimine can be washed off easily before new is applied.

Paint and Varnish Removers

Paint and varnish removers are made of chemical solvents which, when spread over old finishes, soften the finish and permit it to be removed with a steel scraper, putty knife, and steel wool.

There are various liquids which may be used to remove paint and varnish such as caustic soda, wood alcohol, acetone, and ammonia. It is advisable to purchase ready-made removers.

Paint and varnish removers fall into two principal categories - - those with a wax or paraffin base, and removers that are wax-free. They are further classified as inflammable and noninflammable types.

In the wax-base remover, wax forms a floating film over the solvent to prevent rapid evaporation. The wax (or paraffin) must be carefully removed with a cleaning agent such as naphtha, denatured alcohol, turpentine or benzine before proceeding with the refinishing. Otherwise its presence will cause nondrying of future coats and a lack of bond. Alcohol is generally best because it removes the wax without dissolving it. Solvents for the wax frequently cause it to penetrate into porous surfaces where it remains to inhibit the bonding of subsequent coats. The surface should also be washed with some alkaline material such as a trisodium phosphate solution in hot water to remove wax traces. This, followed by flood; rinsing and drying, usually renders the surfaces ready for repainting.

Removers that are wax-free usually work slower than the wax-base removers, but have the advantage that the need for removing the surface with a wax solvent is eliminated.

The advent of the resin-based finishes with their greater resistance to solvents has made necessary the development of entirely new types of solvent removers based on very strong penetrating, high-boiling solvents. Again, the recommendation of the manufacturer should be followed carefully relative to the choice of a remover for a given type of coating.

A painter should exercise great care in handling removers, since they can burn skin and clothing, and can damage other surfaces with which they come in contact. Because of the highly flammable nature of many removers, special precautions should be taken to prevent fire. The manufacturer's instructions should be carefully followed and a neutralizing solution should be at hand to counteract the effects of the remover, in case of accident. Read labels carefully and take the advise given.

Putty, Caulking Compounds and Miscellaneous Materials

Putty and other fillers are used extensively by painters and decorators to conceal defects in wood, fill open grain, cracks and other defects, to fill cracks in plaster and masonry surfaces, and to fill structural gaps between building materials of unlike contraction and expansion.

Putty

There are a number of types of putty, one of the best for general usage is a putty made from white lead, whiting, linseed oil, and a neutral oil to keep it from drying too quickly. Cheaper grades are made of marble dust and cheap oils.

Some painters make their own putty by simply mixing dry whiting with linseed oil on the job. This mixture should age overnight before use. Sawdust mixed with glue or casein can be used to fill large holes in wood and to build up corner defects in unpainted woodwork.

Plaster of Paris (calcium sulphate) when mixed with water sets quickly to form a hard mass which is used to a considerable extent in filling small cracks and holes in interior work. Hardening of plaster of Paris may be slowed by mixing it with a weak glue size or a little vinegar.

Available also are a large variety of plastic wood, crack fillers, and water-mix putties, manufactured for special purposes. The modern painter uses these extensively.

Spackling Putty

Swedish putty should be mentioned because for many years the only smoothing or spackling compounds were made by the painter in his own shop. These were jealously guarded secrets. The basic ingredients were almost always a mixture of whiting and glue into which was emulsified white lead in linseed oil and some varnish. There are many variations and each man considered his product the very best. This soft, smooth putty is knifed on rough surfaces, then when dry, sanded to make a glass-like level paint ground. Modern prepared materials not only supplant this material but are far less hazardous to use.

Caulking Compound

Caulking compound, which usually contains asbestos fiber, a pigment for opacity, fish oil or soybean oil, and drier is used to seal joints or fill crevices around chimneys and windows. It should remain elastic over long periods of time, yet surface dry sufficiently to keep it from collecting dirt. The fact that this material does not completely harden allows it to expand and contract with the movement of wood or other building materials.

Caulking compound comes in two principal types. There is a gun type for application with a caulking gun which forces the compound into cracks and crevices in ribbon-like form, and a knife type for use with a putty knife. The knife type caulking compound makes a durable window sash putty.

Caulking compound is also available in rolls of ready-to-apply strips. Caulking compound may be obtained in several different colors.

Masonry Crack Fillers

Cracks in concrete, brick and stucco, may be filled by using a mixture of Portland cement (one part), sand (three parts) with only enough water added to produce a stiff mix. The cracks must be carefully cleaned out and the edges soaked with water before applying the cement and sand mixture.

Wood Bleaches

Bleaches are used to restore the natural color to stained or discolored woods and to make woods lighter in color.

Woods differ considerably in the ease with which they may be bleached. Birch, oak, mahogany, ash, maple, walnut and beech can be bleached fairly easy. Pine, gum, tupelo, redwood and poplar are examples of wood which are difficult to bleach.

Types of Bleaches

Oxalic acid is a cheap, good bleach. It may be dissolved in hot water or alcohol or a combination of these. It will work only on surfaces free of oils or waxes and is most effective in removing the brownish cast, leaving a pink tone. A ten percent solution of sodium hydrosulfite in water can be used by repeatedly wetting the wood to be bleached with the solution. Ordinary household laundry bleach such as the chlorine solutions will bleach some wood. Chlorine bleaches leave wood slightly yellowish or greenish if used too strong. Calcium chloride can be applied as a paste to pine to "pickle" it. This is a bleaching action that leaves the wood in a fine medley of mellow colors.

The most valuable commercial bleaches obtainable today are the "A and B" or "1 and 2" types. There are several variations of these but they most often consist of sodium silicate solution followed by 100 to 130 percent saturations of hydrogen peroxide. This will bleach most types of wood. The strong hydrogen peroxide is extremely active and will burn skin, clothing, bristles in brushes and will eat glue out of joints in furniture. Glasses should be worn to protect the eyes when using this and other corrosive chemicals. They are applied with fiber brushes.

Cleaning Compound

Removing dirt, grease and smoke from old paint films is one of the most important parts of a repainting job.

Washing soda, sal soda, soda ash, lye, phosphates and commercially prepared products sold under many trade names clean by the chemical action of their alkali bases which turn fats, oils and greases into soap. The soap formed becomes a detergent which surrounds and carries dirt particles away. Many non-soapy detergents and other cleaners are also available.

Waxes

Waxes used by the decorator and wood finisher include: Carnauba, obtained from the leaves of a species of palm grown in Brazil (sometimes called Brazilian wax); Beeswax, obtained from the honeycomb of the common bee; Candelilla, obtained from a shrub grown in Mexico; Japan wax, obtained from seeds of Rhus succedaneum, and the mineral waxes or paraffins.

Two general types of wax commonly used for polishing floors and woodwork are paste wax and liquid wax. Liquid wax is similar to

When working on ladder, set ladder where object can be reached handily. Never lean out too far to one side.

WRONG   RIGHT

paste wax, but has usually been mixed with a solvent which has cleaning properties.

Many of the best waxes in prepared form are compounds of various waxes with silicones. Many synthetic materials are available today for wax formulation. Again, the manufacturer's recommendations are important in choosing a specific wax for a given job.

Know Your Abrasives

Abrasives are materials used by painters, decorators and wood finishers, to smooth rough surfaces and to produce "rubbed" finishes on woodwork and furniture.

The use of the term "sandpaper" as applied to paper coated with abrasive grains was probably started when sand was actually used for that purpose. The term now is obsolete because sand is no longer used in this way. Today, papers coated with abrasive grains should be called "Coated Abrasive" papers or simply "Garnet Paper."

Abrasives used include: Flint, Garnet, Emery, Aluminum Oxide, Silicon Carbide, Pumice Stone, Rottenstone, and Buffing Compounds. Flint, Garnet and Emery are natural abrasives that are mined. Aluminum Oxide and Silicon Carbide are synthetic (man-made) products. Aluminum Oxide is made by fusing the mineral Bauxite at high temperatures, rigidly controlled. Silicon Carbide is made by fusing of silica sand and coke, much as nature makes diamonds.

Backing papers come in different weights, thin for fine curved work and heavy backs with "open" faced coarser grains for leveling flat surfaces. Abrasives are also available on cloth. Jeans is a light flexible cloth and "drills" are the heavier, tougher variety.

Cabinet paper sold by the ream is available in garnet for hand work and the tougher aluminum oxide for machine driven sanding. The range of grits is from 4/0 to 3 1/2.

Finishing paper sold by the ream is for leveling and smoothing sanding sealers. It is in garnet for soft sealers and aluminum oxide for hard sealers and power driven sanding. The range of grits is 10/0 to 1/0.

Waterproof Carborundum paper is for use before finish coats in new or old enameling. It is most used in automotive work but is indispensable for sanding long oil varnishes that would otherwise "seed" or roll. Its grit range is generally given in screen size numbers of 60 to 600.

Some abrasive papers are made flexible in several directions for curved work. The adhesives used to stick the grit to the backing are widely different being merely cheap glue on some coarse flint papers.

It is important to store good abrasive paper in cool (65 to 70 deg. F.) places and at average humidity conditions (with the exception of waterproof finishing papers).

Flint Paper

Flint paper, which is grayish-white in color, appears light tan on finished sheets. What looks like sand is actually quartz. Flint paper is not expensive compared to some other types of abrasive papers, but it has a short working life. It is satisfactory for use by painters in sanding heavy paint, or on gummy woods that clog and ruin more expensive papers quickly. Flint paper has very little use in industry because other abrasives are far superior.

Garnet Paper

Garnet, which is reddish in color and hard and sharp, comes from the same source as the semiprecious jewel by that name. Garnet paper is more expensive than flint paper, but lasts longer and for most purposes is recommended in preference to the flint paper. It is accepted as the most useful in the paint trade today.

Emery Paper

This abrasive comes mostly from Greece and Turkey and consists of crystals of natural aluminum oxide. Until recently it was the acknowledged abrasive for use in metal finishing.

Emery is a slow-cutting, short-lived abrasive, which like flint paper, is today superseded by faster cutting abrasives. However, it is still carried in most hardware stores.

Aluminum Oxide

Aluminum oxide, which is reddish brown in color, is extremely hard and sharp. It is used in making fine grinding wheels and is the basis for aluminum oxide papers. Aluminum oxide papers are widely used on hardwoods, metals and other materials.

	Silicon Carbide	Aluminum Oxide	Garnet	Equivalent In Symbol Series	Flint	Emery
FINE	600			12/0		
	500	500		11/0		
	400	400		10/0		
	360					
	320	320		9/0		
	280	280	280	8/0		
	240	240	240	7/0		
	220	220	220	6/0	4/0	
					3/0	
	180	180	180	5/0		3/0
	150	150	150	4/0	2/0	2/0
	120	120	120	3/0		1/0
					1/0	
COARSE	100	100	100	2/0	1/2	1/2
	80	80	80	1/0	1	1
	60	60	60	1/2		1 1/2
	50	50	50	1	1 1/2	2
	40	40	40	1 1/2	2	2 1/2
	36	36	36	2	2 1/2	3
	30	30	30	2 1/2	3	
	24	24	24	3		
	20	20	20	3 1/2		
	16	16		4		
	12			4 1/2		

Fig. 2-3. Classification of Abrasive Grain Sizes.

Silicon Carbide

Silicon carbide crystals are shiny black in appearance and are very hard and brittle. This type of abrasive paper is used mostly on soft metals such as aluminum and bronze and on plastics, glass and stone. It is too brittle for satisfactory use on hard metals.

Sheet Sizes

Abrasive papers and cloths come in two principal sheet sizes, 9 in. by 11 in. and 9 in. by 10 in.

Grit sizes range from Extra Fine, 12/0 to Extra Coarse Floor Paper, 4 1/2, as shown in Fig. 2-3.

Waterproof Papers

Waterproof abrasive papers have been developed to solve certain finishing problems. Sanding with water makes the abrasive cut faster, easier, and clog less. Water is preferred wherever fine work is done. Some abrasive papers are made to use with gasoline or mineral spirits and will not stand water. Others may be used dry, with gasoline or mineral spirits or with water. Paint that contains lead or other poisonous substances should be wet sanded. For fine furniture finishing waterproof paper is used for wet rubbing with water, turpentine and oil. Wet sanding is never used on untreated wood.

Pumice

Powered pumice, a rock of marine volcanic origin, is good for toning down the luster of finishes that are too glossy, and for giving a smooth surface to a finish. It comes in grades from 4-F (finest), to No. 7 (coursest). In wood finishing, powdered pumice should be kept wet by using water or oil. The work should be inspected frequently by cleaning and drying the surface so the rubbing may be stopped before cutting through the finish.

After completing the rubbing operation, pumice may be removed from the wood by using a chamois and water or a rag dampened in slow mineral spirtis if oil has been used in the rubbing.

Prepared Rubbing Compounds

There are many rubbing compounds made for specific purposes. They differ depending on whether they are to be used with lacquers, enamels or ordinary paints and whether high or low gloss is desired.

Rottenstone (Tripoli)

Rottenstone as used in wood finishing is a type of limestone. It is a siliceous residue which is also called diatomaceous earth, tripoli, and kieselguhr. Softer and finer grained than pumice, it is used with oil as a lubricant to produce a soft satin-like finish. Cleaning the surface is done as for pumice. Rubbing abrasives work faster with thin solvents or water than with oil and more viscous liquids.

Steel Wool

Steel wool, although not an abrasive, is used to remove old finishes and rust and smooth very rough surfaces, particularly rounded surfaces.

Steel wool comes in various degrees of fineness from 3/0, which is very fine, to No. 5, which is very coarse.

In using steel wool strokes should be made WITH the grain to prevent scratching.

SEAL EDGES FIRST. When using exterior fir plywood, make certain you seal all edges first with a heavy coat of high-grade exterior paint. Edges should be sealed before application if possible.

Unit 3

TOOLS AND EQUIPMENT

If a painter has well-selected equipment and knows how to use it properly, he can work efficiently and rapidly.

To prevent accidents, it is essential that every worker in the painting and decorating trades be aware of the dangers involved in the use of equipment and that he try at all times to assure the safety of himself and his fellow workers. Attention is called to the Unit in this book on Health and Safety.

Brushes

In selecting brushes, a painter should remember that quality is a major consideration. A good brush will hold more paint, carry the paint without excessive dripping, paint without spattering, put on a smoother coat, and cut a clean, even edge. The initial cost of good brushes is greater than that of brushes of inferior quality, but the difference in serviceability more than offsets the extra cost.

In order to select brushes properly a painter should know the essential qualities of a good brush. He should be familiar with the various types of brushes so he may choose the ones best suited for each job. To receive the maximum value from his brushes, a painter must use them correctly and care for them properly.

Obtaining Brush Bristles

At one time almost all quality brush bristles were obtained from Russia and China. After World War I it became impossible to obtain Russian bristles. Thus, until the second World War when this source was eliminated, Chinese hogs were the most important source of bristles for paint brushes. Some white Polish hog bristle was imported in small quantities for fine varnish brushes and artists' brushes.

The Chinese hogs, Fig. 3-1, run practically wild, and the bitterness of the winters they face causes their hides to thicken and their bristles, or chu chang, to grow long. Hogs raised under less rigorous conditions do not produce the tough, long bristles of the type required for fine paint brushes.

Fig. 3-1. Chinese hogs grow long hair from which good quality bristles are obtained.

The value of hog bristles over other animal, vegetable, or synthetic fibers lies in the fact that the outer end of the hog bristle divides into two or more branches like a tree, Fig. 3-2. This is called the "flag" end of the bristle.

Fig. 3-2. Value of hog bristles over other animal or vegetable fiber lies in the fact the outer end of the hog bristle divides into branches like a tree. This is called the "flag end" of the bristle.

The flagging provides the brush with ability to hold paint by capillary attraction. The flagged ends will carry more paint from the pot to the surface and also will increase the number and fineness of bristle contacts with the surface, leaving finer brush marks that more easily flow together. Flagging prolongs the life of a brush, for as the bristle wears it naturally becomes thicker and stiffer. If it were not for the splitting quality, the brush would soon be too stiff to use.

Synthetic Bristle

In recent years, ingenious chemists and technicians have developed tough and long-wearing qualities in synthetic bristle.

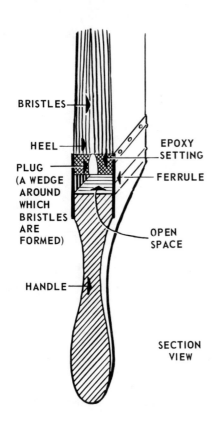

Fig. 3-3. Section view of paint brush showing various parts.

Nylon fiber, although it has about three times the wearing power of hog bristles, is straight sided and without special treatment does not hold paint as well as hog bristles. This condition has been remedied by inserting right angle kinks at intervals, by splitting the fibers, by exploding the tips, and by other means. A minor disadvantage of nylon bristle is that it will soften

in shellac dissolved in either methyl or ethyl alcohol. The alcohol has no permanent effect on nylon and the bristles can be restored by immersing the brushes for 30 minutes in boiling water and drying them overnight.

An advantage of nylon is that water does not soften it as much as it softens bristles, which suits it for water paints of all kinds. Nylon is attacked by coal tar acids found in some creosote products and by very strong solvents such as ketones which are contained in high performance coatings such as two-component epoxies. It is probably that synthetic fiber paint brushes will eventually completely displace those made with natural bristles. Ever since the beginning of World War II Chinese bristles have been increasingly more difficult to obtain, making it necessary to develop substitutes for the natural products.

Other Bristles

Horsehair, which comes from the manes and tails of horses, is substituted for bristle in very cheap brushes. It does not retain its original stiffness when dipped in oil, nor does it have flag ends like hog bristle. It is used mostly in painter's dusters and brooms for dry sweeping.

Tampico, a grass fiber which grows in Mexico and South America, is used to make brushes for floor brooms, whitewashing, and for strong acids, bleaches and other corrosive chemicals.

Hair Brushes

Many fine artists' tools are made of hair from red and black sable, bear, badger, weasel, skunk, and the so-called camel's hair which is actually squirrel's tail.

Badger hair is blended with other bristles for brushes for fine glazing and graining and for short fine varnish brushes. The other types of hair are used in very small brushes for striping, lining, and freehand art work.

Hair does not have the stiffness of bristle and is usually smaller in diameter. Artists who require stiff brushes often use those made of white hog bristle of a highly select quality.

Paint Brush Selection

A good brush is made up of various lengths of bristles so that when the flat ends of the longer bristles wear off, the brush will still have value. Of considerable importance is the solidity of the bristles, (solidity is obtained by using more long than short bristles), and the manner in which the bristles are bound to each other and to the brush handle. The texture or blending of stiff and soft bristles in proper proportion should be such that it will provide proper paint spreading.

Brushes should always have bristles which are set in vulcanized rubber, or fastened with chemically inert cements, Fig. 3-3, which are not affected by water, oil, turpentine, or other solvents.

High quality brushes are clean and feel springy and elastic when pressed against the back of the hand. They should maintain their proper shape when flexed and should have that intangible "balance" that makes for a comfortable day's work.

Types of Brushes

Wall Brushes

Brushes for applying paint and stain to large wall surfaces, both interior and exterior, are flat, Fig. 3-4, and 3 to 6 inches wide. Width

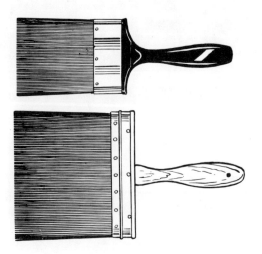

Fig. 3-4. Flat wall brushes.

allowances for various localities differ with trade union agreements. Wall brushes are 3/4 to 1 1/2 in. thick, and have bristles from 2 to about 7 in. in length. "Flats" are usually square-ended and square-edged with the natural bend of the bristles bending toward the center of the brush.

Flat Sash and Trim Brush

The flat sash and trim brush for trimming cornices, window frames, and narrow boards, Fig. 3-5, is similar to the flat paint brush, but comes in widths from 1 to 3 1/2 in. and has bristles from 2 to 4 1/2 in. long. Some sash and trim brushes have chiseled edges - - that is, the working ends of the brushes are beveled on both sides like a cold chisel. Those that are 1 to 2 in. wide are called sashtools. For the average woodwork job a "set" of two brushes, one sashtool and one brush approximately 3 in. wide, is required.

Fig. 3-5. Flat sash and trim brush.

Oval Sash and Trim Brush

Fig. 3-6 shows an oval sash brush which ordinarily comes in sizes from 1/2 in. to 2 in. in diameter. Some painters prefer this type brush to the flat sash and trim brush. Round brushes are also available. These styles, however, are rapidly going out of use in favor of semi-oval shapes and flat brushes.

Fig. 3-6. Oval sash brush.

Angular Sash Brush

An angular cut sash brush, Fig. 3-7, is used by some painters when painting hard-to-reach spots. It is usually available in 1, 1 1/2 and 2 in. widths with bristles from 1 1/2 to over 3 in. long.

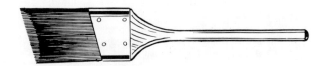

Fig. 3-7. Angular sash brush.

Calcimine Brushes

Calcimine brushes, Fig. 3-8, are available in widths from 5 to 8 in. They are used extensively in applying water-thinned paints and for

Fig. 3-8. Two types of calcimine brushes.

other jobs on which large brushes are required. They are made of very long, tough and elastic gray hog bristles, so-called because the light cream and black mixture is a sort of "salt and pepper" gray color.

Stippling Brush

The stippling brush, Fig. 3-9, generally has its bristles set in rows in a wooden or aluminum block, about 3 1/2 by 9 in. in size. It is built very much like an extra thick calcimine brush without a handle. It is also made of gray bristle set in tufts and is used to tap the paint with the ends of the bristle to form a slight pebble texture.

Fig. 3-9. Stippling brush.

Enamel and Varnish Brush

Enamel and varnish brushes such as shown in Fig. 3-10, are both flat and chisel-shaped. The chisel shape, which contributes to smoother flow and prevention of lap marks, is formed by putting long bristles in the center of the brush and shorter bristles on the outside. This type brush usually comes in widths of 2 to 3 in., with 3 to 3 1/2 in. bristles. It is made of select, fine (small diameter) bristles and must be comparatively short to force high viscosity gloss finishes into an even film.

Fig. 3-10. Brushes for applying varnish and enamel.

Semiovals, a shape nearly flat but with rounded ends and a slight expansion in the center of the width, are used for fine enameling and for exterior wood siding. Three inch and 3 1/2 in. brushes for exterior work are built with extremely long bristle and are called "Thirties" and "Thirty-fives." Four inch brushes are "Forties," although this latter type has not been used much in the last decade.

Stucco and Masonry Brush

The stucco and masonry brush, Fig. 3-11, usually comes in a 5 or 6 in. width with 4 to 6 in. bristles. It is made of bristle, fiber, or nylon and is intended for very rough surfaces and abrasive paints. Some of these brushes look like regular flat wall brushes. Others resemble calcimine brushes.

Fig. 3-11. Stucco and masonry brush of fiber. Nylon brushes for this purpose now resemble wall brushes, as seen in Fig. 3-4.

Roofing Brush

The roofing brush, Fig. 3-12, is useful in painting large shingle roof areas. A popular size for this brush is 7 in. with 3 1/2 in. bristles. It is generally used with a long handle set into the brush at a small angle like a push broom.

Fig. 3-12. Roofing brush.

Bronzing Brush

In applying aluminum or gold color enamel, a wide soft hair bronzing brush can be used to good advantage. This brush is also used for stain, black glass backing and similar fine jobs. It is usually about an inch long by 1 1/2 to 2 in. wide and has a very thin ferrule.

Stencil Brush

The stencil brush, Fig. 3-13, is primarily for use with stencils, as its name indicates.

Fig. 3-13. Stencil brush.

Wire Brush

Wire brushes, Fig. 3-14, have short steel wire tufts set in hardwood blocks or handles. They are useful for cleaning plaster off subflooring, removing rust from metal, and wherever foreign matter must be removed by abrasion. Several other types are available for special purposes.

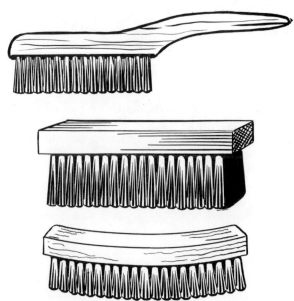

Fig. 3-14. Wire brushes. Above. Shoe handle. Center. Flat back. Below. Curved back.

Dusting Brush

Fig. 3-15 illustrates two types of dusting brushes. These have soft bristles and are useful for dusting sanded woodwork and baseboards. Larger jobs require a broom. Many duster shapes are available. They frequently look like wide woodwork brushes.

Fig. 3-15. Painter dusters. Left. Round duster filled with mixture of black horsehair and black Tampico. Right. Flat duster filled with bristle and horsehair.

Artists' Brushes

Small brushes primarily intended for sign painters and artists are ideal for many jobs handled by painters and decorators.

Caring for Paint Brushes

It is well to remove any loose bristles from a new brush by running the fingers through the bristles a few times and by tapping the brush against the palm of the hand.

Some painters suspend brushes with natural bristles in raw linseed oil for several days before using them. The bristles are porous and absorb the oil which tends to make them more flexible and helps to seal out moisture and thinners. Soaking is unnecessary for nylon brushes.

A thoroughly clean brush is essential to good workmanship. Any brush can be readily cleaned while it is still soft with the thinner of the product in which the brush has been used. Following are the standard thinners.

TURPENTINE, followed by naphtha or min-

eral spirits, will clean brushes used in oil base finishes which must be thinned with turpentine. Otherwise the brush may be put directly into mineral spirits. A follow-up bath of kerosene is good in the summer when warm weather has a tendency to dry a brush too much. In winter, a faster mineral spirits will act in the same way. If a brush is too wet at the start of a job, it will cause the paint to streak and the paint will drip at the heel.

ALCOHOL will clean brushes used in applying shellac or spirit (alcohol) stains.

LACQUER THINNER, preferably a thinner made by the manufacturer of the lacquer, should be used in cleaning lacquer brushes. A cheaper lacquer thinner is generally available for clean-up.

WATER is used for cleaning brushes used in calcimine, casein, water emulsions and other water-thinned paints including various latex emulsions. If paint is allowed to dry at the heel of a brush, lacquer thinner or benzine may be needed to dissolve the dry paint. This treatment is usually accompanied by combining, scraping and flexing.

The brush should be immersed and thoroughly soaked in the thinner. It may then be worked against the sides of the container to release the paint. The bristles should be squeezed between the thumb and forefinger of one hand to work out paint from the center of the brush. Work from the ferrule toward the tip of the brush to

Fig. 3-16. Cleaning brush with a steel comb.

keep paint from accumulating at the heel. A brush with this part clogged with old paint is said to be "heeled up." This procedure should be repeated several times and the brush dip-rinsed each time to help remove the paint.

Brushes to be stored should be washed with mild soap suds and water and rinsed in clear water. The water should be thoroughly squeezed out of the brush, using a flat stick, clean paint paddle or a ruler. Squeeze from the ferrule toward the tip.

Next, lightly comb the brush using a steel comb, Fig. 3-16, or an ordinary hair comb, to make sure the bristles below the surface are straight and parallel. Let the brush dry; wrap it in kraft or wax paper, working carefully so that the bristles are not bent; fasten paper with rubber band or string; and hang the wrapped brush in a cool, dry place until it is needed again. Moth balls or naphthalene crystals inside the paper or closet will protect the brush from moths.

Do not stand a brush on the bristle end, for it will soon have a permanent bend which will cause the brush to work unsatisfactorily. Rather, drill a small hole in the brush handle and then suspend the brush on a wire in an open can of linseed oil as shown in Fig. 3-17.

OIL LEVEL SLIGHTLY ABOVE FERRULE

Fig. 3-17. Storing paint brushes.

There are two schools of thought on whether brushes should be stored in oil. Some painters believe a brush should be washed and dried whereas others could not do without an oil tank. Actually, it is a matter of personal preference when the brushes are being used in normal oil paints. The oil tank method is not too good for brushes used in synthetics or emulsions which are incompatible with oil, unless the brush is washed carefully both before and after storage in oil. This imposes double work on the painter

at the day's end and beginning.

After each day's use, a calcimine, whitewash or paste brush should be washed with warm water and suspended, with the bristles downward, to dry.

Brushes should not be stored in water, for the water may cause the handles to swell and split the ferrules. Also, prolonged water immersion will destroy the elasticity of the bristles and cause them to be flabby.

Renovating Hardened Brushes

Hardened paint may be removed from a brush that has been improperly cleaned by soaking the brush in a container of paint remover or brush cleaner or both in the order mentioned. When the paint has softened, use a scraper to remove the paint on the outside of the bristles and wash out the remaining paint with hot water and soap powder. Use a brush comb as shown in Fig. 3-16 with each of these operations until the comb will completely penetrate the heel.

It is wise to renovate brushes in which the paint has hardened BUT IT IS WISER TO GIVE THE BRUSHES THE PROPER CARE SO THIS TREATMENT WILL NOT BE NECESSARY.

How To Use A Brush

Personal preferences influence how a journeyman grips and holds a paint brush. The type of work and size of the brush also have bearing on this point.

In using all types of brushes, it is advisable to hold the handle almost perpendicular while slanting it to the surface to be painted, in the direction of travel. The brush should be held so that free and easy wrist motion is combined with motion of the arm and body. In spreading paint it is well to press down firmly enough so that the bristles will "plow" through the paint film and level it. However this advice must be tempered by the knowledge that if a brush is flexed too firmly it will wear in the middle instead of at the tip where the wear is supposed to be.

The handle should be pointed in the same direction of travel when removing the brush at the end of the brush stroke to prevent excessive wear and splitting of bristles as well as unnecessary paint splattering.

Varnish and enamel should be "flowed on"

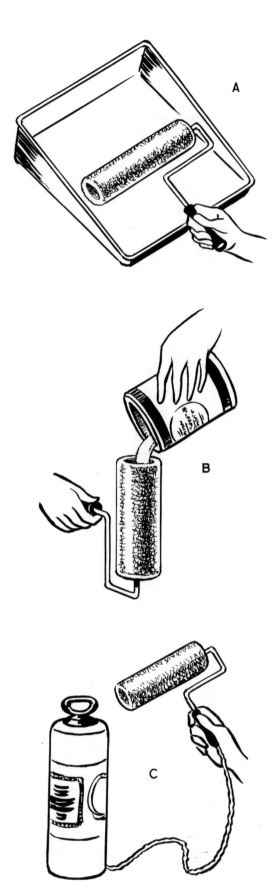

Fig. 3-18. Types of paint rollers. A—Pan-type roller.
B—Fountain roller. C—Pressure-type roller.

with even strokes. Excessive brushing tends to create air bubbles in some paints. Do not try to cover too much surface with one brushful. Dip the brush just far enough into the paint - - not more than one-half the length of the bristles - - to take up a load that will not drip on the way to the surface being painted. In removing excess paint, gently tap the brush against the side of the can. Do not wipe the brush across the can edgewise. It is well to start a new brushful a few inches from the completed portion and to end up by brushing into the finished part. In painting wood, the last strokes should be in the direction of the grain. In painting any surface with full flowing enamels or varnishes the material should be "cross stroked," then "laid off" in the right direction. The "right direction" is vertical on walls and towards the light source on ceilings, especially when the ceilings are painted with high gloss enamel.

Pipe, and other round objects of small diameter should be painted with a brush at least as narrow as the diameter of the pipe.

When too wide a brush is used to paint narrow surfaces, "fish tailing" or excessive wearing of the center bristles often results. Excessive pressure on any brush will also cause "fish tailing."

Another common fault is application of heavy bodied paints by using the brush edgeways. This results in wearing of the corners and lessening the brush's ability to cut into a corner or a sharp, straight line.

Paint Rollers

The three principal types of paint rollers available are the dip type, the fountain type in which paint is poured into the roller itself, and the pressure type, in which paint is forced into the roller by air pressure. See Fig. 3-18. The fountain and pressure types are faster and more practical on large jobs although these types are not extensively used.

Paint rollers can be used in applying many types of finishes, both interior and exterior, including oil, rubber and water base paints, floor and deck paints, masonry paint, and aluminum finishes.

Rollers are ideal for large area painting and adapt well to painting places that are hard to reach with a brush such as high ceilings over stairways. They are also used to stipple finish paint following brush application on ordinary room size jobs in place of block stipplers.

Cleaning Paint Rollers

After use, paint rollers may be cleaned using solvents recommended for cleaning brushes. After cleaning, excess solvent should be pressed from the roller with the fingers and the roller allowed to dry.

Additional information on using paint rollers will be found in the Unit on Coating Application.

Mechanical Spray Painting Equipment

The mechanical method of applying paint with spraying equipment is used extensively since it is a practical and economical means of paint application. Almost all types of protective coatings can be applied with a spray gun in less time than is required for application with brushes or rollers. Most lacquers can be applied by spraying only.

In view of the important place spray painting now holds in the painting industry, it is essential that the painter acquaint himself with available equipment.

Air Compressors

Many sizes and types of air compressors are available, varying from a small electric unit with self-contained compressor, Fig. 3-19, to large units operated by automobile-type engines.

Fig. 3-19. Small electric sprayer with self-contained compressor.

Thus, it is important to obtain a unit with sufficient capacity to do the work expected of it.

A compressor, such as shown in Fig. 3-20, is typical of a convenient portable compressor useful for many industrial maintenance painting jobs.

Fig. 3-20. Air compressor unit powered by 1.7 hp gasoline engine.

How Compressors Work

The two principal types of air compressors are known as the piston type and the diaphragm type. The piston type consists of a metal piston working inside of a cylinder. When the piston goes down, air is sucked into the cylinder; when the piston goes up, the air is compressed.

In a diaphragm-type compressor, a rubber diaphragm is substituted for the metal piston. The diaphragm type is practical for light work, but because of its more sturdy construction and superior performance, a piston-type compressor is considered better for all-around use.

Spray Gun Types

Spray guns used for paint spraying are based either on suction or pressure. The suction feed gun can be compared to the simple mouth spray, Fig. 3-21. Air passing over the tip of the fluid tube produces a vacuum to suck fluid from the

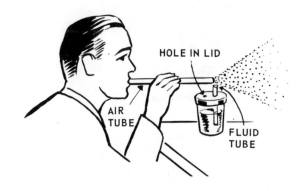

Fig. 3-21. In a suction spray gun air passing over tip of fluid tube produces vacuum to suck fluid from container.

container into the air stream. A suction feed gun can be identified by the fact that it has a vent hole in the cover of the paint cup. A suction feed gun is suited for use with the lighter bodied materials such as shellacs, stains, varnishes, lacquers and synthetic enamels.

The principle of the pressure gun is shown in drawing, Fig. 3-22. Part of the air is diverted to the closed container, forcing fluid up the tube into the air stream. Guns with this positive type of fluid feed may be used to spray heavy materials.

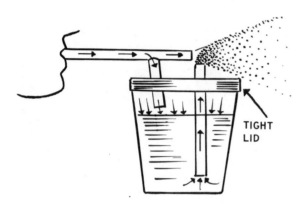

Fig. 3-22. In the pressure type of spray gun, part of the air is diverted into a closed container, forcing fluid up the tube into the air stream.

Spray guns may be of the bleeder type or non-bleeder type. A non-bleeder gun cannot pass air until the trigger is pulled. This type of gun

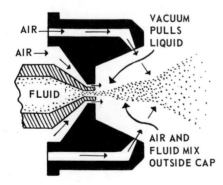

Fig. 3-23. External mix gun; air and fluid mix outside the cap.

is used when air is supplied from a tank or from a compressor having pressure control. A bleeder

gun passes air at all times, thus preventing the pressure of the compressor from becoming excessive. When working directly from a small compressor, a bleeder type gun should be used.

Spray guns may be either "internal mix" or "external mix." These terms relate to whether air and fluid mix outside the cap, Fig. 3-23, or inside the cap, Fig. 3-24. (See Unit on Coating Application, page 129, for details.)

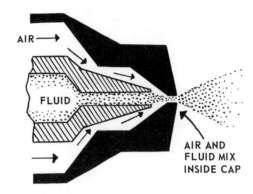

Fig. 3-24. Internal mix gun; air and fluid mix inside cap of spray gun.

Comparison of Suction and Feeder Type Guns

A pressure feed gun will spray heavy materials and may be used with large pressure feed tanks. Thus it is better suited than the suction type gun for use with barn paint, floor enamels, and related coatings. A suction feed gun is ideal for small jobs entailing numerous color changes, if the paint may be thinned sufficiently to syphon. One quart pressure pot guns may be used for small jobs entailing high viscosity or heavily bodied paints.

Information on how to use spray guns, trouble shooting, and spray gun cleaning will be found in the Unit on Coating Application.

Ladders and Scaffolds

Since a painter spends much time working on surfaces that cannot be reached from the ground or a floor, a thorough knowledge of the different kinds of ladders and scaffolds used in painting is highly essential.

It is important, too, to know how to use ladders and scaffolds safely in order to prevent accidents. Local safety rules should always be consulted for local requirements.

Ladders

MATERIALS FOR LADDER CONSTRUC-
TION: Wood generally used in ladder side rails
is Douglas fir, spruce, fir, or Norway pine.
Rungs are usually made of second growth white
ash, hickory or white oak. The lumber used
should be sound, straight-grained, thoroughly
seasoned, free from decay or weakening knots.

Other materials used to make ladders include aluminum, magnesium alloy, iron and
steel. Magnesium alloy and aluminum ladders
are lighter than those made of wood. Painters'
ladders must be portable and convenient for one
man operation for most uses.

Ladders may have either parallel or spreading straight sides. Sides of portable ladders may
also flare at the base to increase stability and
may converge at the top where warranted by
specific uses.

Types of Ladders

SINGLE (STRAIGHT) LADDER: A single ladder, Fig. 3-25, consists of one straight section.
It is not adjustable in length and is non-self-

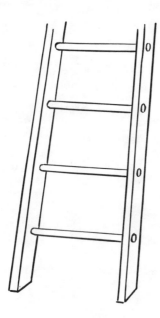

Fig. 3-25. The single or straight ladder consists of but one section. It is non-self-supporting.

supporting. The size of a single ladder is indicated by the overall length of the side rails.
Single ladders over 30 feet long are considered
unsafe.

EXTENSION LADDER: An extension ladder,
Fig. 3-26, consists of two or more sections
arranged to permit adjustment of length. The
size of an extension ladder is indicated by the
sum of the lengths of the sections measured
along the side rails when extended.

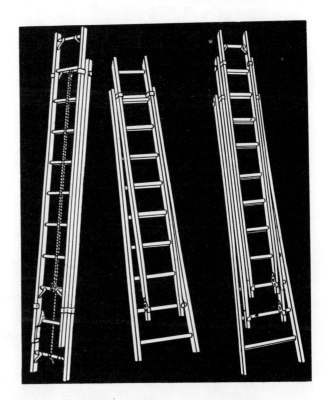

Fig. 3-26. An extension ladder consists of two or more sections
arranged to permit adjustment of ladder length.

High grade rope and pulleys for raising the
upper section are desirable and sometimes
essential features of a well-built extension ladder. Extension ladders should be equipped with
automatic locks. Another important detail is
the allowance of sufficient overlap. Two-section
ladders measuring up to 38 feet should have at
least 3 ft. overlap. A 4 ft. overlap is required
for 40 to 44 ft. and a 5 ft. overlap for ladders
44 to 46 ft. All three-section ladders should
have an overlap of 4 ft. per section. Both two
and three-section ladders must not exceed 46 ft.
fully extended.

TRESTLE LADDER: A trestle ladder, Fig.
3-27, is a self-supporting ladder which is portable. It consists of two sections hinged together
at the top to form equal angles with the base. A
trestle ladder is not adjustable in length. Its
size is determined by the length of the side

Fig. 3-27. Trestle ladder. Also called an "A" ladder.

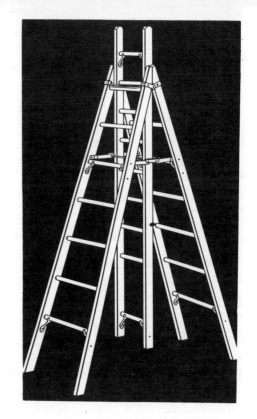

Fig. 3-28. Extension trestle.

Fig. 3-29. Two types of stepladders.

60

rails, measuring along the front edge.

EXTENSION TRESTLE LADDER: An extension trestle ladder, Fig. 3-28, consists of a trestle ladder base, and a vertically adjustable single ladder. Suitable means must be provided for locking the ladders together. The size of a trestle ladder is determined by the length of the trestle ladder base.

STEPLADDER: A stepladder is a portable, self-supporting ladder, which is not adjustable in length. See Fig. 3-29. A stepladder has flat steps, a hinged back and a rack upon which one may rest a pot. This pot rest is definitely not to stand on. Stepladder size is determined by measuring the overall length of the ladder along the front edge of the side rails. Good quality stepladders are equipped with steel safety spreaders, designed so they will not injure the hands when opening and closing the ladders.

How to Use Ladders Safely

No ladder is foolproof but a ladder can be accident-proof. Do not use improvised or makeshift ladders. Obtain only high-quality ladders, made by reputable manufacturers, and constantly inspect them for damage like hidden splits, shakes, and loose rivets, screws and rungs.

Be sure to select the right ladder for the job at hand. This means using a ladder of proper length and size. Fig. 3-30 indicates lengths of ladders for specific heights. The chart takes into consideration the lap required for extension ladders.

Do not splice together two short ladders to provide a long section. The top of a stepladder should not be used as a step. Do not use ladders for guys, skids or any purpose other than for which they were intended.

Ladders are not substitutes for ramps or for

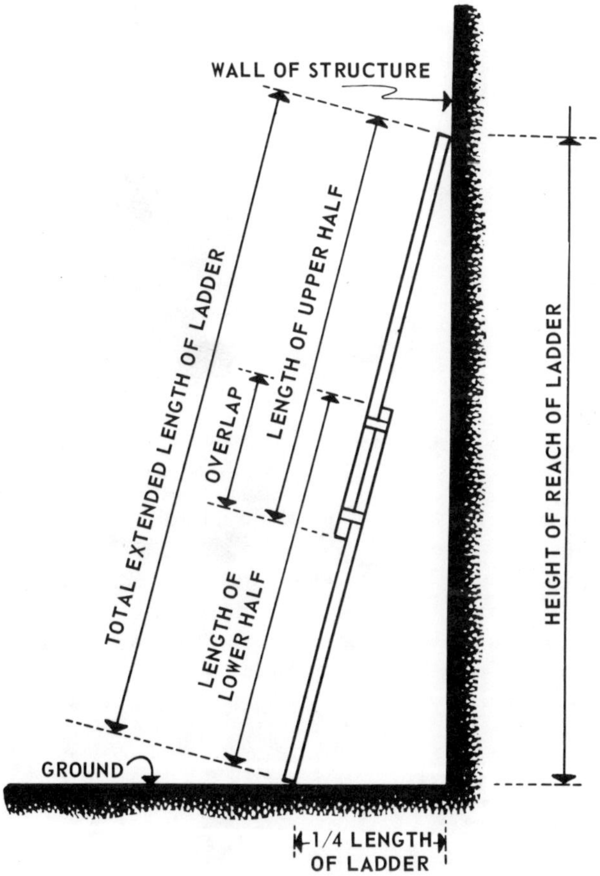

Fig. 3-30. Above. Drawing which shows how ladder would appear at approved angle to building. The distance of the foot of the ladder from the base of the building is one-fourth the total extended length of the ladder. Below. Theoretical ladder sizes for working at various heights.

Size Of Ladder	Length Of Each Of 2 Sections	Total Extended Length – Upper Section And Lower Section Minus The Overlap	Recommended Distance From Bldg. (At Pt. Below Top Of Ladder) To Foot Of Ladder	Height of Reach (To Nearest 6 in.)
14 ft.	7 ft.	11 ft.	2 ft.–9 in.	10 ft.–6 in.
16 ft.	8 ft.	13 ft	3 ft.–3 in.	12 ft.–6 in.
18 ft.	9 ft.	15 ft.	3 ft.–9 in.	14 ft.–6 in.
20 ft.	10 ft.	17 ft.	4 ft.–3 in.	16 ft.–6 in.
24 ft.	12 ft.	21 ft.	5 ft.–3 in.	20 ft.
28 ft.	14 ft.	25 ft.	6 ft.–3 in.	24 ft.
32 ft.	16 ft.	29 ft.	7 ft.–3 in.	28 ft.
36 ft.	18 ft.	33 ft.	8 ft.–3 in.	32 ft.
40 ft.	20 ft.	36 ft.	9 ft.–0 in.	34 ft–6 in.
44 ft.	22 ft.	40 ft.	10 ft.–0 in.	38 ft.–6 in.
48 ft.	24 ft.	44 ft.	11 ft.–0 in.	42 ft.–6 in.

Fig. 3-31. To raise ladder, rest base on foundation or step, raise top end and walk forward under ladder as shown.

stairways. They should be used as ladders and should not be placed at an angle of less than 55 deg. Any angle under 75 deg. (see Fig. 3-30) requires special footing, and any angle over 75 deg. to vertical requires lashing the top of the ladder to the structure in an approved manner and must be described as "a fixed" ladder.

All ladders should support a live load of at least 200 lbs. on the middle of the center rung (as extended to maximum length) with a safety factor of 4. In other words, they should not break up to 800 lbs., but 200 lbs. is the conservative maximum safe load.

Ladders should not be painted. They should be kept coated with spar varnish and the grain structure of the ladder should be visible at all times. Linseed oil may be used but it adds weight to the ladder.

To raise and lower a ladder, rest the base on the foundation or a step. Move your hands from rung to rung as you walk forward or backward, Fig. 3-31.

The correct angle of the ladder with the ground should not be less than 75 deg. The space from the foot of the ladder to the vertical wall should be one-fourth the length of the ladder, Fig. 3-30.

On slippery surfaces be sure to anchor the feet securely. The use of safety shoes is advisable, Fig. 3-32. Check to make sure the ladder has a secure, level footing. Always face the ladder while climbing up or down. Keep both hands free for climbing whenever possible. Be sure your shoes and ladder rungs are free of oil, grease or mud. Never stand a ladder on loose or wet soil without first placing a good broad platform of wood under the feet so they cannot sink.

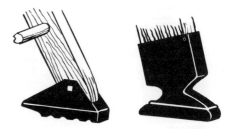

Fig. 3-32. Two types of ladder safety shoes.

When working on a ladder do not lean too far back or to the side. Move the ladder as the work may require. Be sure to watch your balance at all times and it is best to keep a firm grip on the ladder with one hand. Hang the paint bucket from a ladder rung by using a suitable hook, Fig. 3-33.

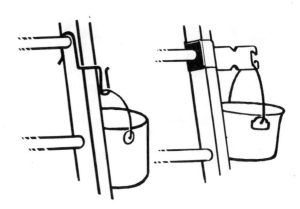

Fig. 3-33. Hooks for hanging paint buckets from ladders.

If the ladder stands in front of a doorway, lock the door or have someone guard it. A ladder should not be placed against a window sash. A board should be attached across the top of the ladder so it will bear at each side of the window.

Do not attempt to erect or extend a heavy

extension ladder without help; this is a two-man job.

Do not permit anyone to climb a ladder with you; never slide down a ladder.

Remember to THINK SAFETY and PRACTICE SAFETY at all times.

Scaffolds

The term "scaffold" means a temporarily located, elevated platform provided for the support of workmen and materials for painting, decorating, paperhanging, washing walls, and sandblasting.

Scaffolds should be provided for all work that cannot be done safely by workmen standing on permanent or solid construction, except where such work can be safely done from ladders.

Most of the information on wood scaffolds which follows was obtained from a booklet on Construction Safety Orders, issued by the Division of Industrial Safety, State of California, and a booklet entitled Navy Safety Precautions issued by the U. S. Navy.

Lumber To Use In Scaffold Construction

All lumber used in the construction of scaffolds shall be Douglas fir not less than No. 1 common or material of equal strength. Such lumber shall be sound, straight-grained, free from such defects as crossgrain, shakes, large and loose knots, dry rot, large checks, brash-

ness or worm holes.

Other material and other designs than required by these orders may be used if equivalent rigidity and strength are provided (for example aluminum beams and plywood platforms).

The minimum size of planks and maximum distance between supports for respective plank sizes are indicated in the following table.

Size Of Plank, Inches	Span Allowed, Feet
2 x 6	6
2 x 8	8
2 x 10	10
2 x 12	12
2 x 14	14
2 x 16	16
2 x 20	20
3 x 20	20

INSPECTION OF LUMBER: All lumber shall be inspected before being used and shall be capable of supporting at least four (4) times the maximum load which will be imposed upon it.

STRENGTH OF NAILS: All nails used in the construction of scaffolds and falsework must be of ample size and length to carry the loads they are intended to support.
1. Size - - Minimum. No nail smaller than eight-penny shall be used in the construction of scaffolding.
2. Driven Full Length. All nails shall be driven full length or to the first head when double-

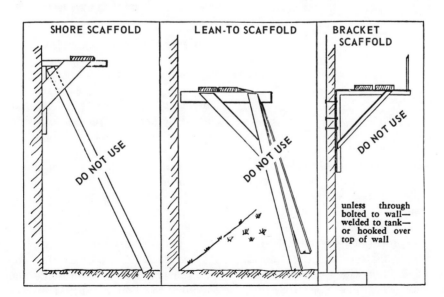

Fig. 3-34. Three types of scaffolds which are considered unsafe and which should not be used.

headed nails are used.

3. Distribution. Sufficient nails must be driven in at each joint of the scaffold or falsework so that it will carry all the imposed loads placed thereon.

4. The following table shows the minimum number of nails per connection for light-trade scaffolds:

	1 in. Material	2 in. Material
Ledgers	5–8d	5–20d
Ribbons	3–8d	
Braces	3–8d	2–20d
Guard Rails	2–8d	2–20d

PROHIBITED TYPES OF SCAFFOLDS: Lean-to, shore or bracket scaffolds, see Fig. 3-34, barrels, boxes, loose tile, loose bricks, loose blocks, or other similar unstable objects shall not be used to support scaffolds or used as scaffolds.

None but skilled workmen shall be employed in the erection of scaffolds, and the work shall be under direct supervision of a man familiar with scaffold erection and who thoroughly understands the dangers that are involved and who knows and will take precautions to insure safety.

No scaffold shall be altered by removing uprights, braces, or other supporting members, except under the supervision of the employer or his representative. In no case shall the strength of the scaffold be impaired to less than that required for the work intended.

Scaffolds shall not be overloaded. Material shall not be allowed to accumulate to such an extent as to subject the scaffold to a load which it is not designed to support.

Runways or ladders shall be erected to platforms of scaffolds 5 ft. or more in height.

Railings and Toeboards

Standard railings shall be provided on all open sides and ends of all built-up scaffolds, runways, ramps, rolling scaffolds, elevated platforms, or other elevations 10 ft. or more above the ground or floor. (Exceptions - Interior scaffolds without open sides, riveters' platforms, ladder jack and horse scaffolds.)

Toeboards shall be solid and extend not less than 6 in. high above the top of platform and shall be provided on all open sides of all bricklayers', stonemasons' scaffolds, or scaffolds having tools and loose material.

SIDE SCREENS. If material on a scaffold is piled higher than the toeboard, 1/2 in. wire mesh or canvas or equivalent shall be provided between the railing and toeboard and secured both top and bottom.

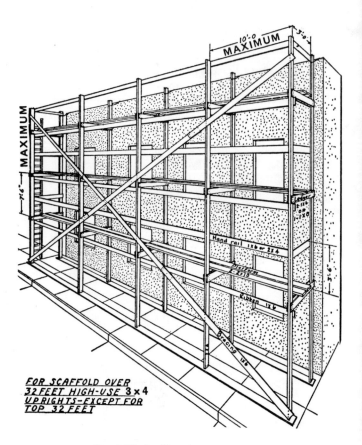

Fig. 3-35. Light trades pole scaffold.

Pole or Built-Up Scaffolds

All pole scaffolds, Fig. 3-35, intended to be used by all trades except bricklayers, stonemasons, stone cutters and concrete workers, shall be constructed as follows:

For heights not to exceed 32 ft., the uprights shall be 2 x 4 in. lumber or heavier, spaced 3 ft. between uprights at right angle to the wall and not more than 10 ft. center to center, parallel to the wall. Scaffolds may be wider than 3 ft. if the platform is correspondingly wider. The inside uprights may be omitted and the ledgers attached to the permanent structure, providing the method of attaching the ledgers to the permanent structure will make the connection as secure as though the ledger were nailed to uprights with 5 eight penny nails. (A suggested

SCHEDULES OF SCAFFOLDS UP TO 75 FT. IN HEIGHT

	Interior	* General
Uprights for scaffolds not over 32 ft. in height	2 x 4 in.	2 x 4 in.
Uprights—first 32 ft. scaffolds 32 to 75 ft.	3 x 4 in.	3 x 4 in.
Ribbons directly under ledgers	1 x 6 in.	1 x 6 in.
Ledgers	2–1 x 8 in.	2–1 x 6 in.
	or	
	1–2 x 6 in.	1–1 x 8 in.
Splice pieces 30 in. long	2–1 x 4 in.	2–1 x 4 in.
Braces	1 x 6 in.	1 x 6 in.
Spacing uprights, longitudinal, parallel to direction of platform planks	10 ft.	10 ft.
Spacing uprights, transverse, at right angles to platform planks	10 ft.	3 in. in clear
Spacing runners or ledgers, vertical	7 ft. 6 in.	7 ft. 6 in.
Railing		1 x 6 in.
Width of platform	at least 2 planks	
Planking	2 in. in thickness and at least 10 in. wide	

* Excluding bricklayers', stonemasons', stone cutters' and concrete workers' scaffolds.

method is to spike a 24 in. piece of 2 x 4 to the stud with 5 twenty penny nails and nail the ledgers to these blocks with 5 eight penny nails.) The platform of the scaffold shall be supported by ledgers made of two pieces of 1 x 6 in. boards or one piece of 1 x 8 in. board or heavier material laid on edge. The ribbons shall be 1 x 6 in. placed on the outer uprights, directly under and shall support the ledger and be spaced not more than 7 ft. 6 in. vertically. (Exception - When ledgers are bolted, ribbons may be placed lower than the ledger.)

The scaffold shall be tied to the building and shall be rigidly braced with 1 x 6 in. boards throughout and every part thereof so secured as to prevent swaying, tipping or collapsing of same.

The upright of the scaffold, when resting on a sidewalk, shall be secured at the bottom to a continuous sill to prevent slipping. Whenever placed on the ground, the uprights shall be secured to sills sufficient to sustain the load. The platform shall be at least two planks wide, and shall be made of planks 2 in. thick and not less than 10 in. wide.

Outrigger Scaffold

An outrigger scaffold is a scaffold, the platform of which is supported by outriggers or thrustouts from or through the wall of a building, and the inner end of which is secured inside the building.

Figure-Four Outrigger Scaffold

One type of outrigger scaffold known as the Figure-Four scaffold is shown in Fig. 3-36.

Constructional details on these scaffolds as contained in the Construction Safety Orders, published by the State of California, are as follows:

"Figure 4 or light outrigger beams shall be spaced not more than 10 ft. apart and shall be constructed of sound lumber as follows:

A. All outrigger beams shall be at least 1 x 8 in. lumber and shall project at least 3 ft. from the outside wall line. The outrigger beams shall be substantially braced and secured to prevent tipping or turning. The knee or angle brace may intersect the beam at least 3 ft. from the wall, and shall intersect uprights or wall at not less than 45 deg. with the horizontal. All joints or parts of the scaffold

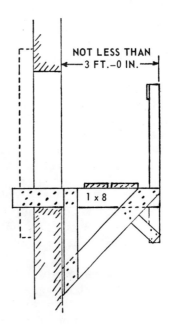

Fig. 3-36. Figure-four, outrigger scaffold. Span limit ten feet.

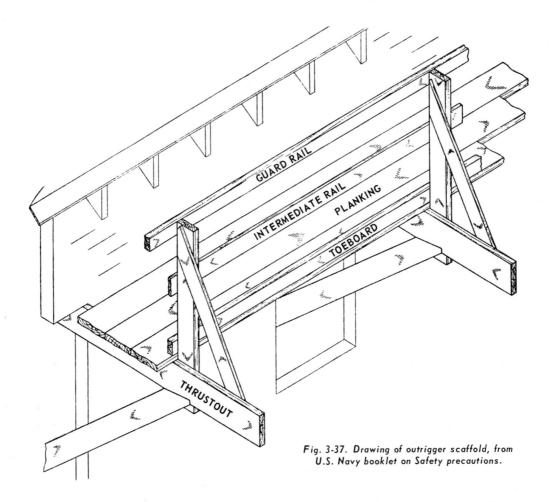

Fig. 3-37. Drawing of outrigger scaffold, from
U.S. Navy booklet on Safety precautions.

must be adequately secured to prevent tipping or turning. The platform shall be at least two planks 2 x 8 in. wide."

Heavy-Duty Outrigger Scaffold

Fig. 3-37 is a drawing of an outrigger scaffold, from SAFETY PRECAUTIONS, published by the U. S. Navy. Constructional details on this scaffold are as follows:

"CONSTRUCTION. Scaffolds shall be supported by thrustouts securely attached to the frame of the building. Each thrustout shall be equal in strength to a 6 in. I-beam at 12.25 lbs. per foot or a 3 by 10 heavy timber set on edge, and shall not extend more than 6 ft. from the building. The inner ends, extending into the building, shall be supported, braced, anchored, and securely fastened in place.

GUARDRAIL. Heavy outrigger scaffolds shall be provided with standard guardrails supported on uprights and securely fastened to the thrustouts. These uprights shall be long enough to

drop 12 in. below the outrigger and the lower end securely braced to it.

TOEBOARD. Standard toeboards and side screens shall be provided.

HORSE SCAFFOLDS PROHIBITED. Horse scaffolds shall not be erected upon the platform of an outrigger scaffold.

WALL AS SUPPORT. Outriggers shall not be built into the wall and left with no other support.

BRACING. The projecting ends of outriggers shall be supported by external braces and struts when extra support is required. These shall not be depended upon as the main support.

SPACING. Thrustouts shall be spaced not to exceed 6 ft. on centers.

BUCKLING. The thrustouts shall be rigidly held to prevent turning or buckling.

CONSTRUCTION OF PLATFORM. The platform shall be constructed of planks 2 by 10 in. securely nailed to the thrustouts and laid close together, except for a 1 in. space along the wall of the building.

PROJECTION OF PLANKS. The ends of all planks shall rest on the back of the thrustouts and shall project not more than 12 in. beyond.

SUSPENDED PLATFORMS. When working platforms are suspended from the thrustouts, they shall be supported by vertical hangers of not less than 2 by 6 in. and shall not be more than 10 ft. long. They shall be securely nailed to the side of the thrustouts and extend at least 10 in. above the top of the thrustouts and to a block resting on the top edge of the thrustouts.

A. Beams. The suspended platform shall be supported on 2 by 6 in. beams, nailed to vertical hangers and rest on a block that shall be spiked to the side of the hangers below the beam.

B. Planks. The suspended platform shall be formed of 2 by 10 in. planks, nailed close together across the back of the bearer and provided with a standard guardrail, toeboard, and side screen protection."

Suspended Scaffolds

The term "Suspended" scaffold means a scaffold, the platform of which is supported from overhead by using rope or cable in a manner which permits raising and lowering the scaffold.

A "Swinging" scaffold, is usually considered to be a form of a suspended scaffold, which is supported from overhead at only two points.

A "Hanging" scaffold is a scaffold which is suspended at a certain or fixed elevation from overhead construction.

Two Types of Suspended Scaffolds

The drawings in Figs. 3-38 and 3-39 show typical suspended scaffolds. Constructional details on the Heavy-Duty Suspended Scaffold, Fig. 3-38 follow:

Each thrustout shall be equal in strength to a 6 in. 12.25 lb. I-beam, and it shall be supported laterally at a point near the center of its support.

Thrustouts shall be suspended by wire rope of at least 9000 lbs. breaking strength, secured to the thrustouts and to each end of the bolster or hoisting machine. Only machines which have been approved by the Industrial Accident Commission shall be used.

Bolsters may be of wood, provided they are equal in strength to 4 x 4 in. straight-grained Douglas fir lumber, free from knots that affect

the strength of the wood.

The bolsters and thrustouts shall be spaced not more than 8 ft. center to center.

The platform shall be not less than 4 ft. wide, and made of not less than 2 in. planks laid closely together and adequately secured to prevent them from slipping, tipping or collapsing.

The scaffold shall be as close to the wall as reasonably possible to prevent falling between scaffold and building wall.

When work is being done above suspended scaffolds, the workmen on such a scaffold shall be substantially protected from falling material by a covering made of not less than 1 in. boards laid tightly together.

The maximum load, including workmen, allowed on this scaffold shall not exceed 100 lbs. per square foot of scaffold platform.

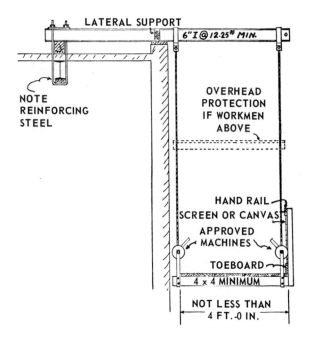

Fig. 3-38. Heavy-duty suspended scaffold. Span limit eight feet.

Typical Suspended Scaffold for Painters

The suspended or swinging scaffold shown in Fig. 3-39 is satisfactory for use where the maximum load does not exceed two men. Constructional details follow:

A. The platform of all suspended scaffolds or stagings shall be made of planks at least 14 in. wide and 1 1/2 in. thickness, and shall be Select Structural Douglas Fir or equivalent. Size of bolster to be 2 x 3 in. net or equiva-

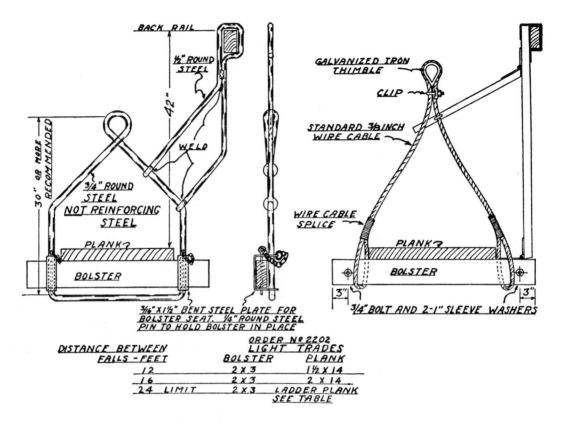

Fig. 3-39. Suspended scaffold for painters where maximum load does not exceed two men.

lent, placed with the 3 in. dimension in a vertical direction.

B. All stirrups or slings shall be made of wire rope of at least 9000 lbs. breaking strength, or of solid round or square steel not less than 3/4 in. dimension, forged or welded in one piece. Loops for the use of bolsters shall be spliced. The top loop shall have a galvanized thimble fastened in place with a clip.

C. An iron or steel bolt 6 in. long and 3/4 in. in diameter shall be fastened through the bolster at right angles to same not nearer than 3 in. to the end to prevent sling from accidentally slipping off the end of bolster. The bolster shall be placed at least 18 in. from the end of plank.

D. The scaffoldings or stagings shall be fastened so as to prevent them from swaying from the building or structure, and all parts of such scaffoldings or stagings shall be rigidly constructed and of sufficient strength to support all loads that may be placed thereupon.

E. The span between falls or hangers shall not be more than 12 ft. when the platform con-

sists of a plank 1 1/2 x 14 in. When the platform consists of a plank 2 x 14 in., the span between falls or hangers shall not be more than 16 ft. When the platform consists of a ladder as specified in the following table, and a 3/4 x 14 in. or a 3/4 x 20 in. plank, the spans between falls or hangers shall be not more than 24 ft. Not more than two men shall be allowed to work between two hangers or falls. Ordinary extension ladders shall not be used as stage ladders.

F. Swinging or stage ladders, Fig. 3-40.

Swinging or stage ladders used for suspended scaffolds shall be reinforced with 3/16 in. rods spaced at least every 5 ft. to prevent side rails from spreading.

G. Safety lines of at least 5/8 in. diameter Manila or sisal rope hanging from the roof, securely tied thereto, shall be provided between each pair of hangers or falls. One such line to be provided for each workman.

H. The hooks supporting the scaffolds or stagings shall be made of mild steel, (reinforcing steel shall not be used), free from flaws or other imperfections, and when formed to

Length In Feet	Minimum Cross Section of Rails In Inches			Minimum Cross Section of Rungs In Inches	
			Round	Oblong	
Up to 16	1 3/8 x 4 1/2		1	3/4 x 1 3/8	
16 to 20	1 3/8 x 5	may be tapered to 4 in. at ends	1	3/4 x 1 3/8	
20 to 24	1 3/8 x 5 1/2	may be tapered to 4 in. at ends	1	3/4 x 1 3/8	

NOTE: When ladders are constructed with truss rods, the above side rails may be reduced in size.

Fig. 3-40. Swinging or stage ladder specifications.

shape each hook shall be capable of sustaining a load of 1600 lbs. without undue deflection. They shall be tied rigidly with at least 5/8 in. diameter ropes secured to an eye on the hook and to a substantial object on the roof.

I. All ropes supporting scaffolds shall be Manila or sisal rope and shall have a factor of safety of at least six, and shall be inspected before being used on each job to ascertain whether they are sound, and free from flaws or deterioration from contact with any solution containing chemicals.

J. Where ropes supporting scaffolds are not attached directly to hooks, the extension from the top block to the support shall be at least a 1/2 in. wire rope.

K. When solutions containing chemicals, or any solution injurious to hemp rope fibers are used, every workman shall be required to wear a safety belt, approved by the Industrial Accident Commission, and said belt shall be securely attached to a safety line by a mechanical safety device or a sliding hitch.

L. Whenever any washing solutions containing chemicals, or any solutions injurious to hemp rope fiber are being used, the free ends of the falls and life lines shall be coiled in barrels or other suitable receptacles.

M. All scaffolds or stagings referred to in this order, suspended more than 10 ft. from the ground or floor, shall have a safety rail of wood or other equally rigid material of sufficient strength to prevent workmen from falling, and said rail shall be not less than 42 in. or more than 45 in. above the platform of such scaffoldings or stagings. The safety rail shall be made of 2 x 3 in. material in one piece.

Sisal rope, when used, shall be considered as only 80 percent of the strength of Manila rope.

Ladder Jack Scaffolds

A ladder jack scaffold is a scaffold the platform of which is supported by jacks attached to ladders. See Fig. 3-41.

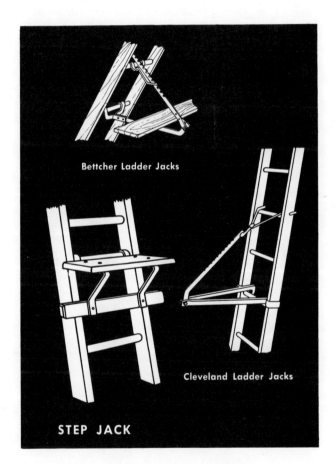

Fig. 3-41. Ladder jack scaffolds.

Ladder jack specifications follow:

A. Ladder jack scaffolds shall not be used when the platform is over 18 ft. above the ground. Not more than two workmen shall be allowed on any such scaffold.

B. The staging shall be Select Structural Douglas Fir or equivalent. The ladders shall not be placed over 16 ft. center to center. 1 1/2 x 14 in. planks shall not exceed a 12 ft. span. 2 x 14 in. planks shall not exceed a 16 ft. span.

C. It is recommended that a safety line of at least 5/8 in. diameter Manila rope, securely tied and hanging from above, be provided for each workman on the scaffold.

Cornice, Ridge Hooks

In using a swinging scaffold, the upper block and pulley is frequently supported by attaching to a cornice or "S" hook, Fig. 3-42, which is fitted over the top of a substantially attached portion of the roof. Single blocks are attached to the scaffold stirrups. In the top of the hook is a ring or eye to which a tie-back rope should be made fast. Tie-back ropes are a very important part of the setup and must be protected from cutting and fraying by the use of suitable padding, usually a sandbag.

The roof or ridge hook, also shown in Fig. 3-42, is a steel hook device which fastens to rungs of a ladder and hooks over the ridge of a building to keep a ladder from slipping off the roof.

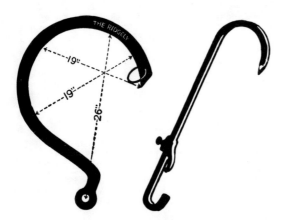

Fig. 3-42. Left. Cornice or stage hook. Ring is provided for tying back securely to some well anchored part of roof. Right. Hook which fastens to rungs of a ladder and hooks over ridge of building to keep ladder on roof.

Steel Trestles, Scaffold Horses

The steel trestles, Fig. 3-43, offer a safe, low-cost method of providing a scaffold for

Fig. 3-43. Steel adjustable trestles form a safe, low cost method of providing a scaffold for overhead painting and decorating.

overhead painting and decorating. The trestles are adjustable in height.

Constructional details on several types of scaffold horses are given in the drawing, Fig. 3-44.

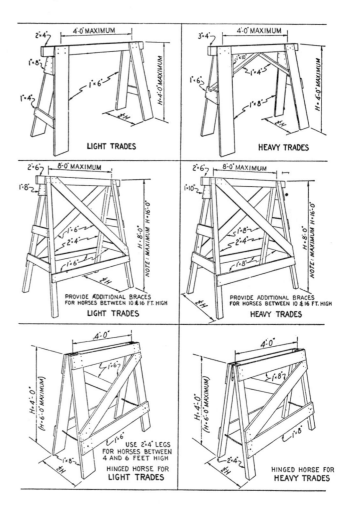

Fig. 3-44. Dimensions and constructional details on several types of scaffold horses.

Knots and Hitches

Safe types of knots and hitches with which the apprentice painter should become thoroughly familiar are shown in Fig. 3-45.

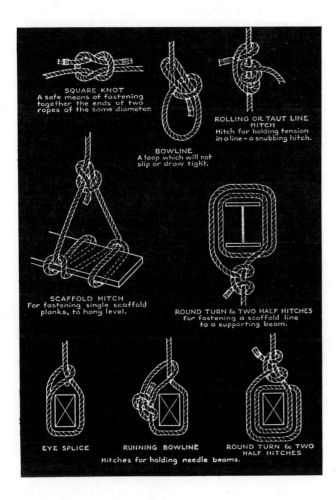

Fig. 3-45. Safe knots and hitches with which the journeyman should be familiar.

Steel Scaffolding

During recent years the use of steel scaffolding by painters and decorators has greatly increased. Steel scaffolds are fireproof and have the advantages of low wind resistance. Dismantling is less hazardous than tearing down wood scaffolding and there is 100 percent recovery of material since the various parts may be used over and over again.

Steel scaffolding is available on either a rental or purchase basis. When the scaffolding is rented, the supplier frequently does the erect-

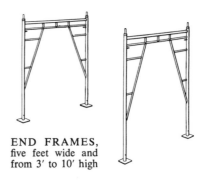

END FRAMES, five feet wide and from 3' to 10' high

plus DIAGONAL BRACES to give various spacings between frames

make this BASIC UNIT, on which other frames can be built, either horizontally or vertically.

Fig. 3-46. Steel scaffolding consists essentially of an assembly of standard patented parts.

ing and dismantling.

Steel scaffolding consists of an assembly of standard patented parts, manufactured from high tensile steel tubing (usually 2 in. O.D.), welded into rigid units. See Fig. 3-46. The flexibility of the equipment, which permits the erection of structures to meet almost any scaffolding requirement, is due to the interchangeable nature of the various parts.

A typical assembly of scaffolding (Safway) is shown in Fig. 3-47. End frames plus diagonal braces are assembled to make a basic unit, on which other frames can be built, either horizontally or vertically. Ladder type frames and casters are available for rolling scaffolds.

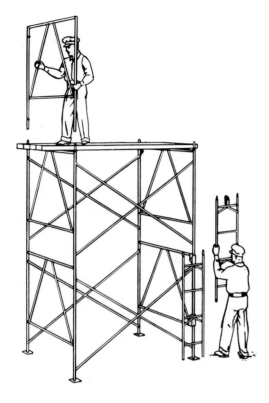

Fig. 3-47. Typical assembly of steel scaffolding.

Aluminum Scaffolding

Aluminum scaffolding has a place too, in the scaffolding industry. Its lightweight makes it practical for ladder scaffolds, Fig. 3-48, and for other uses where a lightweight, small load scaffold is desirable.

In using aluminum scaffolding consideration must be given to the fact that its load carrying capacities are considerably lower than steel. See Fig. 3-49.

Metal Scaffold Safety Rules and Regulations

The following rules and regulations should be strictly adhered to when using both steel and aluminum scaffolding in order to prevent accidents:

1. Provide sufficient sills or under-pinning in addition to standard base plates on all scaffolds to be erected on filled or otherwise soft ground.
2. Compensate for unevenness of ground by using adjusting screws rather than blocking.
3. Be sure that all scaffolds are plumb and level at all times.

4. Anchor running scaffold to wall approximately every 28 ft. of length and 20 ft. of height.
5. Do not force braces to fit. Adjust evenness of scaffold until the proper fit can be made with ease.
6. Guard railing should be used on all scaffolds regardless of height.
7. When climbing scaffold, use ladders rather than the cross braces.
8. Do not use putlogs as side brackets without thorough consideration for loads to be applied.
9. Never tie two putlogs together to accommodate spans of greater than 21 ft.
10. Always use putlog supports where spans are greater than 16 ft.
11. When using 22 ft. putlogs in parallel, be sure to brace between them.
12. Do not omit or fail to tighten all bolts and wing nuts that are a part of the scaffold.
13. Horizontal bracing should be used to prevent racking of the structure.
14. All planking used on a scaffold should be

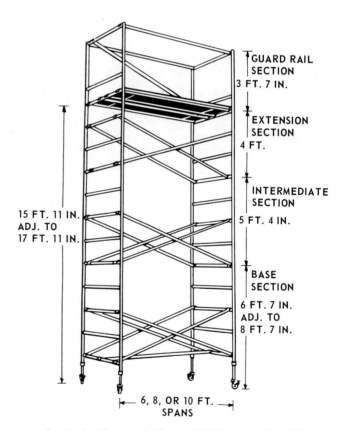

Fig. 3-48. Aluminum ladder scaffold. Tubing is 2 in. O.D. (outside diameter).

of sound quality, straight grained, and free from knots.

15. Handle all rolling towers with additional care.

   a. Narrow towers of considerable height must be guyed at all times.

   b. Apply all caster brakes when not in motion.

   c. Do not ride towers.

   d. Look where you are going with a rolling tower.

   e. Don't attempt to move a rolling tower without sufficient help.

   f. Provide unit lock arms on all towers.

   g. Do not extend adjusting screws to full extent.

   h. Use 5 in. casters on towers under 50 ft. in height and 8 in. casters on everything over 50 ft.

   i. Horizontal bracing is to be used at the bottom, top and at intermediate levels of 30 ft.

16. Guy all towers every 30 ft. of elevation.

Fig. 3-49. Drawing which indicates safe loads for Safway aluminum scaffolding. Safe load for steel scaffolding of same size would be about 5000 lbs. per leg and safe uniform load, 2750 lbs.

17. Do not attempt to use scaffolds as material hoist towers or for mounting derricks without first determining the loads and stresses involved.

18. Keep all equipment in good repair, avoid rusting - - the strength of rusted material is not known.

19. Never use any equipment that is damaged or deteriorated in any way.

20. If in doubt as to ability of scaffold to do a particular job, consult an authority. Don't take chances.

21. Familiarize yourself with the safety requirements of the State Codes and be governed accordingly.

22. Do not permit equipment to be used by anyone not familiar with these rules.

Dropcloths

Painters' dropcloths are available in many different sizes. They are made from heavy cotton cloth or canvas, solvent-resistant plastic and heavy paper impregnated with a waterproofer.

Lightly woven canvas is considered best by most painters. These can be laundered many times, and are strong and flexible.

Masking Tapes, Papers

In applying paint, particularly when using a spray gun, property may be protected by using masking paper or plastic such as polyethylene, pressure-sensitive masking tape, masking paste and liquid masking. The liquid masking and masking paste are applied like paint. After the painting job has been completed, the rubber-like substance is easily peeled off.

There are also masking machines to hold a roll of paper or plastic and a roll of tape. When the paper is unrolled the tape fastens to one edge and unrolls with it making a "skirt" which will adhere.

Blowtorches

Blowtorches used by painters include those operated with gasoline, acetylene, L.P. (liquefied petroleum) gas, and butane.

The essential in a good torch is that it be able to throw an even fan shaped flame of the correct width for the surface and for the operator.

Torches are used principally to soften paint which must be removed from a surface in order to make it suitable for repainting or refinishing.

Miscellaneous Tools and Equipment

Included under the heading of "miscellaneous" tools and equipment needed by the painter and decorator would be included such items as Putty Knives, Scrapers or Broad Knives, Glazing

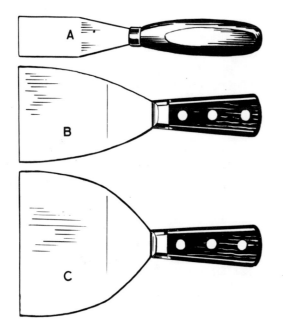

Fig. 3-50. A—Putty knife (1 1/4 in. wide). B—Scraper or broad knife (3 in. wide). C—Glazing knife (4 or 5 in. wide). These knives come with blades which are thin and flexible, medium flexible, or stiff.

Knives, Fig. 3-50; Caulking Guns; Brush Holders; Stripers; Sponges; Wiping Rags; Cheesecloth; Burlap; Paint Strainers; Mixing Paddles; Mixing Tubs; Paint Bucket Holders; and hand tools such as screwdrivers, pliers and hammers.

Electronic Moisture Meter

An electronic moisture meter is used to check the moisture content of both wood and masonry surfaces. A moisture meter, properly used, is of great help in eliminating many avoidable paint failures.

Electric Sander

There are available on the market many types of electric sanders which painters and decorators can use to good advantage, ranging from a large belt sander such as used in smoothing and renovating floors to a small vibrating-type sander such as used in fine furniture finishing.

Unit 4

PREPARATION OF SURFACES
FOR PAINTING

A successful paint job cannot be achieved without the proper preparation of the surface. The surface is one of the three basic elements of a good paint job. If painting is to be successful there must, first of all, be a good paint film. There must, secondly, be a sound surface to receive this paint film. And, third, there must be a strong bond between the paint film and the surface.

Thus, the surface should be studied carefully and should be treated in whatever way is necessary so that it will receive the paint properly. Indeed, the condition of the surface plays an important role in achieving the degree of adhesion required for effective performance. If the surface is not continuous one obviously cannot achieve a continuous paint film. If the surface is covered with loose, chalky paint there may be excellent adhesion between the new paint and the chalky material, but this will be of no value since the chalky material will not adhere to the surface. Dirt, grease, mechanical defects of all sorts and old paint are a few of the factors which contribute to poor surfaces and which must be compensated for by proper surface preparation.

It is an interesting point that if the surface is too smooth or too glossy it may also repel paint, for which reason sanding is necessary to remove the gloss. Metal surfaces provide a special situation, for here the problems of rusting and mill scale may be present to interfere with adhesion. Accordingly, special considerations are involved in the preparation of metal surfaces.

Wood Surfaces, New Wood

New wood to be painted or enameled should be free from all foreign matter such as plaster, grease, dirt, glue and pitch. No painting should be done while plaster is being applied or is drying.

Interior Woodwork (New)

Make sure the wood is clean and dry. Sand to remove any small defects, using 2/0 or 3/0 flint or garnet paper. Work WITH the grain, not across it.

Puttying of cracks, covering nail holes, Fig. 4-1, and other small defects should not be done until after the priming or first coat has been applied and allowed to dry; otherwise, the wood will absorb the oil from the putty and it will crumble and fall out.

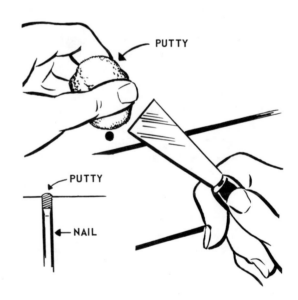

Fig. 4-1. Covering nail heads with putty after priming coat has dried. The putty should be squeezed into the nail hole and cut off with a putty knife while under pressure. The surface of the putty should be slightly convex to allow for shrinkage, as shown in the detail.

Splinters must be carefully glued for later sanding. Small moldings often have sharp edges with loose feathery splinters that must be sanded off. When this condition exists on sash, care must be used to avoid scratching the glass. Also, a sharp lookout for splinters will prevent painful accidents.

Large chunks of plaster or mud can be scraped off with a 3 in. scraper or putty knife before sanding. Avoid nicking the wood with sharp edges on the knife.

Both new and machine-sanded open-grain wood such as walnut, oak, mahogany, and elm require paste wood filler to seal the pores and build up a smooth even surface for painting. Paste filler is not required on close-grain wood such as maple, pine, gum, cedar, poplar and basswood.

One of the most important trends in building materials today is prefinishing. Thus, much of the interior woodwork now utilized in houses is actually prefinished and requires very little attention on the part of the painter beyond the filling of nail holes and cracks and making sure that the surface is clean and dry.

Occasionally the architect specifies that the interior woodwork be "back painted." A good white primer paint should be used and the job should, of course, be done neatly so that paint does not run over the edges onto the front surface.

Additional information on this subject will be found in the section describing hardwood finishes.

Exterior Woodwork (New)

When ready to paint, check carefully to make sure all nails are hammered in tight and set below the surface. Smooth down any rough spots with flint or garnet abrasive papers, working with the grain of the wood. It is very important to know that the wood is dry. Priming too early in the morning when dew or fog wetting occurs or after a rain can shorten the life of the finished job. Paint does not adhere well to moist wood.

It goes without saying that the surface should be free of dust, and any foreign material left on the surface by previous workers should be carefully removed.

Knots and resin streaks should be sealed with shellac, Fig. 4-2, or with knot sealer. This should be done after the first prime coat has been applied.

Nail heads should be carefully primed before puttying. Caulking of joints around window and door frames is usually done after priming. See Fig. 4-3.

Fig. 4-2. Knots and resin streaks should be sealed with shellac or knot sealer after the priming paint coat.

Preparing Previously Painted Interior Woodwork for Repainting

When the surface of previously painted interior woodwork is in good condition, cleaning and sanding may be all the preparation required. Grease, dust and dirt should be removed by using a solution of water and washing powder. Traces of wax, if any, should be removed with turpentine or other solvent, followed by a thorough washing, using trisodium phosphate in hot water. (Solvents dissolve wax but do not remove it. Detergents in water envelop the particles and carry them away.)

Surfaces previously coated with gloss or semi-gloss paint or varnish should be roughened, using abrasive paper, usually after cleaning with a strong washing solution. The surface must be absolutely dry before sandpapering or repainting. Disintegrated, chalked, or powdery

Fig. 4-3. All joints next to door and window frames should be filled with caulking compound after priming.

areas should be sanded carefully and thoroughly. Paint does not adhere on such areas.

Paint which lacks elasticity or which hardens and embrittles on aging may scale or chip. Ideally, paint should expand and contract with the wood whose dimensions are changed by variation in moisture content due to change in humidity. When the paint is scaled or badly chipped it is usually necessary to remove it down to the bare wood. If damage is only spotty, sanding or a liquid paint remover is usually adequate. If damage is extensive a mechanical paint remover (refer to section on paint defects) should be utilized.

The undamaged bare wood which results after removing old paint should be treated very much like new wood with one possible exception. The primer should be less oily or have less binder because old bare wood which has previously been painted does not have the same "suction" or ability to "draw in" binder as does new bare wood. This is because the pores of the old wood have already become filled. If the wood has been damaged or weather-beaten it will be quite porous and may not present a satisfactory surface for long term paint durability.

In redecorating a house it is sometimes desirable to enamel over previously stained and varnished woodwork. On such jobs it is necessary to find out if the stain on the woodwork is a bleeding type stain. This may be done by applying a small quantity of enamel to the old surface, in an inconspicuous spot, but a spot that contains a high concentration of the old stain. (The back edge of a door or the face of the head jamb is generally a good area to try.) After this spot has a chance to dry, examine it carefully. If the old stain was of the bleeding type, the paint will be off-color and show traces of the stain. If this happens it is necessary to remove the gloss from the old finish by using fine abrasive paper (00). Thereafter, apply a full coat of stain sealer such as shellac, before proceeding with the undercoat and final coats.

It is not safe to apply paint over varnish. The varnish is least suited to work over when it is glossy and in good condition. Sometimes economy dictates the necessity for breaking this rule. Adhesion between old varnish and new undercoater is obtained by the use of an additive to the primer to soften the varnish. Either prepared materials on the market or a small amount (two or three tablespoons to a gallon) of toluol can be used.

Worn edges and spackled surface dents should be spot primed before total recoating. This should be done for either a one or two-coat job.

Surface Preparation For Repainting Exterior Woodwork

Repainting exterior woodwork, especially on jobs where the paint has been neglected, often involves major problems.

Adhesion of the paint film to the wood; condition of the building structurally; and kind, quality, and thickness of the old paint film are factors to be considered in determining the work required to achieve a surface for repainting.

Chalking of paint is a normal weathering process. If the chalking is uniform and is not excessive, and if there is a solid bond between what remains of the old coating and the wood, removing loose dust and dirt by sanding and dusting or simply by washing will usually prepare the surface for repainting. On a painted surface that is chalking normally, slight rubbing will produce a dull luster. If rubbing the surface fails to produce a dull luster and if the surface is broken by fine checks or small blisters, more work will be required to prepare the surface for additonal paint. All loose paint, Fig. 4-4, should be removed by scraping, wire brushing, and sanding. In sanding, work with the grain and use 2/0 or 3/0 flint or garnet paper. Rough edges of material around bare spots should be leveled by sanding and the surface treated like new wood. An approved type respirator should be worn to prevent inhaling the paint dust and dirt.

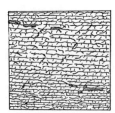

Fig. 4-4. If paint surface is broken by fine checks as shown in detail, loose paint should be removed by wire brushing and by sanding.

Extensive blistering, cracking, and alligatoring of the paint film, Fig. 4-5, are among the most difficult of all defects to repair. Frequently, complete removal is necessary. Paint remover in liquid form is practical for removing

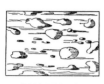

BLISTERING   CRACKING   ALLIGATORING

Fig. 4-5. Blistering, cracking and alligatoring of the paint film are among the most difficult of all defects to repair. Alligatoring often should be removed entirely.

paint from spots and small areas. It is particularly effective for cleaning ornamental work on porches and cornices of old houses.

Where the area is large, burning off the defective film, using a blowtorch and scraper, Fig. 4-6, is usually recommended. Be sure the siding is tight, and handle the torch carefully to avoid burning the wood. Keep the flame away from cracks and glass. Hold the torch in one hand so that the flame is about one inch from the paint and at a slight angle. Move along the boards keeping the flame about two inches ahead of the scraper in the other hand. As the paint bubbles and softens, scrape it off immediately.

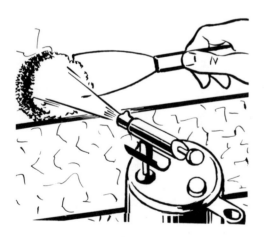

Fig. 4-6. Above. Removing paint with blowtorch. The flame should be moved along siding about two inches ahead of the knife. Below. Using hand scraper to remove loose paint.

Always do paint burning on a day when it is not windy and protect your hands with gloves.

Fill cracks and nail holes with putty. Replace caulking around door and window frames as required to seal cracks. Remove loose putty around windows, prime open rabbet, then apply new putty, Fig. 4-7. Use a brush duster to remove dust from woodwork.

Fig. 4-7. Loose putty should be removed, the rabbet primed and when dry, new putty applied.

Check siding and do minor renailing as required. Splitting of siding when nailing may be prevented by using a small drill to make slightly undersize pilot holes for the nails.

In preparing a building for repainting, any mildew or mold which is present should be removed. Mildew usually occurs where there is dampness and warmth and tends to penetrate the pores of the wood and therefore is difficult to remove. Sanding is the best approach. A good mildewcide in the paint to be applied will prevent further progress of the mildew. Dry mold may be removed by washing with a solution of trisodium phosphate - - one half pound to a gallon of water. After using the trisodium phosphate the area should be sponged with clear water and allowed to dry thoroughly before applying paint.

Quality Must Not Be Sacrificed

On jobs where old paint must be completely removed in order to do a first-class job of repainting, the experienced, scrupulous painter may lose out to competitors who will simply apply new paint and trust to luck for performance. If the scrupulous painter follows his competitor's methods and the job fails, he may seriously damage a fine reputation which has taken years to create.

The painter who is going to get business this

year, and repeat business a few years from now, must learn to distinguish the surfaces that can be trusted to hold new paint properly and those where it is good business to concede to his competitors, when the owner cannot be convinced of the need of proper preparation before painting.

Every house painter encounters the problem of paint blistering because of excessive moisture behind the paint film. This moisture may be caused by wall or flashing leaks or by excessive humidity inside the house. In such instances it is best to call the owner's attention to the problem and wait until it is eliminated before proceeding with the paint job.

Preparing Plastered Walls For Painting

New plaster formerly presented very difficult problems to painters and decorators because of its high water content and chemical reactions. Sizes and primer-sealers have now been developed which surmount these hazards to a considerable extent so that oil paints can be used successfully within a comparatively short time.

Unless moisture present in new plaster is excessive, emulsion paints can be used immediately.

New plaster should be inspected carefully. All cracks and crevices should be filled with spackling compound or patching plaster. It is traditionally accepted that the plasterer will "point up" his own defects on new work. Lumps or high spots should be removed with a putty knife and the areas scraped smooth. Sanding of smooth limecoat walls causes scratching through the trowel polish. Thus, these are very difficult to paint smoothly.

As indicated above, the problems of moisture content of plaster and its alkaline reaction which actually destroys oil paint have, in large measure, been overcome by utilizing the latex or water-based paints. If an oil paint is required, however, the primer sealers, frequently based on acrylics, may be used to allow early job completion. After the plaster has been coated with the priming paint, the surface should be carefully examined for variations in gloss or variations in color difference. These are indications of nonuniformity of the plaster. If many such defects are present a second coat of primer sealer is needed. If only a few such defects are noted a second coat over these areas is

usually adequate. Once a surface appears uniform after the application of the primer sealer coat, the topcoats may be applied. Frequently one coat of flat finish paint serves the purpose. If semi-gloss and gloss paints are to be used one should follow directions carefully, for these sometimes require an intermediate coat over the primed surface.

As already indicated, latex paints are frequently applied on wet plaster. If paint of the calcimine type is to be used, the walls should be sized either with a glue-water size or, if the plaster is dry, with a primer sealer as discussed above. The infrequently used casein paints may be applied directly over the plaster, unless a primer sealer coat is desired in order to compensate for surface defects.

For the application of latex paints the directions of the manufacturer should be carefully followed. If the paint contains some oil, primer sealer coats will certainly be necessary.

In summary, there is no question but that the best results will be obtained if only dry plaster is painted. Since this is frequently not possible the procedures described above may be utilized. However, the painter should be well aware of the defects which may result from painting improperly sealed wet plaster, particularly the scaling or peeling of the film, softening and darkening of the paint and the development of color changes within the paint. Also the film may become sticky and pigments such as chrome green and Prussian blue may become discolored. Efflorescence, the appearance of white powder on the surface, is a possible defect associated with painting improperly cured plaster.

Walls to be painted, from which wallpaper and glue sizing have been removed, should be treated like new plaster.

Preparing Wallboard and Plasterboard

Wall and plasterboards of many types, made from gypsum, paper, pulp and various other compositions, are now used extensively as drywall paneling. The treatment for wallboard and plasterboard is similar to plaster, except for the covering of the joints and nail holes.

Be sure all nail heads are set below the surface. In covering joints, use a broad-blade knife and apply a fairly heavy, even layer of joint cement, four to six inches wide, the length of the joint. Then, place perforated joint tape over the joint and draw the knife firmly over the tape to force cement through the perforations, Fig.

Fig. 4-8. *Covering joint between pieces of wallboard with perforated tape. Left. Filling joint and covering nail heads. Right. Embedding tape in cement.*

4-8. Squeeze out excess cement before spreading a thin finishing coat of cement over the joint. Work several inches on each side to "feather" or taper the edges. When the cement is dry, sand the joint smooth and respackle if needed. In populous areas this is a separate trade.

Preparing Plastered Walls For Repainting

Do not attempt to hide wall defects with paint. Before repainting, check old plaster surface for cracks, holes, dents and other surface irregularities. Fill small holes, cracks, and other defects with spackling compound. Use patching plaster for large cracks and holes and to replace areas where chunks of plaster have fallen out. To fill cracks around bathtubs where moisture crumbles plaster, use caulking compound or special sealer made for this purpose.

Large cracks should be deepened until firm plaster is reached and the edges undercut so bottoms of cracks are wider than the surface.

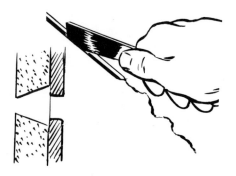

Fig. 4-9. *In repairing large cracks, edges should be undercut so cracks are wider at bottom than at the surface.*

A putty knife or old wood chisel may be used to do this. See Fig. 4-9.

Brush out dirt and loose plaster. Then soak plaster inside cracks and around outside edges with water using a clean sponge, so that new plaster will form a strong bond. After patch is dry, smooth surface with abrasive paper.

Brush off loose dirt, dust, cobwebs, and loose paint. Edges of spots where paint has peeled should be sanded so they taper gradually and will not show under new paint. All patched areas and exposed old plaster should be spot primed before painting.

Wash painted ceiling, walls, and woodwork with soap or detergent to remove dirt and greasy film. Do the ceiling first, then the walls, starting at the bottom of the wall and working upward. Do all washing before patching.

Wall paints and enamels are difficult to apply over shiny finishes such as varnish, gloss enamel and lacquer. The material will film out unevenly and have a tendency to "crawl" and form globules. Bright surfaces should be dulled with abrasive paper or liquid conditioner to provide "tooth" for the new finish.

Painting Over Wallpaper

Latex-base paints may be applied over most wallpaper that is in good condition and is firmly glued to the wall. Go over paper with a clean dry cloth to remove dust and loose dirt. Do not use wallpaper cleaner as this may leave a film which interferes with adhesion of the paint.

Checking to make sure the wallpaper does not contain dyes of water soluble nature, metallic colors or bleeding inks, may be done by applying paint to an inconspicuous area. If colors do show through, the paper should be removed or the colors sealed with a thin coat of shellac.

Bulges or bubbles in wallpaper should be removed by slitting the paper with a razor-blade knife and repasting it. Rough surfaces may be smoothed by sanding.

Generally it is preferable to remove wallpaper before painting. Edges of the paper may come loose after being painted, making it desirable to remove the paper completely. This becomes quite difficult because the paint interferes with soaking or steaming to remove the paper.

Preparing New Masonry Surfaces For Painting

It is quite commonly believed that masonry surfaces such as concrete, stucco, common brick, and concrete blocks are painted only for decorative purposes. These surfaces, because they are somewhat porous, are also painted or finished for protective purposes to keep out moisture and to prevent dusting and spalling.

Paints suitable for use on masonry surfaces include exterior house paint, cement-base water paint, emulsion paint and specialties such as chlorinated rubber-base and latex paints.

Aggregate materials composed basically of specially processed oils and fine silica sand are used as primer-filler coats to fill an unusually porous surface. Coarser grains of sand

Fig. 4-10. Neutralizing masonry surface by application of wash coat consisting of zinc sulphate crystals dissolved in water.

may be added for patching where textures must be matched.

Concrete sets in a short time but the hardening or curing process continues for a considerable period of time. When concrete is completely cured there is no longer active alkali on the surface which will cause paint to discolor, crack, peel and generally deteriorate.

Alkalinity in concrete, which has not fully aged, may be neutralized (aged artificially) by applying a wash coat consisting of two pounds of zinc sulphate crystals dissolved in one gallon of water, Fig. 4-10. Allow the wash coat to dry, then brush off all deposits, before applying paint. The neutralizer is not absolutely required when using latex-base paint but is usually recommended.

A zinc sulphate wash may also be used on old concrete surfaces, not to neutralize them, but to fill pores and to help stop suction, especially on unusually porous surfaces.

Preparing Old Masonry Surfaces For Paint

Masonry surfaces which have been previously painted and are in good condition usually require only removal of dust and dirt accumulations before repainting, using a broom and a wire brush.

Fig. 4-11. Removing loose mortar from joints between bricks.

If in poor condition, they may need extensive preparation. Cracks and crevices should be repaired with cement mortar. Rake out crumbled mortar from joints of masonry blocks and brick surfaces, Fig. 4-11, and replace (tuck point) with new mortar, Fig. 4-12. Allow the mortar to cure or neutralize, as with new masonry, before painting it.

REMOVING EFFLORESCENCE SALTS: Brick surfaces that are in poor condition from exces-

Fig. 4-12. Filling cracks between blocks in masonry wall by tuck pointing.

sive salting or efflorescing should be washed to remove the white powdery crust by using a solution of muriatic acid and water - - three parts water and one part full strength muriatic acid. Add acid slowly to the water; DO NOT add water to acid. Wear rubber gloves and goggles and work carefully. Rinse the surface well with clear water and allow it to dry before painting.

MILDEW REMOVAL: Mildew may be removed from masonry surfaces by using a solution of trisodium phosphate. Rinse well with clean water and allow the surface to dry.

Old, water thinned finishes or cement-base paints that have become porous and crumbly should be carefully wire brushed and treated with a muriatic acid wash as described above.

Concrete and cinder block surfaces that are too porous to be sealed by paint should be filled by applying a thin coat (grout coat) of cement. Allow the grout coat to dry thoroughly, then treat as a new surface. A newer and more effective approach is to use block fillers instead of grout coats.

A concrete floor that is very hard and smooth should be etched so the paint can "grip" the surface. The etching may be done by using a solution of one part muriatic acid to eight parts water. Use a wooden or plastic bucket and apply with a stiff fiber brush. Allow solution to remain on the surface until bubbling stops. Then rinse with ammonia water followed by clear water.

SAND BLASTING: On masonry surfaces where the cracking and scaling is extensive and attachment of the paint to the surface is poor, sandblasting is often the only proper way to prepare the surface for the new paint.

HOW TO CLEAN BRICK SURFACES: Glazed brick on exterior walls may be cleaned by using glazed brick proprietary cleaners. An effective cleaner is made by adding enough trisodium phosphate to a bucketful of warm water to cut the dirt. Experiment and add no more than needed to prevent damage to trim and other surrounding surfaces.

White mortar stains on brick fireplaces can usually be removed by brushing on muriatic acid. Wash off the acid with clean water. Fireplace surfaces that will not clean properly may be freshened by using a mixture of turpentine and linseed oil (equal parts) with oil color added to produce the desired shade.

Preparing Metal Surfaces For Painting

Proper preparation of metal surfaces for the application of paint is frequently more important than the preparation of other surfaces.

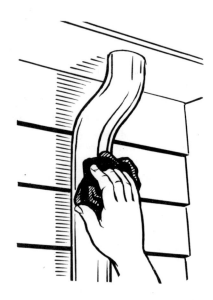

Fig. 4-13. Metal surfaces must be thoroughly cleaned before applying paint so paint film will adhere to surface.

Metal surfaces contain many minute pores which provide anchorage for the paint film. When these pores are filled with dirt, rust, grease, or scale, the paint is unable to adhere properly to the surface and cleaning is required. See Figs. 4-13 and 4-14. When rust is painted over without removing it, the rusting continues.

Preparation of metal surfaces may be divided into the two broad groups of cleaning by physical means and by chemical means.

Physical Cleaning
1. Manual
2. Mechanical -
   Sandblasting
3. Flame Cleaning
4. Heat Cleaning
5. Electrical Cleaning
6. Ultrasonic Cleaning

Chemical Cleaning
1. Solvent
2. Alkali
3. Emulsion
4. Acid
5. Pickling

Physical Cleaning

Mechanical cleaning involves the use of abrasive papers such as flint, garnet, silicon-carbide; wire brushes and chisels. Such cleaning may be done manually or by application of machine power. Revolving steel wire brushes are operated by both compressed air and electricity. Steel brushes can be used to remove dry rust effectively but not large rust scales.

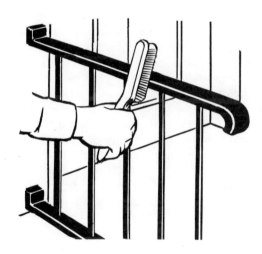

Fig. 4-14. Using wire brush to clean iron surface before painting.

Such scales can usually be removed by using a hammer and a cold chisel. A variety of mechanical tools are now available for removal of rust scale including rotary wire tools, rotary disc tools, rotary impact chippers and needle scalers. A paint scraper is useful in removing scaling paint, asphaltum and other substances.

Abrasion cleaning does not satisfactorily remove oils and greases although sandblasting usually is satisfactory.

Sandblasting

Sandblasting is used widely on plate steel to remove heavy mill scale. It is also used to clean castings. Cracked and scaled paint may be quickly stripped from metal surfaces by sandblasting.

In sandblasting, a gasoline engine or electric motor is used to operate an air compressor which builds up pressure in an air storage tank. Sand is mixed with the air and is driven through a nozzle at the end of a hose. The blast of sand quickly removes old paint, dirt and rust. Brick and stone surfaces may also be cleaned by sandblasting.

The surface produced by sandblasting is suitable for heavy coatings, but is comparatively rough and is not well suited for fine finishes.

Flame Cleaning

Flame cleaning as used on structural steel consists of applying small, intense flames to the surface. The intense heat makes the scale "pop off." This is caused by difference in expansion of the steel and the scale. This treatment should be followed by immediate hand or power wire brushing. Flame burning also removes oil and grease.

Chemical Cleaning

Solvent Cleaning of Steel

Solvents such as kerosene, gasoline and a variety of related materials may be used to remove grease and dirt from metal surfaces. Solvents are health and fire hazards for which reason proper precautions must be taken when using them.

In solvent cleaning, sufficient solvent must be utilized to wash the grease away. Since a layer of solvent invariably remains on the metal there is a tendency to thin the grease out and to end up with a less-concentrated layer of grease than was originally present. The modern chlorinated degreasers have overcome this problem.

Alkali Cleaning of Steel

Alkaline cleaners are usually a blend of alkaline salts, soaps, and resins. A number of types are available. Such cleaners usually come in concentrated form and must be diluted before use. After being cleaned, the surface must be thoroughly rinsed with suitable alkaline rinses to remove the residues.

The cleaned surfaces should be painted before rust starts, for the rust which forms within a few hours is sufficient to be harmful.

Emulsion Cleaning of Steel

An emulsion cleaner is a product in which the minute particles of the cleaning agent remain in suspension like fat globules in milk.

Pickling Method of Cleaning Steel

To remove oxides from metal surfaces by "pickling," tanks of strong mineral acids like sulphuric, hydrochloric and nitric are used. During World War II, a method of pickling was developed which utilizes a molten solution of sodium hydride through which the steel is passed. Descaling is accomplished without fumes and corrosive vapors and has the added advantage of passivating (making resistant to corrosion) the steel surface so that it will not oxidize prior to being painted.

Acid Cleaning of Steel

In acid cleaning of steel, the surface is wet with the acid cleaner by brushing or by wiping the surface with a brush or other applicator.

The painter must, of course, be properly protected with goggles, rubber gloves and protective clothing. After the acid has reacted, it is washed off with clear water. The surface is dried and then treated mechanically. Acid cleaning of steel is generally used in small or confined areas.

Phosphate Coatings for Steel

Steel surfaces are treated with phosphate-containing chemicals not only to clean the surface but also to provide a thin so-called "conversion" coating which is highly receptive to subsequent coatings of paint.

There are several types of phosphate treatments and in their use the recommendations of the supplier should be carefully followed.

Preparing Non-Iron Surfaces

Galvanized Iron

Galvanized iron is sheet metal dipped in hot zinc to produce large protective crystals of zinc on the surface as the zinc cools.

Weathered galvanized iron holds paint better than new galvanized iron. The weathered condition can be produced artificially by the use of various chemical washes to remove grease and form a coating of zinc chloride or other zinc salts to which finishing materials adhere better than to the zinc surface.

Some washes used are:
A. Vinegar
B. 4 oz. copper sulphate, copper chloride or copper acetate in 1 gal. water
C. 1 part commercial hydrochloric or muriatic acid to 4 parts water
D. Weak solution of ammonia

These solutions should be mixed in plastic or glass vessels and applied with a brush. After the solution has dried, the metal should be washed with clean water, allowed to dry, and coated as soon as possible.

Galvanized metal which has been exposed to the weather for six months or more usually does not need a chemical wash before painting.

The first coat of paint on galvanized metal should be a rust-inhibitive primer containing zinc chromate, red lead, blue lead, or zinc yellow. While these rust-inhibiting pigments are highly efficient, they should not be used on children's metal toys or on surfaces that may be chewed by young children. Where such a possibility exists, it is advisable to use primers that are formulated with iron oxide, even though they have less anticorrosive efficiency.

After the primer is dry, it is well to sand it lightly before applying the finish coat. The finishing coat may be any good exterior paint.

An effective coating for galvanized iron is a zinc dust primer, which is generally supplied in a two part container, one containing the liquid portion, the other the zinc dust. The zinc dust primer can be used over new galvanized iron without treatment other than removal of oily material with a solvent. The primer has a pleasing blue gray color and may be used as such. Also it may be coated with any suitable finish coat.

The primer with the zinc dust mixed in may develop some gas pressure if moisture is present. Thus, leftover paint should be handled with caution.

Zinc dust primer is excellent for steel that has been properly cleaned. The presence of the zinc metal tends to prevent the corrosion of the steel in much the same manner that galvanizing does.

Tinplate

Tin-coated metal as used on metal roofs may be prepared for painting by cleaning with a solution of one pound of sal soda to five gallons of water. Rinse the roof with clean water being sure to get the soda out of crevices. Let the metal dry completely before painting it.

Other ways to clean tinplate for painting include light hand sanding and washing with benzine or turpentine. Any acid or rosin stains left by soldering should be carefully removed.

Zinc and Copper

Zinc and copper do not need painting for protection for they do not rust. Down spouts and roof gutters made of these materials are frequently painted, however, to conform to a certain color scheme or to prevent the green discoloration which accumulates on copper. Transparent coatings are frequently used to prevent metal discoloration although these weather poorly. In painting bright zinc and copper no preparation is required other than to remove surface accu-

mulations as described for tinplate. If the surface of copper has weathered, effective cleaning can be accomplished with dilute nitric acid solution followed by clear water rinse.

Aluminum

Chemically, aluminum differs from steel. Its oxides form a protective blanket against further oxidation and ultimate destruction of the metal. Oxide surfaces of aluminum offer good adhesion for paint films.

Several of the methods used to clean steel can be used to clean aluminum. Removing grease and oil from aluminum before painting is desirable.

Mechanical methods of preparing aluminum surfaces find considerable use in decorative work. Scratch brushing is sometimes used to give a satin finish to a surface; sandblasting may be used to produce matte surfaces.

Zinc chromate is an excellent primer for aluminum and will cause paint to adhere very well. Aluminum exposed near sea water must be painted, for even the oxide coating cannot protect it against the action of salt water spray.

The importance of making sure that corners and crevices are well painted is emphasized in this picture.

85

Unit 5

PAINT SELECTION

There are numerous ways to classify protective coatings and the terminology used is far from universal. The most general term is protective coating, for virtually everything which the painter applies to a surface can be described in this way. The term paint, itself, has several connotations. It is considered in some instances as a pigmented protective coating. Others like to use the word only for compositions which are oil-based, reserving the word coatings for resin-based materials. Under the broad heading of protective coatings are varnishes and lacquers which are generally thought of as clear, unpigmented products, the varnishes being based on resin-oil combinations and the lacquers on nitrocellulose or, more recently, on other cellulose derivatives and on the acrylics. On the other hand, lacquers and varnishes may both be pigmented in which case they may be referred to as pigmented varnishes or pigmented lacquers. A pigmented varnish or, indeed, any pigmented protective coating which is highly glossy, may be termed an enamel. Primers and topcoats are pretty much self-explanatory.

Whatever the terminology, however, it is of great importance to select the proper paint for the proper application, Fig. 5-1. Indoor paints normally are not used out-of-doors, and vice versa although, even here, there are notable exceptions. Contract painters normally tend to think of coatings in terms of whether they are used for exterior or interior applications and, accordingly, this is a reasonable way to consider the various types of coatings available. Today, the painter practically always buys ready mixed paints and if he buys them from a reliable source, a great deal of advice is available on how to use the paint and where it will prove functional.

Some General Considerations

One of the most important problems facing the painter is what kind of paint to use in repainting. If the paint originally used has been satisfactory, it should be used again. In recoating over old paint, care must be taken to make sure that the new coating is compatible with the old one. A test patch is frequently advisable. If a paint which dries to a very hard film is used over a soft, oily film, there is a good chance that the job will be unsatisfactory. Certain dark colored pigments have a very high oil absorption. Thus, it is difficult to paint over these with white paints because they will tend to absorb the oil preferentially to the pigments in the white paint with resultant alligatoring. Similarly, house paints should not be used over clear varnish. Paints which dry to hard surfaces such as zinc pigment-containing paints should not be used over paints with so-called "soft" pigments unless the latter have aged for a long time. Also, enamels should not be used over soft house paint. Conversely, ordinary house paints should not be used over enamel, nor should white paint be used over coatings containing yellow ochre.

Repainting should take place often enough to provide protection of the substrate but too frequent repainting can be harmful for two reasons. First of all, the paint will not have weathered sufficiently to provide a good base for the new paint. Secondly, thick films can build up which tend to crack and to lose their adhesion. It is better, usually, to wash a house every year than to repaint it too often. In any case, when repainting it is very important to remove gloss by sanding if there are protected areas where the gloss of the paint has not yet weathered away.

Certain paints are more effective in certain

climatic conditions and, again, the recommendations of the supplier are important. Thus, in warm, humid climates, hard resin-containing paints are usually more durable than high oil content paints. In dry climates the reverse may be true.

The properties of wood markedly effect the durability of the paint. Density and texture are particularly important factors. Defects such as knots, resin and oil content, moisture content and whether or not the wood has a so-called "soft spring" or "hard summer" grain are all important factors. The relationship of these to the adsorptive and adhesive qualities of paint will be found in the Unit on Paint Application.

Primer

A primer is the first coat applied. Each coat of paint, from the first to next to last, must adhere to the surface upon which it is painted and must offer a "tooth" or surface to which each succeeding coat can bond. This first coat must have enough binder to satisfy the absorption of the material being painted and have enough binder left over to satisfy the pigment and make a good hard well bound paint. There must not be too much oily or soft "fat" or rubber-like quality or the primer will not form a stable foundation for the succeeding coats.

Primer-sealer coats for plaster walls and other masonry surfaces should stop the suction so future coats will not be absorbed unevenly. Finish coats over poorly sealed walls do not retain an even color nor can they be successfully washed.

Most good sealers for first coating of walls are now made of alkali-proof vehicles.

Generally, the old rule of the master painter artists of the fifteenth century (and up to now) still holds good: that is to work from lean to fat. Good paints have lasted well for over 400 years

Fig. 5-1. Choosing proper paint product for the job at hand is of utmost importance.

that were painted by this rule. It means that primers and undercoats should be mainly pigment and hard drying vehicle used as scarcely as common sense will permit, followed by coats of ever increasing oil content until the final enamel-like surface has more oil, or is more plastic than all the base coats.

To reverse this procedure is to invite disastrous "alligatoring" or cracking that can be compared to thin ice breaking upon a pond as the movement of the water underneath creates an unsteady foundation.

Primers may consist of varnish, paint sealer, or lacquer, depending on the particular work at hand. The paint manufacturer's instructions should be carefully followed.

Exterior aluminum paint or shellac may be used to prime soft, pitchy and resinous spots when doing exterior painting.

Phenolic-Resin Primer-Sealer

A newer type of finish which is well suited for fir and other softwoods is a phenolic-resin primer-sealer, sold under various trade names, that penetrates into the pores of the wood, dries, and equalizes the density of the hard and soft grains. Staining and painting of the wood thus treated results in an even tone without dark and light streaks which frequently result on untreated wood. Phenolic-resin sealer is light amber in color and is almost as thin as water. It comes as a clear primer-sealer and with both white and colored pigments added. Colors-in-oil may be added to produce almost any color desired.

Topcoat

The topcoat is, of course, the first line of defense against corrosion by the elements and it is also the coat which provides decoration. Topcoats are normally highly pigmented materials which may be either oil, resin or water-based. The choice of the topcoat must, of course, depend on the conditions of service to which it is to be subjected. For use inside a house, it is not necessary for a topcoat to be corrosion-resistant nor is resistance to degradation by ultraviolet light generally important. The reverse, of course, may be true for topcoats for outside use. Whereas outside paints are usually highly glossy, particularly if the utmost in re-

sistance to corrosion is desired, inside paints are frequently of a matte or at the most a semi-gloss finish. On the other hand, it is frequently important that inside paints be washable and stain-resistant. This, of course, is frequently true in a home but it is even more important in food handling institutions, hospitals and rest homes where glossy paints may actually be used to facilitate cleaning. The point of this general discussion, of course, is that the topcoat must be chosen carefully depending on the condition under which it is expected to function.

Enamels

Topcoats are frequently enamels. Enamel is a special type of paint made by grinding or mixing pigments with varnishes or lacquers to form a gloss or semi-gloss finish paint.

The purpose of enamel is to give a high-grade finish which is smooth, hard and long lasting for interior use and highly resistant to weather when used outside.

Enamels are primarily used for finish coats and are preceded by undercoatings. The undercoat which precedes the enamel should overcome differences in porosity so the topcoat will remain on the surface, seal the surface against free lime compounds, and have sufficient body to prevent separation of the vehicle and pigment by suction.

Pigments used for enamels are very finely ground in the vehicle which may be a varnish or more likely an alkyd resin. Vehicles for light colors must be pale and non-yellowing.

Thinners are used as specified by the manufacturer, who has determined which ones best suit the binding vehicles.

Semi-gloss enamel contains less of the transparent or pale varnish and more pigment than gloss enamel.

To meet the demand for various surface effects, manufacturers are producing enamels having high gloss, semi-gloss or eggshell gloss effects. These names refer to about the same gloss surfaces as finishes produced by varnishes with similar names. A true gloss enamel reflects light spectrally from the surface because the fine pigment is almost entirely immersed in vehicle making a smooth mirrorlike surface. Mat or flat paints diffuse light from rough exposed surfaces.

Clear Coatings

Varnishes

Varnish may be defined as a solution of a resin or gum in oil or spirit, which is converted to a solid film by the evaporation of the spirit or other solvent, or by oxidation of the oil or by both means combined.

The two main types of varnishes are Spirit Varnishes, and Oleoresinous Varnishes.

Spirit Varnishes

A spirit varnish is composed of a resin or gum dissolved in a volatile solvent such as alcohol. Such varnishes may be colored by the addition of spirit soluble dyes. They dry as quickly as the solvent evaporates. The principal resins used in making spirit varnishes are the natural resins, dammar, shellac, sandarac, mastic and the synthetic resins, such as certain forms of vinyl and acrylic resins.

Shellac is a spirit varnish.

Oleoresinous Varnishes

Oleoresinous varnishes are composed of a resin or gum dissolved in a drying oil which, after application, hardens as it combines with oxygen from the air. This type of varnish is usually made by heating a mixture of resin, drying oil, thinner and drier to about 600 deg. F. Resins generally used are ester gum, rosin esters, and synthetic resins.

There are many formulas for making each of many types of varnish such as exterior spar, floor varnish, rubbing varnish, interior gloss, flat and semi-gloss varnishes and many mixing varnishes for both interior and exterior use.

Properties of Varnish

The types of oils and resins and the ratio of oil to resin are the principal factors governing the properties of varnish. The selection depends on the compatibility of different oils and resins, and on the intended use of the varnish.

It is generally considered that the oils in the finished coating contribute to elasticity and the resins to hardness.

VARNISH LENGTH: The ratio of oil to resin in varnish is expressed as the number of gallons of oil combined with 100 lbs. of resins. This is commonly referred to as the "length" of the varnish. Thus, where 50 gal. of oil are used with 100 lbs. of resin, the varnish has a 50 gal. length.

Varnish containing less than 20 gal. of oil per 100 lbs. of resin is usually called a short-oil varnish. A medium-oil varnish contains from 20 to 30 gal., and a long-oil varnish is one in which 30 gal. or more are used.

Short-oil varnishes are used primarily where hardness and a high degree of resistance to alcohols, alkalies, or acids is desirable and where elasticity in the film is relatively unimportant. Varnishes for furniture and interior trim are short or medium in oil length. Short-oil varnishes are especially suitable where a "rubbed" finish is desirable. They are too brittle for floors, for which a medium-oil varnish is best suited.

Varnishes for exterior exposure are usually of long-oil formulation because of the beneficial effect of drying oil in providing elasticity and resistance to weathering. Spar varnish (named because of its suitability for wooden spars of a ship), is a varnish of this type.

Recently, by the use of synthetic resins, varnishes have been formulated to provide increased moisture resistance without sacrifice of sunlight resistance. The synthetic resins are equal to and in many cases superior to the natural resins.

In all the above, it must be kept in mind that the selection of the right gum for the formulation is as important as the proportion of oil.

Flat Varnish

Flat varnish - - varnish which dries with a reduced luster or gloss - - is made by adding such materials as silica, wax and metallic soaps to the varnish. Varying degrees of gloss are referred to as satin gloss, semi-gloss, dull, extra dull and many similar expressions.

Black Varnish (Asphalt)

Black asphalt varnish is used mainly for such purposes as shop coating of fabricated iron and steel products, in asphalt-aluminum paints, and for coating tanks. It is made from gilsonite and similar asphalts which take the place of gums. They are used because of a high chemical resistance.

Penetrating Floor Sealer

This is a type of varnish which penetrates into the pores of the wood, rather than remaining as a film on the surface. Scratches made by traffic are less prominent than with regular floor varnishes. In making floor sealers both oleoresinous and spirit types of varnish are used. An example would be a formulation of tung oil and phenolic resin thinned to penetrate.

Shellac

Proper thinning of the shellac purchased in commercial mixtures is an important part of its correct application. Shellac should seldom be used as thick as it comes in the can.

Shellac is furnished in various "cuts," which indicate the amount of resin in pounds added to one gallon of solvent. A four pound cut for example, (which is standard in the architectural field) consists of four pounds of shellac gum dissolved or "cut" in one gallon of pure alcohol. This makes slightly more than one gallon of solution. Therefore, one gallon of shellac contains slightly less than the number of pounds of shellac in its "cut" and slightly less than one gallon of alcohol.

In applying shellac several thin coats are far better than a few heavy coats. Approximately one part alcohol to one part four pound cut shellac makes a workable material for general shop use such as sealing off stains, suction marks in primed plaster walls, and as a primer for patches. Wash coatings for use over primed woodwork to seal in pitch pores may be even thinner, about one and one-half to two parts of alcohol to one part of four pound cut shellac. Some testing and judgment based on experience is always necessary.

Clear coatings may be formulated from the newer resin-based finishes, particularly the epoxy coatings and the urethanes. These have been discussed in the Unit on Materials. Clear coatings from these are used primarily as floor finishes and as finishes for wood and perhaps furniture where high abrasion resistance and resistance to water and chemicals are required. Such finishes, when properly applied, can frequently be highly decorative.

Lacquers

Lacquer is a finishing material that dries by the evaporation of the solvent (liquid capable of dissolving a substance) and thinner, and forms a protective film from its nonvolatile contents. It is characterized by its very rapid drying and distinctive odor.

The prime ingredient in lacquer is nitrocellulose, which is produced by the action of nitric and sulphuric acids on short fibers of cotton or purified wood pulp.

Nitrocellulose lacquers in use today differ greatly from their early formulations but are still combinations of such ingredients as cellulose nitrate, solvents, resins, pigments, and plasticizers.

Sometimes there will be twenty or more ingredients in a formula, each chosen for utility or economy. By proper formulation, lacquers can be made that are hard or soft; dry almost instantly, or so slowly they can be brushed by hand; clear or colored with any desired shade or dye; of very high gloss, or a flat sheen and of both high and low viscosity.

Lacquers are also made from cellulose acetate, cellulose acetate-butyrate, ethyl cellulose, and acrylic resins. Nitrocellulose is still the most important lacquer material. The acrylics, both alone and in combinations with nitrocellulose, are being used on many automobiles where they have exceptional gloss retention.

Lacquer thinners are carefully formulated and should be used according to instructions for the lacquer being used. In humid weather it is sometimes necessary to add a "retarder," a slow solvent, to prevent blushing or a whitening due to condensed moisture.

Stains

A transparent stain is one that dissolves in the solvent and is carried into and around the fibers of the material being colored, like a dye. In fact, clear wood stains are dyes. They are available in water, spirit (alcohol), and oil soluble types, and may be purchased ready for use in the solvent or in dry powder form.

The range of color is very great covering every conceivable need. Most interesting to the painter are the basic colors such as walnut, brown mahogany, red mahogany, cherry red, several shades of oak and maple and many others prepared specially for the trade and eliminating the need to mix colors. These prepared stains are safer to use also because often mixed colors are of varying solubility and separate on application.

Any stain will "bleed" or color the coating

The appearance of a relatively modest home is greatly enhanced by proper painting. Note that the metal flashing around the brick chimney has been carefully painted.

above it if that coating is soluble in the same solvents as is the stain. This is particularly true of oil stains with lacquer or varnish directly in contact with them.

Various colors are more or less permanent within any solubility group, but generally, the water stains are most stable, followed by the oil soluble group and last the spirit stains. Much progress is being made in the field of dye chemistry and all the products are being upgraded to a point where they may be considered safe with few exceptions.

Pigment Oil Stain (Wiping Stain)

Pigment type oil stains consist of finely ground color pigments, such as used in paints, in solution with linseed oil, varnish, turpentine, etc., according to the particular formula being used.

Pigments generally used are the transparent earth pigments like raw and burnt sienna, burnt umber, and Vandyke brown. Raw umber, yellow ochre, and Venetian red are too opaque and make "muddy" stains.

Wiping stains are best suited for use on close-grained woods which do not require filling to the extent that open-pore woods require. Wiping stain serves a dual purpose in that it stains and fills in one operation. Outstanding qualities of pigmented wiping stains are fastness to light, non-raising of grain, non-bleeding and ease of application.

Pigment wiping stain may be applied by brush, dip or spray. It should be allowed to set five to ten minutes, or until the surface becomes dull due to evaporation of the thinner. It should then be wiped using a soft cloth. The depth of color is controlled by the amount of stain wiped off. Pigmented stain should be thoroughly dry before being sealed with shellac, varnish or lacquer, which keeps it from rubbing off.

Pigment stains never have the clarity of dye stains. They always hide some of the satin-like quality of the wood and are therefore seldom used on high quality wood finishes.

Varnish Stain

Varnish stain is a type of stain in which stain is mixed with varnish. This finishing material completes both the staining and finishing jobs with one operation, but has the disadvantage that the stain does not penetrate into the wood and bare wood may be noticed, if it is chipped

off or marred. Also, runs, sags, and laps show dark where the stain is concentrated in heavier layers.

Creosote Stain

Creosote stain, which is made mostly from wood and coal tars, is mixed with linseed oil, Japan drier and thinned with benzine or kerosene. It is used on shingles and for other exterior purposes.

Creosote stain preserves wood from decay, and protects it from wood boring insects and fungus growths. This stain is available in several different colors. Its main disadvantage, a very strong objectionable odor, is hard to overcome. It is also dangerous to skin and eyes, creating bad burns on contact. Some manufacturers have partially overcome these difficulties.

Bituminous Coatings

Coal tar and asphalt coatings are used to a considerable extent for waterproofing, roofing purposes, and for the protection of submerged metalwork. There special suitability is due to the fact they can be applied at reasonable cost in coatings that are thicker than most paint films and create a substantial barrier against attack by moisture and oxygen.

Asphalt

Asphalt coatings derived from petroleum are available as enamels, cold-applied paints and emulsions. They are generally considered to be more resistant to weathering and less resistant to moisture penetration than coal tar products. As a rule, they are also less susceptible to temperature extremes. Both the coal tar and asphalt coatings may be reinforced by epoxy or urethane resins which improve adhesion, flexibility and resistance to chemicals and strong solvents.

Finishes Used Outdoors

House Paint

Of all exterior paints available, the best known is the coating called "house paint." Whereas all house paint was originally oil-based, most of it based on linseed oil, the water-based paints have been making important advances and today one has a choice between water and oil-based paints. Today's house paints are more durable, more color-fast, easier to use and more blister-resistant than the paints formerly available.

The majority of today's light colored house paints are self-cleaning. This means that the rate of chalking is controlled so that any dirt on the surface will be washed away by rain with the accumulated chalk, leaving the paint clean and fresh looking. The self-cleaning quality does not appreciably affect the wearing qualities during the normal lifetime of the paint.

House paint can be used on clapboard siding and wood trim, brick, cement, cinder blocks, asbestos-cement shingles, stucco and stone. It can also be used - - but only if better paints are not available - - on iron and galvanized surfaces, and on metal siding and aluminum and steel windows. House paint should not be used on garden or porch furniture where it will rub off on clothes during the chalking process.

Exterior enamels are suitable for use on garden and porch furniture. Such finishes are also known as trim-and-trellis paints. Outdoor enamels known as farm-and-tractor paints may also be used effectively for this purpose. Exterior enamels may be used on shutters and wood window trim, as well as on metal siding, steel and aluminum windows, iron and galvanized surfaces. Care should be taken not to use these enamels on softwood surfaces with many joints because hardening, cracking and peeling may occur.

Natural Wood Finishes

Natural finishes for wood siding on houses have become increasingly popular during the past few years. Such finishes are most frequently used on redwood and western red cedar. To a lesser extent they are used on cypress, pine and Douglas fir.

Many natural finishes are clear or transparent, but some are slightly pigmented to impart some color to the wood without hiding the grain.

Natural finishes can give satisfactory service, provided a suitable finish is selected and properly applied and maintained. Natural finishes as a whole, however, are much less durable than good quality house paint and must be renewed much more frequently. House paint should serve at least four years before needing renewal. Most natural finishes need to be renewed once a year. On those parts of the house fully exposed to sun, wind and rain, even more frequent renewal may be necessary.

The lowest courses of siding on the south side of the house are usually most severely exposed, and natural finish there needs most frequent renewal. Exposure on the east and west sides is about equal and not nearly as severe as on the south side. The north side is the least affected.

Natural finishes may be classified either as penetrating layers or as surface coatings. Penetrating coatings soak into the wood and do not leave a continuous film of appreciable thickness on the surface. The oil finishes, the wood sealer finishes, and the water-repellent preservative finishes are of this type. Varnish finishes are surface coatings and usually do not contain pigment.

The trivial names of commercial products do not necessarily indicate their application. A material sold as a "log cabin" finish, for example, may be an oil finish, a sealer, or a varnish finish.

Some of the penetrating types contain rot and mold inhibiting creosote which is treated to remove some of the objectionable qualities of the functional material. Any materials containing creosote or asphaltum will bleed into future coats of paint. Thus, they provide a poor base for additional coats of paint unless these are of the same penetrating material.

Information on the application of natural finishes for exterior use will be found in the Unit on Wood Finishing.

Miscellaneous Finishes

Cement-base paints which contain Portland cement are widely used on brick, stucco, cement and cinder blocks. Rubber-base paints can be used on the same exterior masonry surfaces, and in addition, on asbestos-cement shingles and concrete porch floors.

Porch floors, whether of wood or concrete, can be coated with a durable exterior enamel especially formulated for the purpose, a porch-and-deck paint, or an enamel. Awning paint, a product which is devised for a specific purpose, can be used to add new color to canvas awnings.

Another type of exterior coating is aluminum paint. This may be used to protect asphalt siding, as well as galvanized and iron surfaces, brick, stucco and concrete blocks. It may also be used, if properly formulated, as a second coat for new wood to stop pitch burns, and over old finishes that "bleed," to keep the old finish from discoloring the new coating.

	House Paint	Transparent Sealer	Cement Base Paint	Rubber-Base Paint	Exterior Clear Finish	Aluminum Paint	Wood Stain	Trim-and-Trellis Paint	Awning Paint	Spar Varnish	Porch-and-Deck Paint	Primer or Undercoater	Metal Primer
CLAPBOARD SIDING	◪											✓	
BRICK	◪	✓	✓	✓								✓	
CEMENT & CINDER BLOCK	◪	✓	✓	✓								✓	
ASBESTOS CEMENT	◪			✓	•							✓	
STUCCO	◪	✓	✓	✓								✓	
STONE	◪	✓	✓	✓								✓	
ASPHALT SHINGLE SIDING	◪					✓							
NATURAL WOOD SIDING & TRIM					✓		✓		✓				
METAL SIDING	◪						◪						✓
WOOD FRAME WINDOWS	◪						◪					✓	
STEEL WINDOWS	◪						◪						✓
ALUMINUM WINDOWS	◪						◪						✓
SHUTTERS & OTHER TRIM							◪					✓	
CLOTH AWNINGS								✓					
WOOD SHINGLE ROOF						✓							
WOOD PORCH FLOOR											✓		
CEMENT PORCH FLOOR			✓								✓		
COPPER SURFACES										✓			
GALVANIZED SURFACES	◪				◪	◪				✓			✓
IRON SURFACES	◪				◪	◪							✓

◪ Black dot indicates that a primer or sealer may be necessary before the finishing coat (unless surface has been previously finished).

Fig. 5-2. Exterior painting, some suggestions on what to use and where.

Wood Primers

It is necessary to apply primers or sealers under house paint and exterior enamels on new wood unless the surface has been previously finished.

Coating new fir plywood and other soft woods having pronounced soft spring and hard summer growths (grain) with a phenolic-resin primer-sealer before applying spar varnish, enamel or house paint brings the soft growth to approximately the same uniform density as the hard summer growth.

Controlled penetration vehicle primers are also good over woods such as these because they too cover as a film, rather than absorbing unevenly. Uneven absorption weakens the film by creating a discontinuous vehicle at each change of grain structure.

The new vinyl emulsions are excellent masonry and stucco paints. They are good as primers and finish coats and may be used to recoat over other old paints under conditions recommended by the manufacturers.

Always select a paint that can "breathe" for any masonry or stucco to prevent future peeling trouble. Cement paints (made of cement), brush-coats, and most water-based paints breathe.

Additional information on purposes for which various finishes are best suited and which ones require primers, sealers and undercoats may be obtained from the chart, Fig. 5-2.

Interior Surfaces

On interior surfaces the basic choice of finishes is generally determined by whether a transparent or opaque coating is desired. See Fig. 5-3.

The transparent and semi-transparent coatings include varnishes, lacquers, stains, shellacs, sealers and waxes.

There are interior varnishes that can be used on wood paneling, wood trim, stair risers and window sills. Durable floor varnishes, made to withstand foot traffic are available for use on wood floors, stair treads, and wherever heavy abrasion exists.

Also devised for floors are penetrating stains which can be used on wood floors, stair treads and risers as well as concrete floors.

Shellac is often used as a coating for wood floors, stair treads and risers and also on wood trim and wood paneling.

Penetrating wood sealers are often employed on new wood paneling, stair risers, treads and floors.

On most of these surfaces, except stair

Surface	Flat Paint	Semi-Gloss Paint	Enamel	Rubber Base Paint	Emulsion Paint (Incl. Latex)	Casein Paint (Not Latex)	Interior Varnish	Shellac	Wax (Liquid or Paste)	Wax (Emulsion)	Stain	Wood Sealer	Floor Varnish	Floor Sealer	Cement Base Paint or Enamel	Aluminum Paint	Sealer or Undercoater	Metal Primer Sealer or Undercoater
PLASTER WALLS & CEILING	✓	✓		✓	✓	✓											✓	
WALL BOARD	✓	✓		✓	✓	✓											✓	
WOOD PANELING	✓	✓		✓	✓		✓	✓	✓			✓						
KITCHEN & BATHROOM WALLS		✓	✓	✓	✓												✓	
WOOD FLOORS							✓	✓	✓	✓	✓	✓	✓					
CONCRETE FLOORS									✓	✓	✓			✓				
RUBBER TILE FLOORS									✓	✓	✓			✓				
ASPHALT TILE FLOORS											✓							
LINOLEUM									✓	✓	✓		✓	✓				
STAIR TREADS									✓			✓	✓	✓	✓			
STAIR RISERS	✓	✓	✓	✓			✓	✓			✓	✓						
WOOD TRIM	✓	✓	✓	✓	✓		✓	✓	✓								✓	
STEEL WINDOWS	✓	✓	✓	✓												✓		✓
ALUMINUM WINDOWS	✓	✓	✓	✓														✓
WINDOW SILLS			✓			✓												
STEEL CABINETS	✓	✓	✓	✓														✓
HEATING DUCTS	✓	✓	✓	✓												✓		✓
RADIATORS & HEATING PIPES	✓	✓	✓	✓												✓		✓
OLD MASONRY	✓	✓	✓	✓	✓	✓								✓	✓	✓		
NEW MASONRY	✓	✓	✓	✓	✓									✓		✓		

Fig. 5-3. Interior painting, some suggestions on what to use and where.

risers and treads, wax is often used as a final coating. The paste and liquid varieties are used on wood trim, paneling, wood floors, linoleum, rubber tile and concrete floors. Only the emulsion type of wax is suitable for asphalt tile floors. It may be used on other types of floors, too. Wax with solvents (like liquid or paste) dissolves asphalt tile.

Where an opaque coating is desired on floors, durable floor paint or porch and deck enamel may be used both on wood and concrete floors and on stair treads. The chlorinated rubber floor enamels are excellent for concrete as are two-component epoxy finishes.

Opaque coatings are generally available in both gloss and dull finishes. In enamels, the element of gloss is often supplied by the same ingredient which provides the durability. An enamel is generally a smooth finish coating of somewhat less hiding power than undercoaters and generally "long" in the sense of oiliness or high gum content.

In latexes and alkyd flat enamels, the element of washability is present without gloss.

Enamels

The highest gloss finish, an enamel, provides an excellent finish for walls of kitchens and bathrooms, wood trim, stair risers, steel and aluminum windows and window sills. Steel cabinets, radiators and heating pipes also benefit from such a protective and decorative coating, as does both old and new masonry. Enamels for radiators are often specially formulated to resist heat.

SEMI-GLOSS (EGGSHELL) ENAMEL - - like high-gloss enamel - - has an oil base and is suitable for practically all surfaces where high-gloss enamel can be used. It is a little less durable, but has less sheen and is a desirable finish for woodwork as well as for plaster walls, ceilings, wallboard and wood paneling.

FLAT WALL PAINT - - which has no gloss, provides a velvety finish for walls and ceilings. Several types are available. Flat oil paint can be applied successfully to the same surface as the semi-gloss paints, but is not recommended for walls and woodwork of kitchens and bathrooms, nor for window sills or any surfaces that are easily scarred and finger marked. There are so-called flat enamels but they are not as mar resistant as gloss or semi-gloss enamels.

Texture paint, which is paste-like in con-

sistency and applied with a brush or trowel, may often be used with good results on old walls that are full of cracks or are too irregular for other finishes. Such paint may also be used to obtain a rough plaster effect on newly plastered walls, wallboard and plaster board. Such an effect is obtained by rubbing a wad of crumpled paper, sponge, texturing comb, stipple brush, or whisk broom on the wet surface. Raised portions may be flattened slightly by drawing a celluloid triangle or other straightedge across the surface. Thinned and applied with a roller or rolled after application or stippled with a block stippler, this kind of painting belongs to practical house painting as opposed to the above mentioned textures which are generally considered decorative.

Lacquers

Lacquer is used mostly as an industrial finish but is also useful in the home on floors, furniture, fine paneling and cabinetwork. Colored lacquers contain paint pigments and are used to repaint lacquered or enameled furniture and appliances. Lacquers must be spray applied.

Emulsion Paints

Emulsion or latex paints, which were originally available only as flats, are now available also in semi-gloss finishes. These, of course, are the most widely used inside paints and have been discussed in greater detail in the Unit on Materials. The thixotropic latex paints which are now available make the use of these materials even simpler by eliminating to a large extent dripping and splattering and by preventing curtaining or sagging once the paint is applied to a vertical surface.

Water-based paints available today may be used on almost any interior surface although they are used primarily on plaster and more recently on woodwork. Wallboard may be coated with latex paints as may all sorts of interior masonry surfaces.

Important strides have been made in the past few years in paints pigmented with aluminum pigment, particularly from the point of view of improving the pigment itself and providing better methods for combining the vehicle with the aluminum paste or powder. Ready-mixed aluminum paints are available today which are relatively easy to apply.

Aluminum paints have good protective, weatherproofing and waterproofing properties and may be used on a variety of surfaces. For example, aluminum house paint is excellent for weather-exposed wood. Aluminum metal and masonry paint is widely used on hard surfaces such as metal roofs, silos and machinery. Aluminum enamel, on the other hand, with its high gloss, is useful for inside decorative applications as well as to provide heat reflective surfaces for radiators and space heaters.

Aluminum-pigmented silicone resins are the best heat resistant paints known, whereas combinations of aluminum powder or paste with bituminous materials are of value as roof coatings because the aluminum reflects the sun's heat. The bituminous binder, on the other hand, seals leaks around nailheads and covers small cracks. Asbestos fibers add strength and toughness to coatings of this sort. Such coatings are useful not only for roofs but for corrugated steel, slate, tile, stucco, concrete and cinder block surfaces.

It is important to note that the several types of aluminum pigmented compositions cannot be interchanged. Accordingly, one must be sure that he is using an aluminum paint formulated for the specific purpose at hand.

Applying Paint to Metal Surfaces

Metal surfaces such as steel and iron are painted for protection and for decorative purposes. Unless the formation of rust on these surfaces is prevented at the start, a great deal of expense and difficulty in painting results.

Primers recommended for use by painters on most metal finishing jobs are red and blue lead, zinc chromate, and iron oxide.

Lead Primers

Red lead is one of the oldest pigments used for protecting metal against corrosion and rust, and is still one of the most popular metal primers in use today. Currently, red lead is used with alkyd resins, to produce primers that dry quickly, adhere well, and do not saponify (convert into soap) white liquid.

Red lead paints are frequently sold in combination with red lead oxide pigment. Such paints do not have the characteristic orange color of red lead, but still have good rust inhibitive properties.

Blue lead is also used extensively for metal priming purposes.

Zinc Chromate Primers

Zinc chromate primer is usually sold in ready-to-use viscosity. It is yellow in color - - a color which is detrimental to its sale to those who are accustomed to the characteristic orange color of red lead. However, zinc chromate primer is an excellent product, frequently superior to red lead for many metal priming purposes.

Specialized Coatings

Too much emphasis, however, cannot be placed on the importance of analyzing carefully the environmental and functional properties to which the paint must respond. For example, the painting of a bridge, where weight is an undesirable factor, frequently requires a paint with a low density pigment. The painting of radiators, stacks and ovens requires paints which withstand high temperatures. Structures which may be subjected continually or intermittently to blasts of heat should be painted not only with high temperature-resisting paints but with white or light colored paints to achieve the maximum in reflectivity. Aluminum pigment also is excellent because of its reflective properties. Frequently, reflectivity of heat is important for farm buildings in which grain is stored or in which animals live. In still other applications the insulating properties of the paint may be important.

Certainly, careful attention should be given to the environment which the painted surface encounters. In a highly corrosive area, one should never use house paint on a metal surface. Rather, the surfaces should be carefully prepared, properly primed and coated with the more corrosive resistant paints now available, such as those based on epoxy resins.

Finally, the point must be made that economics, in painting, as in all other industries, are of prime importance. However, it is the duty of the painter to impress the consumer with the fact that the cost of the paint is a relatively minor factor. There is hardly an instance where paint accounts for more than twenty-five percent of the cost of the job. Frequently, only ten percent of the total cost is accounted for by the paint. Thus, "cheap" paint is seldom a bargain in the long run. Well-formulated paints using high-grade vehicles and pigments are invariably the best "bargain."

It goes without saying that high-grade paint should be used and applied according to the

Modern homes are requiring elegant decoration as never before. The successful painter must be alert to new and improved products and to the methods for applying them in order to meet the challenges which modern decoration and protection demand.

procedures indicated by the manufacturer. The paint industry has devoted millions of dollars to research to evolve the directions indicated on the label of the paint can. The wise painter makes full use of this hard-won experience.

In the Sections which follow, a variety of specialized coatings will be described.

Multi-Color Finishes

An unusual type of water-based paints are the multi-colored or so-called polka dot paints which have become popular in the past few years. The multi-color paint is a two-phase system in which one phase is water-based and the other is oil-based. When applied on a surface, a multi-colored or speckled effect results because of the way the oil phase has been dispersed in the water phase. The "dispersed" phase is frequently a nitrocellulose lacquer or a synthetic enamel. The continuous phase, on the other hand, is water containing a protective colloid or a stabilizer. The particle size of the dispersed phase can vary from microscopic particles to particles which are visible with the naked eye. It is because of these relatively large particles that the speckled effect is observed.

In preparing the paint, the water insoluble

nitrocellulose lacquer is stirred into the water containing the stabilizer. The droplets disperse and the size and shape of these may be varied by adjusting the speed of mixing, the temperature and the amount and type of stabilizer. Thus, the droplets may be in the shape of circles, ovals or teardrops and their diameters may vary from 1/100 to 1/8 in. If the nitrocellulose is pigmented with only one color, a finish is obtained that will obliterate the grain of most woods, cover knots that do not bleed and will make the appearance of articles from various materials uniform. Thus, the coating is ideal for use on inexpensive lumber, plywood, and masonite. If the nitrocellulose is pigmented with several colors, the polka dot effect will result and the pigment or polka dots will pervade through the entire thickness of the paint.

When the continuous phase of this paint is aqueous, the paint may be applied to damp surfaces. In every instance the paint must be applied by spraying and violent agitation of the material must be avoided since the polka dot character results from a protective coating around each particle of lacquer or enamel. Shaking will tend to break down this protective coating and destroy the spatter effect.

These finishes may be applied to wallboard,

plaster, cinder blocks, wood, metal and areas which have been patched or are unsightly. They are widely used because of their unusual, attractive and decorative effects and also because they provide excellent protection from abrasion and hard usage. Like everything else, however, they have their limitations and should not be expected to provide the protection of a ceramic finish or even of a glossy resin-based paint.

Zinc-Rich Paints

Zinc-rich paints have been described as a means for "galvanizing with a paint brush." Basically, they are paints formulated with a very high content of zinc dust and a very small amount of vehicle. The zinc content may be as high as 92 percent although other types are available with 80 percent zinc. Some zinc oxide may be included, particularly in the paints with lower pigment volume concentrations. Zinc-rich paints are of particular importance for application on galvanized surfaces and for use on steel which is to be protected from salt water and from highly corrosive atmospheres. The zinc-rich paint is normally the primer and is then covered with a protective topcoat. The major virtue of zinc-rich paints is their anti-corrosive character. Thus, they are useful whenever water immersion is a problem. They are particularly valuable because they adhere to galvanized surfaces. They do not, however, adhere well to old paint which must be removed if the zinc-rich paint is to be applied.

Use of zinc-rich paints is indicated wherever galvanizing is useful but where a less expensive type of coating is required.

Fire-Retardant Paints

Fire-retardant paints are based largely on antimony oxide, chlorinated vehicles such as chlorinated rubber, pigments such as zinc borate, a variety of phosphates, nitrogen containing compounds and other materials which, under the influence of heat, provide a degree of heat or fire retardancy.

One of the mechanisms by means of which a fire-retardant paint protects a surface is called intumescence. Here, the paint actually foams to provide an insulating layer to protect the combustible substrate. Other mechanisms involve the fusion of inorganic pigments to provide noncombustible surfaces. A variety of fire-retardant paints are available today, and their use should be considered in both homes and buildings as a means of helping to cut down the tremendous yearly losses from fire.

Highway Paints

A variety of paints are now available for use as highway marking paints. The painting of roads for safety and informational purposes is a rapidly growing area. Special painting devices have been made for this purpose and it is interesting to note that edge striping as well as center striping is now becoming popular. Although most highway paints are formulated from inexpensive vehicles, the use of more resistant epoxy type paints, which provide more prolonged service, is under investigation.

Antiseptic Paints

Paints formulated with germicidal agents of various sorts, particularly with DDT, have been available for several years. The prinicple involved is the volatilization of the bactericide at the surface of the coating to kill bacteria, fungi and algae which may come in contact with the surface.

Antiseptic paints formulated with mildewcides are of particular interest for the painting of houses where mildew-producing organisms are a problem. Zinc oxide is widely used as a mildewcide in house paints.

Antiseptic paints formulated with potent bactericidal agents are useful also for interiors, particularly in bathrooms, kitchens and commercial installations where food is utilized or prepared.

Luminous Paints

Luminous paints are largely a result of improvements made during World War II. These are paints which glow in the dark and can be utilized for decorative purposes. They are also practical as safety guides both inside and outside of the home since they remain luminous and are visible after dark. Many factories and public buildings now utilize luminous paints for this reason. Paints of this sort are now widely used on airplanes and will become more popular as their virtues are recognized.

Swimming Pool Paints

The popularity of swimming pools has made

necessary the formulation of special paints for both decorative and protective purposes. Many swimming pool paints are based on chlorinated rubber. Catalyzed epoxy finishes are highly recommended as are the more conventional types of paints based on cement. A swimming pool paint must adhere to concrete, have excellent resistance to alkali, and it must, of course, resist the problems associated with water immersion and must have excellent abrasion resistance.

Marine Paints

Hand-in-hand with paints for swimming pools are paints required by the individual who has his own boat and is interested in keeping it in excellent condition. Spar varnishes have traditionally provided the bases for marine paints. These are still to be highly recommended although newer finishes such as the catalyzed epoxy resins are valuable because they adhere well not only to wood but also to metal and fiber glass. Such paints, it goes without saying, must have excellent water resistance, a high degree of abrasion resistance and must maintain a decorative appearance throughout their lifetime.

Waterproofing Paints

Waterproofing paints are important for both inside and external use. Internal waterproofing compounds may be used as a base material for filling cracks in walls, mortar joints, and floor-line leaks either above or below grade. These compounds are usually white powders which are mixed with water and applied by a brush or a trowel to the defective areas after seepage has ceased. Again, the painter should be familiar with these materials since they are frequently important in redecorating, particularly, of course, in basement areas.

Exterior waterproofing compounds such as the silicones have become popular in the past few years. The silicones have been mentioned already in relation to their high temperature-resisting properties. They are also excellent for waterproofing untreated masonry to prevent "spalling" as well as damp interior walls, cracking plaster, warped woodwork and peeling paint and wallpaper - - all of which result from the seepage of water through outside masonry surfaces. Silicone masonry water repellents are normally clear solutions which must be applied by spraying or brushing to unpainted masonry surfaces or to masonry surfaces painted with cement-based paints. They cannot be applied over oil-based paints. A single application of a silicone masonry water repellent will usually provide protection for five to ten years. Oil-based or cement-based paints may be applied over the silicone material if a decorative effect is desired.

Roof Coatings

Aluminum pigment-containing roof coatings have already been discussed under aluminum paints. A variety of other roof coatings are available. Thus, thick mastic-like materials for application by troweling are based on asbestos or other fibers and are used for repairing leaks and cracks in all sorts of roofs, including metal ones. Asbestos-based materials may also be of a consistency so that they can be brushed onto a surface rather than troweled.

Asphalt emulsions are, of course, used on roofs as are paints specially formulated for this purpose. Care should be taken in painting galvanized roofs since most paints do not adhere well to galvanized surfaces. Thus, either the galvanized surface should be weathered or else it should be properly prepared by an acid etch.

The use of rubber type vehicles such as neoprene and "Hypalon" in combination with aluminum flakes provides excellent roof coatings.

Aerosol Paints

One of the fastest growing segments of the paint industry has involved the production and sale of aerosol paints. Aerosol paints are packaged in containers varying in volume from six to sixteen ounces and have achieved their high degree of popularity because of the convenience involved. Aerosol paints are not economical for the user, but their acceptance indicates that the consumer is always willing to pay if the convenience factor is great enough.

Aerosol paints have practically replaced quarter pint cans of paint used for touch-up, since aerosols are ideal for this application. They are also valuable for the painting of difficult shapes as chair rungs and bicycles. They are used not only by the homeowner but industrially for touch-up and repair. Thus an important segment of the aerosol industry involves the formulation of paints for the touch-up of automotive coatings.

Aerosol paints are now standard items in maintenance kits for touching up chipped soft-drink dispensers, gasoline pumps, tractors and scores of other such industrial items.

Aerosol finishes are also available for highly decorative effects. The painter should certainly be aware of their utility, particularly for use on surfaces which are difficult to paint well by brushing.

Paints for Porcelain

Several proprietary paints are now available intended for repair and rejuvenation of porcelain surfaces such as bathroom fixtures. Most of these are based on solventless or very high solids epoxy compositions. The materials may be used either to repair nicks, chips and scratches or for complete resurfacing of porcelain fixtures in order to change the color or to provide a new marproof, water resistant and abrasion resistant surface. Such paints are of importance for "putting the finishing touches" on bathroom and kitchen redecorating jobs.

Plastisols and Organosols

The virtues of vinyl paints for maintenance finishes have been discussed above. One of the problems associated with the formulation of vinyl paints is their relatively limited solubility. This means that low solids solutions must be utilized and consequently numerous coats are required to obtain adequate film thickness. A procedure for obtaining thick vinyl films in one pass involves the utilization of formulations known as plastisols and organosols.

A plastisol is a dispersion of vinyl resin in a plasticizer. An organosol, correspondingly, is a dispersion of the vinyl resin in high-boiling organic solvents. By utilizing the proper dispersion technique, it is possible to obtain high solids compositions. Plastisols and organosols may be used for the protection of a variety of items and are normally applied by dipping. Thereafter, the dipped article must be baked either to drive off the solvent of the organosol or to fuse the plasticizer with the vinyl resin in the plastisol. Resulting coatings may be as much as 1/4 in. thick.

Coatings of this sort have not been widely utilized by the paint industry. Most of them are formulated by specialty plastics formulators and used in highly specialized applications. Because they resemble paints in many ways and because they may be applied where paints are now useful, the paint industry should become more familiar with plastisols and organosols.

Proper painting and finishing beautifies and preserves the home--keeps out moisture, protects it from rot, rust, and costly repairs.

Unit 6

PAINT MIXING

In years gone by apprentices and journeymen painters often worked with a single white pigment, a single drying oil, and a single thinner. The ingredients were laboriously mixed according to formulas, often secretive, developed for various types of work. But how times have changed!

House paint became available to the trade in ready-to-use paste, and semi-paste forms. The paste and semi-paste types easily reduce to brushing consistency by adding oil, driers and thinner, according to the manufacturer's specific directions. The paints tint to the desired shade by adding colors-in-oil. Indeed so-called universal colorant machines mix literally thousands of shades of paint automatically, making it possible to match virtually any color for inside decorating or outside painting.

Paints available today are made and mixed with modern machinery. Either they are factory tinted ready-to-use or else they require only machine tinting. The proportions of the various ingredients have been scientifically determined by the manufacturers and the mixing is complete. Much wasteful guesswork has been eliminated. Since the durability of paint is directly affected by the proper balance of pigments in relationship to the other ingredients, proper functional properties will not be obtained unless the paint is thoroughly mixed. The intensity of color depends to a considerable extent on the amount of pigment present in the paint as it is applied. If the paint is improperly mixed the painted surface will vary slightly in color and quality and an unsatisfactory job will result.

MECHANICAL SHAKING: Shaking (agitating) oil paints on a mechanical shaker in a paint dealer's store at the time of purchase followed by a light stirring are usually all that is needed when the paint is to be used within a short time. Latex paints, when agitated mechanically, should always be permitted to set at least an hour before using because the emulsifying agents of some latices cause foaming.

If pigment has settled to the bottom of the can, stirring with a paddle is not adequate. A thorough mixing job involves pouring off the liquid into a clean container. Stir the remainder using a perforated steel stirring paddle or a clean wooden paddle. Scrape the pigment from the bottom, sides and seams of the paint can. Run the corner of the paddle or edge of a clean screwdriver around the bottom to loosen the pigment. Stir thick pigment slowly at first, then a little faster as the pigment and liquid blend together.

After the mixture has blended to a smooth consistency, the liquid which was poured off may be poured back slowly with continued stirring. Thereafter, pour the entire contents back and forth from one can to another several times.

Lumps, "skins," and other particles should be strained out through a wire screen, sieve, nylon stocking, double-thick cheesecloth or cone strainer. Straining freshly mixed paint improves its brushing qualities and, in the case of tinted

Fig. 6-1. In both mixing and applying paint the importance of carefully following the manufacturer's directions cannot be over-emphasized.

paint, prevents the possibility of color streaking.

Varnish, shellac and other clear finishes should not be shaken. If necessary to stir, as in thinning, stir slowly and let the bubbles disappear before starting to use the finish.

Adding Thinner

Many of today's coatings go on without thinning. When using coatings that thin, follow the directions printed on the label. It is very important that the manufacturer's instructions, Fig. 6-1, be followed carefully because the amount of thinner to use has been carefully worked out in order not to upset the balance between the pigment and the vehicle of any given formula.

Thinning of house paint is required in these instances:

1. When regular oil paint is used for a first coat on new, unpainted or badly weather-beaten outside surface, oil must be added to compensate for that which is absorbed by the wood.

2. Some finishes need thinning before they can be sprayed.

3. Paint which has been partially used and stored may develop a scum or "skin" on the surface. If a thick skin is removed it may be necessary to add oil and thinner. (Not applicable to enamels, varnishes.)

4. Resin-base, rubber-base, casein and texture paints may come in powder or paste form. These must be thinned with water.

5. Where the finish must be extra-thin to provide a special effect, thinning is necessary.

For thinning oil-base finishes such as flat paints, house paints, enamels and varnishes, use the thinner specified -- usually turpentine or mineral spirits. Add the thinner slowly and stir thoroughly. A little thinner will go a long way. Do not try to "stretch" paint by adding thinner. Thin paint will not properly hide, cover, or protect the surface. Thinner reduces the gloss of enamel and varnish.

Most rubber-base floor enamels require special thinner. Shellac should be thinned with 188-proof alcohol or shellac thinner. Use lacquer thinner recommended by the manufacturer for thinning lacquer.

Colors-In-Oil

Materials used for tinting house paint are called colors-in-oil. These are color pigments such as yellows, reds and blues, ground in linseed oil to make a paste. The paste is of soft buttery consistency and can be readily stirred into the white paint. Colors-in-oil are available in tubes holding about two liquid ounces, as well as in half-pints, quarts and gallons.

Hand Tinting Paint

White tint base coating colors to a wide range of shades and tints with colors-in-oil, universal colors, or glycol base colors, depending on whether the coating is oil or water-based.

Always add small quantities of color at a time and then stir the color in completely. This not only prevents lumping, but also avoids the addition of too much color. Put in a little color, stir thoroughly, then check with the color that is being matched.

Remember that a dry paint film frequently has a different tint than a wet one. Also, be sure always to compare colors under the same light. Two colors which are identical under artificial light are not necessarily identical under daylight.

If the color is too dark, it can be lightened only by adding more white paint. The simplest colors to mix are those made with only one color. If two or more are called for, follow the relative proportions given in the formula as you mix in the colors, a little at a time.

Unit 7

COATING APPLICATION

To obtain the best results with minimum expenditure of time and effort, the applicator must know how to apply coatings properly. To do this he must know the various types of finishes as well as the types of tools available or required to fulfill the needs of each particular coating job.

Contract jobs involve coating many types of substrates to withstand a wide variety of conditions. Consequently, the applicator must know the various types of surfaces, the proper methods and tools for the required surface preparation, and he must know the proper conditions under which coatings can be applied if lasting coating performance is to be achieved.

The proper handling and selection of accessory equipment such as ladders and scaffolding is essential for the applicator's safety and for the establishment of favorable conditions for full performance of coating application skills.

Confining the deposit of coating material to the area being finished is also of major concern for any good workmanship-like coating application. The proper coating application techniques must be used with a knowledge of protective coverings, masking, and of both wind and coating shielding material to execute a good workmanship-like operation.

Once the applicator has fully familiarized himself with the scope of the job, he is in a good position to complete the job for lasting appearance and performance.

Tools for Applying Coatings

The principal tools used in applying coatings include brushes, rollers and spray equipment. Brushes and rollers can be used virtually on any type of surface, either exterior or interior, with almost any type of coating. Spraying is best adapted to specific coatings and to condi-

tions, for exterior and interior jobs, to be discussed later.

Proper Brushing Methods

Authorities differ somewhat on brushing techniques and methods. The instructions which follow do not necessarily represent the only proper ways to apply protective coatings. Methods described however are used by a representative group of experts and will be found helpful to those who seek practical information on brushing procedures.

Painting is easier if one holds the brush correctly. See Fig. 7-1. The thickness and

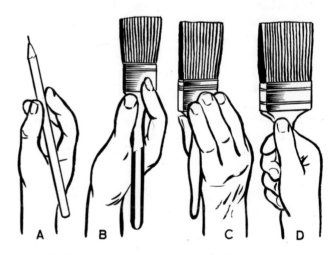

Fig. 7-1. How to grip a paint brush. A and B—Grasping brush with pencil grip. C—Grip used for painting walls and floors. D—Simple grip with all fingers around brush handle, suitable for use when painting ceilings.

smoothness of a paint coat may be controlled to a considerable extent by the amount of paint carried in the brush. The brush must, of course, be clean. It is advisable to dip the bristles of the brush into the paint NOT MORE than half way, Fig. 7-2. Dipping deeper may cause paint to accumulate in the heel of the brush; it also makes paint dripping and spattering more likely.

Fig. 7-2. Paint brush bristles should not be dipped into the paint more than half the length of the bristles.

To remove excess paint from a brush, gently tap the brush against the side of the can as in Fig. 7-3. Do not remove excess paint by wiping the brush against the side of the can; this will damage the bristle of a good brush. Now that the proper method of holding and filling brushes has been described, the various type of brushing strokes used for specific applications will be reviewed. But before learning about application, information on rollers will be needed.

Applying Paint with Rollers

The roller applicator is a fast and convenient means for applying various types of pigmented coatings to large, flat surfaces. The average coverage per day using a roller is 2,000-4,000 sq. ft. or two to four times the amount achieved using a brush.

The roller has gained popularity with the skilled applicator and the do-it-yourselfer. Although the fine workmanship results obtained using a brush cannot be approached using a roller, almost everyone obtains good results from the layman's point of view.

On the other hand, the roller is probably the best coating application tool for rough or discontinuous surfaces like stucco, expanded steel or wire fencing.

There are three principal types of rollers used in applying paint including the dip or pan type, the magazine type and the pressure roller.

The magazine type roller carries the coating inside the cylinder and feeds it through the napped cover. This method has not found wide favor because of the difficulty in obtaining a uniform flow of coating. Likewise, the pressure roller has found limited favor. It is reserved mainly for coating very large areas. The coating is continuously fed to the roller cylinder from the source through a flexible hose fitted to the roller handle.

The conventional dip roller is very popular in the 7 and 9 in. lengths which are either 1 1/4 or 2 1/2 in. in diameter. It is fabricated with a sheet metal or wire cylinder that rotates on an axle. The axle is fitted with a handle frame. The cylinder is covered with a replaceable cover. The cover is composed of a napped material bonded over a plastic tube. The length, texture and composition of the nap are the bases for the difference in rollers.

When coating rough surfaces a long nap length is required; 3/4 in. with enamels, and 1 to 1 1/4 in. for flat coating. Smooth surfaces take a 3/16 to 1/4 in. nap with enamels and a 1/4 to 3/8 in. with flats.

Fig. 7-3. Excess paint should be removed from brush by gently tapping against side of can as shown at left, and NOT by wiping brush across top of can as shown at the right.

Napped rollers made of wool hold more coating and provide a stippled finish. They are used mostly for solvent-thinned coatings.

Mohair is reserved for surfaces that are smooth and produce a smooth finish. Acrylic and nylon covers are useful for water-based coatings because they do not mat or wilt in water. They wear well and can be used on rough

Fig. 7-4. Using narrow trim roller to make starting strip.

textured masonry surfaces. Synthetic resin covers should not be used with coatings containing strong solvents.

Sponge rubber rollers, which produce a good stipple, can be used with equal effectiveness in applying solvent-thinned coatings as well as water-based texture coating.

Special rollers are available in 18 in. length for very large applications. Also, there are rollers in 1 in. length both straight or angled for trim and corners, Fig. 7-4.

The procedure for applying paint with a roller differs materially from brush painting. It is important, first, to study the instructions supplied by the manufacturer of the roller.

Paint is usually applied as it comes in the can. If thinning is necessary at the beginning of the job, or if the paint thickens during use, use the thinner recommended by the paint manufacturer. Paints which come in paste form should be thinned exactly as directed.

If a tray is to be used, pour thoroughly mixed paint into the tray until about half the sloping bottom is covered. Do not mix the paint in the tray.

Dip the roller into the shallow part of the tray where the paint is no deeper than the thickness of the roller cover. Push the roller back and forth until the cover is saturated. Now pull the roller back over the exposed bottom of the tray and across the corrugations to distribute the paint. Do this several times to determine how to charge or load the roller properly. Roll off the excess paint from the roller to prevent dripping. See Fig. 7-5.

Start the application in a corner. Roll in the corner with a 1 in. corner roller or "cut-in" the corner using a brush. The roller should follow brushing promptly to avoid lap marks. Roll in parallel strips whenever possible making sure to overlap each strip to provide even coverage and to avoid leaving lap marks.

Avoid rolling strips longer in length than will maintain a wet edge before parallel strip is started, or else lap marks will remain in the dry coating. Strips 2 ft. wide and 7 to 8 ft. in

Fig. 7-5. Left. Typical paint roller and tray. Right. Surplus paint is removed from roller by squeezing roller against ramp of tray.

length can be handled under most standard conditions.

Coat as rapidly as you can, using a back and forth motion. Change direction as desired, but do not lift the roller when changing direction.

Do not try to work too fast. A steady, methodical stroke will cause the roller to give good contact. The bit of paint which is pushed ahead of the roller flows into surface irregularities and helps provide an even coating.

Exterior Application -- Wood

The painting of exterior surfaces requires detailed consideration to obtain the best possible results. The exterior coatings used serve both an aesthetic (relating to beauty or appearance) and a protective function. The coating must withstand the ravages of nature and perform in unison with the substrate for long term decorative service.

Wood siding is widely encountered today even with the ever increasing use of substitute materials. Because of the complex nature of wood, it presents a great challenge to the applicator to achieve lasting performance on exterior exposure. Since wood is a natural product, little control other than selection and conditioning can be exercised to control its performance. Problems occur as a result of the variation within a single board and because of the differences in behaviors between the so-called "spring" and "summer" woods.

Southern Yellow Pine

Probably the most difficult wood to coat for lasting performance is southern yellow pine. It contains only one type of cell structure in both spring and summer wood and does not have vessels that are associated with hardwood. The summer wood grain is much wider compared to other wood, and the summer wood contains a large amount of resinous material. Yellow pine is subject to wide fluctuations in dimension and resin exudes freely from the summer wood. When coating failures occur, they usually happen over the summer wood.

Because of its availability, southern yellow pine is encountered frequently on both new and old construction.

With new construction, use of special primers or sealer primer material only should be considered. These products are available on the dealer's shelf from many prominent manufac-

turers across the country. As with all new wood, the surface should be dry, free from contamination left by the preceding craftsmen, and free of mud, dust, and other contaminants. Cleaning can be accomplished by dusting or washing with detergent and rinsing with clean fresh water.

Inspection

Before any coating is applied, all knots and pitch-containing areas should be sealed with a shellac or knot sealer such WP-578 developed by the Western Pine Association.

Sealer-Primer Coat-Brushing

The first coat for yellow pine will be either a sealer or pigmented primer. Brushing is the preferred method for applying sealers or primers. Brushing works the coating into the pores and crevices better than roller or spray applications.

A flat brush 3 1/2 to 6 in. wide, but more commonly 4 in. wide, and having bristles extending 4 5/8 in. from the ferrule is used. "Toppy" brushes with all the bristles the same length should be avoided since they do not carry as much coating as brushes having bristles of varying lengths.

The bristles are dipped about 2 1/2 in. into the sealer and the brush is tapped against the sealer can to remove the excess material. The sealer is brushed into the surface, thoroughly brushing in all directions. Short 3/4 length strokes are used making sure not to produce runs or leave excess coating on the laps, end of the strokes, or any other areas. Four or five boards are coated per dip and are coated across to an edge, window or corner. Never stop in the middle of a board.

Primer Clean Up

After the sealer-primer has dried thoroughly, attention can be given to surface imperfections. All nail holes and cracks are filled with first-class putty.

Topcoating-Brushing

Oil Paint Topcoating

Topcoating can be completed with exterior oil paint, oleoresinous finishes, alkyd coatings or water base coatings. The oil and oleoresinous coatings dominated the exterior coating field until a few years ago. But by 1968 over half of the exterior finishes applied to private dwellings were water based, and the percentage increases yearly.

The oil and oleoresinous paint are applied in a somewhat different manner than the other topcoats. The paint is daubed on in spots as in Fig. 7-6, but is spread using long full arm level strokes. Even pressure is exerted at all times to avoid "riding" the brush. Finish applying each brushful with sweeping strokes. Use the tips of the bristle and lift the brush gradually to achieve a thin featheredge at the end of the stroke. Use a free and easy movement of the arm and wrist.

Fig. 7-6. Painting house siding. The paint is daubed on in spots, then spread by using long leveling strokes.

Rough surfaces require extra brushing. Paint should be applied generously and brushed in all directions to make sure pores and crevices are well filled.

Do not poke a surface with a good brush for this turns the flag ends of the bristles and destroys the shape of the brush. Where poking is required to do a good job, always use an old brush.

Alkyd Outside White

The newer solvent-based coatings formulated with alkyd vehicles are faster drying than the oil or oleoresinous paints and, therefore, much less brushing time is available. Only three or four strokes are permitted. Each brush load should be applied using quick 3/4 length arm strokes. Leveling should be accomplished using even pressure at all times making sure to overlap each stroke.

Water Base Coatings

The water base coatings are probably the most satisfying to apply. They are characterized as being thixotropic or creamy and require very little effort to distribute. They dry quite rapidly with a tendency to leave brush marks and a thick edge. To promote leveling and the elimination of the thick edge, the brush should be refilled more often, and extra care exercised to ensure proper edge overlapping and gradual lifting of the brush at the end of each stroke.

General Notes on Painting House Siding

In painting exterior house siding, it is best to paint the highest places first. Stand the ladder so that the distance from the bottom end of the ladder to the wall is one-fourth its height. Do not scale the ladder any higher than the third rung from the top.

Keep in mind the fact that on new wood the priming coat is the most important coat; it is to a good paint job what a substantial concrete foundation is to the entire house. Use only high-grade paint. DO NOT use leftovers or cheap paint of any kind.

Take a moderate brushful of paint, tap the excess off the brush, then paint the edges of siding boards within easy reach, Fig. 7-7. In painting the flat areas in between, lay a brushful in two or three spots, then brush it out well. A thin, even coat of primer which penetrates into the pores of the wood provides good anchorage for the coats which follow. It does not provide as much hiding power as a thick coat,

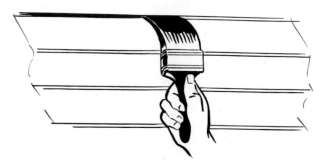

Fig. 7-7. In painting siding the edges should be painted first, then the flat areas in between.

but a thick coat dries slowly and is more apt to chip off later.

It is desirable to paint a band about 3 ft. in depth straight across the house, then drop down and paint another band. Always finish an area which has been started to a wall, door or window before stopping. If you stop on a wall for more than a few minutes the paint will partially set, making it difficult to brush out lap marks. Such a lap may show through several coats of light-colored paint.

Important Painting Don'ts

Don't paint if the temperature is below 50 deg. F.

Be cautious of sudden drops in temperature; paint only when the weather moderates to a fairly even temperature.

Don't paint, after a rain until the wood has dried THOROUGHLY, unless, of course, you are using water-based paint. After a wet period, several days of good drying weather should precede the painting. This does not apply if water soluble or water-dispersible house paints are being used.

Don't start too early in the morning. Give the sun a chance to dry the surface.

Don't paint in the direct rays of a hot summer sun. Move around the house to avoid the sun. Remember that paint does not spread well on a hot surface.

Don't paint in a strong wind as the fresh paint may collect dust and insects.

Exterior Wood-Roller and Pad Application

Roller

Although the primers used for yellow pine are solvent thinned and brushed, the topcoats can be water-based and applied using a roller. The roller is worked across each individual board at a time. The application is started at the top of the building and each consecutive lower board is coated within easy reach. Do not attempt to overreach as this can cause loss of balance and a possible accident.

A brush is handy to have to "cut-in" under the siding edge. "Cutting-in" can be completed four or five boards ahead of rolling provided the "cut-in" holds a wet edge. The board under the last edge cut-in must be rolled before moving to a new section.

Pad Applicator

The pad applicator is fabricated using a plastic pad holder fitted with a spring loaded handle so that the pad is always parallel to the surface being coated. The pad consists of a foam core measuring 4 by 7 in. and is covered with a napped fabric about 3/16 in. deep. The foam core is laminated to a thin spring metal backing that can be fitted to the plastic holder. A tray designed to hold 1/2 gal. of coating in a pail shaped sump beneath a framed grid is used to hold the coating and fill the pad. Filling the grid is completed by tipping the tray and allowing coating to flow from the sump onto the grid. A large amount of coating is allowed to flow onto the grid as any excess coating automatically flows back into the sump. The pad is dipped into the coating wet grid area and the nap fully wet with coating. The excess is scraped from the pad using a light wiping action across a dry portion of the grid. In application the pad is wiped across the siding to deposit an even smooth strip about 4 to 6 ft. long. Overlapping the previous edge 25 percent is suggested for an even application having good coverage. The siding edge can be "cut-in" first using the pad face rather than the edge of the pad. Three or four boards are completed to a stopping-off point such as an edge, corner or window before moving on to a new area.

Wood Siding - - General

Although yellow pine is frequently encountered on new and old construction, there are many types of wood selected for construction.

Some kinds of wood hold coatings of outside house or barn paint longer than others. Even when all boards are of the same kind of wood, some stay coated longer than others. The reasons for this behavior are largely explained by the painting characteristics of wood.

The applicator does not ordinarily have anything to do with selecting wood used in buildings he paints. Thus, he must, to the best of his ability, offset the shortcomings of the wood by careful choice of paints and by using proper painting methods. This is especially necessary the first time the wood is painted.

The information on Wood Properties and Paint Durability which follows is from U. S. Dept. of Agriculture, Publication 629.

PROPERTIES OF WOOD: The properties of wood that affect coating are density and texture;

content of resins, oils and moisture; and defects such as knots.

DENSITY AND TEXTURE: Among softwoods (conifers or needle-leaved trees) the coating characteristics of a board depend primarily upon the amount and distribution of summerwood, Fig. 7-8. Paint oils penetrate farther into summerwood than into springwood, but the oil that penetrates is separated from the coating and does not help to hold the coating in place. New paint sticks firmly to both springwood and summerwood. When the coating becomes old and brittle, it loses adhesion to the smooth summerwood, although it usually is held securely on the springwood. If the bands of summerwood are narrow enough the coating may bridge over the summerwood and remain in place, but if the bands are wide the coating breaks loose from them. Therefore, boards with narrow bands of summerwood are best for painting.

Fig. 7-8. Each year of its life a tree adds an annual ring composed of summerwood and springwood. Summerwood is the dense, dark-colored portion of the annual growth ring, formed in the tree late in the growing season. It has wood cells with thick walls and small cavities. Springwood is the softer and lighter (in weight and color) portion of the growth rings, formed in the early part of the growing season, and has wood cells with thin walls and large cavities.

WIDTH OF SUMMERWOOD BANDS: The width of the summerwood bands in softwood usually varies with the density (weight per unit of volume) of the wood and the rate of tree growth, being narrower when the density is low or the tree growth is slow. The density of softwood lumber is low when the proportion of summerwood is small. If a tree grew slowly, however, the bands of summerwood may be narrow even if the density is high because there are then many growth rings per inch of radius of the log. The manner of cutting the boards from a log also affects the width of the summer-

wood bands exposed on the painting surface. Edge-grain boards (called quarter-sawn in hardwoods) have narrower bands of exposed summerwood than flat-grain boards. They are cut from the logs at right angles to the annual growth rings, and the edges of the growth rings appear on the painting surface of the boards. In flat-grain boards, which are cut at a different angle, the faces of the growth rings appear. In flat-grain boards the side that was nearer the bark often holds paint longer than the opposite side.

Hardwoods (broad-leaved trees) differ in structure from softwoods. Hardwoods have fibers and pores. The size and arrangement of the pores, which are much larger than the fibers, govern the painting characteristics of the wood. Hardwoods such as oak with pores larger than those in birch, are poorly adapted to painting with ordinary house paints because pinholes are left in the coating over the large pores. The pinholes not only are unsightly, but lead to early failure of the coating. The best hardwoods for painting are those of medium to low density, such as yellow-poplar, with pores no larger than those in birch.

RESINS AND OILS: Resins and oils in well-seasoned wood have less effect on painting than is generally supposed. The resin in pine lumber seems to shorten slightly the life of paints containing zinc oxide, but this unfavorable effect can be prevented by using modern priming paints free from zinc oxide. The essential oils in cypress and some of the cedars may delay the drying of some paints, but they prolong the life of the coatings.

In green lumber, however, the effects of resins and oils may be serious. Resin may exude when the painted wood is warmed by the sun or otherwise, and either push through or loosen the coating. Oils in unseasoned wood may completely prevent drying of some paints.

Occasionally on dry wood, but more often on wood that has been only partly dried or has become moist after seasoning, there is a discoloration of white or light-colored paint over the heartwood of ponderosa or white pines. The discoloration comes from brown substances in the resin of the heartwood, which are evidently more active when the wood is damp than when it is dry.

MOISTURE CONTENT: Paints last longest on wood that has been well-seasoned, but which has regained some moisture so its moisture content is 12 to 15 percent. Paints applied to very dry wood are slightly less durable. As a rule, however, it is best to paint wood when it has about the average moisture content that is expected to prevail during service.

Wet wood, the moisture content of which is over 25 percent, is in an uncertain condition for painting because there is grave danger of failure of the coating by blistering, and peeling. Blistering and peeling result from pressure against the back of a coating caused by expansion of air and water trapped in wet wood. Moreover, woods like redwood and red cedar, which contain colored substances soluble in water, may discolor paint applied while the wood is wet. Even if wood is dry when painted but later absorbs enough moisture to become thoroughly wet, there is danger of blistering, peeling, or discoloration.

KNOTS AND OTHER DEFECTS: Knots in wood produce serious blemishes in paint coatings. In pine lumber the paint over knots is often discolored by yellow or brown substances from the wood. End-grain wood in the knots of any wood often absorbs enough oil from paint to destroy the gloss of the paint. Both discoloration and oil absorption can be prevented by applying shellac or knot sealer, such as WP-578, developed by the Western Pine Association, over the knots before painting, but the paint is likely to crack badly and may flake from the knots fairly soon. Large knots are likely to crack even after they are painted, and the cracks may be too large to fill with new paint.

Pitch streaks or pitch pockets in wood mar paint coatings by causing the paint to crack or flake off or by exuding resin.

Blue stain in sapwood can be concealed by paint as long as the wood can be kept dry. If at any time the wood becomes damp, however, the fungi causing the stain may become active and push through, discoloring the paint.

Selecting the Best Wood for Coating

Wherever wood is to be kept well coated for a long time the cost of paint maintenance can be reduced by selecting kinds of wood that hold paint coatings most satisfactorily.

SELECTION BY SPECIES: Since paint-holding qualities are affected by the kind of wood, and woods are marketed by species, the easiest method of selecting woods for painting is by species. Species alone, however, is not the most effective basis for selection because there are wide variations in painting characteristics among boards of any one species. The com-

mercially important native woods, when purchased in lumber of the higher grades, are classified for painting characteristics into five groups:

Group I. Cedar, baldcypress, and redwood, all of which are softwoods. Woods of group I hold all of the common kinds of house and barn paints well.

Group II. Eastern white pine, sugar pine and western white pine, all of which are softwoods. On woods of group II, paints containing zinc oxide are slightly less durable, but other paints are as durable as on woods of group I.

Group III. White fir, the hemlocks, ponderosa pine, and the spruces of the softwoods; aspen, basswood, cottonwood, magnolia, and yellow-poplar of the hardwoods. Paints deteriorate somewhat more rapidly on woods of group III than on woods of groups I and II. On ponderosa pine, paints containing zinc oxide are less durable than paints free from it.

Group IV. Douglas fir, southern yellow pine, and western larch of the softwoods; beech, birch, the gums, the maple of the hardwoods. Paints deteriorate more rapidly on woods of group IV than on woods of groups I, II, and III. On southern yellow pine, paints containing zinc oxide are less durable than paints free from it.

Group V. Ash, chestnut, elm, hickory, oak, and walnut, all of which are hardwoods with large pores. Woods of group V require wood filler to fill the pores before smooth coatings of paint or enamel can be applied.

SELECTION BY GRADE: Most lumber is graded for sale. In softwood lumber the better grades for painting are the select grades. Select grades of lumber permit few knots, pitch streaks, or pitch pockets. Common grades in which defects are numerous cannot be expected to hold paint as well as the select grades.

SELECTION BY KIND OF GRAIN: Some woods are cut into lumber in such a way that the boards in the highest grade are always edge-grain. The term "vertical grain" is sometimes used instead of edge-grain; among hardwoods the term "quarter-sawed" has the same meaning. For good painting, edge-grain lumber should be purchased whenever possible. When flat-grain boards are used, it is desirable to turn them so that the bark side will be the surface exposed for painting, The bark side is the side toward which the annual growth rings are convex.

SELECTION BY DENSITY AND TEXTURE: In commercial shipments of many kinds of lumber there will be found a wide range in density and in width of growth rings. Paint maintenance can often be improved by setting aside those boards that are much above the average in weight or in width of summerwood bands. The heavy, wide-ringed boards may be used for construction that will not be painted, for less important parts of the structure, or for parts that receive little sunshine. (Paint will last longer on any board if it is in a shaded rather than a sunny place.) As a rule, the time for repainting a house is determined by the wearing out of paint on the poorest boards.

Suggestions for Painting the Heavier Softwoods

The forests of the United States produce much more lumber of species classed in groups III and IV than of species in groups I and II. For that reason woods that tend to shorten the life of paint coatings often must be painted. In such cases the unfavorable effect of the wood can be reduced by careful selection and application of paint, particularly the first time the structure is painted.

Painting should be done as soon after erecting the woodwork as is practicable, usually within a week. It is not good practice to allow wood to weather for weeks or months before painting. The first or priming coat of paint may be applied, if convenient, before the lumber is delivered to the site of the building. If this is done, both sides of the boards should be primed to avoid the cupping or warping that might otherwise occur from unequal rate of change in moisture content on the two sides. Although priming of butt ends is often omitted, the best practice is to paint the butt ends with primer after cutting and fitting the boards, but before fastening them in place.

If woods of groups III and IV are primed with aluminum house paint before applying house paint of the desired color, they can be made to hold their paint coatings nearly as long as woods of groups I and II. Aluminum house paint is made for use on exterior woodwork. Aluminum paints or enamels made for other purposes are unsuitable for priming wood. The paint job consists of one coat of aluminum house paint followed by two coats of house paint of good quality. So applied, white paint or any of the light colors should last about four years on woods of groups III or IV before further painting is necessary. Paints of dark colors may last two or three years longer. When repainting, apply only the white or colored paint.

Next best to aluminum house paints for priming woods of groups III and IV are modern house-paint primers that contain no zinc oxide and have the property commonly called "controlled penetration." Many manufacturers of commercial house paint now make such house-paint primers. The painting may be done in either three- or two-coat work. If three coats are applied, the house-paint primer may be thinned with a small proportion of turpentine or mineral spirits and applied so that 1 gal. of the mixture covers about 600 sq. ft. of surface. After that, two coats of house paint in white or a chosen color should be applied, and each coat spread over 700 sq. ft. to the gallon of paint.

In two-coat work the house-paint primer is not thinned and is applied in a thicker coating so that a gallon covers no more than 450 sq. ft. of surface. A single coat of good house paint is sufficient over such a primer coat, provided it is applied so that a gallon covers no more than 550 sq. ft. of surface.

Thus, although the best paint service is most easily obtained when wood of the most favorable kind has been selected, good paint service is possible even on the less suitable kinds of wood if the right kind of paint is applied properly the first time the wood is painted.

Painting New Wood (Types Ordinarily Used for Exterior Siding and Trim)

In painting new wood such as cedar, redwood, white pine, sugar pine, cypress, white fir, spruce and other similar softwoods, the generally accepted practice is to apply three coats of paint -- a priming coat, and two coats of high-grade exterior house paint of the desired color. This applies whether the paint used is factory-mixed paint or paint mixed on the job by the painter.

The paint mixture for each coat varies slightly in the proportion of pigment, linseed oil and turpentine. Ordinarily, the priming coat should contain a greater proportion of oil and turpentine than is used in the second and finish coats. It is considered good practice to tint the second coat slightly darker than the shade desired for the last coat. Caulking around doors and windows and puttying of nail holes should be done after the priming coat is dry. Copper which comes in contact with wood should be varnished to prevent staining the paint finish. Turpentine is seldom used in the finish coat.

On ready-mixed paint, the can label gives

directions for thinning. These directions should be carefully followed.

Painting Hardboard Siding

Although considerable prefinished hardboard siding is used, much is only primed and some is completely unfinished.

Painting unfinished hardboard siding takes special materials and procedures. Care must be exercised to avoid board denting when placing and loading ladders. Cleaning procedures must not abrade the top surfaces removing the surface contamination and as little as possible of the board surface. Soft bristle brushes rather than wire brushes are used for cleaning. Light sandpaper can be effective in some instances with tightly bound contamination.

Usually only light dusting or light detergent washing with fresh water rinsing is all that is required to clean hardboard surfaces. Before painting is started, make sure the board is thoroughly dry.

Painting of unfinished hardboard is completed by first applying a good clear sealer or a heavily pigmented primer-sealer. For some exterior exposure where wide fluctuations of humidity and/or temperature are expected, both a clear sealer and a pigmented primer-sealer are suggested for the best long term performance and appearance.

Clear sealers may be applied with brush, spray gun or roller. Sealer is liberally applied to all ends, edges and face surfaces so that every exposed surface is penetrated. Extra passes with the gun or strokes with the brush and roller are often necessary to prevent runs. The proper method for spraying will be covered later. As with all exterior painting, start on the shade side and follow the shadow around the building.

The metal corners are primed following the sealing operation. Use the appropriate material and procedures required, depending on whether the corners are aluminum or galvanized steel.

All dents, cracks and other imperfections must be filled. Special nails are used with hardboard and the resulting recessed hole is traditionally left unfilled.

The primer-sealer coat is applied to fill or bridge any pores. Also, leveling and hiding the surface profile pattern is accomplished with the primer. The primer may be brushed, sprayed or rolled on hardboard surfaces with confidence as these surfaces accept paint very well. Brush-ing can be used to advantage, however, for best filling. This primer-sealer is used over corners to hide the metal primer.

Topcoating can be completed using the full variety of oil base, alkyd or water-based latex and emulsion finishes. The application procedure used is much like that used for other lap siding. Because hardboard is smooth and uniform, the coating application is easier. Much less brushing is required for wetting and no grain filling or leveling is required. The application of water-based coatings with a pad applicator is easily accomplished on hardboard siding.

Painting Various surfaces

Painting Masonry Surfaces

Masonry surfaces are painted both for decorative and waterproofing purposes. Still another advantage of painting masonry is provided by light-hued coating materials that reflect more light into surrounding areas. This result is especially beneficial in apartment courts and archways where natural darkness is intensified by dark-colored masonry.

Water-Thinned and Solvent-Thinned Paints

There are on the market many types of coatings well suited for masonry. Basically, these coatings may be classified as either water-thinned or solvent-thinned paints. Water-thinned paints may be used over masonry surfaces that are not entirely dry and that contain active alkali. One such paint is cement based paint. It comes as a dry powder and is mixed with water. Also suitable are the latex paints and these are widely used. Cement-based paints may be used on either interior or exterior surfaces. Latex paint, on the other hand, is generally formulated specifically for either interior or exterior use. Most successful masonry paints must be porous enough to "breath," otherwise the natural moisture content of the masonry causes peeling. Solvent-thinned rubber-based paints resist abrasion, moisture and chemical attack somewhat better than do the water-thinned paints. Conventional house paints may also be used in certain cases and will give excellent results, if the masonry is dry.

On new masonry surfaces two coats of paint are usually adequate, a prime coat and a finish coat. All paints should be applied according to the manufacturer's instruction. Since paint films build to thicknesses that cause trouble over the years, it is advisable to apply only what is needed for protection.

Concrete and Masonry Surfaces

Concrete and masonry surfaces need preparation before you coat them. The importance of knowing the various condition of both new and old surfaces and knowing the proper steps for producing lasting coating work cannot be overemphasized. Both previously coated and bare surfaces need cleaning. Dirt, dust, oil, grease, efflorescence, laitance (milky white deposit on new concrete), chalk and loose material all contribute to coating problems if they are not removed before the coating application starts. Although old concrete sometimes presents a chalky, porous difficult surface to coat, new concrete has many more inherent problems. New concrete has problems associated with unbound moisture, the presence of soluble alkaline substance that sometimes forms efflorescence, contamination from curing compounds and smooth dense areas that are nonabsorbent and nearly glazed in consistency. One or several procedures may be needed to prepare concrete surfaces for coating.

Surfaces Preparation - - Masonry

The section on preparation of surfaces for paint provides more information, but a brief outline is convenient here.

CONDITION - DUST, DIRT AND LOOSE MATERIAL: Remove with (1) bristle-brushing and hosing with clean water; or (2) scraping, wire brushing or sandblasting.

CONDITION - OIL, GREASE AND DIRT: Remove by (1) scrubbing with trisodium phosphate (5 percent); or (2) etching with muriatic acid (5-10 percent) followed by neutralizing with ammonia water (10 percent); or (3) sandblasting.

CONDITION - EFFLORESCENCE: Remove with (1) sandblasting; or (2) wire brushing followed by washing with muriatic acid (10 percent) and then by neutralizing with ammonia water (10 percent).

CONDITION - MILDEW OR MOLD: Remove with (1) trisodisodium phosphate (5 percent); or (2) sodium hypochlorite (5 percent) followed by rinsing with clean water.

CONDITION - DENSE, SMOOTH OR GLAZED SURFACE: Remove with (1) sandblasting; or (2)

muriatic acid etching (5-10 percent) followed by neutralizing with ammonia water (10 percent) followed by clean water rinsing.

CONDITION - CRACKS, HOLES AND DAMAGED AREAS: Repair with (1) filling with new synthetic resin based materials; or (2) fill with cement - sand (50/50) grout; or special moisture reactive and expanding compounds.

Aging New Concrete

Aging and weathering is probably the most effective single method of preparing new concrete, glazed asbestos-cement shingles and other masonry surfaces. Setting of concrete occurs in a few hours, but curing and hardening sometimes takes years. With aging, free moisture escapes and migrating alkalinity reduces. Aging is only discussed from a standpoint of academic interest here to help understand the problems associated with coating concrete. With this insight you are better able to choose the proper coating system that will aid you in getting a lasting coating job.

Cement - Water Paints

Cement - water paints need a clean surface, but moisture and alkalinity of new concrete does not present a problem. Just as soon as the concrete has set, cleaning and coating work can start. Portland cement paint, which is made with Portland cement and limeproof and sunproof mineral pigments is particularly well suited for use on concrete masonry surfaces. It bonds with any properly prepared concrete surface, concrete masonry or Portland cement stucco, common brick, soft tile, limestone, or other type of masonry which presents a clean surface having some adsorption.

Portland cement - base paints should be applied according to the manufacturer's recommendations with scrub brushes or fender brushes which permit scrubbing the paint into the pores of the surface being painted. The painted surface should be kept in a moist condition for at least 48 hours following application. A fine water spray may be applied as soon as the paint has hardened sufficiently to prevent damage and at sufficient intervals as needed to keep it moist. This paint "builds" a thick film and only two or three coats at the most are advised. After that, the surface may have to be sandblasted to give secure footing for more coatings.

Properly applied and damp-cured, cement

water paints provide a durable coating for exposed concrete or masonry surfaces above or below grade, inside or outdoors. They are not suitable for floors or other surfaces where abrasion is anticipated.

Latex Coating

As a general rule, a minimum of 4 weeks aging of concrete surfaces is required before latex coatings go on. The surface may be damp, but not wet. A clean (neutralized) surface is required. Latex based paints for concrete fit in one of three general classes: masonry primer, filler or top coat. Latex masonry primers are latex-based paints thinned with a suitable amount of water. They provide excellent sealing of concrete, brick, cinder block, stucco and other porous masonry surfaces. It is a good practice to dampen the porous surface with water when priming with latex based paints. Dampening the surface prevents excess penetration of the paint thereby assuring good holdout.

Latex based block fillers contain some prime pigment combined with fine particle extender pigment and fibrous material such as asbestos. The finished product is characterized as having a thick creamy consistency. Block fillers are widely used on concrete and cinder block construction. They may be used on either exterior or interior exposure. Often they are applied directly over unprimed block. Application can be completed using a brush or spray gun, but for the most part are roller applied. The block filler coats and smooths the rough surface profile of block construction providing a more uniform surface on which to apply subsequent topcoats.

The latex topcoat, as well as the primer and block filler, can be based on resins such as acrylic, polyvinyl acetate, and styrene-butadiene. These latex topcoats have good durability and are easy to apply and clean up. They are used for both exterior and interior surfaces. The acrylic and acetate types generally give the best exterior exposure and the styrene-butadiene type is generally restricted to interior use.

Synthetic Resin Paint

Epoxies, polyesters, polyurethanes and various synthetic rubber coatings apply well on concrete surfaces that have not aged long. The surfaces must be neutralized and dry. Many epoxies, polyesters and polyurethanes require

a sealer undercoat. Usually the sealer undercoat is the same base material as the topcoat thinned to the appropriate viscosity with organic solvent. Filled epoxy coatings and filled or fiber glass reinforced polyester resins apply in thick coats to produce hard, glossy, tile-like coatings having outstanding physical properties, high chemical resistance and great beauty. Polyurethane resins produce tough, durable coatings useful for floors and walls. They are also used in swimming pool paints because of their good water resistance. Widely used for swimming pools are paints based on chlorinated rubber.

Oil-Based and Oleoresinous Paints

These coatings apply safely on thoroughly aged and dry concrete surfaces. New concrete must be "synthetically aged" to accommodate oil-based system. As a result, oil-based paints are usually reserved for topcoat applications over properly primed and sealed concrete.

Bituminous Coatings

Because of low cost, excellent chemical resistance, and resistance to water, these coatings are usually employed for coating the exterior side of below grade masonry foundations and walls in direct contact with water or wet soil. They are supplied from a wide range of base materials derived from coal tar or petroleum asphalt. They go on either as thin primers or in thicknesses of as much as one-half inch when formulated as hot applied mastics. The coal tar base materials are superior for underground work where maximum waterproofing is required. The asphalt base material is more resistant to atmospheric weathering and temperature changes and therefore is more widely used above ground. Concrete surfaces coated with bituminous materials must be clean, dry and aged 4 weeks.

Silicone Water Repellent

Silicone water repellent is not a paint. It is more of a wash coat. It goes on exterior masonry surfaces that are cured and hardened. Untreated concrete and masonry surfaces are porous and soak up water from rain and other sources. This absorbed water can cause damp interior walls, cracking plaster, warped woodwork and a number of other interior defects as well as severe staining on the outside. If the absorbed water freezes, surface cracks and flakes develop which is known as spalling. The silicone water repellent reduces or prevents these problems. The materials apply with spraying or brushing techniques. They are applied directly over unpainted masonry or surfaces coated with cement based paints. They are not applied over oil or resin based paints. The coating may be transparent so that it does not alter the color of the masonry it protects; or it may be a colorful one that improves the appearance of a masonry surface and makes it easier to keep clean.

Painting Concrete Floors

The surface of interior and exterior concrete floors to be painted should be clean, dry, and in suitable condition to receive the paint. Concrete basement floors should age for one year prior to painting. Concrete floors should be painted when the humidity is low. For best results the application of two coats of paint is recommended - one coat of sealer and one of topcoat.

Specially prepared paints are readily available. Where a concrete floor is laid below grade directly on the ground, as in most basements, and where dampness due to condensation is prevalent, latex-paint is often suggested. This paint is not a "cure-all," but is alkali resistant and does not soften when the floor is damp.

Sodium Silicate Hardener

Concrete floors that have been hardened by using sodium silicate hardener in the concrete are usually strongly alkaline. Before painting, such floors should be scrubbed with a solution of hydrochloric acid and water (5:95). (Pour acid into water; not water into acid, wear rubber gloves, goggles, and protective clothing. Do not inhale fumes.) Neutralize the floor with trisodium phosphate or ammonia water (10 percent), wash the floor with clear water and allow to dry before painting.

Paraffin Wax Coating

Concrete floors (in hospitals for example) are sometimes coated with hot paraffin wax. The wax is heated to its melting point and is applied while very hot to the thoroughly clean floor with a large brush. Two or three coats are generally required. This provides a surface that is easy to clean and when properly applied is not overly slippery, unless wet.

Use Old Brushes

Rough masonry surfaces quickly destroy the bristles of a good brush. It is advisable to use old brushes as much as possible.

Repainting Masonry Walls

If a masonry surface has been previously painted and the paint is in good condition, very little surface preparation other than removal of chalk, dirt and grease will be required. Small areas where the paint is flaking or peeling should be wire-brushed and spot-primed. Loose mortar should be brushed away and replaced with fresh mortar. Cracks should be filled using patching plaster, if indoors; mortar or caulking compound, if outdoors.

Painting Cement - Asbestos Shingles

Cement-asbestos shingles have good weather resistance and ordinarily do not need waterproofing. The shingles, however, are porous, and in many parts of the country they become soiled and unattractive.

In painting asbestos shingles any good alkali resistant quality house paint may be used, but especially prepared asbestos shingle paint is preferred. Loose surface dirt must, of course, be removed before applying the paint. If the shingles are covered with mildew, the mildew may be removed by using a sal soda or trisodium phosphate solution (5 percent). Rinse well with clear water and allow to dry before painting.

Exterior Shingles - Stains and Paint for Shingles

Wood shingles may be finished with either stain or paint. Best protection can be obtained by priming the shingles before they are nailed in place by dipping in shingle stain, house paint thinned to shingle stain consistency, or thin boiled linseed oil. To be effective shingle stains should penetrate into the wood.

Shingles used on side walls may be painted like sidings; but applying a pigmented paint coating on the exposed surface of roof shingles is inadvisable because the paint will retard the drying of the shingles after rain and tends to increase warping. Shingle stains should not be applied to surfaces previously painted. Shingles which have been treated with creosote stains cannot later be painted with a light-colored paint because the creosote will discolor the paint. Ordinary paint should not be used on composite shingles or roofs. For this purpose special coated materials such as liquid asphalt, fibrous roof cement, or aluminum-asphalt paints are available. Liquid asphalt roof coating may be applied on either damp or wet surfaces.

Painting Windows

In painting windows you will need a sash brush 2 or 2 1/2 in. wide. Some painters prefer angular brushes, some oval brushes, still others like flat sash brushes best. Whatever type of brush is used, it should be of good quality.

On double-hung windows first lower the outside sash, raise the inside sash, and paint the exposed inside check rail. Then, proceed as indicated in Fig. 7-9:

1. Mullions.
2. Sash horizontals.
3. Sash verticals.
4. Frame verticals.
5. Frame and sill horizontal.

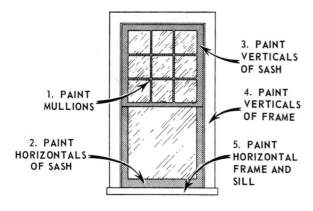

Fig. 7-9. In painting windows, parts should be painted in order indicated.

After painting a window, do not close it entirely, but leave it open about a half inch from both the bottom and top. It is a good idea to open and close painted windows several times daily, from the inside, until the paint has dried. This prevents sticking.

In painting casement windows, paint the top and bottom edges of the windows that face out when the windows are open, then paint the sash stiles, rails, frames and the casings.

Painting Doors

To avoid unnecessary laps and brush marks when painting paneled doors, paint the molded edges of the panels first, starting with the top panel, Detail A, Fig. 7-10. Fill in the panels with light up-and-down strokes, Detail B, Fig. 7-10. Then, paint horizontal crossboards, Detail C, Fig. 7-10. Finish by painting the vertical sideboards, Detail D, Fig. 7-10.

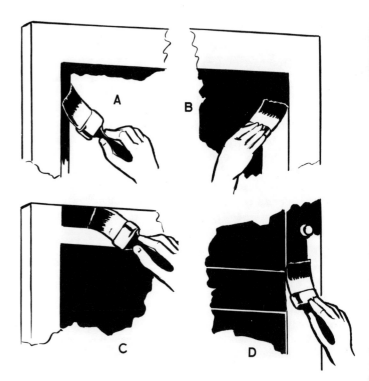

Fig. 7-10. Painting a door. Start with molded edge, A; next paint panel, B; then crossboards, C; and vertical sideboards, D.

If the door swings out, paint the edge with the lock. If the door swings in, paint the edge where the hinges are attached.

Painting Wood Floors

Ordinarily floors in modern homes, with the exception of porch floors and steps, are usually made of hardwood and are finished by using a floor seal, varnish, shellac, lacquer, wax, or a combination of these finishes, such as varnish and wax.

If the floor is made of softwood or of ordinary unselected hardwood possessing no beauty of grain, it may be advisable to apply floor enamel, which being opaque, will cover up the grain of the wood entirely.

A good floor enamel is one that will form a film sufficiently hard and tough to withstand constant wear.

Open-Grained and Close-Grained Woods

Flooring may be classified into two general classes of wood, open-grained and close-grained. Woods of loose, open formation with minute openings between the fibers, such as oak and walnut, are called "open-grained" woods. Woods such as birch, maple, beech and pine where the fibers are fine and are held closely together, are called "close-grained" woods.

Open-grained woods must be filled with paste wood filler to give a smooth surface on which paint is applied. Paste filler is not required on close-grained woods unless the boards have shrunk apart.

In filling open-grained wood be sure to remove all grease spots before applying the filler. To prepare paste wood filler for use, transfer a quantity into a separate container and thin with turpentine or benzine to a creamy consistency. Use a short-bristled, 4 in. flat brush to put on the filler, working first across the grain, then with the grain of the wood. Be sure the pores of the wood are well filled. Let the filler set until the gloss has disappeared, usually 15 to 30 minutes. Then, using a dry coarse cloth (a piece of burlap is satisfactory) wipe off the excess filler. Wipe ACROSS the grain of the wood. Fill only a part of the floor at a time, removing the surplus filler before filling another section.

After the filler has dried, remove the excess from the surface of the wood by using 3/0 garnet paper or coarse steel wool, working with the grain.

Painting of both hardwood which has been filled as well as softwood floors requires a coat of primer and one or two coats of high-grade porch and floor enamel, applied according to the manufacturer's instructions.

Some manufacturers recommend reducing the regular porch and floor enamel with turpentine or other solvent and using this as the priming coat; others recommend using a special primer.

New porch flooring should be primed on all sides, edges and ends before it is laid.

Repainting Previously Painted Floors

Old floors should be clean and dry before being repainted. If soap or washing powder is used in cleaning, rinse afterward with clear water. Wax and oil mop residue should be removed with a turpentine-soaked cloth, rubbing well, or the new finish will not dry properly and will peel.

Any wide cracks in the old floor should be filled with plastic wood or wood putty before applying the new paint.

If the old paint has worn entirely away in spots so the wood underneath is exposed, a coat of floor enamel thinned with a little turpentine, should be applied and allowed to dry thoroughly. Then, apply two coats of floor enamel to the entire floor, making sure that the first coat is dry before applying the next coat.

If the old paint is in bad condition, it should be removed entirely using a power sander or a chemical paint remover. After complete removal, the floor should be sanded smooth and treated in the same manner as a new floor. An old floor that has never been painted should be sanded smooth and treated as a new floor.

Applying Floor Wax

Interior enameled floors, like varnished floors, may be waxed using either liquid or paste floor wax. For best results one coat of wax should not be permitted to wear away before rewaxing.

Finishing Floors with Varnish and Floor Sealers

Finishing of wood floors using stains, varnishes, sealers, etc. will be described in the Unit on Wood Finishing with Varnishes, Sealers, Stains and Lacquers.

Painting Fir Plywood

Fir plywood presents some unusual problems in painting because the grain has a tendency to show through, and hairline checking of paint frequently results.

This trouble may be prevented to a considerable extent by using a phenolic-resin primer-sealer, a penetrating type of finish that dries in the wood and equalizes the density of the hard and soft grains like an undercoat. It is sold under several trade names. When dry, the primer-sealer is sanded or treated with steel wool and the surface is then ready for finish coats of either enamel or wall paint.

This primer-sealer, while perhaps most effective on fir plywood, may be used on other close-grained woods as well, such as redwood, cypress and pine. On open-grained hardwoods it is effective as a sealer over paste filler.

Applying Paint to Metal Surfaces

Metal surfaces such as iron and steel are painted for two principal reasons -- for protection against rust and corrosion and for decorative purposes. Unless the formation of rust on these surfaces is prevented from the start, a great deal of expense and difficulty in painting results.

In painting iron and steel, the surface must be carefully prepared. Information on this topic is given in the Unit of this book on Surface Preparation.

Ordinarily brushes used for house painting are satisfactory for use in painting metal, although some painters prefer oval or round brushes.

Priming Coat is Important

Of considerable importance in achieving a satisfactory paint job on iron and steel is the use of a good primer. Ready-mixed metal primers containing substantial quantities of red lead, blue lead, zinc or zinc chromate, are suggested. Red lead paints are available in combination with red iron oxide pigment which also have good rust preventive qualities.

Following the primer, two coats of ready-mixed metal paint applied according to the manufacturer's instructions, are usually recommended. The application of two thin finish coats is preferable to one heavy coat.

Painting Galvanized Iron

Galvanized iron such as used on roofs, gutters and downspouts is painted not only to make it conform to the color scheme of the building, but also to prevent rust. Even small scratches in the zinc coating provide starting points for rust.

One of the best primers for galvanized metal surfaces, especially surfaces that have weathered less than six months, is a zinc dust, zinc oxide paint. The same kind of paint may be used for the second coat or regular house paint may be used.

Copper Surfaces

Copper surfaces are often left unpainted. They do not rust and do not need paint for protection. Such surfaces, however, are sometimes painted or given a transparent coating to prevent the green deposit which accumulates on weathered copper from dripping down and staining painted areas below.

Copper surfaces should be wiped clean with a cloth dipped in turpentine or benzine, being sure that all acid and rosin stains left by soldering are removed. Rinse well with clear water and allow the copper surfaces to dry before starting the paint job.

Two coats of paint well brushed out and a metal primer are suggested.

Clear Finishes for Copper

Oxidizing of copper including copper gutters, and downspouts, and copper screen, may be prevented by cleaning the metal and coating it with clear spar varnish or transparent metal lacquer.

Tin Surfaces

Sheet iron plated with tin such as used for chimney flashing and on roof decks should be painted. The procedure described for painting copper is also applicable to painting tin-plated surfaces.

Using Paint Tinted Different Colors

In painting metal some painters make it a practice to tint each coat a slightly different color. This helps determine which portions of the surface have been covered. Where particular colors are used for certain coats, it also makes it easier for an inspector to determine how far a certain painting job has progressed.

In painting iron, steel, and other metals the importance of spreading an even coating of paint and covering of every nail, joint, rivet and every inch of the metal cannot be overemphasized. Such coverage is necessary to prevent rust formation.

Painting Wallpaper and Wall Fabrics

Whether to paint over wallpaper or remove it completely is a question that is sometimes rather difficult to decide. Although it is not considered good painting practice, painters are often called upon to handle jobs of painting over various kinds of wallpaper.

First, it is important to determine if the paper adheres tightly to the wall. Paper that has bulges, blisters, or bubbles will not hold paint properly and will give an uneven finish and should be removed.

If the paper is tight on the wall, it is important to test to see if the paint intended for the job will cover the pattern in the paper. Some wallpaper colors will bleed through paint. For a test, pick an inconspicuous corner that includes all the colors in the pattern. Paint over it, and let it dry for several hours. If there is no trace of the pattern or of bleeding, it is safe to proceed with the entire job.

If the color shows through, the papered area will need a priming coat of shellac or aluminum paint to seal the surface. It may also need two coats of paint.

Raised patterns or designs in paper will show through paint. For best results such papers must be removed. Some wallpaper remains sound because it is porous. When it is painted and cannot breathe, it loosens.

Information on removing wallpaper will be found in the Unit on Wall Coverings.

Types of Paint

Latex-base paints are commonly used over wallpaper. They cover most papers in one coat and are reasonably porous. Such paints may be applied with a 4 in. wall brush.

Paints such as flat wall paints with oil bases are sometimes used for covering wallpaper, but they are very difficult to remove if this should become necessary later.

Painting Wall Fabric

Fabric covered walls are as easy to paint as smooth plaster, and the procedure is essentially the same. A coat of primer and two finishing coats are ordinarily required. Primer will not be needed on fabric that has been painted before. Cracks and holes may be repaired in the fabric coated walls using spackle or patching plaster.

Coating of Storage Tanks and Structural Steel

The coating of steel storage tanks and structural steel presents special problems. The painter must recognize various surface conditions and know the proper methods for preparing the surface for the type of coating he applies. The applicator needs to know the service and environmental conditions in which the structure functions in order to select the proper surface preparation method and the proper coating system. He needs to know the properties of various primers, intermediate coats and topcoats and how each applies by brushing, rolling, spraying or gloving. He needs to know which of the different types of coatings combine to achieve maximum performance in a system where each coating complements the total system. In a like manner, he needs to know which coatings are incompatible and which he should avoid using.

Steel

Steel functions widely in industrial construction because of availability, strength to weight ratio, ease and speed of fabricating, dimensional stability and attractive cost. On the other hand, steel has some problems. If these problems are not handled properly they cause the loss of the structural and economical advantages of steel. Steel attracts and is reactive with such things as moisture, gas, chemicals, heat and electricity. It collects dirt, oil and grime.

Steel comes coated with a surface having various amounts of oxide scale and contamination. Steel may oxidize to rust and loses its structural value. This process slows down or even stops if the proper coating is applied over the steel. This process occurs only on the surface and any coating which insulates the steel from moisture and oxygen inhibits this corrosive process.

The same procedure of using proper coatings can prevent other elements from the environment from attacking steel. Coatings selected for typical industrial service must provide excellent adhesion and resist moisture, solvents, chemicals, salt atmosphere, and weather conditions.

Storage Tank Interior and Exterior

With steel storage tanks the applicator is concerned about the interior as well as the exterior. The coating of the interior surfaces requires additional considerations. Coatings are applied to the interior to protect the steel against the usual corrosion developments, to protect the steel against attack from the contents of the storage tank, and to protect the product from contamination caused by the corrosive activity of the structural steel. Maximum emphasis goes to proper surface preparation and the selection of the proper coating in executing interior storage tank applications.

Cleaning for Service and Coating System

The applicator uses many methods of surface preparation to clean the steel for receiving the coating. In service where chemicals, solvents, and salt atmosphere are not a problem, the less stringent cleaning methods are effective with oil based coating systems. Under these conditions, the applicator uses hand cleaning methods. (Reference to the various cleaning methods appear in another Unit of this Encyclopedia.) On the other hand, more stringent methods are needed to prepare steel in the chemical plants, paper mills, refineries, on off-shore facilities and in other highly corrosive industrial locations. The applicator protects these facilities with alkyds and the high performance coatings such as vinyls, epoxies, urethanes and polyesters.

These high performance coatings do not wet steel surfaces which have various amounts of scale and foreign material that remain after hand cleaning. At these locations abrasive blast cleaning is best. It removes rust, dirt, oil, and loose scale as well as tightly held scale. With the removal of loose scale and foreign contamination, the high performance coatings wet and adhere to the steel. But, for the most lasting performance, the tightly held scale needs to come off also.

Tightly Held Scale

Tightly held scale varies in composition from highly oxidized iron on the surface to a very low oxide condition at the steel scale interface. This composition corrodes on contact with moisture and oxygen or chemicals and expands as a unit. As the corrosion continues a condition results where the tight adhesion of the scale deteriorates. When this happens the scale flakes away from the steel or peels away as large sheets. In addition, the process accelerates with

temperature cycling through freeze-thaw and cycling through hot-dry/cold-wet conditions. Although coatings reduce the moisture-oxygen contact with the tight scale, some moisture eventually gets through and starts to work on the scale. Not all scale loses adhesion at the same rate, and not all coatings or the same field-applied system pass moisture and oxygen at the same reduced rate. So painting over scale, or even tight scale, risks early job failure in corrosive areas.

To reduce the risk of early job failure, the steel in corrosive areas receives thorough abrasive cleaning in the field, or chemical or abrasive cleaning at the mill. Written specifications prescribe the degree and methods of cleaning, but only close inspection assures that you achieve the job you want.

Field Removal of Tight Scale

To achieve the best practical abrasive blast cleaning results in the field, the applicator allows the scale to corrode and loosen. The loosened scale comes off many times more quickly and easily than tight scale. To speed loosening of the scale, the applicator wets the surfaces with water frequently. Where possible, he spreads the steel on the ground exposing the greatest surface area to rain, applied water, and sunlight for loosening the scale.

Application

Following cleaning, the applicator coats the steel with a primer. Sometimes he coats with a primer and intermediate coat. Next the steel goes in place and the final coating goes on.

With new steel in place and old steel that requires a new coating job, the applicator generally cleans in the morning and primes the clean area in the afternoon. He cleans only the amount of steel he is able to coat within the same shift. His schedule is flexible. He must coat the cleaned area before it recontaminates or rusts. This will depend on the weather and job location. Cleaning and coating proceed only during daylight hours and only when the humidity and temperature conditions remain within the specified limits. The applicator keeps a handy reference to his specifications and material directions at all times as an aid in maintaining proper job control.

Cleaning and coating start at the top of the job such as on a storage tank. First the roof gets cleaned and primed; then the sides. The sides proceed a ring at a time around the tank with each "drop." Light cleaning with compressed air and solvent wet or dry rags proceeds before the intermediate coat goes on. Solvent cleaning can be harmful with some coating systems. Thus, the directions provided by the manufacturer provide the best guide.

The topcoats follow in order over the primer and intermediate coats from top to bottom.

Scheduling

The scheduling of priming and subsequent coating application depends on the weather and type of coatings used. For instance, oil paints which have advantages in wetting remain wet longer than the high performance coatings at average summer temperatures and remain wet much longer at low temperatures. Scheduling is important from the standpoint of assuring against damage of the applied coating by the subsequent coats due to solvent attack and retarded final drying. Scheduling is important from a mechanical standpoint as well. The applicator does not want to delay the job, but at the same time he does not want to damage the previous coating by getting back on it too soon with equipment, men and additional coating. Proper selection of power staging and scaffolds aid the applicator in preventing mechanical damage to his coating job. Also, the manufacturers material directions provide aids to scheduling under various weather conditions.

Brushing, Rolling and Spraying

Oil coatings, some alkyds, some esters, water based coating, and some specialty coats apply with brush, roller or spray equipment. When brushing select a good flat end brush 4 to 6 in. wide filled with various length bristles trimmed 4 to 7 in. in overall length. Avoid nylon or synthetic bristle when using a specialty coating having coal tar or strong solvents.

The primer needs maximum brushing in all directions to make sure maximum wetting of the surfaces result. The brushing of subsequent coats proceeds with even overlapping strokes using minimum rebrushing. The strokes remain horizontal and start on the dry surface. Work them back into the wet edge by lifting the brush slightly as it contacts the wet edge. Use shorter strokes with fast drying alkyds, esters and the like. More information on brushing and rolling

is in the first part of this Unit.

The high performance coatings do not brush well. Consequently, the manufacturers design these coatings for application by spray equipment. Spray painting does not allow the coating to wet the surface nearly as well as brushing. Thus high performance coatings need clean surfaces for lasting service life. Spray painting is 4 to 12 times faster than brushing, depending on whether or not conventional air atomization or airless equipment is used on the job.

The application of coating using spray equipment is described later in this Unit.

Rolling Interior Paint

Use a narrow trim roller around doors, windows, baseboards, corner and ceiling lines to make starting strips, Fig. 7-11. If a trim roller is not readily available, you can "cut-in" starting strips with a brush. The roller follows brushing promptly to avoid lap marks.

Fig. 7-11. Using narrow trim roller to make starting strip.

In using a roller to paint a room, the ceiling should be done first. Avoid overloading of the roller.

A ceiling is usually painted across the shortest dimension. Start in a corner and paint a strip only as wide as you can reach comfortably, Fig. 7-12. Paint as rapidly as you can, using a back and forth motion. Change direction as desired, but do not lift the roller when changing direction.

Paint as rapidly as you can, especially with oil paints and enamels to avoid lap marks. When one strip has been completed across a ceiling, begin a second strip at the starting side. Proceed in this manner until the entire ceiling is finished.

Fig. 7-12. In ceiling painting, it is best to start at one corner and paint a strip only as wide as you can reach comfortably.

A wall is usually started in the upper left hand corner by a right-hand worker. It is best painted in strips not more than 4 ft. in width. In wall painting, make the first stroke with a freshly loaded roller upward. Overlap the strokes a bit to assure good coverage. In starting out do not try to work too fast. A steady, methodical stroke will cause the roller to give good contact. The bit of paint which is pushed ahead of the roller flows into surface irregularities, and helps provide an even coating.

If, instead of a tray type roller, you are using a fill-type roller, the first operation will be to fill the cylinder of the roller. Prime the roller by rolling it in a half cup of paint poured onto a piece of kraft paper or old newspaper. If this is not done some operating of the roller will be needed to bring paint from the storage cylinder to all parts of the outer surface of the roller.

Brushing Interior Paint

FLAT OIL PAINT: In painting a room where both the ceiling and the walls are to be painted, the ceiling should be painted first. Use a 4 to 6 in. brush, being careful not to overload the brush with paint. Apply paint to the ceiling with overlapping swirl strokes, lifting brush gradually at the end of each stroke in order not to leave

a thick edge of paint. Do a minimum amount of brushing - - just enough to spread paint evenly.

In painting a wall, apply the paint evenly with a well-filled brush, first brushing in horizontal strokes, then stroke with light up-and-down movement as a finish operation.

For inside painting with oil paint, many painters prefer the new thixotropic paints - - paints which appear heavily bodied but which become very fluid on brushing. These paints do not drip, permit high brush loading and can be applied very smoothly.

ENAMEL, VARNISH: The brushing strokes used in applying enamel and varnish are somewhat different from those used in applying oil paint. Use a tapered varnish brush about 3 in. wide. Apply enamel and varnish in short, light strokes, permitting the finish to flow on with the least possible brushing. All varnish and enamel coatings should be cross-brushed before laying off to even the coat and prevent thin edges. After coating remove surplus material from the brush by wiping firmly on the edge of the container. Go over the area just covered, stroking lightly with the tip of the brush. Blend the edges before the finish sets. Watch carefully as the work progresses, so that sags and runs can be recognized and smoothed with light, upward strokes before the finish hardens.

CAUSES OF BRUSH MARKS: Brush marks in paints, enamels and varnishes may be caused by using materials that do not flow out properly to eliminate the marks. They may also be caused by using brushes with too coarse bristles and by brushing a coating too much. On some highly absorbent surfaces, rapid setting of the paint or varnish may cause brush marks. Too much ventilation of a room may also cause a finish to set before the flowing action is complete.

SHELLAC: Shellac should be applied with a

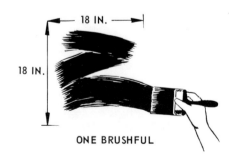

Fig. 7-13. In applying latex-type paint, apply paint to small area at a time. Keep the brush well filled.

soft varnish brush. Brush the shellac on with the grain of the wood, in long strokes, applying a wet, even coat as quickly as possible. Do not brush back and forth over the new coating. Shellac dries very fast, causing the finish to pile up to provide a sloppy, uneven result. Runs, sags and brush marks can be smoothed by stroking the wet surface lightly with the tips of the brush bristles. Remember that proper thinning of the shellac is a vital part of its proper application.

LATEX-TYPE PAINTS: In applying latex-type paint, dampen the brush (4 to 6 in. wall brush) and shake off the excess water. Do a small area at a time, about 18 in. square, Fig. 7-13. Make light finishing strokes toward the painted area.

Applying Paint and Enamel to Interior Wood

The same general principles useful in painting exterior wood surfaces may be applied to the painting of interior wood. However, the mixing of the paint differs somewhat, since the paint to be used for inside work need not be formulated to withstand severe weather conditions.

One of the most important phases of interior painting is the application of enamel to woodwork. In years gone by it was the standard practice to use five or six coats of enamel to finish woodwork. Using the fine finishes now available, a satisfactory finish may be obtained with two or three coats.

Information on surface preparation, brushes,

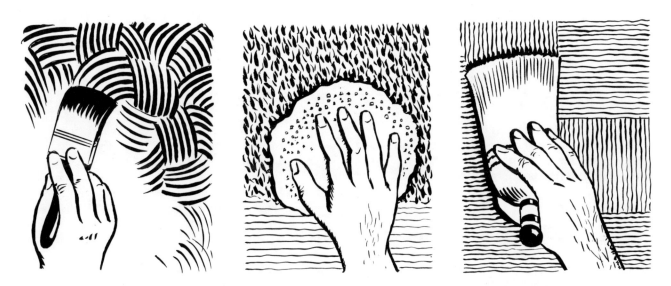

Fig. 7-14. Texture paint. Texturing or creating designs in paint may be done by using short twisting motion of brush tip, with sponge, with whisk broom, and with other texturing tools.

TEXTURE PAINTS: Texture paint, which comes in powder and ready-mixed forms, is used for decorative effects and to cover cracks, taped seams, holes, dents, and other surface irregularities to avoid replastering.

Use a 4 to 6 in. paint brush, and apply finish about 1/16 in. thick. Do a small area, then texture with brush, sponge, whisk broom, or stipple brush. See Fig. 7-14.

Raised portions may be flattened slightly, if desired, by drawing a celluloid triangle or other straightedge across the surface.

Degree of texture will depend somewhat on the thickness of the application. To provide maximum durability a finish coat of paint should be applied.

paint mixing and selection and protection of property is provided elsewhere in this book, and will not be duplicated here.

Paint Ceiling First

If both the ceiling and the walls of a room finished in plywood or hardboard are to be painted it is advisable to start with the ceiling. Hardboard is an all-wood fiberboard made from exploded wood fiber pressed into board form and then heated and shaped by flatbed hydraulic presses.

Begin in one corner and work across the narrow dimension of the room, coating a strip 2 or 3 ft. wide at a time -- never more than you

Fig. 7-15. In painting a ceiling it is advisable to start at one corner and work across the narrow part of the room coating a strip not more than 3 ft. wide at one time.

can reach comfortably. See Fig. 7-15.

Start the second strip on a bare surface a few inches away from the first strip and work backward into the wet edge of the previous strip.

Painting Walls

In wall painting, it is best to start in the upper corner of a wall and "cut-in" a neat line next to the ceiling. This should be done with a partially dry brush angled into the corner so that only the edge bristles come into play. Make light, horizontal strokes, and take particular care to get a neat, straight line.

After cutting in, proceed by painting small areas so that you will always work with a wet edge. It is well to keep horizontal laps well above or below average eye level so they will not be apparent. Complete one wall before starting on another.

Be sure that one coat is thoroughly dry before applying a second one.

Using Enamel

Baseboards, doors, window sash and built-in cabinets, should be finished with great care. Small brush marks which would hardly be noticed on wall surfaces become quite conspicuous on enameled woodwork.

On new woodwork, proper durability may be obtained by giving the surface three coats - - a priming coat, a body coat and a finish coat.

Before applying the priming coat, the surface of the wood should be treated carefully with 3/0 garnet paper. Always work WITH the grain of the wood. Make sure the surface is free from dust before applying the priming coat. Dust and dirt may be removed by careful brushing and by using a vacuum cleaner. Never wipe any surface which is to be enameled or varnished with a rag, unless it is a specially prepared TACK rag.

After the priming coat is thoroughly dry, nail holes, cracks and crevices should be filled with putty or spackle. The putty should be properly smoothed and the filler coat sanded lightly, using 3/0 garnet paper. Spackled areas should be touched up with shellac or paint primer before applying second coat.

Check instructions on the can to see if thinning of the particular paint being used is required for the second or body coat.

When the second coat has dried hard, it too should be sanded lightly before the final finish coat is applied. Usually the enamel for the finish coat is applied just as it comes in the can.

For two-coat enamel finishes, both coats should be applied somewhat thicker than for a three-coat job. Particular care must be taken to prevent runs and sags.

USING ENAMEL ON CEILINGS AND WALLS: An enamel finish for plywood or pressed wood, starts with a coat of primer and sealer. White primer may be tinted with oil colors or with some of the enamel to match the finish coat. The priming coat should be applied carefully, being sure to get complete coverage of the surface. The priming coat should be sanded lightly to remove or "cut" the gloss.

Enamel is more difficult to apply than wall paints. The enamel should be applied in small areas of about a yard square. Start each brushful of enamel a few inches away from the wet edge of enamel and work over to the wet edge. In doing ceilings, it is generally advisable to work on strips not exceeding 2 ft. in width, across the short way. Do one complete strip before returning to the starting side to repeat the operation.

Enameling Successfully

Success in enameling depends to a considerable extent on having the proper type of clean brush, warm, dust-free surface and dust-free room in which to apply the enamel, as well as enamel that is free of specks, and hard particles. It is very important to remove from the enamel all particles that would show up as specks in the finish by using a screen with very fine mesh, or a lintless cloth strainer. Nylon stockings are excellent paint strainers.

Enameling Old Woodwork

Coatings on interior woodwork seldom show the checking and blistering which develops on exterior painted surfaces. The desire for a change in color, or a new and fresh surface, or repairing of mechanical damage are the usual reasons for repainting.

The condition of the surface decides the exact procedure to follow. Areas where the old coating has been removed down to bare wood should be treated like new wood.

Normally, one coat of enamel is sufficient, but if the new enamel is a much lighter color than the original coating, two coats may be required to cover the old finish.

On jobs where enamel is applied over stained woodwork, a test should be made on a small area to see if the old finish will bleed through the new coating. If this occurs, the entire surface should first be sealed with a coat of white shellac, aluminum paint, or sealer made especially for the purpose.

Enameling Furniture

Enamel finishes on furniture are applied by the same general methods and with the same materials as described for enamel finish on woodwork and trim. One exception is that a coat of shellac to seal the pores is sometimes applied before the primer.

Any required repairing should, of course, be done before starting with the finishing operations.

The brush size should be in proportion to the size of the piece being finished.

HOW TO FINISH A CHAIR: In enameling a chair it is usually best to finish all bottom surfaces of seat, legs and back; then stand the chair upright and do the top surfaces, completing the job by enameling the seat. Aerosol paints are particularly effective on chair rungs.

HOW TO FINISH A TABLE: Do bottom (if bottom is to be finished) then the legs - - backs of legs first. Next, do the top edges and finally the top of the table.

HOW TO FINISH A CHEST OR CABINET: First, remove the drawers, knobs and hardware. Start with the panels. Do edges of panels first, then cross-brush panels, using light finishing strokes. Finish remaining surfaces. In finishing drawers, paint to sides about 6 in. back, do the edges, then the front panel.

Wicker furniture can be painted quickly using a spray gun or aerosol paint.

Applying Paint to Plaster and Dry Walls

Plaster is considered one of the most difficult surfaces over which paint can be applied successfully.

Most of the conditions that result in unsuccessful paint jobs on plaster may be detected and avoided. It is, therefore, of considerable importance that the painter be able to recognize the potential causes of paint failures and know how to prevent them.

New plaster contains a large volume of water, which if not allowed to dry out previous to painting, may exert sufficient mechanical action to loosen the paint film. The presence of water, alkali salts and hydrated lime may cause a chemical action called saponification. Here the film becomes soft and sticky and drops of brownish or saponified oil appear on the surface of the paint. Sometimes soluble salts present in new plaster are carried to the surface and appear as a white powder or efflorescence, causing peeling of the paint.

Other conditions in plastered walls that may cause trouble are varicolored areas, excessive cracks, and powdery surfaces.

New plaster should be permitted to dry well before it is painted. Extreme alkaline conditions in new plaster may be neutralized by applying a solution of 2 to 3 lbs. of zinc sulphate crystals dissolved in one gallon of water. Allow the solution to dry, then dust it off. The solution should not be applied to surfaces that are to be painted with latex paints. Areas in which bad powdery spots have developed can best be repaired by replastering.

Choice of Treatments

Although the choice of wall and ceiling treatments is wide, the materials themselves are limited to four principal types of finishes: high gloss paint or enamels; semi-gloss paints; flat paints; and water emulsion paints which are also flat in sheen. Each has its particular merit.

Water emulsion paints are available in the following forms.

EMULSION RESIN PAINTS: Emulsified resin paints consist of a water emulsion of oil and resin in semi-paste form. Additional water is added as a vehicle to facilitate spreading. Such paints spread well, have high light reflection value and are claimed to be washable to a high degree for a water base paint. They dry to a longer lasting film when the weather is warm.

EMULSION PAINTS: Emulsion paints, commonly known as latex paints, consist of a water emulsion of carefully selected synthetic rubber, vinyl resin, or acrylic resin, compounded to produce a paint which applies easily and dries rapidly to form a film which cures to a surface which is readily washable without appreciable film destruction and has very little tendency to absorb dirt of any kind.

Applying Sealer Coat

New DRY plaster in good condition should be given a coat of sealer unless it is to be coated with water paint. This provides a nonabsorbing foundation. Do not use a glue size or any material that is soluble in water, under oil paints.

The sealer coat should be allowed to dry carefully, and should be examined for uniform-

ity of appearance. Any "suction spots" that appear should be given an additional coat of sealer. Next, a priming coat should be applied, for most oil base finish paints. Primer-sealers are now available that combine the functions of priming and sealing in one coat. With many of the new synthetic resin paints priming is unnecessary.

One coat of flat finish paint over a properly sealed and primed wall is usually sufficient although a second coat may sometimes be needed. Oil base gloss and semi-gloss enamels generally require enamel undercoaters before application of the finish coats. To make it easier for the final coat to cover, it is sometimes desirable to tint the wall primer and sealer with colors-in-oil to a shade approximately that of the finish coat.

Painting Previously Painted Plaster

In painting previously painted plaster, all nicks and cracks should be patched and spot-primed. Previously applied water-thinned paints that will dissolve under new applications of water-thinned paints should be removed or sealed with oil-type primers. Glue size may be removed by using steel wool and warm water; water soluble paints with solutions of strong soap and household starch. Glossy finishes should be dulled by washing with a mild solution of sodium silicate, sal soda, or ready-mixed surface conditioner. The gloss may also be removed by using 3/0 sandpaper or steel wool.

In painting over a surface which is not porous and which has been previously painted and is in good condition, one coat of most modern finishes is all that is usually required.

Painting Dry Walls

Wallboard and plasterboard are now used extensively in home building. There is no particular problem in finishing wallboard and plasterboard, except to provide coverings for the joints that are strong and well concealed. Information on covering of joints will be found in the section on Surface Preparation. After the joints have been properly covered, the surface is treated like new, dry, plaster walls.

Cane Fiberboard

Much of the cane fiberboard used in home construction is factory finished and requires no further decoration. New cane fiberboards not finished at the factory may be finished, and factory-finished boards may be refinished by using water emulsion and oil and varnish paints.

Finishing New Cane Board

In using water emulsion paint on new cane board, the surface should be given a coat of preparatory sizing. Sizing is not needed when repainting.

A satisfactory size may be made by adding water to thin the water-based paint. Use about one quart of water per gallon of paint. This must be thoroughly brushed onto the surface to be decorated.

A single coat of high-grade water emulsion paint will ordinarily give fair coverage; two coats are preferable. A thin first coat penetrates small cracks and pores better than a heavy coat.

TREATMENT USED FOR OIL OR VARNISH PAINTS: Factory finishes used on interior cane fiberboard increase obtainable coverage per gallon of certain types of paints. Flat paints may be satisfactorily applied to factory finished products in a one-coat application, but a superior surface is secured by first applying a primer of the type specified by the manufacturer of the paint.

PAINTING INSULATING SHEATHING: Insulating sheathing is intended primarily for use as sheathing, but is sometimes used as an interior or exterior finish. When so used a paint finish is often desired.

Because of the asphalt coating ordinarily found on insulating sheathing, a special primer is necessary to prevent bleeding of the asphalt. Aluminum paint (exterior grade) is a suitable primer for use over an asphalt coated board. Finish coats may be paints recommended for interior and exterior surfaces.

Painting Acoustical Surfaces

In refinishing acoustical surfaces particular care must be taken not to ruin the sound-absorbing properties of the surface.

On most acoustical surfaces, ordinary water emulsion and other types of wall paint may be used, but the finish should be thinned to a viscosity lower than normal and applied in a very thin coat. Apply just enough of the finish to provide a satisfactory surface appearance.

CLEANING ACOUSTICAL SURFACES: Dust and loose dirt may be removed from an acoustical surface by using the upholstery-cleaning brush of a vacuum cleaner. The brush should be drawn lightly over the surface to avoid the possibility of gouging or scratching the sensitive surface. Another method is to use a dry, clean uncolored rubber sponge.

Spray Painting

Applying paint by the spray method is an operation which requires good equipment and trained operators. Spray painting proves most economical where there are large areas, unbroken by windows, doors or trim, which are painted in one color - - such as large barns, factories, tanks, and bridges.

Many products are spray painted in the factory including automobiles, furniture, picture frames, objects of art, household appliances and numerous other fabricated items.

Materials Which May Be Sprayed

There are many finishing materials which can be sprayed such as conventional lacquers, multicolored spatter type paints, house paints, enamels - - in fact, practically any paint product that can be applied by brushing and many that cannot be brushed.

On jobs where some areas receive no paint or paint of a different color considerable masking must be done. The time gained in spray painting may thus be consumed in such extra work. This must, of course, be taken into consideration before deciding whether a job can best be handled by brushing or spraying.

Equipment Needed

Equipment components of a typical spray outfit consist of:
1. Spray gun.
2. Paint container, either cup or pressure tank.
3. Air compressor.
4. Air regulating and purifying device.
5. Air and fluid hose.

Air compressors are of two types - - portable and stationary. A spray gun uses from 5 to 15 cu. ft. of air per minute at normal spraying pressure. A compressor capable of delivering that much air at a given pressure is required for each gun. Excellent portable compressors, driven by both electric motors and gasoline

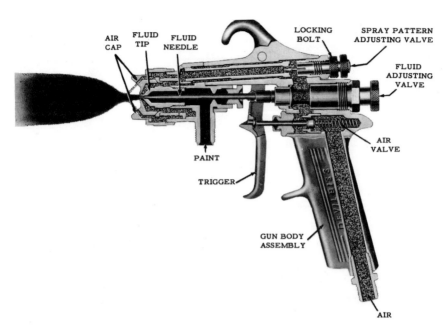

AIR
CAP

FLUID
TIP

FLUID
NEEDLE

LOCKING
BOLT

SPRAY PATTERN
ADJUSTING VALVE

FLUID
ADJUSTING
VALVE

AIR
VALVE

PAINT

TRIGGER

GUN BODY
ASSEMBLY

AIR

Fig. 7-16. Sectional drawing of spray gun lettered to identify principal parts.

engines are readily available.

Air to be used by a spray gun should pass through an air cleansing and regulating device to remove oil, water and dirt by centrifugal force, mechanical filters and expansion.

When using air from a high-pressure line, such as will be found in many industrial plants, the air must be reduced from a main line pressure of 100 or more pounds, to a spraying pressure of 20 to 80 lbs. by using an air regulator. To keep overspray down and to avoid blowing too much solvent into the material mix, the air pressure should be kept at the lowest reading possible.

The air hose used should be flexible, light in weight, kink-proof, and of a diameter which will hold loss in pressure due to friction, to a minimum. Fluid hose used to connect the paint tank to the spray gun should also be of the proper diameter, and made of material that is not affected by solvents in the paint.

Material containers are of two types. Usually suction feed cups which are attached directly to the spray gun are used in small operations. Pressure feed tanks ranging from 2 to 60 gallons are used in major operations.

Spray guns should be as lightweight as practical and designed for ease of handling. A good operator can spray up to 50 gallons of paint per day. The spray gun must, of course, be equipped with the proper fluid metering nozzle and atom-

izing head for the job at hand.

MATERIAL CONTROLS: As mentioned in a preceding paragraph almost any material that can be brushed, may be applied with a spray gun. Unless the manufacturer specifies otherwise, it is best to apply the material as it comes in the can. Hiding capacity of the material may be seriously impaired by using thinning materials. Thinning also encourages sags and runs.

Viscosity control is also important; a cold material cannot be properly spread using either a spray gun, or a brush. A means of insuring uniform viscosity in maintenance painting is with a portable paint heater.

It is also essential that material to be sprayed is strained through a fine screen or through cheesecloth to remove all foreign matter that would detract from the quality of the finish or stop the flow of the paint through the gun.

Air pressure used to spray should be just sufficient to break up the material so it will flow properly. Pressure that is too high wastes material and produces excessive overspray, making the cleanup job difficult and the overspray subject to criticism.

USING HEATED MATERIAL AND CATALYST SPRAYS: Heated materials have been used for several years in product finishing. Heated materials make possible application of high solids paints to obtain thick coatings. These advantages are being recognized and are now being used by many progressive painters.

The use of catalysts to promote more rapid drying, better durability and properties such as sound deadening, corrosion resistance and insulation is also a significant development. Special guns are available for spraying catalyzed systems.

Using a Spray Gun

While handling a spray gun is not complicated, the wisdom of practicing to get the knack of using the gun properly and efficiently should be apparent. Practice spraying may be done on some old corrugated cartons or on sheets of newspaper tacked to a box or carton.

Be sure to experiment with the full range of fluid adjustment, starting with the fluid needle screw backed off from the closed position just far enough to obtain a small pattern an inch or so wide when the trigger is pulled all the way back, Fig. 7-16.

After getting the feel of the gun, gradually back off the fluid adjustment screw to spray more material and widen the pattern. With the increased flow of material through the gun you will find the break-up or atomization becomes a little coarser. A pattern about 6 to 8 in. wide when the gun is held 6 to 8 in. from the surface is about right for most work. Test patterns should be sprayed in both horizontal and vertical positions. The required adjustment for pattern direction is made by rotating the nozzle or air cap, Fig. 7-17.

Spray Gun Stroke

The spray gun stroke is made by moving the gun parallel to the work and at a 90 deg. angle

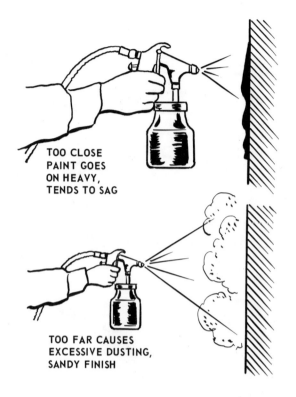

TOO CLOSE PAINT GOES ON HEAVY, TENDS TO SAG

TOO FAR CAUSES EXCESSIVE DUSTING, SANDY FINISH

Fig. 7-18. Above. The closer the gun is held to the work the more paint is deposited. Below. Holding the gun too far away causes excessive dusting and a sandy finish.

to the surface. The speed of stroking should be about the same as for brushing.

One should practice with straight uniform strokes, moving back and forth across the surface in such a way that the pattern laps about 50 percent on each pass. The closer the gun is held to the work, the more paint is deposited on the work surface. The more paint that is applied, the faster the gun must be moved to prevent sags. See Fig. 7-18.

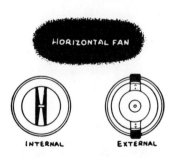

Fig. 7-17. Cap position determines direction of pattern width. Cap should be rotated as needed to suit the job at hand.

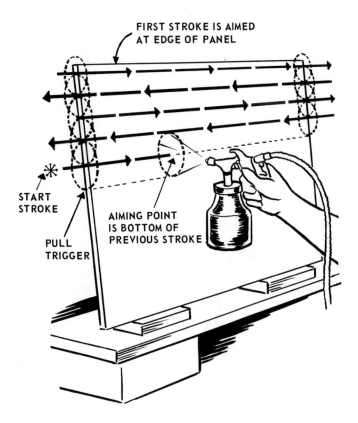

FIRST STROKE IS AIMED
AT EDGE OF PANEL

START
STROKE

PULL
TRIGGER

AIMING POINT
IS BOTTOM OF
PREVIOUS STROKE

Fig. 7-19. Spraying a panel. The stroke should be started with a dry gun, the trigger pulled when the gun is opposite the edge of the work, and released at the end of the stroke.

The relationship between gun distance and stroke speed tends to compensate automatically. The average operator will move the gun in or out as needed to permit a comfortable speed while depositing a full wet coat of paint. When the gun is too far from the work, the stroke must be slowed down beyond average patience; the distant position is also undesirable because of excessive dusting.

When making practice strokes, the results of tilting the gun and arcing the stroke should be noted. On certain types of work it is necessary to tilt the gun but this should not be done haphazardly on surfaces suited to the better gun position. A parallel stroke with the gun held at right angles to the surface will deposit a uniform coating on the surface.

Spraying a Panel

In spraying panels or building sections, Fig. 7-19, each stroke is "triggered." You start the stroke with a dry gun; pull the trigger when the

gun is opposite the edge of the work; release the trigger at the end of the work and continue the dry stroke a few inches before reversing for the second stroke. Hitting the edge of the work and maintaining full coverage without undue overspray is important.

Spray strokes should overlap about one-half. In other words, the aiming point for each stroke is the bottom of the preceding stroke, as shown in Fig. 7-19. This provides double coverage and assures a full wet coat without streaks.

The edges of objects should be sprayed first. The edge of a box is sprayed by aiming directly at the corner. Then the flat sides are treated as panels. The edges of doors and all "hidden" surfaces should be sprayed first followed by the backs of doors. The face of all exposed work should be sprayed last on the finish side of the object or cabinet.

House and Barn Painting

In doing outside work, windy days must be avoided as the breeze will distort the spray. Masking as required to keep the spray off trim and windows can be done with a cardboard shield.

A spray gun is especially appropriate for painting rough stucco. Wood shingles are commonly stained and can readily be sprayed with either suction or pressure feed guns.

Complicated detail work of a nature too difficult to brush is easily painted by spraying. However, exterior paints have a tendency to pile up in some places and the uneven film with thick and thin spots breaks of its own internal stresses to start peeling and alligatoring.

Finishing with Flock

Flock consists of short lengths of rayon, linen, wool or cotton which, when sprayed onto a surface coated with adhesive, will stick endwise and form a pile or nap somewhat similar to velvet.

The flock fibers come in various lengths, including 1/32 and 1/16 in. and in about thirty different colors.

Adhesives

Much of the durability of flock depends on the quality of the adhesive. Commonly used adhesives include water-soluble glues, enamels, lacquers, rubber-base adhesives and polyamide resin adhesive.

Applying Flock

In applying flock the adhesive is sprayed or brushed onto the bare metal or other smooth surface to be coated. Open-grained wood should first be filled with a paste filler. Work in small areas so the adhesive will not set before completing the flock application. To obtain an even color it is best to use adhesive which is the same color as the flock. Two-color effects can be obtained by using adhesive of contrasting color.

It is a good safety measure to wear an approved type of mask while spraying flock to prevent breathing the fine particles.

Spray the flock onto the adhesive coated surface, while still wet, using a flock spray gun with 30 to 40 lbs. pressure. The air pressure used to blast the flock from the gun tends to straighten the tiny fibers and direct them into the adhesive. Sprinkling flock by hand is not satisfactory because the fibers instead of standing upright, will mat down and fail to form the desired velvety nap.

USING HAND SPRAY: On small jobs like coating jewel boxes, lamps, and radios, flock can be satisfactorily applied using an insecticide duster such as used in dusting plants, Fig. 7-20.

Fig. 7-20. On small jobs of flock coating, the flock can be applied using an insecticide duster.

If the hand spraying of flock is done inside a large corrugated box turned on its side, the flock which does not stick to the adhesive can be salvaged.

After the flock adhesive is dry, the surface should be brushed with a soft brush to remove flock which was not anchored to the surface by the adhesive.

To get snow effect when flocking Christmas trees, spray gun containing adhesive is held in one hand and flock gun in the other. Flock is directed into stream of adhesive which carries it onto the tree, Fig. 7-21.

Fig. 7-21. To get snow effect when flocking Christmas trees, spray gun containing adhesive is held in one hand and flock gun in the other. Flock is directed into stream of adhesive which carries it onto the tree.

Trouble Shooting

Trouble experienced with the spray pattern, gun performance, work appearance and the compressor, with suggested cures are given in Fig. 7-22.

Cleaning the Spray Gun

A spray gun should be cleaned promptly after the spraying job is finished or work is stopped for any reason. It is very important not to allow the paint to harden inside the gun.

Before starting to spray, it is a good idea to fill an extra cup about one-quarter full of suitable solvent. Use water for water paint, turpentine for paint and varnish, alcohol for shellac, and lacquer thinner for lacquer. If the gun is of the suction feed type, the cleaning fluid can be held in any open container to clean the gun. Pressure feed equipment requires a spray cup since this type gun will not pull solvent from an open container.

Simple cleaning, involving only the spraying of solvent through the gun, is often sufficient if done promptly after using the gun. With the compressor off, let the fluid tube drip a few seconds and pull the trigger to release fluid trapped in the fluid tube. Second, wipe the tube. Third, spray the solvent, using four or five pulls of the trigger for a period of about two seconds each. Spray at a sheet of newspaper or rag placed over a pan or into an old carton. Next, hold a rag over the nozzle and give the trigger a few quick pulls. This will surge the fluid violently within the cup and fluid tube. Re-

SPRAY PATTERN

Heavy End . . . is usually caused by dirty gun nozzle. Remove cap and fluid tip for cleaning.

Heavy Center . . . results from too much material, too little air pressure. Reduce fluid flow with needle adjustment.

Split . . . may be caused by dirty or partially clogged fluid tip. Correct by thoroughly cleaning cap and fluid tip.

Peanut . . . indicates clogging on one side of cap or nozzle. If fault reverses when cap is rotated, the trouble is at cap; if pattern remains the same, fault is at fluid tip.

GUN PERFORMANCE

Leak at Packing Nut . . . indicates loose packing nut or dry packing. If fault persists after tightening packing nut, remove packing and soften with a few drops of oil.

Leak at Nozzle . . . means the fluid needle is not seating properly, or there is dirt on fluid tip seat. Be sure packing nut does not bind needle movement.

Fluttering Spray . . . results when air gets into the fluid line. Obvious causes are lack of material or tipping the gun too much. Check for a loose or cracked fluid tube, loose fluid tip or damaged tip seat. On suction gun, jerky spray can be caused by too heavy material, clogged air hole in lid, loose coupling nut on lid, loose fluid needle packing.

No Fluid Flow . . . Check first with water or lacquer thinner. If this sprays, the original material is too heavy. If thin material does not spray, the fault is usually a dirty gun. Also, check air supply and connections.

WORK APPEARANCE

Sags and Runs . . . indicate poor gun handling. Beginners should spray test panel before doing actual work. Above all, avoid thin paint — pressure feed gun will handle paint somewhat heavier than brushing consistency.

Misting or Fog . . . is to some extent natural. Do not hold gun too far from work. Avoid cheap lacquer thinners.

Sandy Finish . . . results when overspray is trapped on the freshly-sprayed surface. Occurs only with fast-drying materials. Always spray full wet coat; direct overspray away from surfaces already coated.

Orange Peel . . . is often caused by cheap, fast-drying lacquer thinners. Always spray full wet coat to allow slight flow-out needed for leveling.

Streaks . . . can be caused by improper overlapping of spray strokes. Fault is made worse by heavy end pattern.

COMPRESSOR

Air Filter . . . should be removed when dirty and washed in solvent. Keep the compressor in a clean place.

Starting of Motor . . . should not be attempted with air pressure built up in the hose — the motor may not start under this extra load.

Extension Cord . . . Do not use house lamp extension cords. Extensions to 25 ft. should be No. 16 wire. A 50 ft. run requires No. 14 wire to avoid voltage drop.

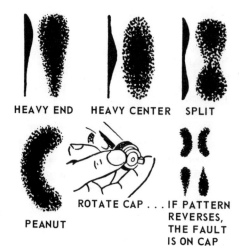

HEAVY END   HEAVY CENTER   SPLIT

PEANUT   ROTATE CAP . . . IF PATTERN REVERSES, THE FAULT IS ON CAP

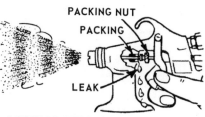

PACKING NUT

PACKING

LEAK

LOOSE OR DRY PACKING WILL CAUSE FLUID LEAKAGE – SPRAY MAY FLUTTER

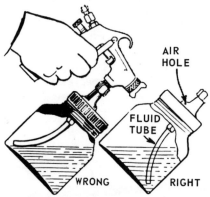

AIR HOLE

FLUID TUBE

WRONG   RIGHT

REVERSED CUP LID WILL STARVE THE GUN WHEN SPRAY IS DIRECTED DOWN

TOO MUCH MATERIAL WILL SAG

THIN MATERIAL WILL RUN

SAGS AND RUNS

GUN TOO FAR FROM WORK

DUSTING OR FOG

SANDY FINISH   APT TO OCCUR ON CLOSED WORK   ORANGE PEEL

Fig. 7-22. Trouble experienced with spray pattern, gun performance, work appearance and compressor, with suggested cures.

move the rag, wipe the cap and then take a final squirt. Lift the gun from the solvent and pull the trigger to release solvent trapped in the fluid tube. Hang up the gun so the fluid tube points down.

For a complete cleaning, after the simple cleaning just described has been completed, take a wet rag and wipe any smudges from the gun. Empty the solvent into a paint cup and clean the paint cup. Wipe the cup dry with a rag. About every second or third cleaning, remove the cap and fluid tip and immerse them in solvent. Use a toothbrush to go over the threads on the cup lid. Wipe the needle. Sharpen a match and push it through the fluid tip. Clean out any paint at the end of the fluid tube. If the gun is of the suction feed type, push a broom straw through the horn holes.

CAUTION: Fluid tips are often made of steel. In order to prevent rusting after spraying water-mix paint, clean the gun first with water and finally with alcohol, then lacquer thinner. Never use a metal object such as a wire or nail to clean out fluid or air holes in the spray tip. Such practice may damage these precision-machined openings and result in a distorted spray pattern.

Keep Compressor Clean

The compressor should be placed where it will receive a supply of cool, clean, dry air. Air filled with dust or vapor entering the air intake will gum or clog the intake screens and intake valves, resulting in decreased efficiency of the unit.

Keep the compressing outfit as level as possible. Drain the air tank daily.

Safety Precautions

Spray painting involves hazards of explosion and fire. Spray in a well ventilated area and make certain that electrical devices are not sparking. It is recommended that motors or gas engines of air compressing outfits be operated outside the spray zone.

When working in close quarters, use a respirator as protection against fumes or vapors. With materials injurious to the skin, wear gloves or apply grease to hands and face.

Flammable liquids such as thinners and lacquers should be kept in safety cans. A fire extinguisher should be readily available for use if needed.

The unit should be provided with an approved type safety valve and an automatic switch to keep the air pressure constant within the limits for which it was designed.

Airless Spray

The use of airless spray equipment is popular for both field and product finishing application work. Airless equipment expands the type of work coated and conditions under which coating proceeds using spray techniques.

With airless equipment, the coating feeds the fluid tip under a pressure ranging from 1300 to 6000 psig. By passing the coating through a small fluid tip .007 to .040 in. in diameter under high pressure into the relative low pressure atmosphere, the coating reduces to a fine atomized mist. The shape of the tip controls the pattern, size and shape of the coating mist.

A basic airless unit has a coating pump, fluid line and spray gun. Compressed air or electricity powers the pump. An air motor pump requires very low volume air (6-10 cu. ft.) on the average, but needs the air at high pressure (100 psig) for effective operation. The air drives a large area piston which in turn drives a small area piston fluid or coating pump. Air at 100 psig on a 27 sq. in. piston pumps fluid at 2700 psig with a pump fitted with 1 sq. in. fluid piston.

Pumps with larger area ratios between the air piston and the fluid pump move the coating at higher pressure. Conversely, the lower ratio pumps put lower pressure on the coating. For most coatings a minimum of 1700 to 1800 psig fluid pressure provides atomization. Mastics and other filled and viscous coatings need a minimum of 3000 psig. The larger size tips require more fluid at the minimum pressure. With any given tip higher minimum pressure allows more coating through per unit time. However, each tip works best with a given coating within a few hundred pounds pressure. Thus, for more paint per unit time one uses a larger tip.

The airless method produces twice the production rate of air atomization methods. There is much less overspray and bounce back in corners for a better job with less coating. There are no extra lines for air atomization nor are there problems associated with wet, oily atomization nor are there problems associated with wet, oily atomization air. About 1/10 the power is required. Thus, airless spraying adds up to a faster, better and more economical operation.

There are certain limitations with airless

since it is not as versatile as conventional equipment. It is not useful for hammer finishes or multicolor finishes and spray patterns must be adjusted by changing tips.

Tip clogging can be a problem. But "Reversa-Clean" tips and clean paint help to avoid clogging problems. Although safety features are on newer airless equipment, the high pressure coating process is always a threat to safety. At short range, paint from the gun under line spraying pressure, with and without the tip attached, can penetrate the human skin and pass through fatty areas.

Spraying Operation

Handle the airless gun the same way as the conventional gun. Trigger each pass and traverse the gun at equal distance from the work for the full pass. Overlap about 50 percent but make fewer passes. The big difference is the need to move faster, put on more paint faster and to stand a little further from the work receiving the paint.

Protection of Property

The proper care and protection of the customer's property during painting should be of MAJOR concern to every painter. Too often the effect of an otherwise first-class paint job is destroyed by paint that has been carelessly spread on electrical fixtures, hinges, baseboards, windows or furniture. Although the workmanship is satisfactory in every other way, failure to observe rules of neatness and respect for another's property often causes a customer to be thoroughly dissatisfied.

Protection Needed for New Interiors

On new work, protection is usually required for cabinets, tiled areas, windows, plumbing fixtures, heaters, electrical fixtures and related items.

Protection Needed for Old Interiors

Vacant property requires protecting all areas that are not to be refinished. Suggestions for protecting these areas follow:
1. Floors should be covered with dropcloths.
2. All hardware should be removed and placed in a container, to prevent loss of screws and small parts.

3. Light fixtures should be lowered and adequately covered.
4. Light switch plates should be removed and all screws replaced in receptacles.
5. Switch toggles and push buttons should be covered with masking tape or with liquid or paste masking.

Property that is occupied presents a more difficult problem than vacant property, since removal and storage of the furniture in the rooms to be painted must be considered. Removal and storage of furniture must be carefully and skillfully done so the furniture and the new finish in the room will not be damaged. After the furniture is removed, the procedure is as follows:
1. The floors should be adequately covered.
2. Hardware on work requiring more than one coat of paint should be removed. For one-coat jobs, the hardware is usually protected in some manner from paint splashes.
3. Switch plates should be removed and screws replaced in receptacles.
4. Switches should be covered with masking tape.
5. Light fixtures should be lowered and covered.

Any furniture that must be left in the room should be covered with CLEAN dropcloths. The importance of having plenty of clean dropcloths available cannot be overemphasized.

When the work is finished, the painter should remove the dropcloths carefully to prevent them from damaging furniture and newly painted areas. Old or soiled dropcloths should be used only for exterior or extremely dirty work. In using dropcloths, the painter should handle them carefully so they will not become torn. Dropcloths should be carefully dried before being stored.

Protection Needed for Exterior Work

When painting the exterior of a house, care should be taken not to splash paint on sidewalks, shrubbery and lawn. Shrubbery should be carefully protected with dropcloths. The careful placement of ladders and other equipment will help avoid unnecessary damage to flowers and shrubs.

Types of Dropcloths

Types of dropcloths which are available include those made from heavy cotton cloth or canvas, solvent-resistant plastic, and waterproofed heavy paper. Painters' dropcloths are available in sizes from 6 ft. by 9 ft. to 14 ft. by 16 ft.

Masking Tapes, Papers

Property may be protected when painting, particularly when using a spray gun, by using masking paper with pressure-sensitive adhesive backing that resists penetration of lacquer and enamel oversprays; pressure-sensitive creped masking tape, masking paste and liquid masking. The masking paste and liquid masking are applied like paint. Rubbing the coating lightly after the painting job is completed causes the rubber-like substance to peel off easily.

Paint Troubles -- Causes and Cures

This section will discuss problems frequently encountered by painters and suggest ways to avoid and cure them.

Alligatoring and Checking

Checking and alligatoring (an aggravated form of checking) are usually due to the application of relatively hard finishing coats over soft priming coats. Such conditions may be caused when the priming or other undercoats are more oily than the finish coats, when insufficient time has been allowed for the undercoats to dry properly, or when the finishing coat lacks elasticity.

Under the influence of changes in temperature, a paint film expands and contracts. If the topcoat is not sufficiently elastic it will crack.

Alligatoring and checking can usually be prevented by making the paint coats, from prime to finish, progressively more flexible and by carefully following manufacturer's directions for thinning. Be sure to allow sufficient time for drying between coats. See Fig. 7-23.

Cracking and Scaling

Cracking and scaling (one follows the other), Fig. 7-24, are generally due to paint which lacks elasticity and becomes hard and brittle, instead of expanding and contracting with the wood.

This trouble occurs most frequently with thick films of paint. The thicker a paint film is, the stronger it is, and the less able to conform to the changes that take place in the shape of the wood during periods of stress.

Fig. 7-23. Checking and alligatoring of painted surfaces is usually caused by application of hard finish coats over soft priming coats.

The best solution for cracking and scaling is to use a high quality paint which will retain its elasticity. It is, of course, important to have the surface properly prepared before applying the new paint. Cracking also occurs on masonry and other porous and often moist materials by applying paint that cannot "breathe."

Excessive Chalking

Paint gloss is due to oil in the surface coat-

Fig. 7-24. Cracking and scaling are caused by using paint which lacks elasticity and does not expand and contract with the wood.

ing. Light, especially ultraviolet light, destroys the oil and leaves loosely bound particles of pigment on the surface. In slight amounts the wearing away or "chalking" is desirable for it helps to keep the paint clean. Heavy chalking that rapidly washes away to leave an unprotected surface is not desirable.

The cause of excessive chalking is usually poor quality paint. Before a heavily chalked surface is repainted, the chalk should be removed by scrubbing or by using a wire brush.

Gas Discolorations

Freshly applied white and light-tinted paints containing lead compounds are sometimes darkened by hydrogen sulphide gas generated from sewage decomposition, industrial plants and other sources. The hydrogen sulphide acts on the lead to produce gray or black lead sulphide, sometimes providing a metallic lustre resembling graphite.

After paint has aged for a few months and has become hard, hydrogen sulphide gas has less darkening action. Even where the paint has darkened, the normal color may be restored by oxidation if the gas is removed.

Where it is desirable to remove the discoloration at once, a very dilute solution of acetic or muriatic acid sponged on the surface will rapidly remove the deposit. The surface should then be flushed with water to remove all traces of the chemicals.

Metal Stains

The staining of paint to a brownish or yellowish color under copper screens, gutters, hinges, and lamps is not uncommon. To prevent this staining of paint, the metal surfaces should be coated. If the owner wants to retain the characteristic color of the metal, clear lacquer or spar varnish should be used. On iron, a rust preventive primer should be used. This may be followed by regular house paint.

Mildew

Mildew is a form of plant life. See Fig. 7-25. The commonest species are black, but some are red, green, and other colors. Mildew feeds on organic matter, like sugar, starch, casein and drying oils. It grows best in warm and humid areas. We find it on the shady sides of buildings, and on the sunny sides if trees or

shrubs protect them from the sun. It is also found on interior walls, especially basement walls, in barns and many other places.

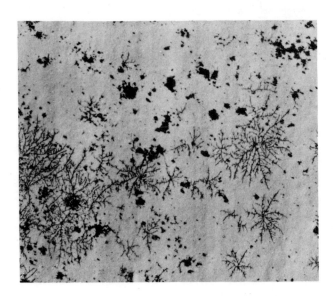

Fig. 7-25. Mildew, which is a form of plant life, feeds on organic matter such as drying oils and casein.

Mildew grows on soft paints more readily than on hard ones - - for example, more readily on exterior house paint than on enamel. It grows very readily on exterior wood where linseed oil has been rubbed in for a natural finish.

Mildew is objectionable because it usually penetrates the coat of paint and resists efforts to wash it off.

Before repainting a mildewed surface, be sure to get rid of the mildew. Dry wiping and scraping are usually not effective. Wash with a mild alkali such as washing soda, trisodium phosphate, or sodium metasilicate. Paint and grocery stores sell these cleaners under these names or under a variety of trade names such as "Oakite" and "Spic and Span." Use about two ounces (six heaping tablespoonfuls) per gallon of water, unless directions on the package state otherwise. Sometimes an abrasive cleaner like "Ajax" or "Comet" is better. These cleaners may remove some of the paint, but this is necessary if mildew has penetrated into the paint. Rinse thoroughly with clean water and allow the surface to dry thoroughly before painting it.

If mildew still remains, treat with a sterilizing solution, such as "Clorox" or "Lysol." Apply with a sponge or brush. Wear rubber gloves. Rinse with clear water and allow to dry.

After the surface has been properly prepared for a new coat of paint, refinish with a paint or varnish to which the manufacturer has added a mildewcide. Or one may add a prepared mildewcide to ordinary paint or varnish. Most mildewcides are poisonous and should be handled with extreme care.

Suction Spotting

On some paint jobs spotting caused by oil absorption by spots or porous areas of the surface will be noticed. When moistened with oil, the original appearance of the paint is restored.

The newly painted areas lack sufficient binder to resist weathering action and they will chalk and show a faded appearance quicker than the other areas. This type of defect is usually noticed in two-coat work over improperly prepared surfaces.

Properly applied dense primers with a sufficient number of paint coats will prevent spotting trouble.

Brown Staining

Discoloration and staining on paint applied to redwood and red cedar siding is generally caused by the presence of large quantities of coloring matter in these woods. Leaching of these woods over long periods of time may make them almost white, thus indicating the high percentage of water soluble staining matter present. The stain is not of a resinous nature, and its effect upon paint should not be confused with staining caused by resins.

The staining matter in redwood and red cedar, if painted when the woods are moisture saturated, may be drawn to the surface by the sun. It then runs down the siding to dry up in blotches that resemble tobacco juice.

On existing surfaces painted white or in light tints that have discolored, removal of the spots may often be accomplished by sponging the surface with a 50 percent solution of alcohol. When the brown stain has aged and oxidized so that the treatment is no longer satisfactory, a repainting job may be necessary. If by such time the plaster in the house is thoroughly dry, there should be no further trouble of this kind.

Blistering and Peeling

The most common form of paint failure un-

der abnormal conditions of exposure is blistering and peeling, Fig. 7-26. Blistering always precedes the peeling of the paint. From their shape it is obvious that blisters are due to water pressure beneath the coating forcing it away from the surface. When examined, the blisters are sometimes found to be filled with water; sometimes they are hollow. If the wood is of a kind that contains colored substances soluble in water, the water in paint blisters is frequently colored.

Fig. 7-26. Blistering and peeling, which is the most common form of paint failure under abnormal conditions, is caused by excessive moisture in the wood.

As the abnormal condition gives way to a normal condition and the wood dries, the blisters often shrink back into place so completely the coating may seem as sound as ever. The appearance, however, is deceiving, because after a few months exposure the paint will probably be subject to scaling.

In scaling, the pieces of paint coating that become detached may include the entire thickness of the coating so the wood beneath is left quite bare. Or the separation may take place between coats of paint. In general, intercoat scaling is most likely to be encountered on repainted surfaces, the newer coats scaling from the older ones. Scaling is occasionally seen on surfaces painted for the first time, especially if the first coat of paint differs markedly in composition from the others, or if the first coat was permitted to dry for a considerable length of time, before applying the others.

Coatings blister most easily soon after they have been applied and hardened.

The only practical way to prevent exterior paint from blistering and peeling is to control the moisture which causes the trouble.

SOURCES OF EXCESSIVE MOISTURE: There are three principal sources of moisture that can affect paint - - exterior leaks, vapor from the ground, and vapor-laden air within the house.

EXTERIOR CONSTRUCTION: Moisture in walls and attics is often caused by actual leaks. These leaks can be prevented by attention to certain important details, such as flashing, gutter replacement, and eave protection as required to provide weatherproof construction of roofs, eaves and outside walls. Flashing should extend under dormer window frames and out over shingles to prevent water backup. Chimney flashing should be secured in mortar joints and overlapped to divert water to top surfaces of shingles. Flashing over doors and regular windows should extend under the siding and out over the top edges of the window and door frames.

Gutters should be placed so the lip is even with the extended shingle line, Fig. 7-27. Where ice is likely to form, gutters should be spaced 3/4 in. away from the house by means of blocks at 16 to 24 in. intervals. Water sometimes

Fig. 7-28. Water sometimes freezes solid in gutters, causing ice dams. As it thaws it may back up underneath the shingles and cause damage to walls and interiors. This may be prevented by laying a course of heavy asphalt saturated felt over the eaves and well past the inside wall line.

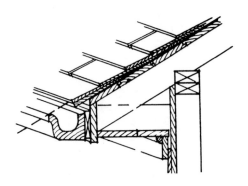

Fig. 7-27. To prevent water damage, gutters should be placed so the lips are even with the extended shingle line.

freezes solid in gutters, causing ice dams. The water may then back up underneath the shingles, and enter walls and interiors. This may be prevented by laying a course of heavy asphalt saturated felt over the eaves and well up past the inside wall line, Fig. 7-28. Electrical heating wires in gutters, downspouts and on the eaves are now used to melt ice and snow.

In fitting wood siding, care should be taken to obtain a good fit at corners and where pieces of siding join each other. Sheathing paper should be water resistant but NOT a vapor barrier, for it must allow moisture vapor to pass through. Wood siding should be at least 6 in. from the ground. Siding should be thoroughly dry when installed and free from dampness or moisture

condensation when painted. Before application, it is recommended that both sides be given a prime coat of paint thinned in accordance with the manufacturer's instructions. To prevent later cupping or splitting, nails should be located above the lap of bevel or bungalow siding, Fig. 7-29. Rust-resisting nails should be used.

ENTRY OF MOISTURE THROUGH CONDENSATION: All air contains moisture in varying degrees. The warmer the air the more moisture it will hold. When warm, moist air inside a house comes in contact with the outer part of the

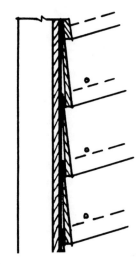

Fig. 7-29. To prevent splitting and cupping, nails should be located in siding just above the lap.

wall, Fig. 7-30, some of the moisture condenses into water. This condensation is most prevalent in today's tightly-built, insulated houses.

When air contains as much water vapor as it can hold at a specific temperature, it is said to be saturated and to have a relative humidity of 100 percent. The temperature is known as the dew point temperature of the air. When the air is cooled more, by coming in contact with a cold surface, such as the exterior wall of a house, condensation will occur, and minute beads of moisture will form on the colder surface.

To prevent excess accumulation of moisture, preventive steps should be taken.

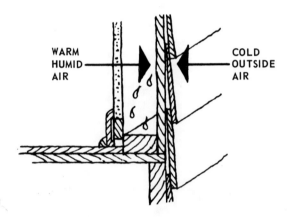

Fig. 7-30. When warm, moist air inside a house comes in contact with the cold, outer part of the wall, some of the moisture condenses into water.

INTERIOR CONSTRUCTION: Condensation of moisture in exterior walls and ceilings varies with locality and type of construction. It is always recommended that vapor barriers be used when insulation is used, and in localities where winter temperatures reach the freezing point or below.

A vapor barrier is a material or combination of materials - - insulation with a vapor barrier on the back, paper backed with metal foil, asphalt-impregnated paper, etc. which stops the passage of air-borne moisture into walls, floors and ceilings. There are different types of barriers but the principle is the same in each; they simply act as a "vapor-proof wrapper" for the home. Vapor barriers are applied on the room side of the studding.

Vapor barriers in ceilings protect against moist attics. The vapor barrier should pass under ceiling joists. Where the attic is occupied, the vapor barrier should enclose the entire room area. Vapor barriers may be placed between the subfloor and finish floor to prevent vapor from coming up from underneath the house. The floor vapor barrier should be overlapped with the wall barrier where the two meet. The vapor barrier around all openings, electrical outlet boxes, heating ducts, etc. should be carefully sealed off, otherwise it loses its effectiveness.

If wood or metal lath and plaster are used, the barrier should be applied slightly loose so the plaster can push the barrier back to form a key.

A vapor barrier may be provided on plywood used in building interior walls, by back-priming the plywood with two coats of asphalt, or aluminum paint.

MOISTURE FROM UNDERNEATH HOUSE: Where there is no basement, the crawl space should have at least 18 in. clearance between the ground and bottoms of joists. All crawl spaces should be well ventilated. Good drainage, so water may not accumulate, is highly essential. Screened vents should be placed as high as possible in the foundation, Fig. 7-31, and located to provide cross ventilation. Total

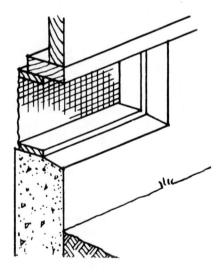

Fig. 7-31. Screened vents should be placed as high in the foundation as possible, and located to give cross ventilation.

area of ventilation openings should be about 2 sq. ft. per 25 ft. of building circumference. The vents should be left open at all times, including winter, unless the openings will make possible the accumulation of drifted snow in the crawl space.

Surfacing the crawl space with a layer of heavy coated, roll roofing lapped about 4 in.

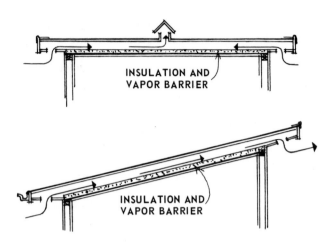

Fig. 7-32. Providing ventilation for flat and shed-type roofs. Vent area should be about one square inch per square foot of area under roof.

will help prevent moisture from getting into the space between the ground and the house.

VENTILATION: Proper ventilation of a house carries away moisture-laden air before the moisture condenses. Shown in Figs. 7-32 and 7-33 are suggested methods of ventilating attic spaces and roofs in different types of home construction.

How to Prevent Excessive Moisture in Existing Homes

Hot running water, steam from cooking and many modern appliances add moisture to home interiors. Any steps which can be taken to eliminate excessive humid air from home interiors will prevent moisture from entering walls and ceilings. Exhaust fans in kitchen, bathroom and laundry will carry much of the moisture outside. Opening windows for short period when steam is excessive will help accomplish the same result.

USING PAINT AS VAPOR BARRIER: In houses where no vapor barriers were used in construction, protection can be obtained by using water-repellent paints such as aluminum paint, applied to the inside of rooms.

ELIMINATE OUTSIDE LEAKS: Installation of proper flashing, repair of rusted or damaged flashing and caulking of cracks will help prevent moisture from entering home through leaks.

USING DEHUMIDIFIER: Dehumidifiers--both the mechanical and chemical types can be used to reduce the moisture content of the air in a

home. Two chemicals which are used are calcium chloride and silica gel. These draw moisture from the air and hold it in the chemical. Mechanical dehumidifiers consist of a refrigerated coil operating at a temperature slightly above freezing. A fan draws the air of the room over the coils where it is cooled. Since the cooled air cannot hold as much moisture as warm air, the excess is deposited on coils. From there it drips into a container.

In cases where humidity is a serious problem, dehumidifiers are frequently used both in summer and winter.

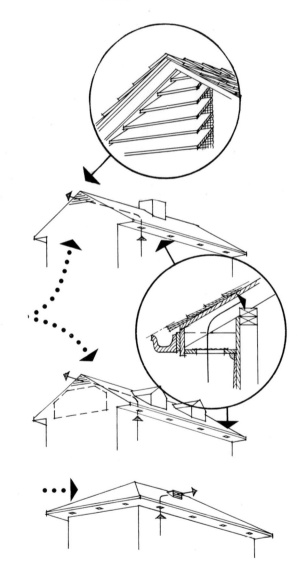

Fig. 7-33. Proper ventilation carries away moisture-laden air before the moisture condenses. Shown here are suggested method of ventilating attic spaces and roofs in different types of home construction. All openings should be covered, using screen of 1/8 in. or smaller mesh.

VENTILATE CRAWL SPACE AND ATTIC: Installing of air vents is helpful in controlling moisture in existing homes, where proper ventilation was not provided during construction.

PROTECT AGAINST GROUND MOISTURE: Proper drainage, elimination of possible water pools under the house and provision for crawl space, all help reduce the problem of ground moisture.

When You Paint

Remember that cheap paint is NEVER a bargain. Your best guide to good paint is the manufacturer's reputation.

Proper preparation of surface, use of quality materials and skilled application are the ingredients of a good paint job - - one which will provide beauty and protection to the home.

Replacing Broken Window Glass - - How to Use Putty

The setting of window panes is ordinarily done by glaziers, but the painter may at some time be required to replace a broken window pane. Consequently, he should have a knowledge of how to remove old glass, mix putty and install new glass. He should, of course, be thoroughly familiar with handling putty and how to replace loose putty in window sashes.

Removing Broken Glass

If the pane to be removed is shattered, Fig. 7-34, use heavy work gloves to pull the pieces out one by one. If the glass is only cracked, it is usually best to remove putty around the edges before attempting to remove the glass.

Every trace of the old putty must be removed, using a jackknife, putty knife, an old wood chisel, or screwdriver. If trouble is encountered the old putty can probably be loosened by running a hot soldering iron slowly along the putty ahead of a putty knife. A soldering iron that holds heat for a long time is best suited for the job. Glazier's points which are encountered, can be pulled out with a pair of pliers.

Size of New Glass is Important

The new glass should measure 1/8 in. less in both length and width than the space the glass is to fill. This reduction is made to provide for any irregularities that occur in the edges of the

glass when it is cut and for warped window sashes.

Wood that will be covered with new putty should be given a priming coat of paint (plain linseed oil is not recommended). The paint keeps the wood from soaking oil out of the putty, and the putty from crumbling so quickly. After the primer has dried you are ready to proceed with the installation of the glass.

Fig. 7-34. Removing shattered glass. A heavy glove should be worn and the pieces pulled out carefully.

Types of Putty

Putty may be mixed as needed, using whiting and linseed oil or paint. Start with a small quantity of dry whiting on a clean board. Add a small quantity of linseed oil or paint and mix with a putty knife. Make a stiff paste, and keep working the whiting and oil until the mass is of smooth consistency.

Putty which will match the paint in color can be made by mixing paint of the desired color with the putty. Use thick pigment from the bottom of the paint can and knead it in until the color is uniform. Colored putty may be made by using colors-in-oil.

Commercial putty which is made mostly of whiting and linseed oil is available in any desired quantity for the painter who does not want to mix his own putty.

Ordinary putty is not satisfactory for sealing glass in metal sash. For this purpose, glazing compounds are used. They differ from common putty in that they dry hard on the surface and remain plastic underneath. The surface to which glazing compounds are applied should be prime-painted before glazing.

Draw putty - - whiting and linseed oil putty thinned with varnish - - is used to some extent by painters in filling cracks and holes.

Inserting New Glass

The new glass should be bedded in a thin layer of putty that is put into the groove in the window sash. The glass is then pressed gently into the putty until all edges are enclosed. This should provide a watertight seal.

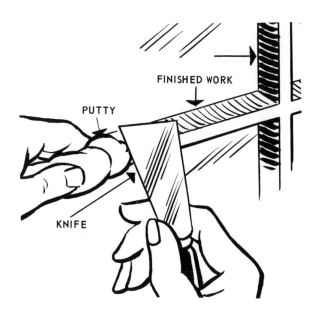

Fig. 7-35. *The putty should be formed with the hands by squeezing it under the knife while following along the muntin bar. The action of the knife to smooth and bevel is simultaneous. Heat the putty to soften it in cold weather.*

The glass is held in place with glazier's points, which are small triangular pieces of metal. Ordinarily, four glazier's points to each side should be used. The points are forced into the wood, using a chisel or screwdriver edge. After this is completed, the outside of the joint between the glass and the wood is ready for sealing with putty.

Sealing with Putty

The putty should be formed with the hands into pencil-size strips, Fig. 7-35. Starting at one corner, lay the strips end to end around the glass. The putty should then be smoothed to an even slope with the blade of a putty knife. Considerable practice is usually required before an apprentice can smooth putty properly and quickly.

Some of the putty used as the bed for the glass will be forced out on the inside of the sash. This should be removed before it dries. Putty on the outside should dry for at least two days before it is painted. Painting is important in preventing the putty from drying out completely.

Glazing Double Pane Glass

Insulating or double pane glass presents no difficult installation problems. However, it differs from glazing of single panes in several ways. See Fig. 7-36.

Removing Sash

In replacing a window pane the sash does not have to be removed from the frame, but the mechanic will find the job easier if he does remove it, and place it on a flat surface where it can be easily repaired.

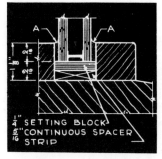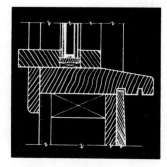

Fig. 7-36. *Typical job of installing double pane glass. Inside dimensions of frames are 1 1/8 in. larger than glass unit to be installed. Left. Glass rests on setting blocks and is cushioned by 1/8 in. bed of glazing compound (A) on each surface of glass. Right. How window stool can be used as backstop for glass unit.*

Unit 8

COLOR, COLOR HARMONY

Because of the great forward strides made in recent years by manufacturers of paint colors, it is now a simple matter to obtain paint in literally thousands of beautiful tints and tones.

If the desired color is not available ready-mixed, it can be concocted quickly. There are several color-mixing systems that make this possible. Fabulous color mixing machines, intermixing, and tube-coloring systems provide nearly all the necessary colors.

Color mixing devices are necessary because ready-mixed colors are not satisfactory for all purposes. One of the duties of the competent painter is to custom-make colors for each room, taking into consideration its exposure, size, use, and of course the all-important factor of customer taste.

It is therefore necessary to learn how to make color schemes, how to mix the colors in paint with accuracy to obtain built-in durability and surface beauty.

The first step toward this goal is to learn what color is, and some of the rules associated with color.

What is Color?

Color may be described as an impression or effect formed on a part of the eye called the retina by light or rays of visible radiant energy (that is, light) of certain wave lengths. The form of an object may be recognized because of the contrast between the color or colors of the object and the color of the background.

Heat or infrared rays, light rays, radio rays, television rays, X-rays and cosmic rays are all forms of radiant energy. These electromagnetic energy rays are identical except for the wave length -- the distance between adjacent wave crests and frequency of pulsation.

The human eye receives and responds only to radiant waves known as light waves, or, the

wave band just below infrared, and generally designated in wave lengths of 400 to 700 millimicrons. One millimicron is one billionth of a meter, and a meter equals 39.37 inches.

The light of sun in normal daylight is white and is composed of a visible spectrum of colors; red, orange, yellow, green, blue, indigo and violet, Fig. 8-1. Violet is a purplish-blue to blue.

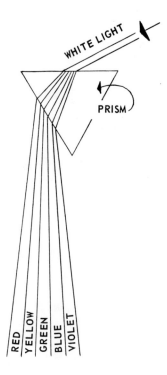

Fig. 8-1. The light of sun in normal daylight is white, and is composed of a visible spectrum of colors--red, yellow, green, blue and violet.

Purple and magenta do not exist in the spectrum but are sensations of the observer when receiving red and blue waves simultaneously.

Light is bent or changes direction when it is passed from one medium to another, as from air to water, or from air to glass. Violet, the shorter wave length is bent the least; red, is bent the most.

Surfaces

Many materials have the ability to absorb only a part of white light and reflect the balance. A red paint is red because it selectively absorbs blue and green rays. Green paint generally absorbs in the violet and red ends of the spectrum. The color not absorbed is reflected to the observer.

Besides being selectively absorbent to regions of the spectrum, paints and varnishes are generally translucent. They are neither completely transparent nor totally opaque. Even if the surface below the film cannot be seen, some of the light penetrates a part of the film. Not only do the pigments absorb some light but the vehicle does also. Linseed oil paints turn yellow when exposed to light and the white pigment is tinted yellowish by the vehicle.

Light is reflected from glossy surfaces just as it is reflected from a mirror. This is called spectral reflection. The light is reflected away from the surface at an angle exactly equal to a perpendicular as the angle of approaching light, Fig. 8-2. When the equal angles are small the percentage of reflection is small, but when the equal angles are large as indicated by the dotted lines in Fig. 8-2, the percentage of reflection is large. This interesting phenomenon explains why gloss paints have more purity and brilliance, especially noticeable in deep colors, when seen with the light nearly perpendicular to the surface.

Mat surfaces, on the other hand, are diffusers of light and are seen with a constant "overlay" of scattered reflection of the light source. This source, considered as normal daylight is white; therefore the mat color is never seen as a pure color but always as a desaturated color lacking the brilliance and depth of gloss paints.

The balance of light not reflected at the surface is absorbed in part by the vehicle, in part by pigment particles or by the surface below, if this penetration is possible. The part not absorbed at these points is reflected back to the surface. And each time the light ray is passed from one medium to another it is refracted or bent in a new direction. In the study of color in opaque paints and its manifold complexities, it becomes increasingly apparent that only a thorough study will suffice as a background for the solution of some of the color problems encountered.

Transparent paints like glazes or water colors are merely filters that subtract light as it is reflected from the background (as a glaze over white enamel or water color on white paper).

Unless absorbed, pigments reflect the light they receive. Gloss paints, with their spectral reflection are not affected as much by the color of the surrounding light as mat surfaces. A red object or light in a normally lit room will create a pink glow on adjacent mat surfaces.

If the light received at the surface is colored, one of several things can happen. The colored light may be completely absorbed and the surface will appear black. This happens if red light is absorbed by a blue-green paint. Or the light may match the reflectance of the surface and it will appear normal or more pure in color because no grayness due to red can show. Still another example is a yellow light which will allow the yellow and green of the blue-green to show but not the blue so that a blue-green object will appear yellow green. There are, of

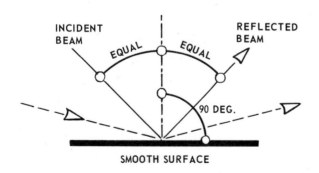

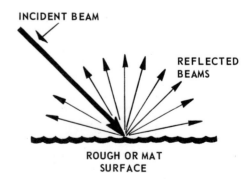

Fig. 8-2. Spectral reflection.

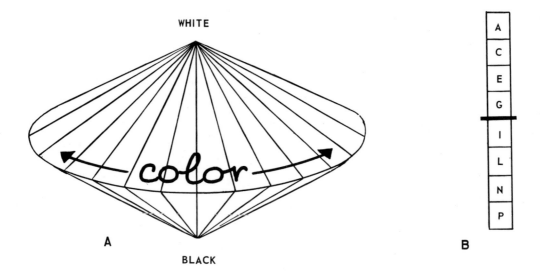

WHITE

color

A

BLACK

B

Fig. 8-3. A—Double-cone solid used in presenting Ostwald concept of color organization and classification. B—Scale used by Ostwald to identify steps of color between A (white) and P (black).

course, many possible examples to demonstrate this phenomenon.

Another disturbing factor to painters and interior decorators is that paints, dyes, and light sources may look alike to the eye but will not be composed of like wave lengths and will, therefore, not match when the conditions are changed. A gray wallpaper made of pure yellow, red, and blue, with white can be matched, it can be assumed, with lampblack and white in daylight. These grays will not look alike at night when the incandescent lights are turned on. Incandescents are strong in red and yellow and are weak in blues and greens. Therefore the gray made of pure colors will have the emphasis of reflection shifted to the yellow and red side. It will become warmer than the lampblack gray and may even be artistically unpleasant.

It is true that the eye cannot distinguish the components of a color. There are innumerable ways to make gray. An incandescent lamp and a fluorescent lamp may appear to the eye to match but their energy output is very unlike.

In order to understand this better, a discussion of the nomenclature and systematic arrangement of color may be helpful.

Color Systems

Many systems have been devised to identify, analyze and measure the innumerable colors perceived by the human eye. Creators of two major generally recognized color systems were Wilhelm Ostwald (1853-1932) and Albert H. Munsell (1858-1918).

Ostwald System

The Ostwald color system sets forth the principle that every color seen by the eye is composed of varying proportions of hue or color, of white and of black, and that all colors are mixtures of these essentials. In the Ostwald system, it is possible by using a number and two letters to give a description of any color covered by this color system.

Ostwald presented his concept of color organization and classification by using a double-cone solid, Fig. 8-3, Detail A. The circumference of the double cone is made up of twenty-four hues, designated by numbers 1 to 24, as in Fig. 8-4. By judiciously spacing the colors of the spectrum plus the purples in a circle in such a way that any opposite two colors (across the center) will be complementary and so that each color will seem to be equally spaced from each other, a usable color wheel may be formed.

Now consider this wheel as a disk with a pole through the center. At the top of the stick is white and at the bottom black. All the colors in between black and white are grays of equal steps. Ostwald identified the steps in this gray scale by using the letters A, C, E, G, I, L, N, P, Fig. 8-3, Detail B. The letter "A" indicates white, the letter "P" black, and the other letters steps in between.

To see how this works, consider an example, such as 2-PA. From Fig. 8-4, we find that the 2 indicates the color is yellow. The first letter "P" indicates there is no white in the mixture and the second letter "A" indicates there is no black. Thus the color indicated by 2-PA would be a relatively pure yellow.

This is the basic skeleton of a "color solid." A color solid is much more useful than a mere wheel and is absolutely necessary to complete arrangement of all the colors.

By mixing one color, yellow for example, on the edge of the wheel with white at the top a series of tints of yellow are obtained. All of the colors can be so mixed and gradually a cone is formed over the color wheel, pointed end up, of all the light colors. By mixing all the colors on the edge of the wheel with black, a dark cone is formed point side down with black at the bottom.

A mixture of any of the tints on the sloping side of the cone with a gray at the core and on the same level will produce a series of grayed tints. Likewise, a mixture of any of the shades (black and color) on the sloping underside with a corresponding gray at the core on the same level will produce a series of grayed shades. This is the general basis for the Ostwald system of color.

Munsell System of Color Notation

The Munsell System is essentially a scientific concept for describing and analyzing color in terms of three attributes, identified in this system as Hue, Value and Chroma. The method of color notation developed by A. H. Munsell, as the principal feature of this system, arranges the three attributes of color into orderly scales of equal visual steps, so that the attributes become dimensions by which color may be analyzed and described accurately under standard conditions of illumination.

Hue

Chromatic colors in the Munsell System of Color Notation are divided into five principal classes which are given the Hue names of red, yellow, green, blue, and purple. A further division yields the five intermediate Hue names of yellow-red, green-yellow, blue-green, purple-blue, and red-purple, these being combinations of the five principal Hues. See color insert, Fig. 8-5 (G-5). The Hue notation of any color indicates its relation to the five principal and intermediate Hues or any of their subdivisions. Capitalized initials such as "R" for red, or "YR" for

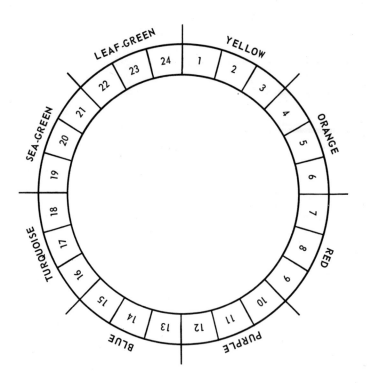

Fig. 8-4. Spacing of colors in Ostwald double-cone solid.

MUNSELL COLOR CHART

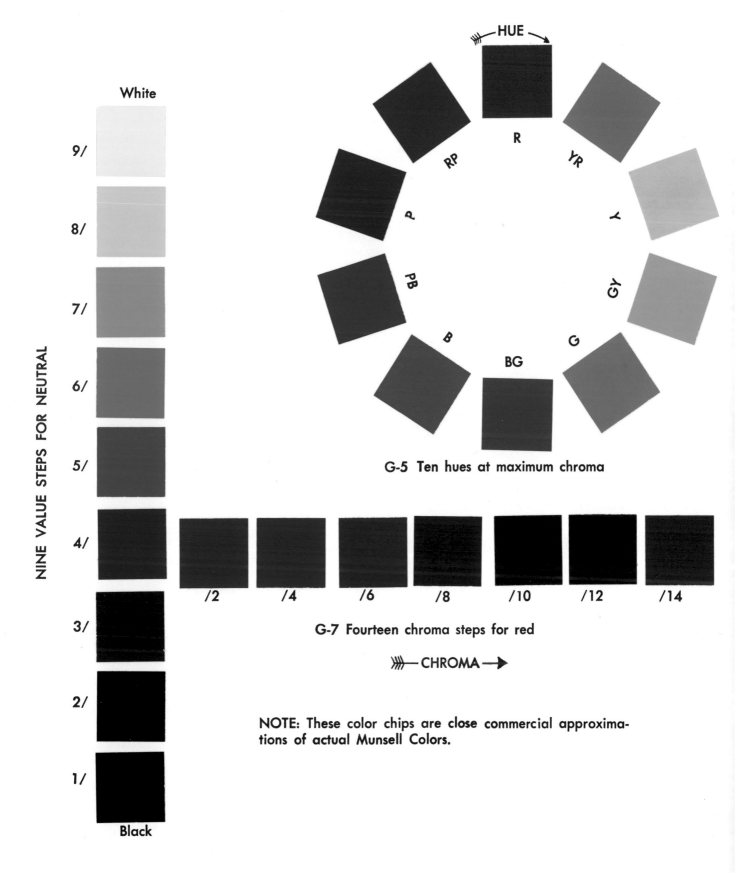

White

9/

8/

7/

6/

5/

4/

3/

2/

1/

Black

NINE VALUE STEPS FOR NEUTRAL

HUE

R

RP

YR

P

Y

PB

GY

B

G

BG

G-5 Ten hues at maximum chroma

/2   /4   /6   /8   /10   /12   /14

G-7 Fourteen chroma steps for red

⟫⟫— CHROMA →

NOTE: These color chips are close commercial approxima-
tions of actual Munsell Colors.

G-6 Value Scale

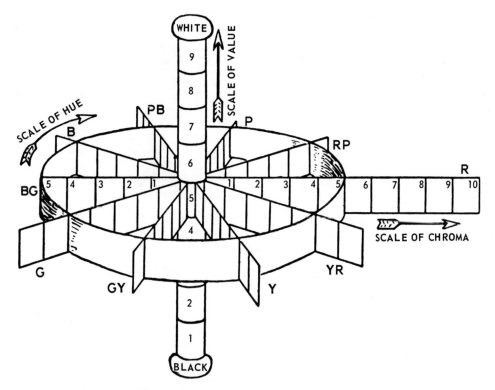

Fig. 8-8. *HUE, VALUE, and CHROMA in their relation to one another. The circular band represents the HUES in their proper sequences. The upright center axis is the scale of VALUE. The paths pointing outward from the center show the steps of CHROMA, which increase in strength as indicated by the numerals.*

yellow-red, are used as symbols for the Hue names. When finer subdivisions are needed, the ten Hue names or symbols may again be combined to produce such combinations as red-yellow-red, which is symbolized "R-YR." For even finer divisions, the Hues may be divided into ten steps each (1R to 10R and 1YR to 10YR), thus increasing the Hue notation to 100.

Value

The Value notation indicates the degrees of lightness or darkness of a color in relation to a neutral gray scale which extends from a theoretically pure black symbolized as 0/ to a 5/. Lighter colors are indicated by numbers ranging above five, while darker ones are indicated by numbers, below five. Refer to the color insert, Fig. 8-6 (G-6).

Chroma

The Chroma notation of a color indicates the strength (saturation) or degree of departure of a particular Hue from a neutral gray of the same value. The scales of Chroma extend from /0 for a neutral gray out to /10, /12, /14, or farther, depending upon the strength or saturation of the individual color. A color classified popularly as "vermilion" might have a Chroma as strong as /12, while another color of the same Hue and Value classified popularly as "rose" might have a Chroma as weak as /4. See Fig. 8-7 (G-7) on the insert.

The complete Munsell notation for any chromatic color is written Hue Value/Chroma, or symbolically H V/C. A particular sample of vermilion might then have a Munsell notation of 5R 5/12, while a particular sample of rose might have a notation of 5R 5/4.

Whenever a finer division is needed for any of the three attributes, decimals may be used, such as 2.5R 4.5/2.4.

The notation for a neutral gray is written N V/. A very dark neutral (black) would be written N 1/0, and N 9/0 would be the notation for a very light neutral (white). For grays of slight chromaticity, the notation is written N V/(H,C), using only the symbols for the ten major Hues to indicate the Hue; thus a gray of a slightly yellowish appearance is written N 8/(Y 0.4).

Color Solid

The Munsell System of Color Notation can be thought of in terms of a color solid or color space in which the Value scale runs vertically from a theoretically pure black at the bottom to a theoretically pure white at the top, while the various Hues are located around it, describing an approximately cylindrical shape with the Neutral Value scale in its center. The Chroma scales radiate from the vertical Value scale in the center to the periphery of the color solid in equal visual steps, Fig. 8-8.

Because of the accurate notation of observed color made possible by the Munsell System, industry has an excellent tool for evaluating certain phenomena in terms of color.

Reflectance is an important consideration in both architecture and interior decoration, and a chart photometer which measures reflectance quickly and accurately for three standard illuminants has been developed using colors with Munsell notations.

The Munsell Book of Color

The Munsell Book of Color available from the Munsell Color Co., consists of charts of color chips representing various areas in the Munsell color solid. It provides an orderly arrangement of standard color papers which serve as guides for the measurement and notation of all colors and appears in several editions each of which possesses certain advantages peculiar to that edition. The charts appearing in the Munsell Books of Color may be used as instruments for the identification and specification of color, as well as useful for tools in teaching color relationships.

Harmony

Every hue has a complementary hue. The complement of a color is that color which the observer tends to see when color fatigue sets in. Thus, the observer sees a yellow object and gradually becomes unable to see yellow for the area and the shape of that object. By shifting the gaze to a white surface, an image of the object in the complementary blue-purple will appear. This experiment may be performed for any color. Under controlled experimental conditions, remarkable results can be secured.

When any two complementary colors are

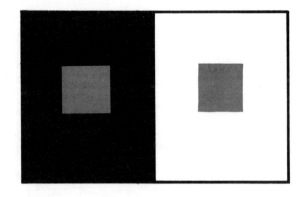

Fig. 8-9. Black surround makes a gray or middle value color seem lighter than some gray with light surround.

placed near each other they tend to brighten and accentuate each other because of this fatigue. This is called the "simultaneous color contrast" phenomena. Red and blue-green are complements. If each were grayed considerably and placed side-by-side on the same plane, color fatigue induced by the red would make it difficult to see the graying blue-green in the red, and sharpen the perception for the grayed blue-green by removing the apparent grayness of it which is due to a quantity of red. This same statement may be made in reverse for fatigue to the blue-green. The net result is that complements tend to seem more pure or higher in chroma than they really are when viewed separately. It is usually wise to gray them more than seems necessary before they are applied, in order to avoid "clashing" colors.

Simultaneous color contrast works in the three dimensions of color. The after image of black is white and vice versa. A black (or dark color) surround makes a gray (or middle value color) seem lighter than that same gray would seem in a light surround. See Figs. 8-9 and 8-10.

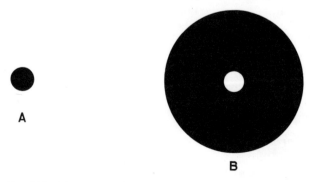

Fig. 8-10. After images. Stare at A for 45 seconds, then look at a blank white paper for a few seconds for after image. Repeat for B.

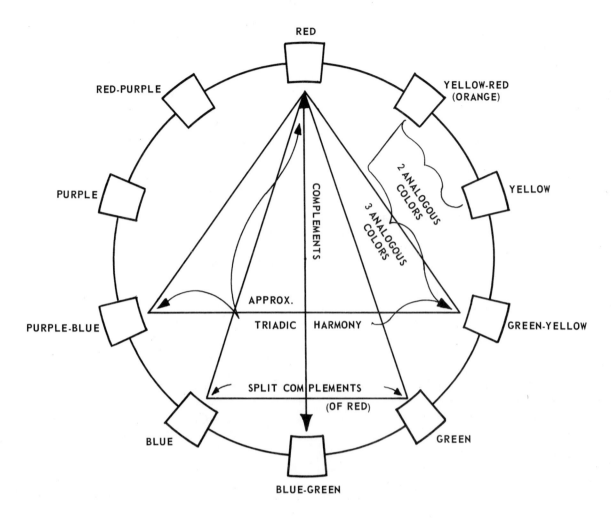

Fig. 8-11. Color harmony systems for HUE only.

Obtaining Color Harmony

Striking one key of a piano does not create harmony; neither does the use of a single color. But, when you combine two or more according to certain rules - - you have either harmony of sound or harmony of color.

There are a number of color wheel patterns or mechanical ways to figure out harmonious color combinations by using the color wheel, Fig. 8-11. Of these, monochromatic is one of the simplest.

Monochromatic Harmony

Monochromatic harmony is formed by using shades and tints of a single color.

Analogous or Related Harmony

In analogous or related harmony a series of neighboring colors on the color wheel are related by containing one color in common.

True Complement Color Harmony

Two colors directly across the wheel from each other are true complements. Red and green are complements or complementary colors; so are red and blue-green, orange and blue, etc. on around the color wheel. See Fig. 8-11.

Split Complementary Harmony

Split complementary harmony is an expansion of the single complement and involves three colors. This is indicated on the color wheel by splitting one end of a line drawn across the color wheel to get a true complement.

Let us set one arrow of our color wheel at blue and point the other to orange; then split the second arrow so the halves divide. One half

151

points to the color next to orange on the left (red-orange) and the other half points to yellow-orange on the right.

Triadic Harmony

To fix clearly in your mind what triadic harmony is, assume that your color wheel has three clock-like hands and that they are always pointed at three equidistant points. Such a device would show you, for example, that red, green-yellow and purple-blue make up a triad.

Which Color Harmony Pattern Should Be Used?

In painting and decorating, it rarely happens that you have a chance to plan a color scheme and then purchase the necessary components to develop it. Most people have such things as certain pieces of furniture, rugs, or drapes which must be used in the redecorated room. These might be called "deciding factors." The coloring of the deciding factors usually supplies the beginning point for determining a color scheme. This is where your knowledge of the color wheel comes into practical use.

Achieving Success

Every paint job and every object of any kind and any place in nature is constantly affected by the observers psychological reactions to the physical scene. And it is important to recognize the facts in order to achieve success in color harmony. It is generally safer to make color a little too gray than too bright because the low chroma colors are easier to live with over a period of time.

However, to follow the safe path seldom leads to some of the outstanding decorative successes due to bold and creative handling of color (for which the rules are more apparent after it is done). A knowledge of color does help in analyzing why we like brown and blue. Brown is a form of low chroma, low value orange, and blue is the complement of orange. Some blue and brown combinations are better than others. Why? Perhaps if the blue is too green, or too dark it will be an off complement or lack contrast. The brown could be too red or too yellow or not dark enough, or too pure. Pale blue-green and maroon is another example of a successful color scheme relying on a strong change in all three-color dimensions. Pale pink also looks well with maroon. This is a harmony of value

contrast in the same color; both are red.

Yellow, yellow-orange and orange are three related colors. Nearly all natural woods are yellow-orange. A scheme of natural wood against a light raw umber gray wall (yellow, low in chroma) all with a terra cotta brown carpet (orange) would have a chance of success. Closely related colors or analogous harmonies can be pleasantly "sparked" with a small touch of complementary color. Blue upholstery in small amounts or a blue lamp base would give life to the yellow-orange scheme. The blue must be carefully chosen as the complement of the average color. If the most used color was lemon or greenish-type yellow, the blue would be purplish, but if the major emphasis were on the warm orange tones, the complement should be blue without greenish or purplish cast.

The above example is actually "split complementary." If the "split" is wide enough, the harmony is called "triadic."

The observer's eye and brain acts as a null instrument that reads differences but not quantities. The observer can make fantastic adjustments for brightness differences. He will see clearly into a shadow surrounded by strong light as no camera can. He will compensate for darkness and recognize a piece of white paper on a dark street even though that paper, in the dark, is reflecting less light than a normally dark gray.

The observer also sees ADDITIVELY. The total components of a color are averaged and are seen as one color when the eye cannot resolve the separate parts. A yellow and purple-blue speckled surface will appear as gray when the spots cannot be optically resolved as separate units. These colors are complements and complements ADD to gray. The same blue and yellow MIXED together as paints would yield a green. But it must be remembered that this phenomena is controlled by a different set of rules, by the subtraction theory governing the subtractive action of filters on light. Many men of the trade confuse these facts and try to base a whole color harmony theory and set of rules on some arbitrary set of three primaries that are actually only suited to help to explain how paint mixes to subtract light. This is obviously a fallacy.

Colored lights add. All of man's "seeing" experiences are added. In fact, all the observer's interpretation of visual experience is additive and all judgments about harmony are based on the idea of the addition of light. Not only do small areas that cannot be seen as separate entities add, but large areas and "schemes" are added psychologically. People speak of rooms decorated in pure, high key colors as being "gay," "exciting," or "happy." They also speak of "rich" rooms or "somber" rooms. In all these areas many colors exist, some perhaps quite bright and pure, but the GENERAL air (or mentally made average) of these schemes is judged in terms of MOOD.

Some of the best scientists of this century have worked hard and successfully to achieve a knowledge of color. First the physical facts of light were defined, then the psychology of the observer. The solution to the problem of standardizing a way of speaking about, classifying and specifying color was to put the two subjects together and call them the psycho-physics of color. A new body of mathematical calculations was made based on this merger of ideas and put into a system called the I.C.I. (International Commission of Illumination). It has a "standard observer" and a standard "illuminant C." This is worth mentioning for the benefit of the student who wishes to do more research, and also as a proof of the need for a more advanced form of thought about color in the paint application field.

The average observer sees best in the range of a yellow-green, in normal daylight. When the light is dim this sensitivity peak shifts to the bluish-green area. There is a probable correlation between this fact and the fact that people in the United States use more green interior furnishings than any other color.

People also are able to see smaller differences in the low reflectance range than for the high range. A difference of 3 percent reflectance between two dark grays near black is equal (as judged by the standard observer) to a 20 percent difference at the white end of the spectrum.

Automobile painters often complain that "blacks" are the hardest to match for touchup jobs. It is easy to see that this is largely due to the observer's increased visual acuteness in the low reflectance areas.

Subtraction

To some extent, opaque paints act like transparent filters. Filters are predictable, but paints are only partly predictable depending on how much is known about the individual characteristics of the material. Filters do not add but each filter removes its "toll" of light depending

on its absorption range and thickness. A color pigment will act very similarly. Some graphic analogies of the action are shown in Fig. 8-12. The horizontal colored lines are to indicate a colored glass filter. The vertical lines are colored light in terms of five primaries: red, yellow, green, blue, and violet.

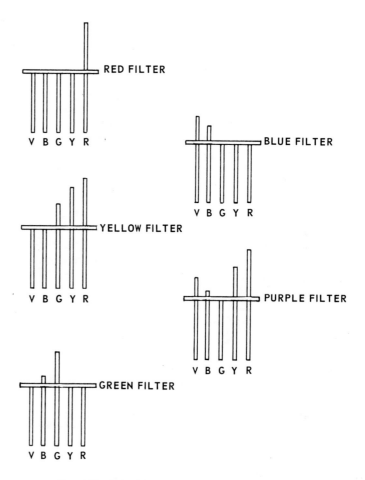

Fig. 8-12. Color filters remove their "tolls" of light.

A mixture of yellow and blue makes green, but the kind of green cannot be predicted by inspection alone. Either the colors must be mixed, or their absorption curves must be compared. Zinc yellow or chrome yellow lemon light mix with Prussian blue to form a fairly pure green; but chrome yellow medium or dark, make grayed greens.

When a color is weakened by the addition of white, it frequently changes in dominant wave length. This action is sometimes mild and sometimes marked.

Ultramarine blue is a dark purplish-blue, nearly black and quite grayed in masstone. When white is added it becomes lighter and more pure; its chroma goes up to a certain point where saturation reaches a maximum peak, after which the further addition of white reduces its chroma. It becomes lighter and grayer (because white is a neutral) as it approaches white. Furthermore, it exhibits a definite loss of purple and is, in the paler tints, nearly a true blue. This is due to an increase in absorption for the red and violet wave lengths.

Colors Shift Toward Green

Most colors seem to shift toward green. They do not become green, but merely move in that direction as they are weakened. The earth color yellows including raw and burnt umber and sienna, shift to yellow (greenward) as they are "let up" with white. Chrome greens defy this rule and become bluer, as does toluidine red and some of the red oxides. All the bright yellows turn so much greener when weakened with black or other dark graying agents that this phenomena becomes a problem to the painter. Lampblack and chrome yellow light makes a definite olive drab color. Copper phthalocyanine blue is nearly free of this effect when mixed with other pigments because it has a narrow reflection curve in the blue region.

The diagram, Fig. 8-13, shows approximate positions of the main useful tinting colors in the practical architectural painter's kit on a Munsell color wheel. Each color is noted by name and by Munsell color specification.

Since this chart has only two dimensions, the Value reading given must be referred to for reflection quality, the lower the value figure the darker the color. Each color shows a loss of chroma as it moves nearer the neutral center (N). The masstone of Prussian and monastral blue is black. Some white has been added to these pigments to produce value level three.

Four Pigments Usually Enough

It is seldom necessary to use more than a total of four pigments to match any color. One of these may be white or black or a base pigment like a standard ready-mixed color. It is white in over 90 percent of the cases in the paint shop. Two colors are needed to bracket the hue, and one is required to gray the color. So these four pigments might be, in order to match a color like terra cotta pink, white base plus burnt sienna, yellow ochre, and burnt um-

ber. Another formula for the same color could be toluidine red, chrome yellow medium, and lampblack. This last color would be more difficult to make and would be less permanent. It could also be made of any bright yellow, red, and blue; or yellow, red, and green and so on for a multitude of ways. The chart, Fig. 8-13, can help by showing the nearest hues to the one to be matched.

Whenever complements are mixed together, light reflection is quickly lost. Pink and green paint will most often combine to form a grayed purple (mauve) but the resulting color will not have the same value. It will be substantially darker than either component. If these same two colors were painted as small spots on a surface and viewed from sufficient distance to merge them into one color, the result would be an average of the two reflection percentages and would likely be a gray with a yellow cast instead of a darker mauve as in the case of mixing. So if it is impossible to match two colors in a wallpaper, mix them and arrive at a color to harmonize with the paper.

A little red will turn a dark blue-green to a nearly black gray with astonishing speed because they are subtractive complements and both are dark at the start. Surface grains of blue-green and red also add to gray. (The additive effect of exposed surface grains are always present in opaque paint.)

Color changes as it dries. The "wet" color usually darkens if it has tinting colors in it that are darker than the base color. This situation is generally true but may be reversed if titanium is used in small quantities to lighten the color of a coarse ground dark color.

The trade term for this darkening is "floating." Floating, however, occurs on the ceiling just as it does on the walls and floor, so the term is not quite accurate. It is a process of squeezing the lightweight, fine particles out of the mixture to the free surface. This happens more often in viscous paints like enamels and floor paints than it does in "short" paints like lead and oil exterior or interior stipple paint.

A rule of thumb for predicting the extent of floating is to remember that the dark, graying type tinting colors like lampblack and deep strong, but lightweight colors like Prussian blue have more tendency to darken the paint film than heavy chrome yellow.

After enamel darkens it dries without substantial further change. Mat paints darken and then lighten. The darkening action usually makes

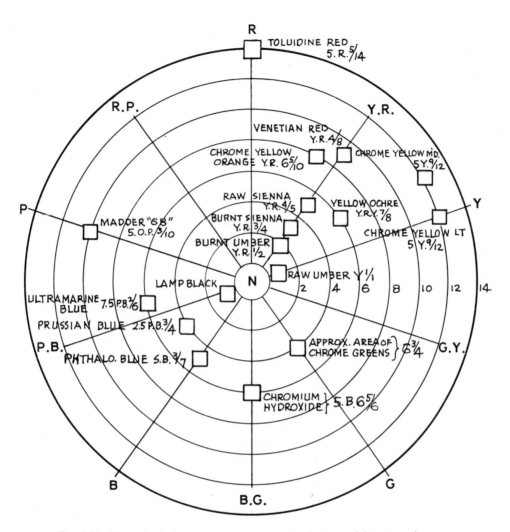

Fig. 8-13. Chart which shows approximate positions of main useful tinting colors in
painter's kit on Munsell color wheel.

them more gray also. When they lighten on drying and move toward neutral white there is a
further graying action. It is never possible to
mix flat paints to a maximum black or to a
maximum deep rich saturated color because of
this "bleaching action." The action is partly due
to the scattering of reflected rays and partly to
a lack of difference in the refractive indexes of
the pigment and the air to which it is exposed.
Some of the pigment in flat paint is not immersed in the binder. The drying away of the
thinners exposes it to air and this also creates
the rough diffusing surface. There are other
factors such as scattering of rays by diffraction
from particle size spacing and colloidal conditions, but the functions of surface diffusion and
loss of refractive index differences due to lack
of immersion in vehicle are the dominant fac-

tors. Another important fact to remember is
that as the color undergoes this double graying
or weakened saturating, it suffers a change in
dominant wave length or color and generally
shifts toward green. An exception to this is in
yellows leaning toward red. These become redder on drying by losing yellow. The comparatively new latex emulsion paints exhibit such a
marked tendency to lose yellow on drying that
strong measures must be taken to counteract
the loss. Wet vinyl emulsions must also be
much yellower than the dried color.

Preparing Special Colors

"Custom" or special colors may be produced
in two ways:

1. Intermixing colors of the same type, being

155

sure to use identical brand and type. Do not mix oil-base with water-thinned or rubber-base paints. Gloss will be reduced if gloss finish is mixed with flat or semi-gloss paint.

2. Tinting paint with concentrated colors (paste or liquid). In most cases in actual mixing, you will be working with colors-in-oil. These are pigments, finely ground in oil, so they can be conveniently used in tinting many different products. Colors-in-oil are used in tinting all kinds of opaque coatings except lacquers and water-thinned paints. These paints require special tinting materials. Color-in-oil is not used in large quantities in any paint because it upsets the formulation and reduces the quality.

Deep tones in flat wall paint are to be made with flat colors ground specially. Oil color makes gloss streaks when used in quanity in mat paints.

As a professional painter you should become acquainted with the names by which colors-in-oil are known and learn how to use them to obtain the desired effects. Naturally, you will use the modern color mixing and matching facilities of your paint dealer in most instances. Even so, it is important that you be familiar with the art of color mixing.

Information on color mixing which follows was furnished by National Paint, Varnish, Lacquer Association.

	Pigment Name	Color Family
REDS	Indian Red	Purple-red
	Rose Pink	Purple-red
	Crimson Lake	Purple-red
	English Vermilion	Orange-red
	American Scarlet Vermilion	Orange-red
	Venetian Red	Orange-red
	Tuscan Red	Orange-red
	Toluidine	Red
	Permanent Red	Orange-red
ORANGE	Burnt Sienna	Orange
	Burnt Umber	Orange
YELLOWS	Chrome Yellow, Dark (Chrome Orange)	Yellow-orange
	Chrome Yellow, Light (or Lemon Chrome Yellow)	Yellow
	Chrome Yellow, Medium	Orange-Yellow
	Golden Ochre	Yellow
	Yellow Ochre	Yellow Grayed
	Raw Umber	Yellow
GREENS	Chrome Green, Light	Green
	Chrome Green, Medium	Blue-green
	Chrome Green, Dark	Blue-green
	Chromium Oxide	Yellow-green
	Chromium Hydroxide	Blue-green
	Phthalocyanine	Green
BLUES	Prussian	Blue
	Ultramarine	Purple-blue
	Phthalocyanine	Blue
PURPLES	Madder Lake	Purple-red

Pigment names and color family names with which you should become familiar.

Color, Color Harmony

To aid you further, here is a table which provides the nucleus of a list which will be invaluable to you in your business. In addition to a general description of the hue listed is a suggested way of obtaining it by combining the necessary pigments. Experience and observation will, in the future, constantly enable you to add to your "color prescriptions."

Color Name	Description	Pigments to Use to Obtain It
Apple green	Moderate yellow-green	White for base. Add light chrome green and orange chrome yellow.
Apricot	Pale orange	Medium chrome yellow for base; Venetian red and carmine lake. If a light tint is wanted, lighten it with white.
Bottle green	Dark green	Lampblack and Prussian blue for base; lemon chrome yellow.
Browns and brown drabs-all shades	Dusky orange	Venetian red for base; add ochre and lampblack in various proportions according to shades of brown wanted. For the brown drabs, add white to reduce the above brown tints.
Cafe-au-lait	Light brown	Burnt umber for base; add yellow ochre and Venetian red and white.
Canary	Moderate yellow	Use lemon chrome yellow for base, lightened with white.
Chamois	Weak yellowish-orange	White for base; add ochre, medium chrome yellow to suit, redden it with a little burnt sienna.
Chartreuse	Light yellow-green	Lemon chrome yellow for base; add some medium chrome green.
Cinnamon	Weak orange	White for base; add burnt sienna, ochre, medium chrome yellow.
Crimson	Strong red	Toluidine red. If desired very rich, add some of the crimson lakes or glaze with them.
Colonial yellow	Moderate yellow	White for base; add medium chrome yellow, tinge with a trifle of orange chrome yellow.
Copper	Weak reddish-orange	Medium chrome yellow; tinged with burnt sienna.
Coral pink	Moderate yellowish-pink	Vermilion for base; white, medium chrome yellow.
Cream color and all the buffs	Weak yellowish-orange and moderate orange	White for base; add ochre to make the color desired. Gray with burnt umber for buffs.
Ecru	Weak yellowish-orange	White for base; add ochre, burnt sienna, lampblack.
Electric blue	Weak blue	Ultramarine blue for base; add white and raw sienna.

Color Name	Description	Pigments to Use to Obtain It
Emerald	Strong green	Very light chrome green or phthalocyanine green.
Fawn	Light brown	White for base; add medium chrome yellow, Venetian red, burnt umber.
Flesh color	Weak yellowish-orange	White for base; add medium chrome yellow, French ochre and Venetian red, or burnt sienna plus any yellow.
French gray	Light gray	White for base; add lampblack with a faint tinge of ultramarine blue and madder lake or carmine.
Golden brown	Moderate brown	Ochre for base; add burnt sienna or Venetian red and lampblack. Lighten with white.
Gray green	Weak green	White for base; add ultramarine blue, lemon chrome yellow, lampblack.
Gray stone	Pale brown	White for base; add lampblack, Venetian red, and ochre.
Grays, all shades	Gray	White for base, lampblack in various proportions to obtain shade wanted, plus color desired.
Ivy green	Moderate olive green	Ochre for base, add lampblack, Prussian blue.
Jonquil	Moderate yellow	White for base; add medium chrome yellow and a tinge of vermilion.
Lavender	Pale purple	White for base; add ivory black, ultramarine blue, tinge with carmine or madder lake.
Lemon	Moderate yellow	Use lemon chrome yellow.
Magenta	Deep red-purple	Vermilion for base; add carmine or madder lake with a tinge of ultramarine blue, or Alizarin red plus ultramarine blue.
Marigold	Strong orange	Medium chrome yellow for base; add white, orange chrome yellow.
Maroon	Very dark red	Venetian red and lampblack.
Mauve	Strong red-purple	Ultramarine blue for base; add white, tint with madder lake.
Navy blue	Dusky purple-blue	Ultramarine blue for base; add ivory black.
Nut brown	Weak brown	Lampblack for base; add Venetian red, yellow ochre.

Color, Color Harmony

Color Name	Description	Pigments to Use to Obtain It
Old gold	Light olive brown	White for base; add medium chrome yellow, ochre and a little burnt umber.
Olive green	Moderate olive	Lemon chrome yellow for base; add Prussian blue and lampblack. Some shades of olive can be made by substituting ochre for lemon chrome yellow. Then, of course, the tone will not be so bright.
Orange	Orange	Orange chrome yellow as it comes from the can.
Peach	Moderate orange-pink	White for base; add pale Indian red and chrome yellow.
Pistachio	Weak yellow-green	White base; add ochre, medium chrome green.
Pink	Very pale red	White for base; plus any red as desired.
Plum	Very dusky purple	White for base; add Indian red, ultramarine blue.
Primrose	Moderate yellow	White for base; add lemon or medium yellow chrome, according to the color desired.
Robin's egg blue	Pale blue-green	White for base; add Prussian blue.
Russet	Strong brown	White for base; add orange chrome yellow, a trifle of lampblack and burnt sienna.
Sage green	Dusky yellow-green	White for base; add medium chrome green until the tint is nearly but not quite a pea green, then add lampblack to shade it.
Salmon	Moderate orange-pink	White for base; add ochre, burnt sienna, a trifle of vermilion.
Sapphire	Dark blue	White for base; add ultramarine blue.
Sea green	Moderate yellow-green	White base; add Prussian blue, raw sienna.
Scarlet	Deep reddish-orange	Pale English vermilion or any of the scarlet toned vermilion reds.
Shrimp	Moderate reddish-orange	White base; add Venetian red, burnt sienna and a trifle of vermilion.
Sky blue	Pale blue	White for base; add Prussian blue as desired.
Straw color	Moderate yellow	Medium chrome yellow for base; add ochre; a little Venetian red; lighten with white.

Color Name	Description	Pigments to Use to Obtain It
Tan	Dark orange	White for base; add burnt sienna and a trifle of lampblack.
Terra cotta	Dark orange	Ochre for base; add Venetian red and white. Some shades of it require the addition of Indian red. If rich colors are wanted, use orange chrome yellow in place of ochre, add Venetian red and a trifle of burnt umber.
Turquoise	Light greenish-blue	White for base, Prussian or phthalocyanine blue; pale chrome green.
Violet	Very dusky blue-purple	White for base; add lake red to ultramarine.

Mixing Two Colors of Same Type Paint

In mixing two colors of the same brand and type of paint, mix the colors slowly; usually by adding a little at a time of the darker color to the lighter while stirring well. Make frequent tests, if possible, on a surface that is similar to the one to be painted. If time permits, let the sample dry, then check the color.

Keep accurate record of proportions, so if necessary, you can mix a similar color again. Always mix ample paint for the job at hand, allowing some extra as a margin of safety. It is difficult to get two batches that match perfectly. Information on estimating quantities of paint required will be found in the Unit on Estimating Costs.

If two or more separate cans or batches of painter-mixed paint must be used on a job, it is well to change mixtures only when starting on new walls, new panels, or intersections - - never in the middle of a ceiling or wall. Even the same color from various paint cans may vary in hue.

Using Color-In-Oil

Colors-in-oil in paste form should be mixed with enough thinner to make a smooth, lump-free liquid; then mix slowly into the paint, Fig. 8-14. Do not add a dab of color to a whole can of paint and expect it to stir evenly into an even tint.

Colors-in-oil which come in fluid or liquid form may be mixed with paint, without pre-thinning.

Fig. 8-14. Color-in-oil in paste form should be mixed with enough thinner or linseed oil to make a smooth lump-free liquid, then mixed slowly into the paint.

"Warming" and "Cooling" Other Colors

Some colors "warm" other colors; others "cool" the colors. To warm any color except green, add a little red. To "warm" green add a little yellow. Add a little blue to pink, green or gray, to "cool." A very little green plus a touch of blue cools ivory, yellow, cream or tan. To make a color softer (less bright) add a bit of black or gray. To lighten add white. To brighten use more color.

Color Matching

As a journeyman painter you will not only have to match paint products to color names but to all kinds of samples.

In drying, some colors dry darker, some lighter; some change quite a bit. The surest procedure is to brush on a sample on the surface to be painted, or a similar surface, and let it dry.

Study the sample under artificial as well as natural light for its color and the way it looks in relation to other colors that will be in the room. Be sure to consider the lighting. Remember that different kinds of light produce unusual effects on some colors of paint.

In making a decision on color, it is important to keep in mind the fact that the finished job will look darker than the sample; particularly if the paint is being used on a large area. The size of the area in many cases has considerable influence on the value of colors. Wall areas that reflect each other intensify and purify each other. The general affect is a removal of grayness.

As you check the color sample against various color factors in a room, be sure to check it against colors which are visible when doors to adjoining areas stand open. Smooth color transitions from room to room are important in achieving complete color harmony.

Talk "New" Colors

Important as the names on the color wheel and standard names of colors-in-oil may be, it is frequently unwise to use them in selling colors to most customers - - especially women. Whether you are talking about paint for a closet or a thousand dollar decorating job, distinctive and imaginative color names help pave the way to sales. In "selling" jobs of decorating the use of a little psychology often pays big dividends.

Though a woman prospect may not have an accurate mental picture of the colors you describe as "cardinal" and "citron" which you have learned about from decorator's and women's magazines, it is quite possible she will be intrigued by your romantic terminology and will enjoy using it, in turn, when she describes the finished job to her friends.

As an aid to selling high-quality decorating, a scrapbook collection of distinctive color samples, clipped from magazines devoted exclusively to the home or from "prestige" magazines, will be very helpful.

The use of information of this sort will invariably impress your customers with the fact you are on your toes and are wide awake to cur-

rent color trends. It will give them added confidence in what you have to tell - - and sell.

Styling with Paint

Basically, paint styling is a means of making possessions appear to the best possible advantage. It is a method of using colorful coatings in such a way that the good features of a room, a house, a barn, a piece of furniture - - or any object, in fact - - are emphasized and the not-so-good features are minimized.

The good features of a piece of furniture may be emphasized by surrounding it with an area of a different color; tint, or shade so the good features stand out.

Bad features may be minimized by painting a piece of furniture to match the surrounding areas so that it becomes less noticeable.

Paint styling also emphasizes how color can deceive the eye. As an example, paint stylists point out that a light-colored house and a dark-colored one - - of the same size and at the same distance - - will not look the same size. The light-colored house will seem larger.

Indoors, if you paint the walls and ceiling of a room in a light tint and the walls and ceiling of another room of equal size in a very dark color - - the light-walled room will seem much larger than the dark-toned room.

Of importance are colors which convey the feeling of warmth: the reds, oranges, yellows, yellow-greens. These seem to advance toward you, to bring things nearer, Fig. 8-15. The

Fig. 8-15. The reds, oranges, yellows, yellow-greens, convey the feeling of warmth - - - seem to advance toward you.

Fig. 8-16. Blues, violets, greens are "cool" colors—which seem to retreat.

"cool" colors - - the blues, violets, blue-greens and blue-grays - - seem to retreat and to push things away, Fig. 8-16.

Some colors seem "heavier" than others. The cool colors generally seem lighter than the warm ones.

Then there is the point about bright colors. The brighter the area, the larger it seems. That is not all illusion, either. The brightness in a color stimulates the nerves of the retina of the eye. It produces an image that tends to "swell" in dimensions. The "largest" color is white, then yellow. Next comes red, then green, blue and finally, black.

These factors are taken into consideration when you use the principles of paint styling, but most important of all the angles are the emphasizing of good features and the minimizing of bad features.

Minimizing House Defects

To see how the minimizing of defects applies to a color scheme for the outside of a house, let's take a chimney - - the type that shows from the outside as it rises from the ground to the roof.

If a chimney is too large in relation to the size of the house, painting it the same color as the house will make it blend with the background color. A chimney that is too small and weak-looking for the house will also benefit from being painted the same color. Refer to Fig. 8-17.

Now let's look at a roof-line - - one that is cut up with too many gables. With color "sleight of hand," you can draw the eye away from the roof area by using eye-holding hues to feature the front door and shutters, and make everything on the roof dark.

Perhaps a house may have a light-colored roof that seems much too high for its width.

Fig. 8-17. Painting a chimney that is too large in relation to the size of the house, the same color as the house, will make it blend with background color and minimize defects. A chimney that is too small will also benefit from being painted the same color.

The owners of this house could "lower" their house visually by painting the roof a dark color, Fig. 8-18.

Assume we have a house which has window openings of so many different sizes and shapes it gives the house a jumbled look. If the trim is different in color from the body of the house it adds to the poor impression. It would be much better to conceal this lack of unity by painting the trim the same color as the house and by removing the shutters from all the small windows. Shutters should be left only on the larger, more uniform-size windows.

side, if they are very close. Their coloring should be considered in deciding on the colors for the home to be redecorated. No matter how wisely you choose paint color, if the colors "fight" with the neighbors' homes the results will be disappointing.

If you plan to use a strong, definite color for a front door, keep in mind - - especially if the door opens directly into the living room - - that the door will probably stand open in the summer. It should, therefore, harmonize with the scheme of the room of which it will then be a part.

Fig. 8-18. A house with a light-colored roof that seems too high for its width may be "lowered" visually by painting the roof a dark color.

Just as windows of various sizes can break up the overall unity of a building, so can the use of too many types of building materials. Here, again, paint styling can help because the same color on the different materials used can improve the appearance of the house and make it look larger.

Small homes lend themselves especially well to styling. It is the detail of the small home which makes it attractive. This same detail makes it possible to have a truly distinctive color-styling job. Well-designed doorways, window boxes and shutters are the areas where you can have interesting color accents. These accents are especially important in areas where many homes of the same design are built.

In planning a color scheme for the exterior of a home you must have a starting point. This logically may be the roof, especially if the roof is constructed of a material which cannot be painted and changed in color. See Fig. 8-19. Usually several unchangeable factors affect the color decisions. In addition to the roof the deciding factors may consist of the houses on each

Room Styling

Formerly, all walls in a room were given the same color treatment simply because they were all wall surfaces. The new concept is that all surfaces should be colored so they contribute the greatest amount of beauty and utility to a room.

Employing the principles of paint styling, we know now that if a room seems too small, we can make it seem larger by using light colors on the largest surfaces.

In a large, barn-like room that is well lighted, we can use the knowledge that walls in a darker tone will make the room seem smaller and more friendly.

Then, of course, light tints make rooms lighter by reflecting more of the light that falls upon them, and cool colors make warm rooms seem cooler and vice versa.

We have learned that long, narrow rooms can be made to look wider by placing a dark color on the wall at each of the narrow ends and a lighter color on the remaining walls and

If a house has a ROOF that is ...	It will look well if the BODY of it is painted ...	With these, as a TRIM could be used ...	And for SHUTTERS or DOORS such colors as ...
GRAY	SOFT YELLOW OYSTER WHITE PALE GREEN LIGHT GRAY PINKISH BEIGE	Same Color as Body, White, Cream or Gray	Blue-green, Dull Blue, Lettuce Green, Coral, Rust, Yellow, or Turquoise
GREEN	WHITE CREAM GRAY PALE GREEN	Same as Body, White, or Cream	Blues, Blue-greens, Gray, Straw Color, Rust tones
REDDISH	SAND CREAM GRAY WHITE	Same as Body, White, or Cream	Dull Blue, Rust, and Brown tones
BROWN	BUFF CREAM WHITE	Same as Body, Cream, or White	Old Blue, Verdigris Green, or Russet tones

Fig. 8-19. In planning a color scheme for a home the roof makes a logical starting point.

ceiling, Fig. 8-20.

We have discovered that rooms that are square and uninteresting in shape can be improved by making one wall a focal point of interest. If there is a fireplace in the room, the decorative interest is usually placed on the fireplace wall. If there is an alcove this frequently can be dramatized to advantage.

We know too, that ceilings which seem too high can be made to seem lower by painting them a color darker than the side walls, Fig. 8-21.

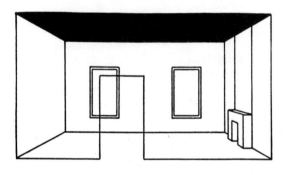

Fig. 8-21. A ceiling which seems too high can be made to seem lower by painting it a color darker than the side walls.

Reflecting Powers of Paint Colors

When you want to make the most of natural and artificial lighting, use paint colors that reflect rather than absorb light. In rooms with large wall areas of glass, where too much sun and sky glare are disturbing factors, dark paint - - colors with low light-reflectance - - will help solve the problem.

Light reflecting powers of various paint col-

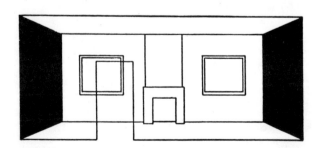

Fig. 8-20. A long, narrow room can be made to look wider by placing a dark color on the wall at each of the narrow ends and a lighter color on the remaining walls and ceiling.

ors for both exterior and interior use are as follows:

WHITE	70-90 Percent
IVORIES AND CREAMS	55-71 Percent
LIGHT YELLOWS	65-70 Percent
LIGHT BUFFS	40-56 Percent
LIGHT GREENS	40-50 Percent
MEDIUM GREENS	15-30 Percent
ORANGES	15-30 Percent
MEDIUM BLUES	15-20 Percent
DARK BLUES	5-10 Percent
MEDIUM GRAYS	15-30 Percent
REDS AND MAROONS	3-18 Percent
MEDIUM AND DARK BROWNS	3-18 Percent
BLACK	1-4 Percent

Different light sources produce light of somewhat different spectral composition which accounts for the fact that a red surface, for example, has a somewhat higher reflectance for the light from filament lamps than for the light from cool white fluorescent lamps. A blue surface, on the other hand, has higher reflectance for cool white fluorescent light than for filament light. These differences in reflectance, however, amount to only a few points at most, and are more of academic interest than of practical significance.

How Light Affects Color

The most-used sources of artifical light are filament lamps and fluorescent lamps. Filament lamps produce light that is rich in red and relatively deficient in blue. This light emphasizes the warmer hues and creates a psychological warm atmosphere - - which incidentally has been acceptable for most lighting applications for many years.

Information on how lighting affects colors which follows, furnished by the Westinghouse Electric Corporation, discusses the coordination of artificial light with colors, particularly as related to the problems presented by fluorescent lamps. See Fig. 8-22.

Light is produced from the fluorescent lamp by the physical action generated in the phosphor coated interiors of the lamps by the impingement of short ultraviolet rays. These phosphors are of prime importance in the rendition of colors. The advent of the fluorescent lamp emphasized color rendition because it tends to bring out blues, yellows, and greens rather than reds, like the incandescent lamp. At the present time there are seven tints of white fluorescent lamps in general use which use different phosphors to produce various tints of white light.

In comparing these different tints, natural daylight is apt to be used as a standard. Of course, no single light source can duplicate the spectral characteristics of daylight. Daylight changes in color value from one hour to the next, as well as through the seasons of the year. It is, of course, necessary to know the properties of the various types of white fluorescent

COLOR CHARACTERISTICS OF WESTINGHOUSE FLUORESCENT LAMPS

Lamp Designation	Ordering Abbreviation	Apparent Color Appearance Of Lamp	Principal Application*
Daylight	D	Blue-White	Factories, Displays
Standard Cool White	CW	White	Stores, Offices, Factories, Schools
DeLuxe Cool White	CWX	White	Stores, Offices, Homes, Color Inspection
White	W	Creamy White	Stores, Offices, Factories, Schools, Homes
Standard Warm White	WW	Yellow-White	Stores, Homes
DeLuxe Warm White	WWX	Yellow-White	Stores, Offices, Homes, Restaurants
Soft White	SW	"Peach" White	Stores, Homes, Restaurants

*Selection is often governed by personal preference.

Fig. 8-22. Color characteristics of fluorescent lamps.

lamps before any selection can be made. The effects of the spectral distributions for the seven standard fluorescent tints are:

DAYLIGHT - The bulb surface appears a bluish white color. The light from this lamp simulates north sky daylight. It is widely used in industry and in some store displays.

STANDARD COOL WHITE - The bulb surface appears white and the illumination creates a cool atmosphere at high efficiency. It blends well with natural daylight and is a favorite for use in stores, offices, factories, and schools.

DE LUXE COOL WHITE AND DE LUXE WARM WHITE - Bulb surfaces of these lamps appear like those of the corresponding standard lamps except that they have a slightly lower brightness. Light from De Luxe lamps is flattering to human complexions, and provides a good color rendition of house furnishings and decorations, merchandise, and other colored objects. The use of De Luxe lamps is recommended in stores, homes, restaurants, and for noncritical color inspection where the best single standard source is desired.

WHITE - The bulb surface appears cream white. The color temperature of the illumination rendered lies between the "cool" and "warm" lamps. Since its luminous efficiency is high, this lamp is most often used in industry, stores, general office areas, and classrooms.

STANDARD WARM WHITE - The bulb surface appears yellow white. The illumination from this lamp creates a warm atmosphere at high efficiency. It is best suited for use in installations combining fluorescent and incandescent lamps because of the appearance of the lamp closely matches that of filament types. This lamp is used in stores, homes, and general offices where economy of light production is of primary importance.

SOFT WHITE - The bulb surface appears a peach white. The illumination rendered is flattering to the human complexion. It is used in lighting for homes, restaurants, and showcase meat displays.

The selection of the proper white for a particular application not only depends upon the color of the object, but also upon the importance of the color rendition and the amount of illumination desired. How successful any final result will be depends entirely upon your skill in selecting colors of materials, in juggling contrasts, and in the design of the lighting equipment. Also, there are some factors which are somewhat divorced from the lamps themselves

which must be considered in attempting to present the best color design possible. Color depends not only upon the inherent pigment of the object - - it depends upon at least four additional factors:

1. The spectral characteristics of the light by which it is seen.

2. The physiological condition of the eye observing it. (Color blindness, for instance.)

3. The contrasting colors of surroundings.

4. The psychological color experiences of the observer. (Color adaptation, for instance.)

There may be other factors, but these are the ones the designer considers most in his work.

These four factors, incidentally, tend to discourage the practice of observing materials for interior designs in neat little cubicles with soft gray backgrounds lighted by sources of various tints, and then basing selection entirely upon the results observed. It is a safer practice to surround the pigments under investigation with other materials to be used and view them as a whole.

Effect on Human Skin

Widespread use of fluorescent lamps in commercial establishments, especially beauty parlors and shops catering to women, has often induced the question of the appearance of human skin under this lighting. The following opinions, based on tests made with several trained observers, indicate some solutions to these problems.

The Soft White lamp is the most flattering to ruddy complexions while the De Luxe lamps are more flattering to tan complexions. Makeup looks best under De Luxe lamps which enhance the red while rendering other parts in their natural flesh color.

Good appearance of the complexion is only part of the problem in many cases. It is often just as important to render the colored surroundings, clothing, etc. to their best advantage. In such cases, the De Luxe lamps give the best rendition since they have the most balanced spectrum. Whether Cool or Warm De Luxe is used is a matter of personal preference.

De Luxe lamps can usually solve most noncritical color problems satisfactorily. Under De Luxe, complexions take on a natural, fresh, healthy glow, and improvement over their appearance under other fluorescent or even incandescent lighting.

Effect on Wood Finishes

Samples of several wood finishes have been tested and the lighting effect of each fluorescent lamp compared with that of incandescent light. The following results represent the majority opinion of a group of observers.

BLOND OAK FINISHES: The yellow-white pigments in this type of wood were best brought out by the Soft White and De Luxe lamps. In fact, under these lamps rendered a richer brown appearance than incandescent lamps. Daylight lamps gave the wood a blonder appearance but other fluorescent lamps overemphasized the slightly greenish tint of the wood.

MAHOGANY FINISHES: Incandescent lighting was preferred, but fluorescent lighting did not materially reduce the beauty of these woods. The Soft White lamp was preferred, since it enhanced the red pigments, but De Luxe lamps rendered the colors well.

BLEACHED MAHOGANY AND BLOND MAHOGANY FINISHES: The yellow-brown grain in these types of finishes were overemphasized by incandescent light while the yellow-white pigments were more predominant under the Soft White and De Luxe lamps. The "natural" color was slightly distorted by both renditions but the incandescent was generally preferred with De Luxe lamps a close second choice. The main objection to other fluorescent lamps was that the greenish pigments were enhanced.

GOLDEN WHITE MAHOGANY AND KNOTTY PINE FINISHES: The De Luxe Cool White, the Standard Cool White, and the Daylight fluorescent lamps were preferred for these finishes. The incandescent and warm colored fluorescent tended to overemphasize the brown and red pigments.

WHITE MAHOGANY FINISHES: The gold appearance of this type of finish was best brought out by incandescent and soft white fluorescent lamps. The De Luxe lamps gave a fair rendition. Other fluorescent lamps, including the De Luxe types, overemphasized the green pigments.

DARK MAPLE FINISHES: Soft White fluorescent was again preferred by the observers, who selected incandescent and the Warm Whites as second best in this instance. The other fluorescent lamps again overemphasized the greenish tints in the wood.

LIGHT MAPLE FINISHES: With the exception of Soft White, the fluorescent lamps came out second best to incandescent due to the emphasis given to the slight greenish tint.

KNOTTY LEMON PINE FINISHES: The De Luxe fluorescent lamps were preferred for this finish with incandescent and Soft White fluorescent acceptable. Other fluorescent lamps gave a yellow-green cast to the wood.

Although Soft White was often given preference over other types of fluorescent lamps, the problems involved in the use of this "tinted" source in offices and stores should be considered before a decision is made to use it.

One might well raise the question: "What effect does illumination level, that is, amount of light, have upon the rendition of color?" Tests have been conducted at three levels of illumination which were most likely to be used in new installations -- 25, 50, and 100 foot candles.

No obvious influence of levels on relative "attractiveness" of colors was observed, although higher intensities allowed a less balanced spectral distribution to be as satisfactory as a more balanced distribution was at lower levels. However, since economy is a factor, and since there is a limit as to how high one can go in intensity, it is preferable to resort to illumination with a balanced spectral distribution such as De Luxe lamps. The psychological effect of different color temperature should not be neglected. Cool temperatures are not as satisfactory as warm at a low level of illumination. As the level of illumination is increased, cooler sources become more pleasant in effect.

Admittedly, color and color effects are so much a matter of taste and opinion that there is always room for doubt and question, but the usual problems connected with lighting with fluorescents can be eliminated if careful attention is paid to the selection of the type of lamp.

Paint Styling as Aid to Industry

Paint styling may be used to safeguard health and safety in buildings other than dwellings. Paint may also be used for color coding in industrial areas. See Fig. 8-23.

In factories the way in which surfaces are coated can mean the difference between tired, aching eyes that can no longer detect mistakes and well-cared-for eyes. Colors that are selected may mean the difference between the physical safety of men and women who run the machines and their injury resulting from disregarded dangers.

The wide and careful use of paint color in industrial maintenance is an important investment.

THESE PAINT STYLING POINTS ARE THE SIGN POSTS
TO GUIDE YOU TO WISE COLOR DECISIONS

LIGHT COLORS.... reflect more light, seem lighter in weight; make things seem larger; make things seem farther away; make you feel cheerful.

DARK COLORS..... absorb light; seem heavy; make things seem smaller; make things seem closer; depress you if used on too large surfaces.

BRIGHT COLORS... seem larger in area than they are; attract the eye....are sometimes used to draw attention away from unattractive features; are distracting.

WARM COLORS.... seem to advance toward you; convey the feeling of warmth; (Reds, oranges, are stimulating.
yellows,
yellow-greens)

COOL COLORS..... make things seem cooler; seem to retreat from you; are (blues, violets, subduing.
blue-greens,
blue-grays)

Also remember that: Broken-up surfaces lack unity--seem smaller than they are; Vertical lines give the appearance of added height; Horizontal lines give the appearance of additional length; "Too square" rooms can be made more attractive by endowing one wall with focal interest.

NEVER FORGET TO emphasize that which is good by painting it in a color, tint, or shade different from its surrounding area.

NEVER FORGET TO minimize that which is not-so-good by painting it the same color as its surrounding area.

WATCH CURRENT COLOR TRENDS....USE PAINT STYLING AS A POWERFUL SELLING TOOL.

Fig. 8-23. Paint styling points.

Industrial Color Code

The Industrial Color Code is a move toward having all industry use the same color to warn employees of plant hazards.

A suggested Color Code (from the book "Paint Power") follows: YELLOW - - because it is the color of greatest visibility - - is employed to indicate dangers in the plant itself, also for traffic markings. ORANGE - - the color of greatest attention value - - is used for hazardous parts of machines or equipment, which if not properly handled, might crush, cut, or otherwise injure the workman. RED - - the traditional "Fireman's red" is used for fire alarm systems, sprinkler pipes, all fire-fighting equipment. GREEN - - the traditional safety color for traffic lights, etc. is used for marking first aid cabinets, stretchers, etc. and for marking floor or wall spots where they are kept. BLUE - - the "thoughtful

color" inspiring caution and deliberation is used as it is in railroad practice, to warn against starting or moving cars or equipment, and to caution against moving, touching or starting equipment so marked. Examples of the use of blue would be self-operated elevators, furnaces, pumps, compressors, starting and stopping devices, and vats containing chemicals.

The Piping Code

Another form of safety code is the piping code for the identification of piping systems. The code of the American Standards Association divides plant piping into five categories as follows:
RED--sprinkler systems, foamite pipes, etc.
YELLOW OR ORANGE--pipes carrying acids, gases, live steam, etc.
GREEN--safe contents, such as drinking water,

steam below 212 deg. F., brine, etc.
BRIGHT BLUE--protective materials.
PURPLE--safe materials of more than ordinary value.

Styling in Offices

The selection of paint color for offices is of considerable importance. Colors chosen must work in harmony with natural and artificial lighting. The eyes of desk workers need thoughtful consideration. Paint color may also be used to "sell" the standing of a company to its employees and to its business prospects. Clean, smoothly painted surfaces in colors that are carefully selected speak well for the efficiency of a firm, the firm's pride in itself and its consideration of its employees.

Basic Points to Remember

Space limitations will not permit us to discuss here the color problems which are encountered in the innumerable types of structures varying from beauty shops to boiler factories. With few exceptions, the problems are but little different from the examples we have discussed with the important exception that paint in a boiler plant must be highly corrosion resistant. From a decorator's point of view, however, you can solve your problems by reflecting on your basic paint styling knowledge.

Colors do not have to be novel or overly exciting to be effective. Usual colors used imaginatively will provide a successful job with outstanding appearance. The finished job can "look like a million" without costing more than an ordinary job through the use of good color.

To properly estimate a paint job four main factors must be considered
--Cost of materials, cost of labor, general overhead, profit expected.

Unit 9

WALL COVERINGS

Hanging wall coverings is an important phase of modern decorating. To turn out professional-quality work requires a thorough basic knowledge of materials and procedures plus acquired skill.

Most of the wall coverings used today are made from vinyl resins. In other words, vinyl plastic has, to a large extent, displaced the more traditional types of wallpaper because of its ready washability and long life. In addition, it can be made highly decorative. Of the remaining wall coverings, one-half to one-third is the traditional wallpaper made from such materials as cotton, linen, hemp, wood and wastepaper. The remainder are more expensive, high fashion coverings such as the grass cloths, flocks and the foil-based materials.

There are three procedures for printing wall coverings. The first is roller printing which is the oldest form and the most widely used. After the background color has been applied to the paper, usually by a so-called ground coating machine, the paper passes through a roller coating machine with as many as thirteen printing units. This means that thirteen different colors can be applied in order to achieve the desired design. Each printing unit consists of a color roller immersed in a color pan. The color is picked up by a metal roll revolving in the pan. It is transferred to a rotating felt which in turn transfers it to the print roller from which it is applied to the wall covering. After all the colors have been applied, the wall covering is festooned or hung in large loops for drying. Finally, it is cut, rolled and wrapped for storage and shipping. One machine can make 3,000 to 12,000 single rolls of wallpaper per day, or enough material to cover 300 to 1200 average size bedrooms.

A second procedure, less widely used because it is newer, for printing wallpaper is the rotogravure method. Here, printing is done by rollers with many indentations which establish the pattern. The depth of the indentations on a given roll may vary for which reason many values of the same color can be produced with a high level of accuracy. Each given color, however, must be applied by a different roller. However, fewer rollers are needed than in the printing process described above because each roller may contribute several depths of color. The rotogravure process is a very rapid one. It is, however, expensive and is most effective for very long runs.

A third procedure is silk screen printing. This process is used for small runs of high quality product and involves a high degree of hand labor. The "screens" look very much like the frames in a double hung window screen. A different screen is necessary for each color and the designs are blocked out on the screen so that the color passes only through the desired areas. The thick color is placed on the screen, the screen is placed over the area to be printed and a rubber squeegee is used to press the liquid color through the silk screen onto the wall covering. After this has been done with the proper number of screens to achieve the desired pattern, the paper is dried, cut and rolled as in the previous process.

Types of Wall Coverings

Wallpapers may be identified by the paper stock used, and by the color and design. Traditionally, the commonly used papers include the following:

LINING PAPER: A blank paper without a ground (overall background color). This is used mostly for wall conditioning.

MICAS: Papers in which mica is used in printing the designs.

PULPS: Papers colored in the process of manufacture of the stock.

SILKS, SATINS, VELVETS, CHINTZES, ETC. Papers made to imitate fabrics from which the names are derived.

FLOCKS: In flock printing, adhesive is applied, then short lengths of fiber such as nylon or wool, are applied to achieve a raised or velvet effect.

DUPLEX PAPER: This consists of two separate papers pasted together to create a highly embossed effect.

GRASS CLOTH: Grass cloth is made by gluing woven native grasses onto a paper backing. The product originally came from Japan. Although the original material is still widely used for high fashion decorating, the effect of grass cloth can be duplicated with vinyl wall coverings.

CALENDERED PAPERS: Papers with a hard finish.

EMBOSSED PAPERS: Paper run through rollers with raised areas to provide a light relief effect such as texture.

GROUND PAPER: Wallpaper coated with an overall background color.

UNGROUNDED PAPER: Paper without a basic background color.

OATMEAL: Plain paper made by sprinkling sawdust over adhesive surface.

TILE: Paper made to imitate tile. This may be varnished, waxed or plain.

PIN STRIPES: Papers with fine stripes.

PLAIDS: Papers made to resemble plaid cloth.

HAND PRINTS: Papers printed by hand, usually with the silk-screen process.

BRUSH TINTS: Plain papers coated with water color.

WOOD PAPERS: Papers made to imitate the appearance of various woods.

Modern wall coverings include the following of which, as indicated above, the vinyls are by far the most important.

VINYLS: Currently, there are six types of vinyl wall coverings. These include:
A. Vinyl film laminated to paper.
B. Paper laminated to lightweight woven cloth and then coated with a vinyl resin.
C. Vinyl film laminated to lightweight woven cloth which may be a synthetic like nylon or a natural material.
D. Vinyl film laminated to light nonwoven cloth such as the nonwoven materials used for "wipes" and baby diapers.
E. Vinyl film laminated to nonwoven paper-fabric webs.

F. A synthetic base impregnated with a vinyl resin. The surface of the coating is printed very much like ordinary wallpaper.

FOILS: Wall coverings which are metallic in appearance are made from very thin sheets of flexible metal laminated to a paper or fabric backing. The foil is then printed with either transparent or opaque dyes and pigments to achieve mottling which resembles marble, tortoise shell and a variety of other decorative finishes.

WALL CARPET: As the name indicates, this is simply carpeting applied to a wall frequently for acoustic reasons but also for the unusual decorative and tactile effects that may be achieved.

How Wall Covering is Measured

The standard of measurement for American-made wall covering is a roll (single roll) containing 36 sq. ft. After trimming, approximately 30 sq. ft. are available in terms of actual coverage on the wall. The paper usually comes in bolts containing two or three single rolls. This is done for purposes of economy, since more full strips can be cut from one two-roll bolt than from two separate single rolls. Wall coverings vary in width, the narrowest being 18 in. wide and the widest 54 in.

The most popular widths are 20 and 27 in. In the 20 in. width, a single roll is 21 ft. long; a double roll 42 ft. In the 27 in. width, a single roll is 16 ft. long; a triple roll 46 ft.

Foreign-made papers vary in length and width and the amount considered a roll by American standards is only approximate.

English-made wallpapers are usually 22 in. wide (about 21 in. trimmed) and come in rolls 36 ft. long, containing one and one-half single rolls.

French papers are generally 18 in. wide, 27 ft. long, and are classified as single rolls.

Other Wall Coverings

Coverings in addition to vinyls and wallpaper applied by the paperhanger include the following:

Muslin

Bleached and unbleached muslin materials are used to cover plaster walls when preparing them for further decoration. Since muslin usually shrinks, it must be handled accordingly.

The pores of the cloth must be filled with a prepared filler. Muslin is frequently used on walls to hide hair cracks in preparation for painting or papering. It is also used as a base for very expensive wallpaper, which can be removed from the wall and rehung, as has been done with scenic papers of historic and decorative value.

Oiled Fabrics

Oiled fabrics which were frequently used instead of plain muslin have been made obsolete by wall coverings made from vinyls on fabric.

Burlap

Burlap is used as a wall covering to provide a heavy cloth texture to a wall. Raw (unfilled) burlap is applied in the same manner as muslin. A filled burlap, which is also available, is easier to apply. It can be hung so the seams do not show. Burlap comes in natural and dyed colors. Most burlap sold for walls today is laminated to a paper backing for ease in hanging.

Chintz

Glazed and unglazed chintz and other printed cotton fabrics are sometimes used as wall coverings.

Silk

Silk fabrics are used as decorative wall coverings. The Japanese make a paper with a silk covering that is quite delicate to handle, creating special problems. Silk fabric coverings are often hand-painted either before or after hanging.

Grass Cloth

This material is made of woven rice straw, root fibers, paper fibers, hemp and synthetic threads pasted onto a paper backing in hundreds of combinations and colors. Interesting designs can be obtained by reversing the grain of the straw and by hanging it in shapes such as squares and rectangles. The concept of grass cloth originated in Japan.

Linen

Pure linen is sometimes used by decorators as a backing for hand-painted wall decorations.

It is excellent for the purpose as it does not shrink. Most linen used today is laminated onto paper or a filled background for ease of hanging.

Lace

Lace, such as used for curtains, is sometimes applied to walls to provide an embossed painted effect. The lace is pasted on the wall and then a gloss or flat paint is applied.

Tools and Equipment

In order to perform his job efficiently, the paperhanger must have the right kind of tools and know how to use them. Paperhanging equipment includes hand tools, paste table and acessories, scaffolding and proper attire or uniform.

Shears

Paperhangers' shears come in two principal types, high carbon steel and forged steel. Shears made of forged steel are usually considered the best. The shears come in lengths from 10 to 14 in. These are overall measurements. A pair of 12 in. shears, for example, would have blades about 7 1/2 in. long. See Fig. 9-1. Long shears

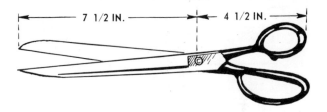

Fig. 9-1. 12 in. paperhanger's shears.

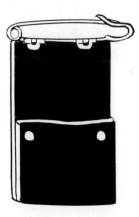

Fig. 9-2. Shear holder. Leather slip-pocket holder with safety pin fastener; assembled with rivets for sturdiness.

are convenient for cutting paper quickly. A pair of small shears is useful when hanging fabrics and for fine cutting. Shears having handles which offset are preferred by some workmen. A leather holder fastened to the side of the uniform should be provided to hold the shears, Fig. 9-2.

Rollers

Rollers are used by paperhangers to press the paper tightly to the wall at the seams and the space along woodwork and moulding. Many kinds and shapes of rollers are available. Some have flat surfaces, some convex; the surfaces may be smooth, ribbed, padded, or covered with abrasive paper. Wide padded rollers are frequently used in place of smoothing brushes on fine, delicate papers. A 2 in. padded roller is used to roll seams on paper that has a tendency

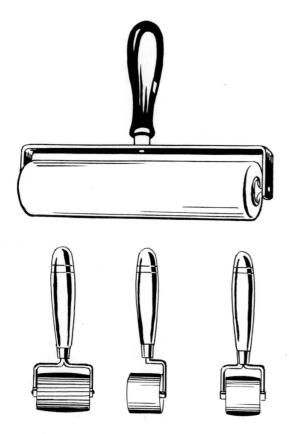

Fig. 9-3. Above. 9 in. smoothing roller with detachable cover. Below. Left—Oval roller. Center—Flat roller. Right—Roller with ribbed surface.

to shine. A flat roller covered with fine abrasive paper or soft rubber can also be used to prevent shine but must be used with consider-

able caution. A 1, 2, or 3 in. plastic roller can be used to roll seams on ordinary wallpaper. Angle rollers, made of wood or plastic, either flat or conical in shape, are used to roll corners, angles and irregularly shaped woodwork. See Fig. 9-3.

Brushes

Smoothing brushes, Fig. 9-4, are used to brush the paper tightly to the wall. These are made in widths of 10 to 16 in.; the bristles are usually 2 1/2 to 4 1/2 in. long and are set in tufts in aluminum or wood blocks and are vul-

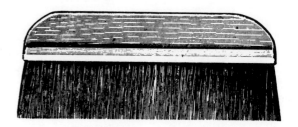

Fig. 9-4. Typical smoothing brush. Width 12 in., thickness 11/16 in., bristles 2 1/2 in. long.

canized in rubber. Types of bristles include pure hog bristle, nylon, plastic and fiber. A paperhanger's tool kit should include brushes with both soft and fairly stiff bristles.

A good paste brush is a very essential tool for the paperhanger, yet many paperhangers give but little consideration to its selection. A paste brush must be able to hold a lot of paste and be stiff enough to brush it out well, Fig. 9-5. Paste brushes are made in various styles and sizes, the 7 and 8 in. widths being the most popular. Very important is the fact that many applicators now use paint rollers to apply wallpaper paste.

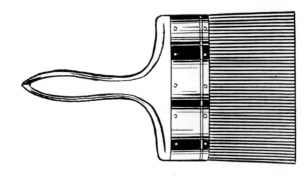

Fig. 9-5. Typical paste brush. Width 7 in., thickness 7/8 in., length of bristles 4 1/8 in.

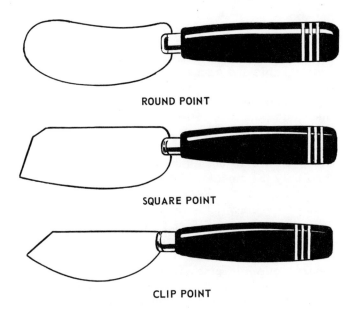

Fig. 9-6. Paperhanger's knives.

Paperhangers' Knives

Another very important tool to the paperhanger is a sharp knife. The knife blade should be of rigid material and should be sharpened with a long bevel on one side only. The side used next to the straightedge in cutting should not be beveled. The choice of a knife varies with the job at hand; it may have a round point, square point, or clip point, Fig. 9-6. A broadknife, Fig. 9-7, is used for trimming wet paper around woodwork and for scraping off old paper or cloth. In sharpening, be sure to maintain the original bevel.

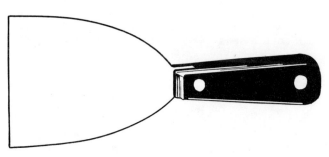

Fig. 9-7. Broadknife, width 3 1/2 in.

Safety razor blades make good cutting tools for paperhangers and in many cases are preferred over regular knives. Suitable blade holders should be used to prevent accidents.

"Razor Knives"

"Razor knives" which are simply single-edge razor blades inserted into a convenient holder, Fig. 9-8, are used for cutting wet paper at casings, base, moldings, and related boundaries. Wheel knives which were formerly widely used are not effective with vinyl or thick papers popular today.

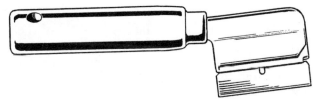

Fig. 9-8. Razor knife.

Mechanical Trimmers

Various types of mechanical trimmers or machines are available for trimming off the selvedge (unprinted portion along edges of paper). Some trimmers are used to trim both edges dry; others are used for trimming pasted paper. See Fig. 9-9.

Fig. 9-9. One type of paper trimmer.

Measuring and Ruling Instruments

The straightedge is a very important piece of equipment for the paperhanger, Fig. 9-10. It comes in 6 and 7 ft. lengths, in both wood and metal, and either with or without a track for a wheel trimmer. The edges are usually bound with steel or brass, and may be screwed or clamped on. Those that are clasped on are considered safer. Screws on the screw-type may loosen and interfere with the knife, causing it to

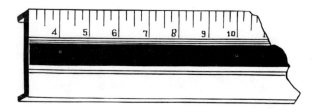

Fig. 9-10. Paperhangers' straightedges come in 6 and 7 ft. lengths, in both wood and metal.

jump and possibly injure the operator. The wood straightedge should have a hole in one end so it can be hung up when stored to prevent warping.

A spirit level, Fig. 9-11, is also widely used by paperhangers. A two-foot level is generally recommended, since it can be used both in connection with the straightedge to make vertical or horizontal lines and as an aid in cutting wet paper on the wall and at the paste table.

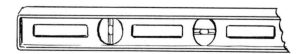

Fig. 9-11. A 2 ft. spirit level should be included in paperhanger's tool kit.

A 50 ft. chalk line, blue chalk, and a plumb bob, are used in making vertical and horizontal lines. See Fig. 9-12. An awl may be used to hold the chalk line and to help hang fabric wall coverings. A yardstick is needed to measure wall space and may also be used as a tear stick at the paste table. Another measuring tool that can be used to good advantage is a 2 or 3 ft. folding rule. A steel tape is convenient when hanging wide fabrics and for measuring around outside corners.

Fig. 9-12. Plumb bob, chalk line and blue chalk are used in making vertical and horizontal lines.

Sponges

Clean sponges should be on hand to wipe paste from woodwork and from the paper. Some

paste is bound to be spattered on every job, regardless of how expert the paperhanger is.

Paste Table and Accessories

A table for cutting and pasting paper is a necessity, as are pails for paste, stepladders, and drop cloths. See Fig. 9-13. In selecting a table, solidity and ease of handling are important factors to consider. A table 6 ft. long is probably the most convenient length.

FOLDING TABLES: Folding tables with legs attached are available in different lengths, usually between 6 and 8 ft. long. An extra board may be attached when working with 30 in. paper.

SEPARATE BOARD TABLES: Straight-grain boards of white pine, 12 in. wide, 1 in. thick, and 6 ft. long placed on separate legs or trestles make a sturdy and convenient table. The pine boards furnish a good surface for cutting with a knife.

MISCELLANEOUS: Scaffolding for hanging paper on ceilings and high areas can be constructed from two stepladders and an adjustable extension plank. See Fig. 9-14. The length of ladders and planks needed will vary according to the work being done.

Pails for water, paste and size must also be provided. A used five gallon paint can with a lid is convenient for carrying dry paste. Clean drop cloths should be available to keep paste, cuttings, and waste paper from soiling rugs, carpets, and furniture.

The paperhanger's uniform is of more importance than may be evident at first. He should wear white overalls with several convenient pockets. One-pocket uniforms are not recommended because time may be lost searching for the right tool. It is better to have more and smaller pockets in which to place specific tools. As each tool is used, it should be put back in its proper place immediately.

Wall Preparation

One of the most important requirements of a good paperhanging job is the proper preparation of the walls. The paperhanger should be able to judge the condition of the walls and know how to prepare them for papering.

Painted Walls

Painted walls can be papered if the paint is still adhering firmly to the plaster. Paint that

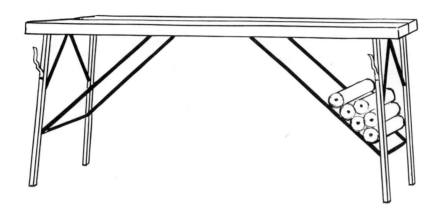

Fig. 9-13. Typical folding paste table. Length 6 ft. Height 33 in. Basswood top,
heavy metal rails and braces. Straightedge holders attached.

is not adhering firmly may be pulled off by the paper. In some cases the application of a lining paper will help, since the papers that have a strong pull will not pull directly on the paint. Another solution is to cover the wall with prepared canvas. This has very little pull on the surface.

Besides determining the condition of paint, the workman must consider the kind of paint which is to be covered with paper. An enameled surface is usually hard and glossy, requiring a size made elastic by adding sugar or syrup to glue size, or by adding a few crystals of sal soda or small amount of trisodium phosphate to glue or cereal size. The gloss may be removed by washing the painted surface with a solution of 1 part ammonia and 6 parts water. Rinse thoroughly, dry, then size. Sanding is also an effective way to remove gloss to assure good adhesion. In hanging vinyl wall coverings, adhesion problems may be encountered if the wall has been sized. Accordingly, sanding is a safer procedure.

Calcimined Walls

Since wallpaper will not adhere to calcimine, it must be removed. Wash with warm water,

using a sponge. Allow to dry, then size. If washing will not remove the old calcimine, scrape the surface.

Resin, Casein Painted Walls

Such walls require only sizing, before papering. However, the manufacturer's recommendations should be checked relative to the exact sizing method.

Textured Walls

Textured walls that are not too rough can be smoothed and papered. Indentations should be filled with plaster of Paris, and the entire surface scraped and sanded smooth before applying the size. Blank stock is advised on all rough walls as a means of creating a smooth surface for better joining in the final hanging. Recently, a "liquid liner" has become available for filling the indentations of a textured wall to make it smooth.

Sand-Finished Walls

Paper should not be applied over sand-finished walls without first conditioning them.

Fig. 9-14. Adjustable extension plank.

Such walls must be given a hard or solid surface and smoothed so the sand will not penetrate the paper.

On sand-finished walls, loose sand should be scraped off with a scraper, stiff broad-blade knife, or wood block. The wall surface may be hardened by applying a good penetrating sealer and a coat of glue size applied. Walls that are very soft may be prepared for papering by first applying prepared canvas. The canvas does not exert as much pull on the soft surface as blank stock.

Painted sand-finished walls should be treated the same as unpainted walls, except that no penetrating sealer is needed.

Old Paper Should be Removed

To provide a good foundation for new wallpaper, old paper should be removed. The old paper may become loose and spoil the whole job. Also, laps in the old paper may show through. Modern wall coverings are frequently "strippable" which means that they can be stripped from a wall simply by pulling in the proper way. These, however, are relatively new and, accordingly, most wall coverings must be removed by the procedure which follows.

The modern way to remove wallpaper is by using a steamer. This eliminates much hard work and speeds up the job. The steam penetrates and moistens the paper quickly and the heat helps to soften the old parts.

The old way to remove paper is by the use of water, a scraper and considerable manual labor. The paper is thoroughly saturated with warm water containing additives which speed up the penetration of the water and soften the paste. The solution is brushed on with a paste brush, sponge, or sprayer. Wet the paper at the top first and then work downward. If it is possible to wet all the walls of a room several times before the scraping is started, the job is made easier. Care should be taken to keep water off the woodwork. To remove the thoroughly saturated paper, use a broad knife or a painter's scraper. After the old paper has been removed, and before the wall or ceiling has had time to dry, wash it with clean warm water and sponge, to remove old paste and wall size. While the wall is still damp, fill holes and patch cracks.

Varnished, lacquered or vinyl coverings and paper which has been painted with oil, casein or resin emulsion paint, as well as paper with a waxed surface, must be removed before re-papering, because paste will not adhere to these surfaces.

Such papers cannot be wet sufficiently to scrape off until the surface coating has been cut through to permit penetration of water. The penetration may be effected by scratching the surface with No. 2 flint or garnet paper fastened to a sanding block or by using a wire brush.

Papering Over Old Paper

While applying new wallpaper over old paper is not considered the best practice, the average paperhanger is called upon to handle such jobs. He should be thoroughly familiar with the problems involved.

Wallpaper has a tendency to come loose at the molding and around woodwork. If the paper is tight elsewhere the loose sections should be shaved off with a paperhanger's knife to leave a beveled edge. The beveled edges should then be sanded or "feathered." Old seams should also be smoothed by shaving them off with a paperhanger's knife or by sanding. Any indentations caused by scraping must be filled.

Wall Sizing

New plaster walls and ceilings, which are thoroughly dry and ready for papering, newly patched walls, as well as old walls that have been washed after removal of paper, must be sized before being papered. Newly plastered walls should be treated with a solution consisting of two pounds of zinc sulphate to one gallon of water. This neutralizes the lime and alkali in the plaster. Sizing should be applied after the neutralizer is dry. Glue is the foundation of size used to prepare surfaces for wallpaper. There are available on the market several prepared sizes in various stages of partial preparation. Some have special characteristics such as resiliency.

The size seals porous walls, prevents paste from soaking into the plaster and makes a tight wall surface to which paper will adhere firmly.

Glue is made into a size by adding water. Glue will absorb a considerable quantity of water - - as much as 15 to 18 times its own weight. Finely ground glue is much easier to dissolve than flake glue. Instructions furnished by the manufacturer of the size being used should be closely followed.

Glue size is applied to the wall with a large paint brush.

Glue size can be preserved and prevented from souring by adding pulverized borax (usually three ounces to one gallon of size will be adequate) or by adding carbolic acid (CAUTION!), or formaldehyde.

Many of today's adhesives may be diluted and used as a size following carefully, of course, the manufacturer's specifications.

Paste for Wallpaper

Wallpaper as it comes from the paper mill, is brittle and must be softened before it can be applied to the wall. Adhesives containing water serve this purpose. Water softens the paper so it will not break and tear easily when handled.

Paste used in wallpapering may be one of the many prepared pastes available at paint stores, or it may be made from cooked flour or starch and water. Modern prepared pastes are fast replacing the old homemade pastes, but many paperhangers still prefer to make their own paste. There are many recipes for making wallpaper paste, but the basic methods are similar.

A good wheat flour paste can be made as follows: Pour about one-half gallon of water into a clean, rust-free pail, and stir in three or four pounds of winter wheat flour to make a batter, (spring wheat makes thin, watery paste). Next, pour in about two gallons of boiling water, stirring rapidly. The paste will turn from milk white to slightly yellow and will stiffen as the starch in the flour changes to gluten.

If the boiling water does not completely cook the paste, place it over heat and stir until well cooked. If the paste is not to be used immediately, a preservative, such as carbolic acid, boric acid, alum, or an antiseptic that will not stain the paper should be added to the paste batter. Alum added to the paste will make it harder drying. If it is desirable to make the paste more elastic and more adhesive, glucose, molasses, corn syrup, melted brown sugar, or an elastic size can be added. Such materials also retard drying and make the paste more effective. Strain the paste before use to remove any lumps.

For use with the modern vinyls and foil-backed papers, ready mixed adhesives designed especially for these are required.

Moisture in the paste causes wallpaper to expand. It will be both longer and wider after dampening. Paper expands from 1/16 to about 1/4 in. in width, depending on the type of paper and consistency of the paste. Thus, the impor-

tance of considering the dimension of the PASTED strip rather than the dry strip during fitting is obvious. Sufficient time must be allowed for complete expansion before the paper is applied. If it continues to expand after it is hung, wrinkles and blisters may result.

Evaporation is another important factor in paperhanging. One of the most difficult tasks of a paperhanger is to have the paper just right at the time it is applied to the wall. Some papers require more time to absorb moisture and to expand than others. This is especially true of the new, strippable papers.

It is frequently necessary to have windows and doors closed so there will be no draft to dry out the edges of the paper while hanging it. In very hot weather, it may be necessary to place pasted strips under a cloth to prevent too rapid evaporation during the expansion and softening period.

Cost Estimating

One of the most important jobs of the paperhanger is that of figuring the quantity of paper needed and the time that will be required to do a particular job. Information on these phases of paperhanging will be found in the Unit on Estimating Costs.

Paperhanging Procedure

Besides acquiring a knowledge of types of wallpaper, paste, and surfaces to be covered, the paperhanger must develop the skill required to fit paper and other wall coverings into a given space. Paperhanging involves a great deal of physical activity. The worker should develop a routine that can be repeated with machine-like precision. The procedures described here are suggested as a basis from which the paperhanger can work out a technique that best meets his individual needs.

Preliminary Steps

1. Spread the drop cloth so the paste table can be placed on it to receive the proper light for pasting and trimming of the paper.

2. Set up and place the table where it will be convenient to the work.

3. Check the straightedge for accuracy. This may be done by placing it on a strip of clean paper, drawing a line with a sharp pencil, then turning the straightedge end for end and drawing

a second line over the first line. If the second line falls on the first line for full length, the straightedge is true.

4. Provide a sufficient quantity of good-quality paste.

5. Place the paste in a spot where it will be convenient, yet will not interfere with the various operations.

6. Provide a pail of clean water and a sponge. Place the pail of water on the floor beside the paste pail. Water should be changed frequently.

Checking the Paper

Before applying any paper to the wall, it is advisable to check the paper for several details. First of all, check to make sure there is plenty of paper to complete the job. If not, it is advisable to obtain an additional bolt right away, because paper from a different mill run may be of slightly different shade. Full-bolts can usually be returned to the retailer, within a specified time limit, if not required on the job.

The worker should examine the paper to make sure he has the right pattern before doing any cutting. The selvedge on some papers contains valuable information, including name of manufacturer, pattern number, register marks to show size of pattern, trim marks, marks to indicate the match, mill run number to aid in obtaining paper that was run in same batch, and marks to show top of pattern. If top of paper is not marked, the hanger may determine which is the top of patterned paper by studying the pattern. On flower design, the heaviest leaves usually hang down, and the heaviest shading is found in the leaves at the bottom of the design. On plain or textured goods, indicate the top of the strip by marking. Some plain goods require reversing of every other strip.

Cutting and Matching Paper

Cutting and matching wallpaper is done at the paste table. To avoid the possibility of getting paste on the sidewalls, the professional paperhanger hangs the ceiling paper first.

In learning how to hang paper, however, the apprentice should practice on sidewalls before attempting a ceiling job.

In using paper with a design, it is necessary to match the strips at the table before cutting the paper. Join or match marks on the selvedge are helpful. Carelessness in matching can easily ruin an otherwise fine job of paperhanging.

There are two principal ways of matching patterns: the pattern that matches straight across, called a STRAIGHT PATTERN MATCH, or SQUARE PATTERN PAPER; and the pattern which is staggered, called a DROP PATTERN, or HALF MATCH.

UNCURLING PAPER: In starting with a roll of paper, the first step is to uncurl the paper so that it is easy to handle. Unroll a few feet, and with the left hand pressing lightly on the paper as it passes over the edge of the table, pull the roll gently to the right and up, Fig. 9-15.

Fig. 9-15. Removing curl from rolled wallpaper.

Measure the height of the walls to determine the length of strip you need. Do not cut the paper too short - - allow at least two inches excess at top and at bottom. Since wallpaper expands when pasted and walls are seldom uniform, it must be fitted to exact size after it is placed on the wall. Ends of rolls are used for spaces over and under openings. It is not good policy to cut more than two bolts of paper at a time.

To place patterned wallpaper on the wall correctly, the paper should be torn so a full pattern appears on the wall nearest the ceiling line. The pattern must run uniformly around the room. Extremely large designs should be centered when possible.

Unroll paper for the second strip and uncurl end, Fig. 9-16. Before cutting, move the paper along the right edge of the first strip, until it matches with the least amount of paper extending beyond the bottom of the first. Cut even with

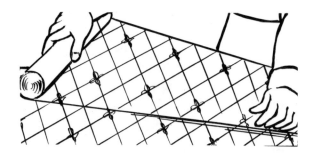

Fig. 9-16. Matching pattern. Paper for second strip is unrolled and moved along right edge of first strip until it matches with least amount of paper extending beyond bottom of first strip.

the top of the first strip. Cut each succeeding strip in the same manner, matching it carefully with the preceding strip. Always keep the strip cut last on top. Turn the entire stack of strips face down without reversing ends and take curl out of the tops by rolling all together over a yardstick. Strips must be pasted and hung in the same order they were matched and cut.

Fig. 9-17. Pasting. Stack of cut strips is turned pattern down, at rear side of table. Strip to be pasted is pulled toward worker so paste going over edge will go on next strip.

Pasting

Place stack of cut strips of paper at rear side of table. Pull strip to be pasted first toward you, so paste going over the far edge will go on the back of the next strip, Fig. 9-17. Do not overpaste on next strip when hanging silks, grass cloths or flocks. Paste half the length at one time. Do not use too much paste. Begin in the middle of the strip, work toward end, brushing paste evenly from center to edges. Take care to get no paste on face of paper. Use thicker paste for heavy embossed and varnished paper.

Folding

Wipe paste from your hands, pick up the corners of pasted end of strip and fold over, pasted side in. Do not fold beyond the pasted portion in the middle. Be sure that both upper and lower edges are exactly even for the entire length of the strip. Press down lightly but do not crease.

Slide pasted half to end of table, and apply paste to remainder of strip. Fold second half of strip to center as you did first half, Fig. 9-18. Check all edges to make sure they are even. This IS VERY IMPORTANT. Make sure there is no excess paste at edges of paper.

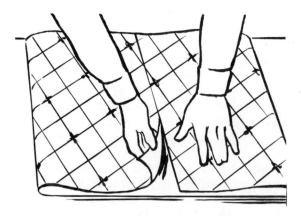

Fig. 9-18. Folding. To make paper easy to handle. Ends are folded toward middle, pasted side in. Edges must be even.

Trimming Paper

In trimming pasted paper use a straightedge, run knife along edge with enough pressure to cut selvedges away cleanly, Fig. 9-19, or use a

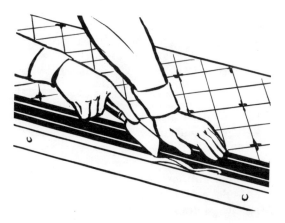

Fig. 9-19. Trimming. Sharp knife is run along a straightedge with enough pressure to cut selvedge away cleanly.

PLAIN BUTT SEAM

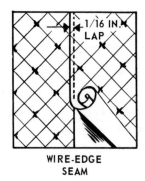
WIRE-EDGE SEAM

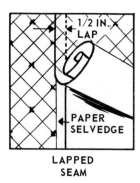
LAPPED SEAM

Fig. 9-20. Three types of seams: Butt, Wire Edge, Lapped.

trimming machine, if available.

The point at which the papering is started determines the arrangement of the pattern in the room. Papers with geometric arrangements should be centered on one wall. A wall having one window or equally spaced windows is usually the best one on which to start, for it enables the hanger to work from the light. However, the space considered most important may be a mantlepiece, an archway, or the space for a picture or a piece of furniture. After the starting point has been selected, the finishing point must also be considered. It should be the most inconspicuous spot in the room. The space back of a door near a corner is a good place for the mismatch which frequently results. It is a good idea to make the mismatch above the door in a corner, and from the top of the door to the corner.

Types of Seams

In paperhanging three types of seams or joints are used:

The BUTT JOINT is made by trimming both selvedges and butting the edges together. This is used in the highest type of work.

The WIRE EDGE JOINT is made by trimming both selvedges and lapping one edge slightly over the other.

The LAPPED JOINT is made by trimming one selvedge and overlapping the other. See Fig. 9-20. This procedure, however, is seldom used on present-day wall coverings. Almost all modern applications are butted.

The apprentice who attains proficiency in making butt joints will have no trouble with the others.

Different types of paper require different techniques in making the butt joint, depending on the amount of handling the paper will stand.

Hanging First Strip

In hanging wallpaper the first strip which serves as a guide in hanging must be hung perfectly straight. It is not safe to assume a door casing or corner is square and start hanging paper true with either.

For a vertical starting line use a chalked line and a plumb bob. Use ice pick or drive nail

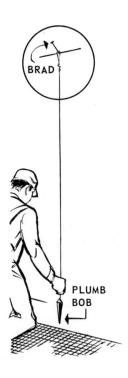

Fig. 9-21. Chalk line and plumb bob are used to get vertical starting line.

at ceiling 16 in. to right of casing or corner. Tie line to ice pick or nail, so plumb bob swings clear of wall. At point where bob comes to rest, hold line taut, Fig. 9-21, and snap it against the wall, leaving guide mark for edge of first step.

Mount ladder or platform and unfold top half of strip. Allow lower, unfolded half to rest on your extended foot to break paper's fall and prevent tearing. Place upper right hand side of strip against chalk line. Hold it there, and raise or lower left side until strip falls along chalk line. Then smooth left hand side of strip against the wall, Fig. 9-22.

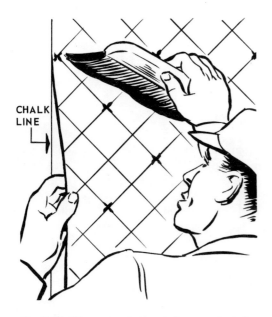

CHALK LINE

Fig. 9-22. First strip of paper is hung to plumb line.

After smoothing top half of strip, unfold lower half, pulling it down gently. Make sure lower half is also right on chalk line. This is important because the first strip is a guide for all the rest.

Smoothing Paper

With smoothing brush, work down the center of the paper first, pressing gently but firmly. Then smooth out from the center to both edges. Take out all bubbles and wrinkles, and make certain the edges are well pasted down. Work paper firmly against door casing or into corner, using patting motion with smoothing brush so paper adheres securely.

Special smoothers are available for vinyls and for heavy wall coverings to force out the air trapped behind the sheet. These should be used for best results with modern wall coverings.

Care should be taken not to put too much pressure into smoothing the paper. Such pressure may cause paper to stretch. If this happens, it will contract when dry, and may split. Also, embossed paper should be smoothed gently, otherwise the embossing will be flattened.

Trimming at the Door

A careful job of trimming around woodwork and molding is essential for a professional job. Each strip of sidewall paper should be trimmed as it is hung before the paste sets.

Having worked paper against the door casing with smoothing brush, crease it and trim it with either shears, a trimming knife, or razor knife. When you have completed trimming along entire length of door, smooth paper down again.

Always have a clean, well moistened sponge at hand to remove promptly any paste that gets on woodwork. Paste is very difficult to remove if allowed to dry and set. It is often necessary to sponge seams. This cleans off paste, but more important, it adds moisture to help paste to stick. This is only possible on waterproof papers. Water should be changed frequently.

Trimming at Baseboard

When paper has been smoothed down to baseboard, use a piece of cardboard or a scraper to push the paper against the wood, making a crease at the baseboard line. Turn the paper back, fold on crease, trim with shears, a trimming wheel, or knife, Fig. 9-23. Brush the paper down firmly.

Fig. 9-23. Cutting paper off at baseboard, using trimming wheel. As indicated in the text, razor knives are most effective with modern vinyl wall coverings.

For the finest appearance of the room, work the edges of the paper under the woodwork - - door and window casings, moldings and baseboards. This can be done by using a thin knife or other metal edge to force the edges of the paper under the wood. Care must be taken not to gouge or mar the paper.

Hanging Second Strip

Using the first strip as a guide, hang the second strip. Match the pattern carefully. Hang remaining strips in same order they were cut, making sure pattern matches at seams. Trim the top same as bottom unless a border is used that will cover any unevenness at ceiling line. Hang spaces over and under windows and doors, as they are approached. Match short strips in these places, splitting when necessary.

Rolling Seams

When the strips have been on the wall from 10 to 20 minutes, or when the paste has started to dry, use a seam roller to press down the seams, Fig. 9-24. This will aid in getting perfect joints. Do not use too much pressure on the roller. If you do it will polish the paper and leave an unattractive shiny streak. The bristle edge of a smoother is often used to tap seams down. Any paste squeezed out should be washed off at once.

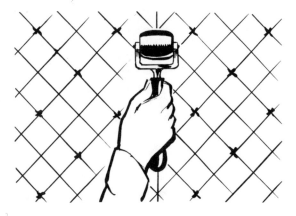

Fig. 9-24. Using seam roller to press down seam.

Do not use a seam roller on heavy embossed papers or on flocks, use a soft cloth and press the edges of the paper down. Do not rub with a cloth. This will shine the paper and leave a streak.

Turning Corners

Do not try to paper around corners, for wrinkles and, later, cracking may result. Measure distance to corner from last strip on wall. If space is too narrow for full strip, trim strip to fit into corner and extend 1/4 in. onto next wall. Smooth firmly into corner. Then take piece which was trimmed off and paste where it would have been before cutting, butting the seam. If the corner is crooked the next piece must be lapped over at the corner so the open edge is plumb to start the new wall.

For outside angles, such as a chimney breast, trim paper so it goes around corner onto the next wall. The overlap should be one-half inch or more, depending on the weight of the paper. Then paste on remainder of strip, butting seam, if possible. Cut edges should never occur directly on an exposed turn.

Piecing Out

Short full width strips above and below windows are cut from stub rolls left after cutting full-length strips. Care must be taken to see to it that the pattern matches the long strips on the wall. Hang everything in sequence. Do not "dutch in" even on plain goods.

Hanging Border

Border is the finishing touch to your job. Cut the border in strips convenient to handle - - about 5 to 6 ft. Paste and fold like sidewall. Trim both edges after folding, using straightedge and knife, or shears. Hang from right to left, starting at point 4 in. to right of corner. Turn corner, continue around room.

Unfold half of border, hold in position along ceiling edge. Brush smoothly against wall. Keep top of border close and parallel to ceiling. Match pattern carefully each time you start new strip. Always use butt seams - - never lap border. Fit last strip into corner, overlapping the extra 4 in., of the first strip. If vinyls are being hung, be sure that the special paste recommended by the manufacturer is used.

Decorative Borders

Many unusual, attractive effects can be achieved with wallpaper border. They offer relief from plain or sparsely patterned wallpaper and furnish accents on painted walls. Following are a few suggestions:

For dropped ceiling try border under the molding. Place border along top of dado or chair rail at baseboard. Create appearance of dado by applying border on a plain wall several feet above baseboard. Line inside surface of arch or doorway, or outline door and window casings.

Horizontal Hanging

Streamline or horizontal hanging of wallpaper can be very effective especially with striped patterns. Measure a strip the length of one wall, allowing extra inch for each corner. Work from right to left and from top to bottom.

Unfold first half and start at corner, allowing strip to lap one inch around corner to right. Keep trimmed edge of first strip close and parallel to ceiling. Unfold remainder of strip and brush on smoothly. For lapped seams apply second strip so trimmed edge covers selvedge of first. For butt seams, push edges together, matching the pattern. Trim around woodwork and roll seams.

Working Around Obstructions

In papering sidewalls, take off switch plates. Hang the paper over the switch, then cut an opening large enough to expose the switch. Replace the switch plate.

To paper around a wall thermostat hang strip of paper down to the thermostat. Cut across into the paper over the thermostat and push it through the opening. Smooth down paper and trim around the thermostat using a sharp knife or razor blade.

Loosen or remove ceiling fixtures so they are not in the way. Make sure wall switch is OFF before handling fixture. Disconnect circuit if possible. Let paper extend over opening, then cut paper in way of fixture, using razor blade or knife.

Remove radiators when possible. Otherwise roll paper down behind radiator, reach in and smooth tight to wall.

Hanging Paper on Ceilings

To avoid the possibility of getting paste on the sidewalls, always hang the ceiling first. Start at side from which the most light enters, to avoid shadows on your work. If paper is hung crosswise of room, strips will be shorter, easier to handle. If hung lengthwise, strips will be

longer, but you will have fewer seams. To start out, drive tack at each end of ceiling at point from sidewall 2 in. less than width of strip. Draw chalk line tight between tack, snap against ceiling to provide starting line.

With half of pasted strip unfolded, apply paper to ceiling with outer edge along chalk line. When it is in position, use an extra roll of paper to support the unfolded end, Fig. 9-25. Use the smoothing brush from right to left, smoothing paper firmly into joint between wall and ceiling. The 2 in. allowance for unevenness in walls is lapped onto the sidewall if a border is used, otherwise it must be trimmed.

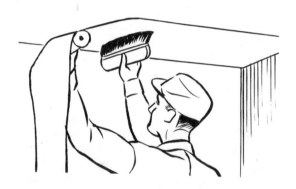

Fig. 9-25. Hanging paper on ceiling. Extra roll of paper is used to support paper.

Unfold and apply second half of strip, being careful to keep outer edge along chalk line. Smooth firmly, as before, especially into joint of wall and ceiling. Hang next strip, using first as a guide. Handle seam rolling and oozing of paste as in sidewall instructions. Work across room using previous strip as a guide. If last strip is too wide, trim it.

Hanging Specialty Papers, Fabrics, Prepasted Papers

In hanging prepasted wallpaper the walls are prepared as you would for regular wallpaper. The paper is cut into strips, then each strip is soaked in water before placing it on the wall. No pasting, and ordinarily no selvedge trimming is necessary. The new strippable papers mentioned earlier require more soaking time than do the conventional wallpapers.

In applying another type of prepasted paper the full double roll is inserted in a water-filled dispenser. The wallpaper is pulled upward from the dispenser and applied to the wall. It is smoothed on the wall, then trimmed at the top and the bottom.

Varnished and Plastic-Coated Paper

Creasing varnished and plastic-coated paper must be avoided as the pattern will be harmed. The selvedge should be trimmed from both edges of each strip before it is pasted. Varnished and plastic-coated paper should always have butted seams, as paste will not stick well to the coated portion of overlaps.

Engraved Paper

Handle engraved paper as you would varnished paper. Use care in handling these heavier papers, since their weight, when pasted, will be greater, and the paper will be more easily torn.

Muslin

Unbleached muslin is used to cover walls, particularly those with a lot of hairline cracks, in preparation for further decoration. It is made in various qualities and weights. A 9 ft. width is frequently used to eliminate seams. Muslin shrinks when handled; therefore it cannot be trimmed around openings and at the ceiling and base until it has shrunk. In cutting, allowance must be made for the shrinkage.

Muslin is usually applied dry to a pasted wall. The material is of such large size that it would be difficult to paste it before hanging. Ceiling jobs can best be handled by two men working together. To hang a ceiling with 9 ft. material, two planks and four stepladders should be used to provide a wide working space. The muslin should be rolled onto a pole and unrolled onto the pasted ceiling and brushed on with a smoothing brush. Awls are useful in fastening the material at the starting end.

Subsequent ceiling strips and sidewalls are hung in the same manner, with seams being overlapped 3 or 4 in. to allow for shrinkage. After several strips have been hung, they should be gone over with thin paste or a glue size to help fasten the material solidly on the wall and to fill the fabric for painting.

The muslin, after setting for about an hour, will have shrunk sufficiently to trim around woodwork and to cut the seam. This may be done with a knife and broadknife. The hanger should cut through both thicknesses of material in a long wavy line and be careful not to cut into the

plaster. A special canvas cutter is best for this purpose.

Oiled Fabrics

Oiled fabrics are frequently used in place of muslin. They require only one or two coats of paint to produce a finished job. Oiled fabrics are also available with a washable finish, plain and patterned.

Oiled fabrics come in 2 and 4 ft. widths. There are 16 square yards in a bolt of 4 ft. material.

The selvedge should be trimmed from the edges of each strip before it is pasted. Do not crease the folds. The seams should be butted, not lapped, then pressed down securely with brush or broadknife. DO NOT use a seam roller.

Chintz and Other Cottons

Chintz is a closely woven fabric and the colors are generally waterfast. It usually shrinks slightly, even though preshrunk, and the back should be dampened slightly with sponge and water after the lengths are cut and the selvedge trimmed.

Materials that are not waterfast should not be moistened with sponge and water because the colors are likely to smear. In hanging this type of material the possibility of shrinkage must be taken into consideration and allowances made. If the shrinkage is too great, the material may have to be overlapped and cut on the wall.

In hanging chintz and cottons a heavy paste should be used. An awl can be used to advantage for holding top edges until they are securely fastened. The strips must be handled carefully after trimming to prevent unraveling the edges.

Japanese Grass Cloth

In hanging Japanese grass cloth, which is made of paper and straw, the walls are prepared in the usual way. This wall covering comes in double or triple rolls, 3 ft. wide. A blank stock wall liner should then be applied, because the alkali in plaster has a tendency to stain grass cloth. The stains become more apparent after the material has hung for a while.

Grass cloth should be hung with low water content paste. Paste with a heavier than usual mixture of the adhesive and work on one strip at a time to prevent separation due to saturation.

Seams of grass cloth may be butted, but vertical seams will show because the product is hand made.

Filled Burlap

Filled burlap is frequently used as a wall covering, to achieve a heavy cloth-texture appearance. It is sold in 50 yard rolls and usually comes one yard wide. It can also be obtained by the single yard. Filled burlap is filled with glue and is very stiff. Most burlap is now laminated to paper for easier hanging. If it is not, however, a paper lining must be used on the wall first.

In hanging burlap a heavy paste should be used. Edges may be trimmed either before or after hanging. Sharp cutting tools, such as a razor knife, are required. The worker must be certain the paste is still wet when the material hits the wall.

Canvas

In applying canvas the strips should be allowed to overlap about an inch and the edges trimmed afterward. Because of shrinkage, it is not advisable to cut the seams until the entire wall has become fairly dry.

In cutting the seams, use a sharp knife or canvas seam cutter, and cut through both thicknesses of canvas at the same time in a long wavy line, being very careful not to cut into the plaster. Open the seam, remove the edge of the lower strip, then paste both edges down. Cracks that show up when dry, may be filled with white lead, putty, or spackling compound.

"Remodeling" with Wallpaper

Architectural defects such as irregular walls and uneven ceilings can be hidden from view or at least made less conspicuous, by using wallpaper with an allover print. If a room seems cramped or confined, wallpaper can be made to give it an illusion of space. A scenic panel makes a room seem larger by creating a vista. Vertical climbing patterns can add a feeling of height; horizontal patterns seem to provide length.

Papers with an outdoor pattern may be used to turn a bay window into a garden alcove; allover prints may be used to blend the point in attic rooms where walls and low sloping ceilings meet.

The new three-dimensional papers can change the mood of a small room by providing an illusion of spaciousness.

From the wide selection of wallpaper available, you can find special papers to create a mood in any room, from a fairytale town for a child's room, to a collection of liquor labels for a home bar.

How to Take Care of Wallpaper

CLEANING: A good quality, dough-type, non-crumbling cleaner will usually give good results. These mixtures are easy to handle, and will do a thorough job of cleaning wallpaper or window shades.

REMOVING SPOTS: If your paper is washable, smudges and marks can be quickly and easily removed with a damp sponge and mild soap and cold water. If the paper is a nonwashable quality, a commercial cleaner as just described will give you the best all-around cleaning job.

REMOVING PENCIL MARKS: An art-gum eraser will remove the marks. Be sure that you do not use an eraser containing any grit that will damage the surface of the paper. Removing crayon marks can be most successfully done with a solvent, such as naphtha followed by the use of an art-gum eraser.

REMOVING GREASE SPOTS: Spots of an oily character can often be removed by using a mixture of Fuller's Earth and a nonflammable dry cleaning fluid. Make a paste of these two ingredients, and apply over the spots not more than 1/4 in. thick at center. Smooth down thin at the edges. Blow on the edges while you are applying the mixture to avoid the formation of a ring. When thoroughly dry, remove by brushing lightly with a soft cloth. Several applications may be required to remove completely a stubborn spot. A variety of proprietary spot removers are now available.

REMOVING INK SPOTS: An ink eradicator can be used. Be sure to exercise care in applying and using it, because it is often a very powerful substance. It is best to practice removing a small spot in an inconspicuous place before attempting larger and more prominent spots. There is no question but that the new vinyl wall coverings offer the greatest ease of maintenance and the longest life. This accounts for the great popularity they have achieved in the last few years.

Unit 10

WOOD FINISHING WITH
SHELLAC, VARNISH AND LACQUER

Interior Finishing

Basic Steps to Achieve a Fine Finish

To obtain a fine finish on new woodwork and floors or woodwork from which the old finish has been removed requires a series of operations carried out in the proper order.

Basic steps for achieving a fine finish with varnish, shellac or lacquer include: sanding to smooth the wood; bleaching (for blonde finishes); staining to provide color and bring out the grain; applying filler to level the surface (open-grain wood only); sealing to seal in the filler and provide a good bond for finish coats; applying top coats to provide wear surface; and waxing. Some variations are required, depending on the type of wood, quality of furniture or other item being finished, and on the need for a standard or novelty effect.

Groups of Woods

Wood used in home construction, by furniture manufacturers and by home craftsmen may be divided into two main groups; hardwood, which are for the most part products of broad-leaved trees, and softwoods, which are mostly products of needle-leaved trees or evergreens. The hardwoods and softwoods may in turn be divided into the general classifications of open-grained or porous wood, and close-grained or nonporous woods.

Open-Grained Woods

Lumber from most broad-leaf trees contains large vessels and is very porous. When such lumber is cut and planed at the mill, the tubular cells are ruptured, leaving minute openings or pores. These pores must be "filled" in order to obtain a smooth finish.

Open-grained woods which require the use of a filler include Oak, Walnut, Chestnut, Mahogany, Ash, Bubinga, Padouk, Teak, Amaranth, Prima Vera, Rosewood and Zebrawood.

Close-Grained Woods

Examples of close-grained woods which require no filler are Pine, Birch, Gum, Maple, Poplar, Cedar, Cherry, Fir, Basswood, Hemlock, Spruce and Cypress.

Determining whether wood is open-grained or close-grained is not difficult and can be done by inspection. When wood is open-grained it is porous and the pores or minute openings are quite obvious. There are no such pores in close-grained wood.

Sanding (The First Step)

The finish coat can be no smoother than the surface to which it is applied. On most finishing jobs it is necessary to sand to remove some unevenness and fuzziness from the surface. On new, unfinished furniture, the chances are that a light sanding with fine garnet or aluminum oxide paper (4/0 or 6/0) will be satisfactory. On interior woodwork of a home a little more sanding may be needed since the surface may be marred or scratched. At least two grades of abrasive paper will usually be required - - 1/0 and 3/0. In using abrasive paper always work WITH the grain of the wood. Sanding across the grain results in scratches which will require more sanding to remove. See Fig. 10-1.

Power sanders can be used to good advantage for large areas. A belt sander is practical for most jobs, and a vibrating type sander is ideal for small jobs where a particularly smooth surface is desired.

DAMPENING TO RAISE GRAIN: Additional smoothness may be obtained by going over a surface with a sponge moistened with warm water to raise the grain, and sanding when dry to remove the fuzziness.

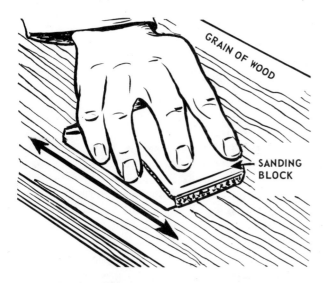

Fig. 10-1. In hand sanding best results can be obtained by using a rubber sanding block or padded hardwood block. Always sand WITH the grain.

Smoothing Abrasive Paper

Rubbing sheets of abrasive paper together with the grit sides against each other, will scuff off sharp grit that protrudes too far above the surface of the paper and will enable the worker to do a better job of sanding with the paper. See Fig. 10-2.

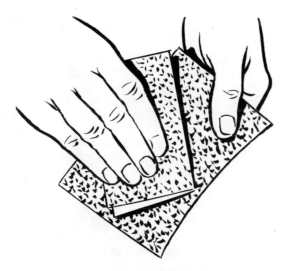

Fig. 10-2. Rubbing sheets of abrasive paper together to scuff off sharp grits.

Cleaning up Abrasive Dust with Tack Rag

Before applying any finish to a surface which has been sanded, the abrasive dust should be carefully removed. One of the best ways to do this is to use what is called a Tack Rag. Tack Rags may be purchased at paint stores, or can be made from a piece of soft, lintless cloth. Wet the cloth with water and squeeze lightly. Sprinkle turpentine liberally over the cloth, then sprinkle two or three teaspoonfuls of varnish over it. Squeeze the cloth until almost dry. The cloth should be completely damp with the varnish. Such a tack rag, if kept in a closed can or glass jar, will remain tacky for a long time.

Bleaching Wood

In the past the main reason for bleaching wood was to provide uniform color to the woods used in a piece of furniture. Today, woods such as walnut and mahogany, which are naturally dark in color, are often bleached, in conformity with the demand for light-colored or blond furniture and to achieve novelty finishes.

Types of Bleaches

Bleaches commonly used include Oxalic Acid, Hydrogen Peroxide, Sodium Hypochlorite and the commercial bleaching solutions.

Oxalic Acid Bleach

Oxalic acid is frequently used as a wood bleach. Recommendations for the proper concentration vary, but on most jobs a mixture consisting of 10 to 16 ounces of the crystalline or powdered oxalic acid to one gallon of water will work out satisfactorily. The addition of alcohol will increase the solvent ability of the water for a stronger bleach.

Oxalic acid should be dissolved and used in glass, earthenware, or enameled iron vessels. The bleach is most effective when used hot, almost boiling, but it may also be used unheated. Several applications may be made, until the desired color of wood is obtained. Then, the acid should be removed using hot water, or neutralized with a solution of one ounce of borax to one quart of water. Remove the borax solution by washing with hot water.

The wood must be allowed to dry thoroughly before sanding. In sanding, be careful not to inhale dust particles which may be coated with the poisonous bleach. A dust mask should be worn if a large amount of sanding is to be done.

Hydrogen Peroxide Bleach

One of the more powerful bleaches is a strong solution of hydrogen peroxide, 30 to 100 percent strength (not to be confused with the 3 percent antiseptic solution. The wood is first coated with a solution of sodium hydroxide (caustic soda, or ordinary lye) containing four pounds of the solid to ten gallons of solution. After this has dried for about 30 minutes, an even coat of hydrogen peroxide is applied. The sodium hydroxide renders the hydrogen peroxide unstable and decomposes it to liberate a large amount of oxygen in a chemically active state to do the bleaching.

Liquid on the surface of the wood should be' allowed sufficient time to dry, during which time bleaching occurs. Then, the wood should be rinsed with cool, clean water. Any remaining traces of sodium hydroxide may be neutralized by washing or spraying the surface with a solution consisting of 1/4 lb. of acetic acid (the active ingredient of vinegar) to two gallons of water. Let the acetic acid solution stand about 15 minutes; then rinse it off with clear water.

Sodium silicate may be used as a first coat in place of sodium hydroxide. It is recoated with hydrogen peroxide immediately while wet and foams to hold the oxide action to the lumber. When dry it may be sanded clean and smooth readily. Hydrogen peroxide of this strength will burn and blind and eats holes in clothes. It also digests brushes. Every precaution such as goggles, rubber gloves and fiber brushes must be used.

Miscellaneous Bleaches

A satisfactory bleaching solution may be made by first applying a solution of potassium permanganate, made by dissolving one ounce to a gallon of water. This solution should be applied freely to the wood. While still wet apply a solution of sodium bisulphite (photographer's "hypo") made by dissolving 4 ounces to a gallon of hot water. Allow this solution to cool before using it.

A 10 percent solution of sodium hypochlorite in water can be used by repeatedly wetting the wood to be bleached with the solution. Ordinary household laundry bleach containing weak solu-

tions of hypochlorite, such as "Clorox," will bleach some woods, using a solution of 1/2 pint per gallon of water. The laundry bleach should be applied liberally and allowed to dry. The application should be repeated if necessary to obtain the desired shade, and the wood finally rinsed with clear water.

Commercial Bleaching Solutions

Perhaps the simplest and best way to obtain a good bleach is to purchase one of the available commercial bleaches. Two general types of commercial bleaches are available. One consists of two solutions which are applied in separate coats. The other consists of two solutions which are mixed together just before using, Fig. 10-3. In using both types the manufacturer's instructions must be carefully followed to obtain best results.

Fig. 10-3. Using commercial bleach. The two solutions are mixed together and applied as a single coat.

On small jobs or in bleaching selected areas, such as mineral streaks or dark individual boards or pieces of veneer, the bleaching solution or solutions, may be applied with a brush, cloth swab, or sponge.

In large-scale production work, bleaching solutions are frequently applied with a spray gun. A gun for such purposes should be one with a glass jar and its construction should be such that the solution can touch no metal except stainless steel or other corrosion-resistant alloy. The gun should be washed after use by spraying water through it.

After bleaching, wood must be sanded lightly to remove the fuzziness which results, and the abrasive dust carefully removed. Commercial bleaches are based on strong hydrogen peroxide and should be used with proper safety measures. They are extremely hazardous when sprayed.

Staining to Enhance the Beauty of Wood

Staining is a very important operation in wood finishing. It is used to darken and intensify colors, emphasize wood grains, and to impart color to the wood surface. Stain is not a protective finish in itself.

Wood stains of the dye class may be classified according to the solvent used in their manufacture. These include water, oil, and alcohol.

Water Stain

The coloring matter used in water stain is usually an aniline dye in the form of a dry powder. Water stains are available in primary and secondary colors, from which may be mixed any shade of stain desired. They are also available in wood colors such as mahogany, walnut, and maple. In mixing water stain the water is heated to just under the boiling point, and the aniline dye added while stirring slowly. An ounce of the powder makes about a quart of concentrated stain.

Water stain is low in cost, is nonfading, and provides brilliant colors. It penetrates evenly and deeply into the pores of the wood and gives clear even tones. A disadvantage of water stain is that the water raises the grain of the wood, requiring extra sanding to level the surface.

Before applying water stain, the sanded surface should be moistened with water to raise the grain. Use either a sponge, cloth, or spray gun. Only enough water to moisten the surface is needed. Allow the surface to dry, sand lightly using 3/0 abrasive paper. Be sure to remove glue, grease, oil and fingerprints as stain will not spread properly over them.

Water stain may be applied by using a spray gun, or a brush. The spray gun provides the easier way to apply the stain and will result in the most uniform coverage.

In applying water stain with a brush, a full-chisel brush as large as practical and of good quality should be used. Work with the grain and use long, straight strokes. Apply the stain freely; spread the stain as far and as quickly as possible. Continue brushing the stain into the wood until there is no more stain on the brush. Avoid applying stain to the same spot twice, or a darker brush lap may result. After an even coat of stain has been applied, the surface should be wiped to an even tone and let dry.

Darkening of end grain may be controlled by using a separate lighter stain (stain thinned down more); by treating the end grain previous to staining with a thin glue size; by sponging with water just before staining; and by removing excess stain with a cloth before it soaks into the wood.

EXPERIMENT ON ROUGH STOCK: To learn how to use stain, it is advisable to experiment on rough stock, preferably stock of the same kind that is subsequently to be finished.

A light sanding after the surface is dry, is required to remove raised grain. If any difficulty is experienced in sanding off the fuzz, apply a wash coat of shellac to stiffen the raised fibers. Water stains are most permanent and are clearer than others but are extremely hard to handle.

Non-Grain-Raising Stains (NGR Stains)

The powders used in making water stains may be used in making non-grain-raising stains by dissolving them in special solvents provided by manufacturers. The colors have the same permanence as those of water stains. In using NGR stains, not only is extra sanding avoided, but the NGR stain dries much quicker than water stain.

Because of its quick-drying quality NGR stain is best applied with a spray gun. By skillful manipulation of the gun, it is possible to stain and shade at the same time.

When brushing NGR stain, use a large brush and apply a wet coat of stain. Follow immediately with a soft cloth, wiping off the excess and making the color uniform.

Oil Stains

Oil stains are of two principal types: Pigmented or Wiping Stain and Penetrating Oil Stain.

Pigmented Oil Stain

Pigmented type oil stains are like thinned paints. Suitable stain can be made by diluting enamel or paint with turpentine until it is of watery consistency, or it may be purchased in ready-to-use form. Colors in pigmented oil stains, like those used in paint, are of a permanent nature. The pigments are finely ground, insoluble minerals uniformly mixed in a suitable vehicle such as linseed oil. Pigmented oil stains will not bleed. Since the coloring matter consists of pigment instead of dyes, and is opaque, such stain has a tendency to cover up the grain pattern more than water or NGR stains.

Pigmented oil stains are best suited for use on close-grained woods such as maple, pine, birch, cherry, gumwood, and basswood. These stains are frequently used where it is desirable to obscure the characteristic grain of wood, and to impart the color of the wood being imitated. When used on open-grained wood like oak they tend to clog up the pores producing a "muddy" appearance.

Pigmented oil stain should be stirred well before use, because the pigment coloring matter settles to the bottom of the can when the product is stored.

The stain may be applied with a spray gun, brush or rag. Spread it liberally over the surface. Allow it to set for a short period of time, usually 2 to 8 minutes depending on the product and the type of finish required, then wipe off to a uniform tone. Wipe with the grain. If wiped too soon, the color may be lightened too much; if too late, the stain may be gummy. Instructions furnished by the manufacturer of the stain should be carefully followed, and some experimenting should be done on rough stock.

As pigmented stains do not penetrate into the woods like aniline dyes, they can be used to produce blond finishes. White pigmented wiping stain may be used on maple and birch to get an attractive blond effect. For woods that are a little darker, an off-white stain may be used. White pigmented wiping stains may also be used to obtain some interesting color effects by tinting them with oil colors.

Penetrating Oil Stains

Penetrating oil stain may be obtained in ready-to-use form or in the form of stain powder or dye which is dissolved in turpentine, naphtha, benzol and other light oils. Penetrating oil stain does not raise the grain of the wood like water stain, but has the disadvantage of bleeding into top coats and of not being lightfast. The bleeding and fading however, may be controlled to a considerable extent by using proper finish coats.

Penetrating oil stain is usually preferable to pigmented oil stains in finishing the open-grained woods such as oak, walnut, mahogany, and chestnut.

Apply penetrating oil stains with a brush, using long, full strokes with the grain. Brush strokes should be started on unstained portions of the wood and carried to the stained portions without overlapping. When staining end grain, the stain should be wiped off quickly to prevent too much penetration and darkening of the wood. Excess penetration and darkening can also be avoided by using a sealer on the end-grain prior to staining. The sealer should be thinned as directed by the manufacturer and applied as a light coat and care should be taken to apply the sealer only to the end-grain so that other grained areas are not spotted. After the sealer has been applied, stain should be applied to all surfaces as outlined above.

On flat surfaces, the stain should be wiped off, using a soft cloth, a few minutes after its application. An area that is too dark may be lightened by use of a cloth saturated with turpentine.

Additional darkening or coloring of the wood may be obtained by applying a second coat of stain, or allowing the stain to remain on longer before wiping off the excess. Oil stains' main advantage is its easier workability.

Spirit Stains

Spirit stains are made by dissolving aniline dyes in spirits, such as alcohol or acetone. They dry very quickly and are best applied by using a spray gun. Brush marks and streaks are almost inevitable when applying spirit stains with brushes. Spirit stain is a bleeding type of stain and will strike through almost any kind of finish. It fades quickly when exposed to strong light, unless protected by finish coats.

Spirit stains are used to some extent as "shading stains." Lacquer is usually added to the stain for body. By proper adjustment of the spray nozzle and skillful use of a spray gun, fine shading can be done. Shellac may also be added, particularly for brush work.

Applying Filler

Woods having open pores, such as walnut, mahogany and oak, require a coat of paste wood filler to provide a level surface for the application of top finish coats. A filler is used on all finishes except a true "Old World" finish which requires that the pores be left unfilled. The filler is usually applied after staining, and sometimes after a light sealer coat after which the surface is sealed and finished.

The filler helps to color the wood and to emphasize the pattern. The grain pattern may be emphasized by using filler a shade darker than the color of the stained wood. The grain pattern may be brought out even more prominently by using a filler that is very dark, almost black. Novel two-tone effects are obtained by rubbing a white or colored filler into a surface that has been stained a different color. The filler fills the pores of the stained wood, leaving them the color of the filler, while the rest of the surface is the color of the stain.

Paste wood fillers are usually made of silex or silica ground in linseed oil and drier with various pigments added for coloring. These fillers come in standard wood colors such as mahogany, light oak, dark oak, maple, walnut, black, white and natural.

Most fillers come in paste form and are too thick to use without thinning. Thinning is done by adding turpentine, naphtha, or special thinner according to the manufacturer's instructions. The degree of dilution depends on the size of the pores in the wood to be filled and the effect desired. A heavy-mix (about 1/2 pint thinner to one pound of filler) is required for coarse, open-grained woods such as Philippine mahogany, oak, and chestnut; a medium-mix (about 10 ounces of thinner to one pound of filler) for closer-grained woods like walnut, rosewood, mahogany, and zebrawood.

MIXING THE FILLER: In mixing silex wood filler, add the thinner a little at a time, being sure to stir well. Turpentine used as a thinner will provide a slower setting filler than naphtha. The use of boiled linseed oil as a thinner will slow up the setting of the filler still more.

The surface of the wood to be filled should be clean and dust-free. Use a stiff, short-bristle brush not more than 4 in. wide. Do not try to cover too large an area at one time. Brush with the grain.

As soon as the surface of the filler begins to get dull or lose its shine, it is time to begin the wiping operation.

In wiping use a burlap pad (section from a burlap bag folded into several thicknesses) or a felt block. Use circular and cross-grain motion to work the silex particles well into the

pores of the wood. The surplus filler should then be wiped off using clean pieces of burlap or coarse-textured rags, again working ACROSS the grain, Fig. 10-4. If the filler sets before the excess has been cleared off, put a little turpentine or naphtha on the wiping rag. The final clean-up is done by wiping very lightly WITH the grain to remove the streaks. Care must be taken not to remove any of the soft filler from the pores.

Fig. 10-4. Surplus paste wood filler is removed by using coarse cloth or burlap and wiping ACROSS the grain.

In finishing nonporous and semi-porous woods, wiping stains may be used to serve the same purpose silex fillers serve in finishing open-grained woods. These are similar to filler in some respects but do not contain as much inert materials as the silex fillers.

Changing Color of Filler

Paste fillers are available in a number of different colors as well as natural, which is about the color of linseed oil. It is often necessary to change the color to match the color of stained wood by adding to the filler small amounts of pigment color ground in oil. Mix the colors in small quantities of turpentine; then add them to the filler gradually, until the desired color is obtained.

Filler may also be stained by adding a little oil stain to the filler, but the use of pigment oil colors is preferable.

Thorough drying of the filler is necessary for good finishing. It is then sanded, using 6/0 paper, working with the grain.

Applying Sealer Coat

The next step in producing a good finish on a surface that has been filled and sanded is to apply a sealer coat. In finishing nonporous wood where filling is unnecessary, the sealer follows the stain.

Sealer prevents absorption of finish coats into the wood, ties down the stains and fillers which have been applied, and helps provide good adhesion of the top coats to the filler or wiping stain. A sealer coat is also used to prevent bleeding of certain types of stain into the top coats.

TYPES OF SEALERS: Sealers are of three principal types: shellac, varnish and lacquer.

Sealer for a Shellac Finish

The sealer for a shellac finish should be either orange or white shellac - - four pound cut thinned to the proportion of one part shellac to six parts of denatured alcohol. Orange shellac is satisfactory for dark woods like mahogany and walnut; white shellac should be used on light woods such as maple, and in applying blond finishes.

Sealer for Varnish Finish

Shellac may also be used as a sealer for varnish finish, or else a varnish sealer may be used. Most professionals recommend a varnish sealer in preference to a shellac sealer.

A varnish sealer may be made by thinning varnish with an equal quantity of turpentine or thinner specified by the manufacturer of the varnish, (one-to-one proportion).

If a natural or light finish is desired, it is advisable to use varnish with dammar gum. Oil varnish sealers may be used over water stains and spirit stains, but if used over oil stains without filler, the stain causes the varnish to dry very slowly.

Good results with a varnish finish may be obtained by using a water or non-grain-raising stain, followed by a paste filler and a wash coat of shellac. This provides an excellent base for the varnish.

Sealer for a Lacquer Finish

Lacquer sealer is a "must" with lacquer. Both brushing and spraying types of lacquer sealers are available. Lacquer as it comes in

the can is reduced with thinner - - one part lacquer to six parts thinner. Applying the sealer by spraying is preferable because it provides better uniformity.

SEALER SHOULD BE SANDED: The sealer coat, when thoroughly dry, should be sanded lightly, working with the grain, using 6/0 paper. Be careful not to cut through the coat, especially along the edges.

Glazing

Glazes are pigments finely ground in oil, which are brushed, wiped and blended over a sealer to give a high-lighted, shaded or antiqued effect. The glaze is generally wiped clean from the flat surfaces and edges that are to appear worn, and left in the recesses in order to provide an antiqued effect. Tinting colors-in-oil are usually satisfactory for glazing, if reduced to brushing consistency with turpentine or mineral spirits.

Applying a Shellac Finish

Shellac finishes dry fast and hard and wear well.

Some disadvantages of a shellac finish are poor resistance to water, easy staining, and no resistance to alcohol. Wet glasses and flower vases will produce white rings on a shellac finish. Hot dishes also damage a shellac finish. For these reasons shellac should not be used on dresser or table tops, or other furniture on which hot objects, wet glasses, or alcoholic beverages may be placed or spilled. Shellac is recommended as a top coat for floors, and is frequently used as a base coat or undercoat.

In buying shellac always get a top-quality product. Avoid shellac substitutes. Shellac darkens with age and should not be purchased in a quantity that will last more than six months. Shellac is sold in three, four and five pound cuts. By "cut" we mean the number of pounds of shellac gum that has been dissolved in each gallon of alcohol. Best for general use is the four pound cut. A four pound cut is reduced close to a three pound by adding 1/2 pint alcohol to one quart shellac, to a two pound cut by using one quart alcohol to one quart shellac, and to a one pound cut by using three quarts of alcohol to one quart of shellac.

On most shellac finishing jobs three coats of shellac are recommended. For the first coat, mix one part white shellac (four pound cut) and three parts denatured alcohol. Apply with the grain of the wood and avoid overlapping of brush strokes. Let this dry, sand light, then mix shellac and alcohol - - one part shellac, one part alcohol, for the second coat. Allow at least three hours to dry. Sand lightly, then apply the third or finish coat, using the same mixture as specified for the second coat. Sand lightly when dry, using 6/0 paper.

For a shellac and wax finish, apply a coat of good paste wax. Make sure the entire surface is covered. Allow 20 to 30 minutes time for the wax to dry, then polish with a soft cloth. Additional coats of wax may be applied if desired.

Never use wax on bare wood as the soft wax will catch and hold dirt. Wax used in this manner is very difficult to remove for application of other types of finish.

Varnish Finishes

Varnish makes an excellent clear, transparent finish that reveals the full beauty of the grain and color of wood. It possesses good durability and hardness.

Types of varnish in use today include:

1. Natural Varnishes which are the secretions of trees. These were developed in Asia and are known mainly as Oriental lacquer, Chinese lacquer or Japanese lacquer. Their principal use is finishing of jewel boxes, wood vessels and certain types of furniture.

2. Catalyzed Varnishes take their name from the fact a catalyst is added just before application to speed the drying of the resinous contents. These varnishes, which are highly resistant to water, alkali, acids and solvents, are used primarily for industrial finishing.

3. Water Varnishes include the fixatives employed by artists to protect pastel drawings and other types of art work, the sizes used to stiffen straw hats and various hair-dressing goods. They are emulsions or dispersions of resins in water.

4. Spirit Varnish is composed of a resin or other film-forming material combined with a volatile liquid. When the liquid has evaporated, the resin remains on the coated surface in the form of a film. Large quantities of spirit varnishes are used for coating such familiar objects as playing cards and food cartons. They are also used in the antifouling paints that discourage the growth of speed-impeding organisms on the hulls of ships and in paints that safeguard our lives by marking traffic lanes on highways.

5. Most familiar of all types and most widely used are the oleoresinous varnishes which are mixtures of resin, oil and drier, dissolved in a volatile liquid which serves as a thinner. The resin and oil are usually processed by cooking.

Oleoresinous varnishes include many types. The names may describe the ingredients, some special characteristic, or end use. There are tung oil, phenolic, asphalt and epoxy varnishes, long and short oil varnishes (oil length is proportion of oil to resins - - number of gallons of oil used for each 100 lbs. of resin), flat varnish, air drying and baking varnishes, spar varnish, aluminum varnish (for mixing with aluminum pigment), floor, furniture, electrical insulating and heat resistant varnishes, and many others.

Varnish Application

"MUSTS" IN APPLYING VARNISH: A clean brush is essential. A regular tapered or wedge-shaped varnish brush 2 to 3 in. wide is recommended. One way to be sure the brush is clean is to put a small amount of varnish in a separate container and brush several brushfuls of varnish from this container across a knife edge or the edge of another can until all dust and dirt are removed. Be careful not to damage the bristles of the brush. Throw away the small amount of varnish which contains dust and dirt from the brush.

Work in a room as free from dust as possible. Dust is the worst enemy of varnish. If you cannot arrange to work in dust-free surroundings do not attempt to apply varnish. Do not try to apply varnish in a cold room. The temperature should be 70 deg. or more.

Make sure the surface to be varnished is dust-free. Use a Tack Rag to pick up dust from the surface just before applying the varnish. Remember that a varnish brush will pick up every speck of dust and every speck will be magnified in a glossy finish. Dust specks may be picked up by using the moistened tip of a small artist's brush or a clean sliver of wood. This should be done before the varnish has a chance to set.

Varnish brushes should not be dipped into the can in which the varnish was obtained, because of the danger of getting dirt in the can and ruining the varnish. A clean can of appropriate size should be provided. Left-over varnish should be discarded instead of pouring it back into the original container.

FIRST COAT: Assuming that the wood has been stained, filled and sealed as required to prepare it for varnish, we are ready for the first varnish finish coat. The manufacturer's instructions for thinning should be followed. In most cases thinning of the varnish for the first coat is required. To avoid bubbles handle varnish with care and do not shake it or stir too vigorously.

BRUSHING TECHNIQUE: Brush varnish on liberally with the grain of the wood, but exercise care to avoid running and sagging. On flat areas it is well to crisscross the varnish horizontally, and then vertically to level out the varnish and provide a uniform film. Uniformity of film does much to prevent sagging.

NUMBER OF VARNISH COATS: Two coats of varnish will usually provide a good surface if the wood has been carefully filled and sealed. Three and four coats of varnish are frequently used where a fine finish is required.

RUBBING AND POLISHING: Although there are satin-finish varnishes which dry to subdued, satiny finish without rubbing, many finishers prefer to hand-rub their furniture or woodwork. By hand rubbing they can dull down a gloss finish to just the depth of sheen desired. Rubbing also eliminates small imperfections, dust specks and waves, making the surface perfectly smooth.

Much of the success of getting good varnish finishes depends on proper drying of the various coats of finish before sanding and rubbing. Varnish may appear to be dry on the surface, but it takes considerable time for most varnish coatings to dry all the way through.

You can test for hardness of finish by pressing a thumbnail against the finish. If an impression can be made more drying time is required.

The first coat of varnish should be rubbed dry (water or oil are used in rubbing down other coats), using 6/0 paper. Sanding should be done with the grain of the wood. Be careful not to sand through the finish.

Sanding after the second and succeeding coats up to the final coat should be done with 6/0 waterproof paper. The paper should be backed with a felt pad or sanding block faced with sponge rubber. Water should be used as a lubricant. After sanding, wash the surface with a clean, damp cloth to remove the dust. Allow the surface to dry before applying the next coat of varnish.

For obtaining a fine finish, pumice is the standard abrasive for rubbing the final coat. This comes in the form of a powder. In rubbing the final coat most wood finishers prefer to use oil with the pumice instead of water. Regular rubbing oil, paraffin oil, or light mineral oil may be used. Proceed by dipping a felt pad into the oil and then into the pumice. Use plenty of oil so the pumice will not cake up on the felt. Pumice may also be applied to the surface by using a sifter top can, or by sprinkling by hand.

Rub with long even strokes. On most work only a few strokes will be required. Be careful not to cut through the finish at any point. Carvings and moldings may be rubbed with a stubby brush, such as one made by cutting the ends of bristles off an old paint brush.

Inspect the finish by cleaning a small area. When finished, remove all oil and pumice with a clean cloth. Rottenstone which is finer and softer than pumice, is used for final rubbing and polishing. Rottenstone does very little cutting but will bring up a surface from satin to near-gloss by continued rubbing. After obtaining the desired finish, use a clean wet cloth to remove the rottenstone. Complete the clean-up job by using a soft cloth and benzine.

RUBBING MACHINES: In production shops rubbing machines are used to eliminate much of the strenuous labor required in hand rubbing. Both electric and air-driven units are used.

Spraying Varnish

All types of varnish may be applied by spraying. The varnish is usually sprayed at container consistency with the larger units. A reduction of 25 to 30 percent is sometimes required when using small units with suction feed guns.

Varnish-Stain Finish

On pieces where a varnish finish is desired but the grain of the wood is unattractive or uneven and it is desirable to cover it up, varnish-stain may be used. As the name indicates, this is a combination varnish and stain. In addition to producing an imitation of wood color, it provides a protective finish.

A disadvantage of varnish-stain is that when the varnish is worn off or chipped, the color comes off too.

Varnish Defects

Defects that develop in varnish finishes include: crawling, blistering, bloom, crazing, withering, tackiness, sweating, runs and sags, livering, skinning, and specks in the finish.

Varnish Crawling

Poor wetting of the freshly applied varnish to the surface in some spots causes crawling (the gather up of varnish into globules) instead of covering the surface. This may be caused by applying varnish over a greasy, wet, cold or wax covered surface, or a surface that is too glossy. It may also be caused by adding too much drier to varnish, or mixing two different types of varnish together. Varnish that is thinned with benzine instead of turpentine or applied too thick may also have a tendency to crawl.

Blistering

This defect can be easily identified by the swelling of the varnish into bubbles or blisters. Blistering is usually caused by excessive moisture present in the wood at the time of varnishing or moisture which gains access to the wood after varnishing. Heat of the sun or heat from inside the house moves moisture through the wood to the underside of the film and loosens the adhesion of the varnish. If vapor pressure is built up, blisters are formed.

Blistering caused by construction faults can be avoided only if the faults are corrected. Be sure the material to be varnished is dry. Before revarnishing a blistered surface, remove all the old varnish.

Bloom

Bloom or clouding of the transparency of a varnish finish may be caused by applying varnish in rooms when the humidity is too high and an excess of moisture has collected on the surface. Increasing the ventilation usually corrects this trouble.

Another cause of bloom in a varnish finish is rubbing of the finish with pumice and water instead of pumice and oil.

Crazing

This defect in a varnished surface may be identified by fine interlacing cracks which appear to be on the underside of the varnish coating. Crazing is frequently noticed on the finish of old cars. This defect is caused by sudden temperature changes and failure of the varnish to contract and expand to the same degree as the metal.

Withering

Withering or loss of gloss is often caused by varnishing open-pore woods without filling the pores, use of improper or insufficient undercoating, and applying a top coat before the undercoat has thoroughly dried.

Sweating

Sweating or changing of a varnished surface that has been rubbed from a glossy to a dull finish, back to a "greasy" gloss, is often caused by applying varnish over an undercoat which was not thoroughly dry.

Runs, Sags, Curtains

Runs, sags and curtains (heavy fluid sags in flowing lines like a draped curtain) are caused by applying too much varnish or by not applying it evenly. The same factors that produce crawling can also cause runs and sags.

Livering

Livering of a varnish finish is coagulation of the finishing material into a viscous, rubber-like mass. Livering is usually a chemical reaction between two or more substances.

Tackiness

Slow-drying or nondrying of varnish may be caused by applying a heavy coat of varnish over open-grained wood on which the paste filler has not been allowed to dry thoroughly; on jobs where the ventilation is extremely poor; and on surfaces that have not been properly cleaned. Varnishes containing too much oil are frequently slow drying. Some stains inhibit the drying of varnish and should be sealed off with shellac.

Skinning

Some varnishes skin over when left exposed to the air in an open can or in a partially filled container.

Varnish skin can be removed by straining the varnish. Varnish should not be stored in partially filled cans; instead it should be poured into smaller cans which are completely filled. A thin film of turpentine over the top of varnish will also prevent it from skinning over.

Specks on Varnished Surfaces

Specks on varnished surfaces may be caused by spraying varnish containing skins. When forced through a spray gun, the air breaks the skin into small particles which appear as specks.

Another cause of specks in a finish is allowing a newly varnished surface to become chilled before the varnish has had a chance to set. Specks which develop are bits of gum resins, oils, or driers which have congealed.

Specks in a varnish finish may be caused by improper cleaning of the surface, dirt in the air, or dirty brushes.

Penetrating Stain Waxes

Penetrating stain wax finishes, which combine the essential finishing ingredients in one material, are available for use on trim, wood paneling, furniture and floors. Such a finish produces the color of a penetrating stain with the luster of wax.

The wood must be clean, dry, and carefully smoothed by sanding. The stain wax may be applied with either brush or cloth. It will not raise the grain and does not show lap or brush marks. Allow the finish to penetrate into the wood five to fifteen minutes then remove excess, using clean cloths. Allow to dry overnight and apply a second coat in the same manner.

When the second coat of stain wax is dry, paste finishing wax should be applied and polished. This finish is not to be used where spar finishes are required and where surfaces are subject to heat or water stains.

In finishing open-grained woods, paste filler is usually applied between the first and second coats.

Procedures vary somewhat according to the specific product being applied, so be sure to read and follow the manufacturer's instructions.

Finishing with Wax

Wax provides a pleasing semi-gloss finish for furniture, woodwork and floors. The durability of a wax finish is largely dependent on the base on which it is formed. Wax always demands periodic renewal in order to retain its appearance. Wax finishes will not stand excessive heat or water and should not be used where these elements will be encountered. Wax comes in two principal forms; paste and liquid.

Best results are obtained with wax, if the work is first coated with shellac, varnish or lacquer. Wax may be applied with a brush or soft cloth. It should be put on in a thin, even coat, permitted to dry until it is dull in appearance, and then polished to a luster, with a wax buffer, soft woolen rag, or cheesecloth, using long sweeping strokes with the grain of the wood. Two or three thin coats of wax are better than one heavy coat. A wax coating should be allowed to dry at least an hour before applying an additional coat.

A wax finish should not be permitted to wear through before rewaxing. If this happens, the remaining wax coating should be removed with turpentine or benzine, and a completely new wax finish applied.

Self-Polishing Waxes

Floor waxes of the self-polishing type, differ from regular furniture waxes and should not be used on furniture or woodwork.

Colored Wax

Colored wax, as required for some types of furniture finishing operations, may be obtained by adding a small quantity of color in a suitable vehicle to paste or liquid wax. Adding powdered rottenstone will give a "dusty" appearance, which is suitable for antiquing.

Penetrating Wood Finishes (Wood Sealers)

Penetrating wood finishes like varnishes, are made of resins, drying oils, thinners and driers. A penetrating wood finish sinks into the wood cells nearest the surface without forming a continuous coating of appreciable thickness over the surface.

While penetrating finishes made by various manufacturers differ considerably in composition, the same general procedure is followed in their application.

The finish should be applied full strength to smoothly sanded wood, either raw or stained. In applying the finish either a brush or cloth may be used. With this finish, streaks, laps and brush marks are never a problem. It is advisable to cover the surface liberally so the wood will become thoroughly impregnated with the finish.

Unabsorbed finish should be wiped off when the finish starts to become tacky. If the film has become too stiff the excess finish can be removed by using a pad of 2/0 steel wool moistened with turpentine. On some jobs a single application may suffice, although two are usually recommended. After the first coat is thoroughly dry, the second coat is put on the same way as the first. Since the surface has already absorbed a good deal of the finish, more time will be required for the second coat to become tacky. Excess finish should be removed before the finish sets, leaving a sort of burnished effect.

When dry, the last coat of finish may be rubbed to a satiny surface with a soft cloth. The finish may be left this way or a coat of paste wax may be applied.

Finishing Floors

Sanding Floors

New floors should be sanded just before application of the final coat of finish to the base molding and after all other interior work has been completed. Sweep the floor clean; no water should be used.

The sanding should preferably be done with an electric sanding machine. Large machines are not efficient near walls, in corners and in small closets. Such areas should be sanded manually or with a small, power-driven hand sander.

Three sanding cuts or traverses are usually recommended for the average floor, although acceptable results sometimes are achieved with only two. If a drum or belt type sander is used, the first cut may be made crosswise of the grain or at a 45 deg. angle. Succeeding cuts should be in the direction of the grain. It is generally advisable to use No. 2 open-coat paper for the first traverse, No. 1/2 for the second, and No. 0 for the third. If an unusually smooth surface is desired, four or five cuts are in order, using finer abrasive paper on each cut. After the last machine cut, the floor should be gone over manually, working with the grain of the wood, using 3/0 paper or correspondingly fine steel wool. The floor should not be walked on until the stain, filler or first coat of finish has been applied and has dried thoroughly.

Staining Floors

It is important that the first coat of stain or other finish be applied the same day as the last sanding. Otherwise the wood grain will have risen and the finish consequently will be slightly rough. Stain is not used if one desires a finish

retaining the natural color of the wood. When used, it is applied first, before wood filler or other finishes. It should be put on evenly, preferably with a brush 3 or 4 in. wide.

Wood Filler for Floors

Paste wood filler customarily is used to fill the minute surface crevices in oak and other hardwoods having large pores. It gives the floor the perfectly smooth surface required for a lustrous appearance. Filler is applied after stains and sometimes after floor seals but always before other finishing materials. It should be allowed to dry 24 hours before sanding and before the next operation is begun. Wood filler may be colorless or it may contain pigment to bring out the grain of the wood more contrastingly. For residential oak flooring, wood filler is always recommended.

Filler is not required on close-grained woods.

Types of Floor Finishes

The ideal qualities of a finish for hardwood floors are:
1. Attractive appearance.
2. Durability.
3. Ease of maintenance.
4. Capacity for being retouched in worn spots without revealing a patched appearance.

Additionally, when a finish is applied to high grade flooring of considerable natural beauty, it usually should be transparent in order to accentuate that beauty. The three principal types of finishes are floor seal, varnish and shellac. Lacquer is used occasionally.

Floor Seal

Floor seal, a relatively new material, is being used on an increasingly larger scale for residential as well as heavy-duty flooring. It differs from other finishes in one important respect. Rather than forming a surface coating, it penetrates the wood fibers, sealing them together. In effect it becomes a part of the wood itself. It wears only as the wood wears, does not chip or scratch and is practically immune to ordinary stains and spots. While it does not provide as shiny an appearance as other finishes, it has the advantage of being easily retouched. Worn spots may be refinished without presenting a patched appearance. Floor seals are available either colorless or in color.

It is difficult to give specific directions for applying floor seal, for directions of different manufacturers vary widely. Generally, however, it is applied across the grain first, then smoothed out in the direction of the grain. A wide brush, a squeegee or a wool applicator may be used. After a period of 15 minutes to 2 hours, depending on specific directions of the manufacturer, the excess seal should be wiped off with clean cloths or a rubber squeegee. For best results the floor then should be buffed with No. 2 steel wool. An electric buffer makes this task relatively simple. If a power buffer is not available, a sanding machine equipped with steel wool pads may be used; or the buffing may be done by hand. Although one application of seal sometimes is sufficient, a second coat frequently is recommended for new floors or floors that have just been sanded.

Varnishing Floors

Varnish provides a glossy appearance, is quite durable, fairly resistant to stains and spots, but will show scratches. It is difficult to patch worn spots, however, without leaving lines of demarcation between the old and the new varnish. Some varnish finishes dry in eight hours or less. Like the other types of finish it gives satisfactory results if properly waxed and otherwise maintained. The newer urethane varnishes provide more durability and scratch resistance and dry in a few hours. They are one of the most widely used floor finishes.

Precise directions for application of varnish usually are stated on the container. Varnish made especially for floors is much preferred. So-called all-purpose varnish ordinarily is not so durable when used on floors. As a rule three coats are required when varnish is applied to bare wood, but two coats usually are adequate when wood filler has been used or a coat of shellac has been applied first, as is sometimes the case. Cleanliness of both floor and applicator is essential to a smooth finish. Drying action is hastened when room temperature of at least 70 deg. F. is maintained and plenty of ventilation provided.

Shellacking Floors

One of the chief reasons shellac is so widely used is its quick-drying property. Workers,

starting with floors in the front of a house and shellacking toward the rear, may begin applying the second coat by the time they have finished the first. Shellac spots rather readily if water or other liquids remain on it long. It is transparent and has a high gloss. It does not darken with age as quickly as varnish.

Shellac to be used on floors should either be fresh or should have been stored in a glass container. If it remains too long in a metal container it may accumulate salts of iron which discolors oak and other hardwoods containing tannin. It should not be adulterated with cheaper resins but before use should be thinned with 188-proof No. 1 denatured alcohol. Recommended proportion is 1 quart of thinner to a gallon of 5-pound cut shellac. A wide brush that covers three boards of strip flooring is the most effective and convenient size for application. Strokes should be long and even with laps joined smoothly.

The first coat on bare wood will dry in 15 to 20 minutes, after which the floor should be rubbed lightly with steel wool or sandpaper, then swept clean. A second coat should be applied and allowed to dry for 2 to 3 hours. Then the floor should be rubbed again with steel wool or sandpaper and swept. A third coat then is applied. If necessary, the floor may be walked on about 3 hours after being finished, but preferably it should remain out of service overnight.

Lacquering Floors

Lacquer is a glossy finish with about the same durability as regular varnish but less durability than urethane varnish. Because it dries so rapidly it requires considerable skill in application. Worn spots may be retouched with fairly good results, since a new coat of lacquer dissolves the original coat.

Waxing New Floors

To protect the finished floor and increase its wear, it is well to go over the surface with a good grade of paste or liquid floor wax about ten days after the final coat of varnish has been applied. An electric polishing machine is the best means of applying the wax, but hand polishing with a weighted brush provides a satisfactory job. Wax on varnished floors tends to make them slippery unless the coating of wax is kept thin. To insure a non-slippery surface, allow the wax to dry from thirty minutes to one hour before polishing the paste or the liquid floor wax.

Prefinished Hardwood Flooring

Some manufacturers produce flooring which is completely prefinished at the factory. It is ready for use immediately after being laid.

Care and Maintenance of Floors

When properly laid and finished, wood floors may be kept in good condition almost indefinitely with a little care and attention.

A floor should be refinished before an old finish has worn down to where unfinished wood is exposed.

Floors, shellac finished or wax polished, should never be scrubbed with water or unnecessarily brought in contact with water. Sweeping or mopping should be all that is necessary for routine cleaning. A soft cotton floor mop, barely dampened with a mixture of three parts of kerosene and one part of paraffin oil, is excellent for dry mopping. When the mop becomes dirty it should be washed in hot soap and water, then dried and again dampened with the mixture of kerosene and paraffin oil. If patches of dirt cannot be removed in this manner, rub slightly with a fine steel wool moistened with turpentine. When the finish is of the sealer type, badly soiled spots can be sanded by hand, patched with sealer and rubbed with a pad of fine steel wool.

In addition to the regular sweeping and mopping, wax polished floors should be waxed at least twice a year or oftener, depending upon the wear to which they are subjected. Follow waxing procedure given for new floors. Liquid and also water-emulsion waxes that are merely mopped on the floor and allowed to dry are also used for polishing. Water-emulsion waxes should not be used on shellac finished floors. If unusually severe usage wears the wax down in certain areas, an additional coat of wax should be applied immediately to the worn area and thoroughly rubbed in.

Never allow one coat of wax to wear entirely away before rewaxing. When wax and top finish wear down in spots so the bare wood is exposed, it becomes filled with dirt and cannot be satisfactorily patched. Shellac or varnish finishes, after three or four renewals, are likely to become dark in color and should be removed completely with a high grade liquid varnish remover

or by sanding or scraping; and a new finish applied to the bare wood. Shellac can be washed off with trisodium phosphate in hot water and alcohol (3 parts water, 1 part alcohol) made into a saturated solution. Some skill and care is needed, but this works well and also removes the wax.

Finishing with Lacquer

Lacquer is a fast-drying finish favored by most furniture manufacturers. A basic lacquer schedule does not differ materially from a basic varnish schedule. You simply use stain, filler, and lacquer; instead of stain, filler and varnish.

Stains best suited for use with lacquer are water stains and non-grain-raising stains. The stain may be applied either by spraying, or with a brush.

Lacquer is available in many different types -- for application by brush, and by spray gun. The spray gun method is preferable. A spray gun permits a fast, even application of the finish without fear of leaving brush marks, or having the coating dry before it has been properly applied.

Lacquer is highly volatile and must be kept away from fire. This is especially important when spraying, as a careless spark may cause an explosion.

Furniture finishing lacquers are supplied in various grades, including Gloss, Medium Rubbed Effect (medium gloss) and Dull, or practically Flat. The application methods and drying characteristics of the various grades are essentially the same.

After the final coats of finishing lacquer have dried thoroughly, they are often rubbed. Sanding is usually not done between coats unless roughness or irregularity of the surface has developed. The procedure described for rubbing down varnish finishes is also applicable to lacquer finishes.

In using lacquer, as in using other types of finishes, a considerable amount of trial-and-error work must be done to get the knack of using the finishing materials, before professional quality finishing can be expected.

SHADING LACQUERS: Because of the lack of uniformity of color in some woods, regular staining and filling may not make the piece uniform. In such cases, shading lacquers (lacquers which contain permanent, light fast dyes) may be used. In addition, the shading lacquers may be used to create desirable highlight effects.

Wood Finishing (Interior)

Step-By-Step Procedures

Recent trends in interior decorating and wide-spread use of wood paneling has increased emphasis on finishing techniques that capitalize on the natural beauty of these materials.

Most of the finishes covered in this section are suitable for use not only in finishing woods, wall panel, trim and doors, but modern furniture as well.

The schedules suggested are typical schedules for average conditions. Finishing results can be affected by many factors. Results obtained are dependent upon such conditions as the kind and quality of wood used, condition of surface, quality of finishing materials, and careful attention to details in applying the finishes.

There are no industry-wide standard procedures for obtaining certain effects. The procedure followed by one wood finisher to obtain a particular effect is often considerably different from the procedure followed and recommended by another finisher.

On most furniture-finishing jobs application of wax, after other finish coats, is advisable.

In wood finishing, it is always advisable to experiment on scrap stock, preferably the same type of wood that is to be finished, before starting a finishing job.

Ambered Walnut

Bleach. Apply amber stain. Apply natural filler. Seal with wash coat of shellac. Finish with clear varnish or lacquer. Wax.

Natural Walnut, Mahogany

Bleach slightly. Sand. Apply filler of shade to match color of wood. Seal. Apply varnish or lacquer finish. Wax.

Stained Walnut, Mahogany

Same as natural except no bleach used.

Bone White Walnut, Oak

In this finish the grain shows through white undercoater. Apply thin coat of white enamel undercoater, making no attempt to hide grain or obtain smooth finish. Sand lightly. Apply weak glaze of raw umber in oil reduced to wash consistency by thinning with turpentine. Wipe off glaze immediately, and blend with grain, using rag or badger-hair blender, so only gray haze remains in wood pores. Finish with white shellac and wax or varnish.

Pickled Walnut, Mahogany, Oak

Bleach. Apply wash coat of white shellac. Apply natural paste filler tinted to light oak color. Apply second wash coat of shellac. Sand. Apply antique glaze made by dissolving 2 ounces Van Dyke brown Japan color in about 1/4 pint turpentine. Let set a few minutes, then wipe off. Apply finish coat of shellac or varnish.

SECOND FORMULA: Apply natural paste filler mixed with about 20 percent synthetic resin sealer. Rub filler into pores and wipe off. Apply coat of lacquer. Sand or steel wood. Apply second coat of lacquer. Wax.

Heather Walnut, Mahogany

Bleach. Fill open pores with white paste filler. Seal. Sand. Finish with clear varnish or water-white lacquer.

Tweed Walnut, Mahogany

Bleach wood. Fill pores with red paste filler. Filler may be colored by using red color-in-oil. Seal. Sand. Use clear varnish or lacquer for finish.

Dusty Antique (Walnut, Oak, Ash, Chestnut)

Apply dark brown walnut stain. Apply white filler tinted with small quantity of raw umber in oil, to provide dusty gray cast. In wiping filler DO NOT follow usual procedure. Wipe, using burlap, in diagonal strokes. Do not wipe clean. Effect desired is that of generations of dust accumulating on museum pieces. Seal. Apply flat varnish.

Blond (Any Open-Pore Wood)

Bleach. Sand. Apply natural filler. Seal. Sand. Finish with varnish or lacquer.

Harvest-Wheat Mahogany

Bleach to wheat color. Fill with natural filler tinted with raw sienna color in oil. Sand. Seal. Finish with varnish or lacquer.

Ebonized Mahogany

Apply black water stain. Flow on coat of shellac, reduced with equal amount of alcohol. Steel wool lightly. Apply second coat of thinned shellac. Finish with paste wax.

Pigment Grain Mahogany

Bleach. Fill using filler mixed with dark red, brown or other color of your choice. Sand, being sure all color is removed from surface of wood. Seal. Finish with varnish or lacquer.

Limed Oak, Mahogany

Bleach. Fill pores with white paste filler. Sand. Seal. Finish with clear varnish or water-white lacquer.

Silver Fox (Black Background White Pores. All Porous Woods)

Apply black enamel. Sand. Apply second coat of enamel. Mix natural paste filler quite thick, with high-grade white enamel. Wipe clean with burlap or other rough cloth, working across grain. Sand very lightly. Seal. Finish with varnish or lacquer.

Silver Gray Oak (Frosted Finish)

Apply coat of silver-gray water stain. Apply white filler. Seal. Finish with white shellac or varnish.

Fumed Oak

A fumed finish is formed on white oak by fuming with ammonia. Oak contains a substance called tannin which reacts with ammonia gas to change the color of the wood to a rich gray brown color. The process is complicated and has been used very little for the past several years. It involves putting the item to be finished in a closed box or room of ammonia fumes.

Simulated Fumed Oak (May Also Be Used On Mahogany, Chestnut, Gum, Pine)

Raise grain of wood by sponging. Let dry and sand. Apply acid solution, mixed as follows: 1/2 oz. tannic acid powder to 1 quart water, or, 1/3 oz. pyrogallic acid powder to 1 quart water.

Sand. Apply solution: 1 oz. bichromate of potash and 1/2 oz. caustic potash to 1 quart water. When dry rub with a solution of 1 part boiled linseed oil and 3 parts turpentine.

Natural Oak

Bleach lightly as required to equalize colors. Sand. Fill with neutral paste filler. Sand. Finish with shellac, varnish, or lacquer.

Interesting variation: Mix tint of red, green or brown with wood filler for grain-toned finish.

Honeytone Maple (Any Light Close-Grain Wood)

Bleach. Sand. Stain with honeytone (light amber) maple stain. Seal. Sand. Finish with shellac, varnish, or lacquer.

Blonde Maple

Bleach. Sand. Seal. Finish with water-white lacquer. Quick blonde effect may be obtained by using white wiping stain on bare wood.

Colonial Maple

Apply coat of water or non-grain-raising maple stain to entire surface. Seal with a wash coat of orange shellac. Apply a maple pigmented wiping stain. Let stand until the surface of the stain begins to dull, then wipe off most of the stain with a clean, lintless cloth. Be careful not to leave too much stain. Dark smudges of stain should be left in corners and recessed portions of turnings. In shading panels sharp contrasts should be avoided. Aim at gradual blends from dark to light. A soft badger blending brush is useful for this purpose. Seal. Finish with varnish or lacquer.

Harewood

Harewood is pale gray finish applied to curly maple veneer in effort to imitate genuine English Harewood. Stain using solution consisting of four grains of blue-black nigrosene aniline dissolved in one gallon of hot water. Sand lightly. Finish with white shellac or clear lacquer.

Light Stain Glaze - Cypress, Pine, Fir, Cedar, Redwood, etc.

TO WHITEN WOOD: Apply coat of interior white undercoat thinned one part undercoat to one part turpentine or mineral spirits. Before paint film becomes tacky (10-15 minutes) wipe with rag or dry-brush for grain show-through. Sand. Seal. Apply coat of flat varnish.

TO PROVIDE COLOR: Apply one color coat. This may be interior undercoat or enamel, thinned one part undercoat and one part turpentine or mineral spirits. Or white undercoat or resin primer-sealer tinted with colors-in-oils may be used. If tube oil colors are used, mix color pigment separately with a little turpentine or mineral spirits, until fluid enough to mix readily with finishing material. Light stains may also be used. Apply thinly and wipe or dry-brush to proper color tone. Sand lightly. Apply coat of flat varnish.

Frosted Fir

Apply coat of high-grade enamel of desired color to raw wood. Much of coating will sink into soft wood. Brush on diluted white enamel or white synthetic sealer. Wipe, blending white "frost" color as needed for best appearance. Finish with varnish.

Natural Pine

Brush on boiled linseed oil. Let stain penetrate for about two hours, then wipe off excess. Wax. Golden-brown color develops as wood is exposed to light.

Antique Pine

Apply wash coat of orange shellac. Mix weak wiping stain of raw sienna in linseed oil, experimenting on rough stock to get golden-brown color desired. Darken slightly using raw umber, if desired. Let stain set for about ten minutes, then wipe off. For walls apply coat of wax; for pine furniture, apply varnish.

Pickled Pine

This intriguing term does not signify the same color of finish to all persons. The range of colors usually lies between olive-green, gray and driftwood gray. The name implies the color of weathered wood in vinegar and pickling vats. Bleach. Antique surface with coat of white paste filler tinted with raw umber and black. Skillfully wipe surface to leave dust-like coating. Seal. Finish with varnish or lacquer.

Knotty Pine Finish Highlights Knots

Apply oil stain to raw or unfinished wood. Allow stain to penetrate for about ten minutes then remove stain on up-turned grain around knots by wiping with cloth. After stain has dried, highlight further by sanding lightly around knots or along ridges of a milled pattern to produce "worn" or burnished edges. Seal. Finish with varnish, lacquer, or wax.

Ebony Jet Black

Fill, if wood has open pores. Seal. Apply black lacquer primer. Sand. Apply second coat black lacquer primer. Sand. Apply three coats water-white gloss lacquer, sanding lightly between coats. Rub and polish.

Old World Finishes

"Old World" is a term used to describe a finish that is shaded or antiqued to produce the effect given by age.

OLD ENGLISH WALNUT: Apply light walnut stain. Fill using walnut filler reduced to thin consistency by thinning with turpentine, or omit filler and use pigmented wiping stain. Seal. Shade with dark brown wiping stain, or glaze made by thinning color-in-oil. Finish with flat varnish or flat lacquer.

OLD ENGLISH MAHOGANY: Apply red (colonial) water stain. Fill using filler reduced to thin consistency by thinning, or omit filler and use pigmented wiping stain. Seal. Shade with dark mahogany pigmented wiping stain, or glaze. Finish with flat varnish, or flat lacquer.

FRENCH PROVINCIAL: For chestnut or walnut. Follow procedure described for Old English Walnut.

SWEDISH PROVINCIAL: Usually applied to oak. Apply stain-grayish brown or deep brown. Omit filler. Seal. Antique glaze. Finish with shellac and wax.

Notes on Wood Panel Installation

On new construction, all plaster work should be completely dry before paneling is delivered or installed. Its installation should be one of the last items to be done.

Masonry and concrete walls are subject to moisture penetration. They should be waterproofed if paneling is to be applied over them.

Use hot coal tar pitch; or two coats of colloidal solution of asphaltum in water, brushed when dry with mineral spirits to complete uniting together. Backpriming of the paneling with a good primer paint, aluminum, shellac or knot sealer, offers additional protection.

If the woodwork is to be finished naturally or stained, rather than given an opaque coat, avoid using more than one species of wood in any one room. Use of a single species for doors, casing and small moldings as well as for paneling will insure consistent finished tones.

Patching and Repairing Furniture Finishes

Injuries to furniture finishes such as burns, scratches, alcohol spots, heat and water marks, and stains can often be successfully repaired.

Minor Scratches

An application of paste furniture wax, with 4/0 steel wool will hide many minor scratches and blemishes. You might also try coloring the break in the finish with colored, wax-type shoe polish or liquid shoe dye. The dye comes in various shades of brown and is good on walnut. Wax coloring crayons such as used by school children can often be used to good advantage.

Fig. 10-5. Scratches on dark stained furniture can often be "cured" by applying iodine or mercurochrome.

Scratches on red mahogany can often be concealed by using iodine or mercurochrome; new iodine or mercurochrome for red mahogany, iodine that has turned brown for brown mahogany. For maple, iodine should be diluted about

50 percent, with denatured alcohol. See Fig. 10-5. Also try oil from a black walnut, or a Brazil nut. Break the nut meat in two and rub well into the scratch or blemish.

A method for restoring luster on a surface is by using rottenstone and oil. Dip pad of fine-mesh cloth in a bit of rubbing oil, boiled linseed oil or paraffin oil. Sprinkle on some rottenstone - - enough to make a paste. Rub briskly with grain of the wood. Wipe frequently and compare gloss of damaged area with the original finish.

Severe Scratches, Blemishes, Burns

When a finish is damaged too much to be repaired by simple remedies as just described, methods which are most professional should be tried.

First, clean off the damaged finish. Scrape damaged finish with sharp jackknife or razor blade taped for safe handling. Sand with 8/0 abrasive paper, or smooth with steel wool. Rub lightly with the grain of the wood. Apply wood stain of proper shade with small brush or cotton-tipped toothpick, wiping with cloth. Continue to apply stain until stain matches the original finish. Let stain dry then seal with white or orange shellac, using fine brush. Repeat shellac application until scratch is filled, allowing three hour drying time between treatments. Smooth with rottenstone and oil.

In repairing severe blemishes caused by cigarette burns, the charred wood should be removed with a sharp knife, and the damaged area cleaned with a cotton-tipped toothpick dipped in naphtha. Smooth damaged area with 4/0 steel wool wrapped around point of orange stick or wooden skewer. Sand lightly, using 8/0 paper. Next stain, matching the finish as closely as possible.

Filling Damaged Area with Stick Shellac

The deeper the damage on wood finishes, the more difficult the treatment required. Deep blemishes caused by burns may be filled by using melted stick shellac. Stick shellac comes in about seventy-five different colors and in opaque and transparent types. Two or more colors of shellac can be melted together to provide still more colors. Opaque shellac of the proper color should be used for deep scratches which go down to bare wood; transparent stick shellac of the proper color for shallow scratches where the stain color is intact. Use ordinary stick shellac for varnished surfaces, lacquer stick for lacquer finishes.

The burning-in knife should preferably be heated with alcohol flame or an electric heater, Fig. 10-6. If heated with gas or a candle, soot which forms should be wiped off the knife before using it to melt shellac.

Fig. 10-6. Above. Electric burn-in knife for melting stick shellac. Below. Filling deep blemish in furniture with melted stick shellac. Knife used to melt shellac is heated over alcohol flame.

A kitchen paring knife may be converted into a tool for burning in shellac by grinding it off square across the end. One may use a tool made for the purpose or an electric burn-in knife, Fig. 10-6.

In using a knife and alcohol burner, the knife is held in the flame until it becomes hot enough to melt the shellac. Frequent trials are advisable. If the shellac boils and bubbles, the knife is too hot. Shellac is picked up on the end of the hot blade and is dropped into the hole to be filled. Otherwise it may be deposited near a crack or hole to be filled and worked into the hole using the hot knife. The latter procedure eliminates trouble caused by forming of bubbles when the shellac is dropped directly into the hole. Danger of burning the surrounding surface with hot shellac can be prevented by using masking tape around the hole being filled. A thin layer of opaque shellac of the proper color should be placed in the bottom of the hole and smoothed with the hot iron. Then the hole should be filled with clear or transparent shellac.

If the shellac is either too light or too dark in color, dig out the shellac and start over.

To rub down shellac and blend the patch and the surrounding finish use 6/0 wet-or-dry finishing paper and rubbing oil or naphtha. Finally, the gloss of the finish may be matched by rubbing lightly with 4/0 steel wool, or by using pumice or rottenstone and oil.

Removing Water Marks and White Spots

Marks or rings from wet glasses, vases or flower pots are common on tables, especially if the surfaces have not been waxed. Wax will not prevent damage caused by allowing liquids to stand on a finish indefinitely. It will, however, keep water from being absorbed immediately, providing time to wipe up spilled liquid before it causes damage.

To remove water marks here are some ideas to try:

1. Place a clean, thick blotter over rings and press with a warm (not hot) iron.

2. Apply liquid wax to surface, with 4/0 steel wool. Work WITH the grain of the wood.

3. Use rottenstone and oil.

4. Try camphorated oil, oil of peppermint, lemon oil. Stroke spot lightly with cloth moistened with the oil. Do not use linty cloth since fuzz may stick to wood. Wipe immediately with clean cloth.

5. Try a mixture of table salt and light mineral oil; also, try a mixture of cigarette ashes and butter, vegetable shortening, salad oil.

6. A light, swift, wiping with alcohol will remove water spots. The second they disappear the area must be bathed in raw linseed oil.

Removing Alcohol Spots

Perfumes, beverages and medicines containing alcohol can cause serious damage if not wiped up promptly.

Suggestions for removing alcohol spots are:

1. Try a quick application of ammonia. Put a few drops of ammonia on a damp cloth and rub the spot. Follow this with an application of wax.

2. Rub with cloth saturated with liquid wax, paste wax, silver polish, linseed oil, or moistened cigar ash.

3. Try rottenstone and oil. If necessary use FFF powdered pumice instead of rottenstone (pumice provides considerably more abrasive action).

4. Use alcohol and raw linseed oil as in removing water marks and white spots.

Many manufacturers of finishing products now produce materials especially designed to dissolve crystals which have formed beneath the surface from such effects as heat, cold and water.

Removing Paint Stains

To remove spots of paint which have dried, cover spots with linseed oil and let stand until paint is softened. Wipe off paint, using cloth dipped in linseed oil. If any paint remains, remove it using rottenstone and oil.

Fresh paint can usually be removed by using cloth dipped in turpentine. The turpentine removes the wax too, so rewaxing will be in order.

Removing Shallow Dents in Wood

Dents in wood can frequently be removed by applying a ball of water-soaked cotton or paper to the spot and heating it with a soldering iron or flatiron. The moisture and heat cause the wood fibers to swell and the surface of the wood to return to its original form.

Dents which cannot be removed by using the method just described, may be filled by using a mixture of sawdust and liquid glue, or one of the many preparations which are on the market.

Using Furniture Polish

In using furniture polish, care should be taken not to use too much polish which serves only to make a coating to which dust clings.

Lemon oil polish is a product that is well known in furniture and piano shops for cleaning and preserving a finish. A dust rag may be very lightly impregnated with such polish by placing a small quantity of the polish in an empty glass fruit jar with a screw cap. Place in the jar a square of old soft flannel, screw on the cap and leave until the polish has uniformly penetrated the cloth.

An oil-impregnated cloth such as this should be stored in an airtight glass jar, or metal container.

Exterior Clear (Natural) Finishes

Woods that are rich brown or red in color, such as redwood and western red cedar, lend themselves well to natural finish. Woods that are paler in color such as pine, cypress and Douglas fir are also frequently finished in this way.

The first thing to learn about natural finishes is that they are much less durable and must be renewed much more frequently than coatings of house paint. House paint usually lasts three or four years. Most clear finishes need renewing at least once a year - - some as often as every six months.

There are many factors that contribute to early failure of the clear finishes but the three principal causes are: Sunlight, Moisture and Lack of Knowledge about Proper Choice and Application of Materials.

Sunlight

Basically, the resins that make up varnish and paint films are very similar; that is, they are both composed of chemical compounds which have the ability to polymerize (interreact) in the presence of heat, air, and sunlight to form solid films. This is how the coatings dry or "set up." Polymerization is a continuing process and may occur even after the films feel dry and are hard to the touch. As polymerization progresses, the films become harder and extremely brittle. This is what happens to exterior varnish coatings; the increasing brittleness makes them less tolerant to the dimensional changes that take place in wood and consequently the films crack and the coating scales off.

In paint films, the influence of sunlight, in this polymerization process, is not nearly so great as with clear coatings because of the pigment particles which prevent most of the destructive light from reaching the resin. Therefore, the embrittlement process is extended over a longer period of time, giving a much longer service life to pigmented finishes than to clear coatings.

Sunlight also causes changes in the wood structure. Clear finishes do not protect against these changes nearly as well as pigmented finishes. The change in wood structure contributes to the short life of clear films.

Moisture

Moisture represents the next greatest offender contributing both to film breakdown and to wood damage. The water (in the form of free water or water vapor) penetrates under the clear coating, usually through the very hard-to-seal end grain, and promotes the formation of blue stain and mold growths. This results in a very unsightly appearance of the siding and is one of the most common causes of trouble with natural finishes. The effect of water-saturated wood on the clear finish is equally disastrous as it causes the coating to lose its adhesion and ultimately peel, leaving large areas of exposed wood where more water may enter to continue the deterioration.

With new construction there are several things to be considered which will prolong the service life of a clear coating. A large roof overhang (eaves) will extend the life of a good finish from 50 to 60 percent over one which is not protected by eaves. When using vertical siding, it is very important to protect the upper ends of the boards with metal flashing. The bottoms of vertical siding should be left free to insure good drainage and adequate free air circulation. Molding strips on the bottoms of the siding panels merely act as water reservoirs and promote water absorption through the end grain of the wood. Care should be taken that the open lower siding ends are not subject to direct saturation with water.

For best protection, backs and edges of exterior siding should be given one well brushed out coat of a high quality exterior or marine spar varnish prior to installation. Open grain ends of the siding should be given two or three coats of the same varnish (enough to form a good continuous varnish film over the very absorptive end grain). These precautions provide the best known protection from varnish failures caused by moisture under the varnish film.

Protecting From Rot, Termites, Beetles

Wood has natural enemies which constantly attack it. Rot, termites, and powder post beetles are the most common.

ROT: Rot (decay) in wood is caused by small plant-like organisms called fungi. These fungi are everywhere. Their "spores" or "seeds" are carried by the air. They cause spoilage of food, mildew on walls, as well as rot in wood. The fungi need moisture or dampness in order to thrive. Rot on wood will be found where conditions are right for its development.

TERMITES: Subterranean termites live in colonies in the soil (moist) below the frost line. They feed on dead wood - - whether fallen trees, wooden buildings, or lumber. They do not like light. They must have moisture and must keep constant contact with the nest. Thus, they are forced to enter wood from the ground or build mud tunnels up over foundations to the wood.

Dry termites cause similar damage. They do not need moisture, do not build nests in the ground and attack untreated wood above the ground.

POWDER POST BEETLES: Powder post beetles which are common the country over, are most likely to attack hardwood such as beech or hickory. The presence of these beetles can be recognized by the "shot holes" left when the adult beetles bore out of the wood.

OBTAINING PROTECTION: The best way to obtain protection from rot, termites and beetles is to treat the wood with a chemical. Pentachlorophenol (chlorinated phenol) is such a chemical. Many water repellent solutions containing pentachlorophenol which provide protection not only against rot and insects but also help reduce warping, checking, and swelling are available. Wood treated with water repellent takes up water very slowly, even when soaked in water. That is why the repellent helps reduce warping, checking, swelling and grain raising, all of which are largely caused by moisture moving unevenly in and out of wood.

Pentachlorophenol water repellent solutions may be applied by brushing, spraying, and by soaking or dipping. Commercially treated wood is available in many areas.

Best protection can be obtained by soaking the wood. The wood is immersed in a container (trough or tank) of solution. If the container is not large enough to take the entire piece, dip treat as much as possible, then flood the remainder with a brush. If the wood is to be used above ground, but under cover, where it will not be exposed to the weather, a short dip of three to five minutes is usually sufficient. Always follow instructions furnished by the manufacturer.

Wood to be installed above ground and painted after treatment usually requires three to fifteen minutes soaking. If the wood is not to be painted, soaking time should be increased by fifteen to thirty minutes. The thicker the wood the longer treating time required. Wood to be exposed below ground or at groundline, should be soaked from twenty-four to forty-eight hours.

Where it is not practical to soak wood, water repellent can be applied with a brush. Use a wide, thick brush. Flood the solution on the wood, using a tub or other container under the pieces being treated, to catch the run-off or excess.

Existing structures which cannot be dipped, or large areas difficult to protect by brushing may be sprayed. Wood must be unpainted and dry. In applying the solution with a spray gun, use a coarse, low-pressure spray.

In applying water-repellent solutions avoid skin contact because the solution is irritating to the skin of some people. In case of contact, wash immediately with warm water and soap. Rubber gloves and apron should be worn. In spraying, avoid breathing mists or concentrated vapors. Wear goggles and respirator if exposure is unavoidable. Be sure to provide adequate ventilation. Water-repellent materials stick to glass when they harden. When applying them around windows it is advisable to use the same precautions as for painting.

A water-repellent solution may penetrate into end grain of sapwood as much as two or three inches. It also goes into heartwood about the same amount. It seldom penetrates into side-grain more than one-sixteenth inch. After treatment very little wood can be removed from the surface without exposing bare untreated wood. In cases where cutting must be done, the newly exposed surfaces should be treated before the parts are fastened in place.

Oil Finishes

The oldest and probably the simplest penetrating finish is linseed oil. The oil may be either raw or boiled. Boiled linseed oil contains driers; raw linseed oil does not. Either may be applied in warm dry weather. During cool or damp weather it is better to use boiled oil. Turpentine or mineral spirits is sometimes added to the oil. This makes spreading easier and provides better penetration. Not more than one-half gallon of thinner should be added to a gallon of oil; more than that seriously reduces the protection provided by the oil.

An oil finish penetrates completely into the wood and imparts very little luster or gloss to the surface. However, it darkens the color of the wood more than other natural finishes, and continues to darken and age more than other natural finishes.

Bodied oils do not penetrate the wood so deeply as raw or boiled oils, and therefore do not darken the wood so much. They are made by treating the oils chemically, or heating them for some time to increase the viscosity. Bodied oils must be thinned with paint thinner to a viscosity suitable for application. Most trade-brand

oil finishes are of this type.

Oil finishes may be applied by brushing, spraying or mopping. For new wood two generous applications are advisable. If, after the second application of oil, there are glossy spots where excess oil stands on the surface, it should be wiped off before it dries. Surface coatings of linseed oil are not satisfactory because they are too soft, hold dirt, and become mildewed easily.

In renewing an oil finish after it shows signs of wear, one application should be sufficient. Any oil not drawn into the wood should be wiped off.

ADDING PIGMENT: Oil finishes, like other natural finishes of the penetrating type, may be markedly improved by adding a small amount of pigment. Some oil finishes on the market contain pigment. Those that do not can be pigmented by adding a small amount of color-in-oil sold at paint stores for tinting paints. One-half pint or less of a mixture of equal amounts of raw and burnt sienna-in-oils added to a gallon give the oil finish a color resembling that of the heartwood of redwood or red cedar. The colors-in-oils should first be mixed thoroughly with a little of the oil finish until free of lumps, then stirred smoothly into the rest of the oil.

Oil finishes serve best in dry regions, where there are no prolonged periods of dampness. In areas where excessive dampness prevails, the oil finishes may be attacked by fungi (mildew) that cause dark brown to black discoloration. Mildew, however, can be prevented by adding suitable preservatives to the oil finish.

One way is to add a concentrated solution of pentachlorophenol or other chlorinated phenol to the oil instead of adding turpentine or paint thinner.

Another way to protect the finish from mildew, is to buy one of the paintable water-repellent preservatives now sold at many lumber yards, and some paint stores.

Wood Sealer Finishes

Another penetrating finish is wood sealer. Wood sealers are made of resin, drying oils, thinners and driers. A wood sealer finish sinks into the wood cells nearest the surface without forming a continuous coating of appreciable thickness. Any sealer left on the surface of the wood should be wiped off before it becomes too dry to wipe. Sealers do not penetrate wood as deeply as oils and therefore do not darken the wood as much. For the same reason, they impart more glossiness to the surface than oils. If excess sealer remains on the wood, it forms a glossy, varnish-like finish.

Some commercial wood sealers contain pigments for the same desirable purpose described for oil finishes. Pigments may be added to clear sealers by the methods suggested for pigmenting oil finishes.

Spar Varnish Finish, A Surface Coating

Unlike penetrating finishes, spar varnish covers the wood with a coating of appreciable thickness. It may also be used on galvanized and copper surfaces. With most spar varnishes, the coating is highly glossy, but varnish may be obtained that is less glossy or even dull or flat. At first, varnish may not darken the wood much more than a sealer, but in time there is likely to be more darkening caused by chemical changes in the varnish.

Ideally, the best varnish to use on large areas is one that disintegrates by a very fine crazing, followed by fine crumbling, as the old fossil-resin varnish used to do, and some ester-gum varnishes still do. The newer synthetic varnishes may remain free from crazing and maintain gloss for a relatively long time, but in the end they tend to crack, curl and scale badly. Unfortunately, labels seldom tell exactly what a varnish contains. Terms like "spar" and "marine spar" mean different things to different manufacturers. Marine spar varnish intended for use on boats is apt to be more durable than ordinary spar varnish.

For best protection, three or four well-brushed out coats of spar varnish should be applied, allowing plenty of drying time between coats to make sure that each coat is completely dry before the next coat of varnish is applied.

Spar varnish is also used to a considerable extent as a finish coating over colors-in-oil stains which are used to change the color of the wood. These stains in themselves do not provide wood with adequate protection from weathering. Let the stained surface dry thoroughly, then apply three coats of spar varnish, being sure one coat is thoroughly dry before applying another.

NOTE OF CAUTION: Wherever clear finishes have been used, it is essential that the condition of the finish be checked frequently so periodic refinishing may be done before the finish deteriorates to the state where it must be removed before refinishing.

In general, refinishing will consist of washing the surface with a detergent, light sanding of any rough spots which might have developed, and application of a thin coat of spar varnish. When refinishing, the same type of varnish as was applied previously should be used. This prevents difficulties which might arise from the components of one varnish being incompatible with those of another.

Old Construction

The problems involved in applying clear finishes to houses which are already built and have the siding in place, and those involved in trying to correct unsightly clear finishes which have passed the condition of being refinishable, are for the most part more complex and far more costly to correct than an appealing clear finish may be worth. In most cases it is most advisable to clean the surface as best as possible and paint with a pigmented house paint.

In most situations where varnish films are completely broken down, black molds, blue stain, and other discolorations will probably have set in. The first step in refinishing involves the removal of all old finish. If the old finish is a varnish, it may be removed quite readily by scraping. Shellac, lacquers, and old paint may be removed by sanding or with universal paint and varnish removers which are obtainable at most paint stores.

Every attempt possible should be made to correct construction defects which may be contributing to film breakdown. This involves the installation of metal flashings where applicable, filling cracks with putty which has been tinted with burnt umber or burnt Italian sienna to match the wood color, replacement of boards which are badly cracked and checked, and providing ample ventilation for the lower edge and back of the siding. Each wall void should be vented in this manner. This ventilation is essential where it is suspected that water vapor from the interior of the structure is one of the main contributing factors to finish failure. To insure that the wood will be dry prior to refinishing, it is best to remove the old finish in late spring and allow the surface to weather normally until late summer, finishing just prior to the start of the fall wet weather.

Changing From Natural to Paint Finish

Some house owners who originally apply a

natural finish to their house decide to change to house paint.

Since no natural (transparent) finish serves ideally as a prime-coat for paint, certain precautions must be taken to obtain satisfactory results. Oil and sealer finishes may be painted over if the finishes are entirely within the wood. If some of the area remains glossy, the surface should be sanded to remove the glossy material. Then a priming paint suitable for use under the paint chosen for finish coats should be applied just as it would be on new wood.

A natural finish of the surface-coating type should be removed completely before paint is applied. This may be done with a varnish remover. The surface should then be sanded lightly, and a priming paint applied. Suitable topcoats may then be applied.

Log Finishing

One of the most satisfactory methods of finishing log construction, according to the Western Pine Association, begins with a dip treatment of the material in a 5 percent solution of pentachlorophenol in diesel oil to protect the sapwood from blue stain. Allow sufficient time for the oil to penetrate the surface and then stain with a high quality logwood oil or color-in-oil creosote stain. Inasmuch as it is very impractical to try to form a continuous film over logs with a varnish, this step should be eliminated.

It will be necessary to renew the oil treatment every eight months to a year. Even with this precaution the logs may tend to show signs of greying and weathering quite rapidly. Care must also be taken to apply no more oil than can be absorbed in a week's time to prevent film buildup. After the oil has been on for about a week, any glossy areas should be rubbed down to work the oil into the wood.

Fence Post Preservation

Fence posts, need protection from termites and decay. Such protection may be provided for untreated posts by long soaking in pentachlorophenol water-repellent solution.

Creosote has been in general use for preserving fence posts for a long time. It may be used where its color and odor are not objectionable and where the wood is not to be painted.

Copper naphthenate is a preservative developed during the war. It colors wood a bright green. It is odorless and is similar to pentachlorophenol in that it gives a "clean treatment."

Unit 11

SPECIAL FINISHES
FOR SPECIAL JOBS

Antique Glazing

Glazing is a superimposed transparent finish, which may be used to give an effect of age or to impart a decorative effect. A glaze finish may be applied over either a stain or enamel finish with equal appropriateness.

Antique glazing over stain is frequently used to provide an effect of greater age than is possible with stain alone. It may be applied over any type of stain, provided the stain is first sealed with a wash coat of shellac.

Glaze may be purchased ready-made in various shades or it can be shop-made by thinning down colors-in-oil. Usually about two ounces of color-in-oil is required to a quarter pint of a mixture consisting of half raw linseed oil and half mineral spirits with an adequate amount of drier. Add sufficient fine silica to prevent creeping of the thin mixture when wiped and stippled or blended.

Japan colors thinned with turpentine should be used under lacquer finishes.

Glaze is applied with a brush to all stained parts of the piece; it is allowed to stand until it begins to show dull and is then wiped off using a clean, lintless cloth such as cheesecloth. A certain amount of the glaze will stick in pores and carvings. On flat surfaces such as table tops, a circular motion should be used to wipe off the glaze partially from the middle, leaving only a small amount at the edges. Blend the darker glaze at the edges toward the center. Complete the blending with a dry brush, brushing lightly over the surface from the center toward the edges and back again.

Some experience is required to get the knack of applying glaze to provide pleasing effects. If the effect obtained the first time is not satis-

factory you may apply glaze over the entire surface again and repeat the antiquing process.

After the glaze is thoroughly dry, finish with shellac, varnish or lacquer.

Antique Highlighting

Antique highlighting is applied to a stained finish to give the piece the appearance of wear such as would come about naturally through many years of regular usage.

Antiquing requires the application of a wiping stain of a deep shade, one dark enough to achieve an effect of contrast at the proper points. The stain is applied over the piece in the usual manner, but where a "highlight" or worn effect is desired, the stain is wiped immediately and lightly with a soft cloth. Use a lifting or circular motion to feather or blend the tone gradually from dark to light.

Some experimenting will be required to obtain an authentic appearance. Of considerable importance too, is to know where to highlight. Study the piece and decide where the effects of wear would most likely show if the piece had been used for a long time. A careful study of old museum pieces or good reproductions, will be found very helpful in this regard.

Spatter Finish

A spatter finish is a "trick" finish. There are several ways to obtain a spattered or speckled effect. The decorative effects are added after the surface has been given a base coat - - usually a solid color of neutral shade. See Fig. 11-1.

One way to spatter paint is to use a piece of fine-mesh window screen tacked to a frame such as an old picture frame together with a stiff-bristle brush. The tip ends of the brush are dipped into the paint about 1/4 in., and the paint is flicked from the brush through the screening onto the object being spattered.

Another way to obtain such an effect is by using a hammer to lightly tap the handle of a long-bristle paint brush containing a small amount of paint. The consistency of the paint will help determine the size of the spots applied. The taps will cause the paint to spatter on the surface. For broad surfaces, a spray or "flit" gun makes an ideal tool for applying the spatter color over the base paint.

Fig. 11-1. Spatter finish. The decorative effect is applied over a base coat of solid color.

On some spatter jobs, such as floors of an old home, a spatter applied in several colors is very attractive. A new color cannot be added until the previously applied color has set.

Before starting a job of spattering, experimentation should be done on cardboard or old boards to see if the consistency of the paint is correct and to determine the exact technique needed to obtain the density of pattern desired.

Multicolor Spraying

A spatter effect may also be obtained by using multicolor spray enamel. With this type of material it is possible to spray a surface with one, two or three different colors at one time from one gun. No special equipment or application technique is required. The multiple colors exist separately within the material and when sprayed create an interlacing color network with each color retaining its individuality.

The basic colors may be combined in varying quantities, and in either large, medium, or fine particle size, to give an overall color scheme individualized for the customer.

Sponge Stippling, Mottling

Interesting effects may be obtained by stippling paint with a sponge or sheet of newspaper crumpled into a ball. A base or foundation coat of paint is applied and allowed to get fairly hard - - fully dry if on a floor.

An overlay of contrasting color is then applied. In using a sponge, the sponge should be soaked in water and wrung out to soften and open it. A small quantity of the stipple color is poured or brushed onto a piece of board or tin. The sponge is dipped into this, and then tapped once or twice on a board to remove the surplus paint, after which the second color is stippled directly on the wall or other surface, in effect printing from the sponge. When stippling, tap the sponge straight onto the surface without any turning or twisting motion. A firm but not too heavy stroke is desirable. In stippling a large surface, the sponge may become loaded. If this happens, rinse the sponge out in benzine or turpentine, squeeze and wipe dry; then wring it out in water again to open the sponge.

A full sheet of newspaper crumpled into a ball may be used in place of a sponge. Dip the bottom of the ball of newspaper into the paint. Then gently touch the surface with the newspaper and you will find that the odd, irregular shape of the wrinkled newspaper forms an attractive pattern. Or paint a glaze on the wall and remove with dry crumbled newspaper.

A regular stippling brush may also be used to obtain a two-tone effect. The surface is painted and allowed to dry. The contrasting color is brushed on and while still wet is gone over with a stippling brush, Fig. 11-2. This causes the under color to show through.

Fig. 11-2. Using stippling brush.

Designs may be created on walls first coated with base wall paint, by means of twin rollers, Fig. 11-3. Fastened on a single handle are a fabric covered roller, and a molded plastic roller on which a design is embossed. The fabric roller picks up the wall covering material

Fig. 11-3. Creating designs on wall by means of twin rollers; a fabric roller which picks up the wall covering materials, and a molded plastic roller on which the design is embossed.

(Applikay) from a paint tray and distributes it over the design roller in the process of application. The design repeats itself with every roll over the wall surface.

Texture Paints

Texture paint is used to provide a coating which covers imperfections and disguises or camouflages blemishes, fills cracks, and in general does a job of plastering and painting at one time.

Broadly speaking, texture paints can be separated into two types; dry or powder, and wet or ready-mixed.

Texture paints come with various bases as does regular paint. They are ready-mixed with latex bases, with rubberized alkyd and with oil bases. Some contain finely ground silica; others coarser grinds.

Effects which may be achieved with texture paints include a smooth finish with brush application, brush swirl pattern, and textured effects with a roller or by stippling with a sponge, Fig. 11-4.

Striping and Lining

Painters are sometimes called on to paint stripes or lines of various widths on doors, floors, cupboards, and furniture, and should be familiar with striping procedures.

Stripes may be applied by using a fountain-type striping tool that feeds paint to a wheel which is in contact with the surface, such as shown in Fig. 11-5. As the tool is drawn along a straightedge, the color is transferred onto the surface. Wheel widths range from 1/64 to 1/4 in.

Pressure-sensitive masking tape is useful when doing striping work. Lines are drawn, one on each side of the area to be striped. Long lines can best be drawn using a chalk line. The chalk line will make a clean straight line which will serve as a guide in placing the masking tape. When the masking tape is in place, a small brush is used to apply paint, enamel or bronze to the exposed surface between the two strips of tape. The tape may be removed immediately, leaving the stripe.

A "free-hand" method of striping is shown in Fig. 11-6. The handle of a beveled bristle striping brush is held between the thumb and first two fingers of the right hand. In use, the metal ferrule of the brush comes in contact

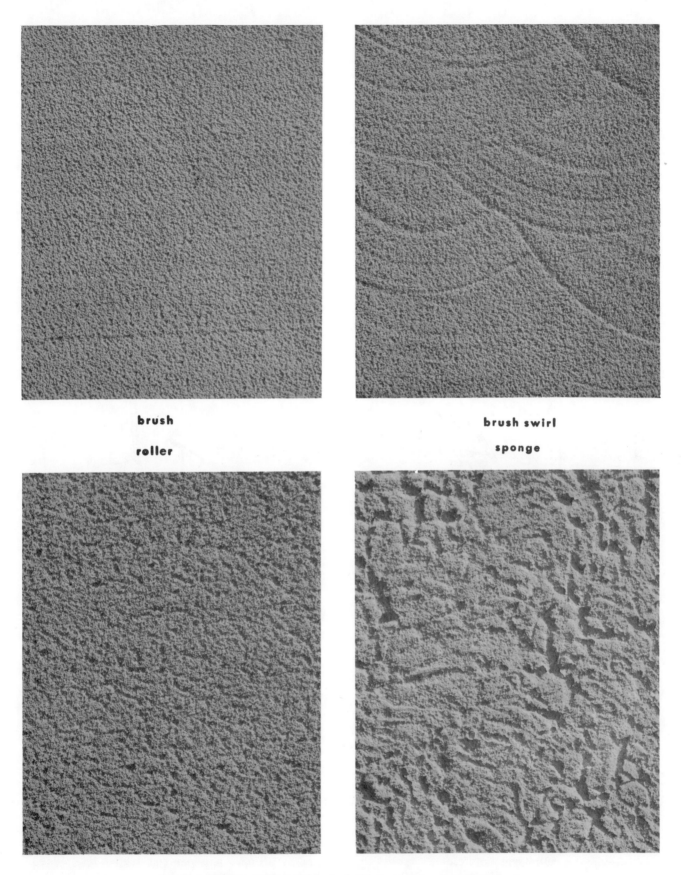

brush

brush swirl

roller

sponge

Fig. 11-4. Effects which may be obtained with texture paint. Upper Left—Brush. Upper Right—Brush swirl. Lower Left—Roller. Lower Right—Sponge.

with the side of a yardstick, which serves as a guide. The brush is pulled along slowly but steadily. A smooth, dry surface, even pressure, a steady hand, paint of thin but short consistency and a good straightedge, are essentials of a good job.

Metal Finishing (Obtaining Special Effects)

Brass, copper and bronze have in common the characteristic that the salts or oxides formed by their corrosion tend to prevent further corrosion. Many architectural details and objects of art made of these metals are allowed to corrode. Newly fabricated metals are often aged artificially to achieve the beautiful bluish-green patina that accompanies the darkening of the metal.

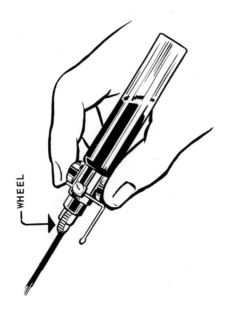

WHEEL

Fig. 11-5. Using painter's striping tool.

Darkening with Acid

Objects made of brass, copper and bronze cared for by periodic cleaning and polishing eventually develop a dark color in the low parts of the detail. This effect can be obtained quickly by first cleaning the metal with a wash of sulphuric acid - - one part acid to four parts water-- followed by a quick dip in liver of sulphur. In preparing the sulphuric acid cleaning solution, pour the acid into the water; DO NOT pour water into the acid. In applying acid solutions, the painter must wear closely fitting goggles

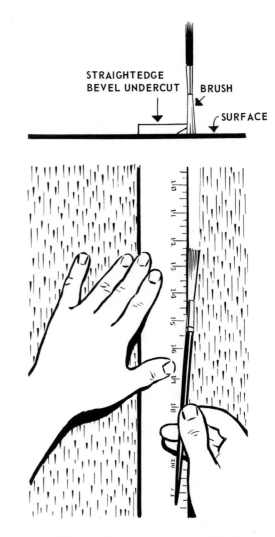

STRAIGHTEDGE
BEVEL UNDERCUT   BRUSH

SURFACE

Fig. 11-6. "Free-hand" striping using yardstick as a guide. Handle of striping brush is held between the thumb and first two fingers of the right hand, in the position shown.

and long, heavy-duty rubber gloves. This treatment causes the metal to turn to a dark, rich brown. Highlights may be produced by polishing with fine steel wool before the sulphur solution is entirely dry. After the surface is dry, the color can be protected by applying clear lacquer.

Darkening with Glaze and Colors

A common way of coloring metal to imitate the effects of oxidation is by using a paint coating. Brown color on brass can be simulated by using burnt sienna, burnt umber and Vandyke brown. Copper and bronzes deepen in shades of chocolate brown to black, and can be fairly well imitated with Vandyke brown to which is added some maroon oxide of iron.

Verdigris effects on metal can be simulated by the use of two or three colored glazes ranging from pale, pure green to deep, brilliant blue-green. These glazes are used in varying strengths to duplicate various degrees of corrosion. For the effect of a very old corroded copper roof, for example, a combination of rag-wiped glaze, paper-stippled glaze, and sponge-mottled glaze would come close to duplicating the patterns of natural corrosion.

Finishing Wood to Imitate Metal

Ground colors can be applied over wood to imitate copper, brass, bronze, iron or silver. Copper and bronze effects may be obtained by using colors ranging from burnt orange to deep chocolate brown or deep chocolate bronze powders. For brass, ochre and chrome yellow-orange mixtures may be used with enough white to bring the color to a golden yellow-orange. Bronze powders in all shades of brass are available.

The effect of rust showing through paint on old iron can be simulated by using in glaze form, red and yellow iron oxides (yellow ochre, raw sienna, burnt sienna, Venetian red). These should dry without gloss.

Silver is comparatively easy to imitate. The ground coat should be aluminum bronze with drop black or Vandyke brown, or a combination of these colors glazed over the top.

Using Bronze Powders, Liquid

Metallic paint may be applied by brushing, spraying, dipping or by roller coating. Such paint is available in ready-mixed form; or the ingredients, metallic powder and bronzing liquid may be purchased separately and mixed on the job. Metallic powders available include pale gold, white gold, natural copper, brushed brass, antique copper, light blue, green, aluminum and others.

In preparing the paint for use the manufacturer's instructions must be carefully followed to assure ease of application and smoothness of film. In applying metallic paint with a brush, use a soft-bristle brush to avoid brush marks. Use light pressure and brush out the final strokes toward the already painted surface. Do not go over the painted surface a second time as rebrushing disturbs the leafing effect and reduces the brilliancy of the coating.

Gilding with Metal Leaf

Gilding is the process of obtaining a finish by using metal leaf (metal hammered into very thin sheets). Briefly, the process consists of applying an adhesive called size, placing sheets of metal leaf on it, smoothing down the metal and burnishing.

The kinds of metal leaf most commonly used in the painting industry are gold, imitation gold, palladium (color similar to silver), and aluminum. Because it tarnishes quickly, silver leaf is seldom used on wood but is satisfactory for use on glass.

Gold leaf comes in sheets 3 3/8 in. square, 25 leaves to each paper book, and 20 books per pack. It also comes in the form of ribbon in rolls from 1/8 to 5 in. wide and 67 ft. long. Gold leaf in ribbon form is used in making lines and is applied by using a tool called a gilding wheel. Gold leaf is sold in various grades. Some types are made especially for use over glass; others for use over wood, metal and other surfaces.

Palladium leaf comes in 3 3/8 in. squares.

Aluminum leaf and imitation gold leaf come in sheets 5 1/2 in. square, 50 leaves to a book and 10 books to a pack.

Types of Size

There are two principal kinds of size: water size and oil size. To apply gold to glass, water size is used; oil size is generally used when applying gold to metal and wood unless it is to be burnished.

WATER SIZE: Water size for gilding glass comes in capsule form.

In preparing the size greatest care must be taken. The pan in which the size is made must be thoroughly cleaned so there will be no trace of oil or other foreign matter. In fact, utmost cleanliness is required throughout the preparation of the size and application of the leaf to obtain a bright burnish or "good gild."

The size is prepared by dissolving a gelatin capsule in about a cupful of water. Heat the water over a stove until the water boils, stir, then add enough clean (preferably distilled) water to make a pint of size. The size may be used cold during warm weather but should be heated before use during cold weather.

Liquid size should be strained through a piece of cheesecloth or unbleached muslin prior to use.

In applying silver leaf a stronger adhesive is needed than when applying gold. About a third more of the dry ingredient should be used. It is important to follow the manufacturer's specific instructions. Size that is too strong will produce a clouded effect which tends to destroy the burnish. Size that is too weak will not permit the washing process and will require replacement, resulting in a loss of time as well as materials. Making tests before starting on a regular lettering job is always advisable.

Unless a preservative is used, water size should be prepared fresh each day. By adding a small quantity of grain alcohol size can be retained for several days, if kept in a tightly sealed jar.

Gilding Procedure

The first step in applying gold leaf on a window lettering job, for example, is to lay out the lettering or design on the face or outside of the glass. The leaf is put on the inside. The outside of the glass should be washed, and the design laid out very accurately using a glass-marking pencil. On some jobs a perforated pounce pattern is used to transfer the pattern or design onto the glass with powder.

Next, clean the inside of the glass. A very thorough job of cleaning is necessary to remove all traces of oil, even finger prints. A cleaner such as Bon Ami and water may be used and the glass polished, when dry, with tissue paper.

Flood the glass with clean water, using a size brush (flat camel's hair brush) to remove any specks of dust. Apply a coat of size to the entire area to be gilded. During the gilding operation, the entire surface, except the portion that has been gilded, must be kept wet. Allowing the size to dry in places, before gilding, will result in a poor job.

In gilding, (if worker is right-handed) it is advisable to start at the upper left-hand corner of the job. A left-handed worker should start at the upper right-hand corner. This prevents the workman's hand from obscuring the view of the part of the job that has been completed, enabling him to make proper joints as leaf is applied. The job should be started at the top because the size must NEVER be allowed to run down over leaf that has already been applied.

LAYING ON GOLD LEAF: To lay gold on glass a camel's hair brush or gilding tip, as shown in Fig. 11-7, is required. In applying silver leaf a badger's hair brush is used.

Fig. 11-7. Camel's hair brush or gilding tip, such as used in applying gold leaf.

The cover of the book is folded back with the right hand, to expose the gold. Cutting of the gold leaf is done with the nail of the little finger of the right hand, Fig. 11-8, by running the nail across the gold. The folded book leaf serves as a guide. The book of gold leaf is then held in the left hand, a piece of heavy cardboard the same size of the book is placed under the book to strengthen it when the leaves are cut. The gold leaf that has been detached from the book is picked up with the gilding tip which has been prepared to pick up the leaf, Fig. 11-9. You prepare the tip by drawing it across the hair on your head or across your cheek to charge the tip with static electricity. Too much "charge" will cause the leaf to adhere to the tip too persistently. The book should be held close to the spot to which the gold leaf is to be applied, preferably about 6 in. away, and the gold picked

Fig. 11-8. Leaf of book (not gold leaf) is folded back and nail of little finger is run across gold leaf to cut it.

up by the charged tip and applied to the area to be covered. The tip must not be allowed to come into contact with the glass.

Gold leaf should be applied to the design or letters, allowing the sheets to overlap about 1/8 in. After the gilding has been completed, it must be allowed to stand until the size is thoroughly dry before taking the next step. An electric hair dryer can be used to hasten the drying. When dry the entire surface should be rubbed lightly and briskly, using cotton batting (top quality batting as used by physicians is best). This removes the leaf that did not adhere and burnishes the gold.

Next comes the patching of small holes and imperfections. Despite all precautions there are bound to be areas that are not covered with leaf. To patch the holes, the entire surface is again

this from the inside, the lettering would be reversed.

Then, the gold is covered with specially prepared oil-free paint. Asphaltum, rubbing varnish and brushing lacquer are suitable for backup paint when used indoors.

When the backup paint is dry, the gold extending beyond the edges of the letters should be removed, using cotton saturated with water, and the letters trimmed with a safety razor blade.

Lettering on glass that is exposed to the elements should be coated with high grade oil paint and spar varnish to protect it from dampness, frost and wear caused by cleaning. Apply the paint, being careful not to overlap the edges; let this dry, then put on a coat of spar varnish, allowing the varnish to overlap the edges of the

Fig. 11-9. Left. Gold leaf which is detached from the book is picked up with a gilding brush or tip. Fig. 11-10. Right. Applying gold leaf to wood surface. Page of book is turned back and gold leaf is placed on size-coated surface.

coated with size. The size brush is dipped into the size and is drawn across the surface from left to right. Each stroke of the size brush should barely lap the previous stroke. Small pieces of gold leaf should then be applied to the spots that need touching up. The size is allowed to dry, and the surface is again burnished with cotton. All loose particles of gold must be removed.

Washing gives the gold a brilliant burnish. Clean water heated to boiling should be used. The water is applied hot, using the size brush.

Backing up Gold Leaf

The lettering or design to be left on the glass should next be traced onto the gold. Looking at

letters about 1/8 in. The overlapping of the varnish prevents dampness from penetrating under the edges of the letters.

Silver Leaf

Silver leaf is put on, backed up and finished, following the procedure described for gold leaf.

Gilding Wood and Metal Surfaces

In applying gold or aluminum leaf to wood or metal, oil size is most often used. This comes in slow, medium, and quick-drying types. Quick-drying size dries in 30 minutes to an hour; slow-drying size may require as much as 24 hours time for drying.

Wood Must be Sealed

Gold leaf cannot be expected to stay on wood unless the surface is first sealed to prevent moisture from working up under the gold and literally "pushing it off." To prepare a wooden surface, it should be thoroughly smoothed by sanding, finishing with 6/0 paper, primed, and at least two coats of lead and oil paint applied, allowing plenty of time between coats for drying.

Metal Should be Painted

Sheet metal should be primed and painted as required to prevent corrosion before applying gold leaf. Each coat should be thoroughly dry before applying the next coat.

Gilding Plaster

Plaster may be gilded, if it is thoroughly dry and free from alkali. It should be coated with wall primer or sealer before applying gilding size.

Size is applied to the area to be gilded, like paint, using a paint brush. Care must be taken not to apply too much size as it may sag.

Slow size used for gold leaf is usually mixed with a bit of yellow ground in oil. The gold color tends to cover small imperfections or "holidays," and adds to the covering qualities of the size.

When the size is dry enough to be gilded, that is, when it possesses a barely perceptible "sticky" feeling, the gold leaf may be applied, following the procedure shown in Fig. 11-10. The cover of the book is turned back, and a leaf of gold is placed face downward onto the size, rolling it on slowly. Considerable practice is required to lay gold evenly without excessive waste. After the work has been covered with the gold leaf and all broken places in the leaf have been patched, the gold leaf is "patted" down using cotton batting. Following this, the sign is rubbed lightly, but briskly with cotton to burnish the gold and to remove leaf not securely fastened in place.

Water Gilding

For fine picture frames or antique furniture, the work is built up of whiting and clay over a sealed surface. Each succeeding coat is sanded carefully. The whiting is used first and the base coats are heavily bound with glue. As each coat is added the percentage of binder is cut until the last coats of gilders clay are applied with little or no glue at all. When this surface is hard and dry, a flood of size like that described for glass gilding, is applied and while glossy wet, the gold is put on. The suction of the clay pulls the leaf to the surface helping to gild the hard-to-reach deep parts. When the whole is bone dry the gold can be burnished to a bright luster with an agate.

Using Aluminum Leaf

Aluminum leaf is much stronger than gold and can be handled more easily without breaking. Aluminum requires a stronger tack than is required for gold.

Stenciling

Stenciling a design on a wall, or piece of furniture is accomplished by painting through a template cut out of thin, flat paper or metal.

Most stencils used today are obtained from paint stores, but on a job such as restoring an authentic old pattern the craftsman may be required to make his own stencils. For this reason, the apprentice should become familiar with the principles of stencil layout, design and cutting. Good stenciling requires the use of good templates, neatly and expertly cut and handled.

Stencils that are to be reused frequently should be cut from heavy, tough paper stock. Those that are to be used only a few times can be cut from lighter stock. Specially prepared, oiled stencil papers are available, and are desirable for average work. Heavy papers called tagboard are also suitable for making stencils. Drawings should be made in a color easy to see on the stock. Paper used for stencils should be strong enough to support itself, even when loaded with paint, to the extent it will not sag or curl, or tear at sharp corners when the stencils are used.

LAYING OUT STENCILS: In laying out designs on stencil paper you will need a drawing board, T-square, triangle, curve, compass and a cutting tool. Stencil layout is very exacting work because all cutouts used in repeating the design must be in exact duplicate. A space of at least 3 in. should be left all around the stencil cutouts so the stencil will be stiff enough to handle and to keep the brush from contacting the wall surface outside the stencil while it is being used.

If regular oiled stencil paper is not used, the paper should be oiled before the cutting is started. Designs drawn in pencil should be marked in heavily so the lines will not be eliminated by the oiling process and because the reduced contrast due to the darkening of the paper color will make the lines more difficult to see. Oil used should be one-half mineral spirits, one-half boiled linseed oil. The oiling is most effective when done immediately preceding the cutting. The oiled paper will cut easily and with clean edges. After it is cut a wash coat of shellac makes it last longer.

In cutting a stencil the curves must be smooth and the lines clean. Clean cutting is the mark of good craftsmanship. A cutting surface of plate or safety glass is desirable. The knife should have a thin blade and be shaped so it is comfortable to hold. Special stencil knives are made of thin steel and are about 1/4 in. wide. See Fig. 11-11. An oilstone should be kept at hand for frequent sharpening of the knife, for a razor-sharp edge is required to do clean cutting.

Fig. 11-11. Stencil knives. The knife shown in lower drawing is swivel cutter which revolves to follow curves, but may be locked in position.

The knife should always be drawn toward you with the blade erect in order to make a perpendicular cut. If the stencil is "undercut," it will catch paint and cause smearing. "Ties" which hold the pattern together should be carefully placed.

Stencil brushes which are round and have short bristles, Fig. 11-12, come in 13/16 to 2 1/8 in. diameters. In stenciling a design, the paint to be used - - usually a mixture of tube paints and turpentine - - is applied to a piece of metal or glass with an ordinary paint brush. The end of the stencil brush is dipped into this paint and the stencil brush is tapped against the surface, coating the wall through the openings in the stencil. The stencil may be held against the wall by hand, Fig. 11-13, or by using mask-

Fig. 11-12. Typical stencil brush.

Fig. 11-13. Stenciling design on wall.

ing tape.

A chalk guide line is snapped for the top, bottom, or center line of the border and the stencil is made to follow the line. In order to facilitate following the line, notches can be cut in the extreme ends of the stencil so the points of the V's in the notch line up with the chalk line. The chalk used should be of the type that is easy to erase. The traditional blue chalk used in the building trades is not recommended as it is apt to stain the surface.

When a unit has been completed, pull the stencil carefully from the wall. Clean the back and place it in its next position. Repeat this procedure all the way around the room.

Stencils that are to be reused should be cleaned, separated with layers of wax paper to prevent them from sticking together and stored flat in drawers or on shelves.

Wood Graining, Marbleizing

Graining is a process employed to make the surface of one wood look like that of another. For example, birch may be finished to resemble oak, walnut, or mahogany. Graining is also used to make surfaces such as plaster and metal look like wood.

In marbleizing, the surface to be treated is finished to look like marble.

Basically, both graining and marbleizing consist of applying ground color, and then working in a pattern of wood or marble grain with other colors, using graining tools.

Skillful graining requires much practice, and

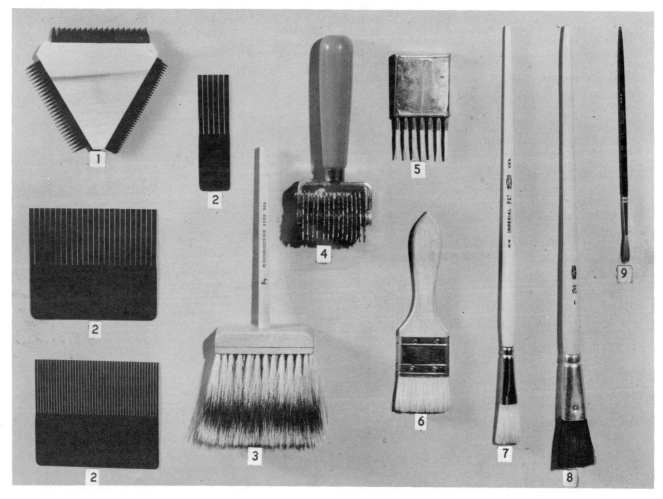

Fig. 11-14. Typical graining tools. 1—Triangular rubber graining comb. 2—Steel combs. 3—Badger blender. 4—Check roller. 5—Piped over grainer. 6—Bristle mottler. 7 and 8—Liners. 9—High liner.

keen observation. To become familiar with the characteristics of various woods and marbles, it is advisable to study actual samples of these materials.

In graining, keep in mind that nature never produces two patterns exactly alike, and that too much repetition of pattern should be avoided.

Tools Required

Tools used in graining and marbleizing include steel and rubber graining combs; fitch brushes for veining, knots; sable pencil brushes; hog hair mottlers; camel's hair mottlers; piped overgrainer; badger's hair blenders; stipplers; and graining check roller. See Fig. 11-14.

Ground Colors

An essential for providing a good imitation of wood grain is a properly mixed and properly applied ground color or foundation on which the graining color is applied. The ground color should match the light colors in the wood to be imitated.

A desirable ground finish is one that leaves the surface hard, nonporous, and not too glossy. Ready-mixed ground color available from paint stores may be used, or a satisfactory ground color may be mixed using white T_1O_2 paste tinted with colors-in-oil to obtain the proper shade. This may be thinned with a mixture consisting of two parts turpentine and one part spar varnish. A bit of Japan drier should be included to hasten the drying of the ground color.

The ground coat should be allowed to dry thoroughly before proceeding with the graining, or marbleizing.

Graining Color

Graining stain may also be purchased ready-mixed or mixed on the job using one part raw linseed oil and two parts turpentine with colors-in-oil to provide the desired shade. To this should be added a little Japan drier.

Graining Procedure - Oak

A typical graining procedure is one in which an imitation oak finish is to be applied on a panel of birch or pressed wood. See Fig. 11-15. Assuming that ground color, a deep cream, has been applied and allowed to dry, we are ready to proceed with actual graining procedure.

Produce the pores first by water color stippling; then grain over with oils. Mix a beer color stain, using stale beer or vinegar and sugar as the thinner and binder and dry raw sienna and burnt umber color. Add to this mixture one-third its volume of water. Apply this stain on the panel and while wet, stipple the area with the flat side of a long bristled flogger. A calcimine brush could also be used. The mottling is done from the bottom up. When this is dry, continue with the figure work.

The graining stain should be applied (rubbed in) and allowed to set until the surface appears a bit flat or dull--from 10 to 30 minutes depending on the graining stain used. Then, start with the figure work, using a rubber graining comb.

Hold the rubber comb loosely with the teeth lying in front on the rubbed-in area. Using a free movement, wipe the figure out with the comb. The comb must be held flat and the teeth used on the figure work should be at a right angle to the grainer.

Walnut Grain

The walnut grain effect in Fig. 11-16 is obtained by first applying a buff ground color. The pores are produced by water color stippling and mottling. When the water color is dry, continue with the figure work. Mix a thin stain of three parts turpentine and one part oil and color with

Fig. 11-16. Panel grained to imitate walnut (kidney shape knots).

burnt umber and Vandyke brown. Rub in the area previously stippled in water color. Use a 2 in. brush or top grainer which is cut out as if having three separate brushes, and proceed to grain the figure with thinned Vandyke brown. This brush should be held and used in the same manner as the rubber comb.

Fig. 11-15. Panel grained to imitate oak.

Figured Walnut Swirl

To obtain a figured walnut swirl effect, Fig. 11-17, the ground color should be cool buff similar to the ground for regular walnut graining. Rub in sparingly an oily glaze of Vandyke brown or umber. With a small brush rub in thin glazes of burnt sienna and touches of black. The brush should be twisted or dabbed, and in some spots a dragging motion should be used to remove part of the color. Uneven distribution of the color is desired. Crush a greaseproof paper into a ball and break up the color in areas where a lighter tone is wanted. Add color to a sponge and a few drops of turpentine and soften the color in certain areas, thus forming a design.

Fig. 11-17. Panel grained to produce figured walnut swirl effect.

Brush Graining

In brush graining, a ground coat is applied, allowed to dry, and graining stain is then applied.

Brush streaks are added by drawing a coarse, dry brush or whisk broom down through the color from top to bottom, while the graining stain is still wet. The brush should be wriggled as it is pulled along, to produce a wavy grain in some places. In this type of graining, no particular attempt is made to imitate actual grain and figure of a particular wood, but the overall effect obtained, if properly done, will be pleasing.

Brush graining may also be done using a calcimine brush. The brush should be held as nearly flat as possible, and the surface pounded with the side of the brush to produce a stippled effect as the brush is brought downward.

Marble is a variety of limestone which has become crystalline due to heat and pressure changes in the earth. Marble is composed of crystals of the minerals calcite or dolomite, which when pure are white. Colored marble results from the presence of other minerals or staining matter mixed with the calcite or dolomite. Many colors of mottled and banded marble are formed by nature - - white, pink, greenish, reddish, gray, and black.

Serpentine marbles are principally green and yellowish-green silicates. Fossiliferous marbles are limestones containing tiny fossil shells. Cross sections of the fossil shells can be seen when this marble is cut and the surface polished.

In marbleizing, it is desirable to have a sample of the marble being imitated at hand, to serve in a general way as a guide to the colors needed and the effect to be obtained.

Sienna Marble

A typical marbleizing job involves imitating Sienna Marble, Fig. 11-18, a very popular type of marble from Italy. It consists of fragments of multicolored stone held together by veins of various colors.

The ground should be a light cream. When dry, paint the area with a thin white paint. While the paint is still wet, put in patches of buff color and blend. The parts outside of the patches should be shaded with a thin blue mixed with black. Using a soft, clean rag, dab lightly to soften the outlines. Put in dark veins by using an artist's brush and then blend. Follow the dark veins and blend, using a thin, white paint.

Black and Gold Marble

Paint the ground a gloss black and let it dry. Using a small sponge, with thin white paint in it put in the lights and shadows. Place the following

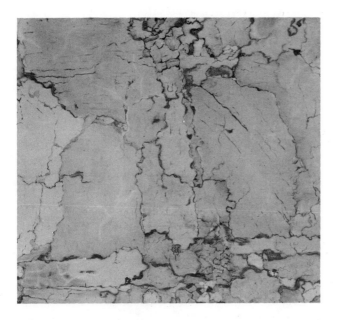

Fig. 11-18. Sienna marble effect produced on pressed wood panel.

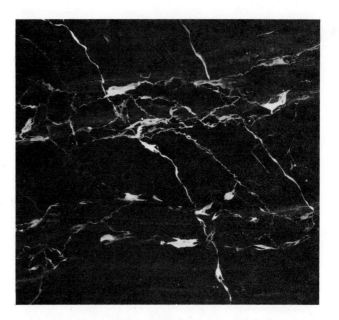

Fig. 11-19. Black and gold marble effect produced on pressed wood panel.

colors on a palette: white, chrome yellow, raw sienna and burnt umber. Using a fine pencil brush, dip into a Japan drier and benzine. Pick up some white and raw sienna and begin veining. As the vein progresses, add into the brush a little yellow and burnt umber. Add intense veins of white using a dagger stripper. When this is dry, overglaze only over the veins with a thin Vandyke brown. See Fig. 11-19.

Burned or Fiery Finish

A burned finish in which the hard portion of the grain stands out in relief can be applied to any wood that has a decided difference in texture between the spring and summer growths. Typical examples are redwood, fir, Western cedar, Ponderosa pine, cypress and yellow pine. Such a finish is suitable for outdoor furniture, various rustic pieces and panels in amusement rooms. To produce a burned finish only two items of equipment are needed - - a blowtorch and a stiff-bristled brush. In doing the charring or burning, the torch is moved back and forth WITH the grain. See Fig. 11-20. CAUTION: Be very careful in handling the torch to prevent fire. The degree of darkness is controlled by length of burning.

Brush the charred surface to remove excess charring and sand lightly with 4/0 paper. If the object is to be used indoors, apply a coat of

white shellac. Rub down the shellac lightly when dry and apply a second coat of shellac. Lightly rub down the second coat of shellac, using 4/0 paper, and apply a coat of furniture wax. Spar varnish should be used instead of shellac and wax if the piece is to be used outdoors.

Wrinkle Finishes

A wrinkle finish is a one-coat job. It is obtained by using a finish made especially for the

Fig. 11-20. Using blowtorch to produce burned or fiery finish. The torch is moved back and forth WITH the grain of the wood.

purpose. Porous objects such as plaster and open-grained woods should be sealed with shellac before the finish is applied.

Wrinkle finishes are available for both wood and metal surfaces and may be applied with a brush, or spray gun (pressure fed). The finish should be applied as a heavy coat. With most wrinkle finishes the heavier the coat, the coarser the wrinkles.

Heat is necessary to form the wrinkles. Some types may be dried with infrared heat lamps; others by over baking or with electric or gas heaters.

In applying wrinkle finishes, as in other finishes, the manufacturer's instructions should be closely followed.

Crackle Finishes

A crackle finish, which is one of the oldest of the novelty finishes, is obtained by applying a specially prepared quick-drying lacquer finish over a slow-drying elastic finish. Cracking of the finish reveals the undercoat in an intricate pattern of irregular lines.

Actually three coatings are required - - lacquer undercoat, crackle coat and a finish coat. Various color arrangements may be obtained. Red crackle lacquer over black lacquer is frequently used to produce a Spanish or Oriental effect.

In applying a crackle finish, the surface is smoothed and cleaned and coated with lacquer of the desired shade. When dry, the crackle finish is sprayed on. This will hold together as a solid coat for a short time and then it will start to crack. Crackle lacquer dries sufficiently for application of the final or finish coat of clear lacquer in about a half hour.

Crystallizing Lacquer

Crystallizing lacquer, another novelty finish, comes in several different colors. As it dries, it crystallizes, forming unusual crystal and floral patterns. This is a one coat finish and may be applied with a brush working in one direction or with a spray gun. Both air-dry and oven-dry types are available.

French Polishing

French polishing is a process for obtaining a high-grade wood finish by applying refined shellac or French varnish with a cloth pad, and using linseed oil as a lubricant to prevent the pad from sticking.

Steps to be followed prior to the application of the French polish are the same as for other finishes. The wood should be carefully sanded, stained and if open-pore wood is being finished, it should be filled.

In preparing to apply the French polish, equal parts of denatured alcohol and French varnish are poured into a cup or dish. Boiled linseed oil is poured into another dish. A wad of cotton or pad of cheesecloth is placed in a small square of muslin which has been washed. The muslin is folded over the cotton or cheesecloth and the corners tied with a string. The pad is first dipped in the French varnish, picking up a small quantity of the varnish. Then it is dipped in the boiled linseed oil, picking up even less of the oil. The pad is squeezed to remove excess varnish and oil.

In applying the finish to the wood, the pad must never be permitted to touch the surface except when it is in motion, either circular or straight-back-and-forth strokes. Even a slight pause will cause the pad to stick and lift the finish.

The pad should be dipped in the varnish and oil occasionally, each time squeezing out the excess before applying the finish to the wood. Three or four times over the surface constitutes a coat.

The first coat should be allowed to dry before applying another. Several coats of finish will be required. The first coats should contain a high proportion of varnish to oil; the varnish should be decreased and the percentage of oil increased as the finishing progresses.

After considerable film has been built up, the pad should be discarded and the surface polished with the heel of the hand, using a bit of linseed oil as a lubricant.

Unit 12

HEALTH, SAFETY RULES

Most disabling injuries to painters - - in fact, four out of every five injuries - - are caused by four things:

1. Falls from scaffolds and other elevations.
2. Slips and falls on the same level.
3. Over exertion.
4. Striking objects and structures, or being struck by them.

If you prevent injuries from these sources, you will prevent almost all painting injuries.

When do these injuries occur, and how can they be prevented?

Falls From Scaffolds (And Other Elevations)

One out of every four painting injuries results from a fall from an elevation, usually a scaffold or staging.

They frequently occur when scaffolds are raised or lowered or are moved from one place to another or when painters are climbing around them or reaching from them.

To prevent these injuries:

1. Be sure that all scaffolds, ladders, and related equipment conform to State Safety Commission and Local Safety Ordinances.
2. Be sure that swinging stages have at least one safety hand line from the roof to the ground for each man on a scaffold.
3. Be sure all scaffolds are in safe condition.
4. Don't use handrails and platforms that are splintered or cracked.
5. Don't use hooks and other tackle that are cracked or deformed.
6. Place painter's hitch carefully, so the load line will not slip off the lower block hook and thus allow one end of scaffold to fall.
7. Be sure that planks or ladder stages are long enough to extend well beyond the supports. Stirrups that support staging should be at least

18 in. from the end of the plank or fastened so that the plank cannot slip.

8. Know the ropes!

a. Check for worn and broken fibers on the outside.

b. Inspect the inner fibers by untwisting the rope in several places. If the inner yarns are bright, clear and unspotted, the rope is probably fairly strong.

c. Unwind from the rope a piece of yarn about 8 in. long and break it with your hands. If you can break the yarn easily, the rope is probably unsafe.

d. Rope used around acid or caustic should be inspected frequently. (Some make a daily inspection.) If black or rusty-brown spots are noted, test the fibers as described in c. Discard all rope whose fibers do not pass the test.

e. If rope cannot be easily bent or worked, or if its fibers seem to be dry and brittle, it might be better not to use it, especially for scaffolding.

f. Don't use wire rope that has many worn or broken wires (three or four broken wires in a foot of wire rope would not be hazardous if the rope was otherwise good, but 10 broken wires in a foot of wire rope would call for a careful check).

g. Wire rope, not fiber rope, should be used near sandblasting, or where there is exposure to chemical washing solutions.

See also Metal Scaffold Safety Rules and Regulations, in Unit on Tools and Equipment.

Slips and Falls (On the Same Level)

One out of every seven painting injuries results from slips and falls on the same level.

These injuries usually occur where rubbish and waste and slippery materials are allowed to remain, or where walkways and working surfaces are uneven.

To prevent such injuries:

1. Remove waste and litter to a place provided for them.

2. Fill in holes around the place where you are working.

3. Clean up spilled oil, grease, paint and other materials at once.

Striking Objects or Structures (Or Being Struck By Them)

One out of every four painting injuries results from painters striking objects or structures, or being struck by them.

This occurs where materials or objects fall or roll; when sudden movements on the part of workmen or equipment are made; when vehicles are moved without warning; or when workmen are inattentive.

To prevent such injuries:

1. Watch where you are going.

2. Make sure you have a clear working space around you.

3. Avoid roads or ramps usually used by vehicles on the job, if possible.

4. When handling, piling, or storing materials, do so in such a manner that you will not be likely to drop them or cause them to move to the danger of yourself or others.

5. Have a proper place for all tools, material and equipment, and keep them there when not in use.

Overexertion

One out of every seven painting injuries results from overexertion.

These injuries usually occur while objects or materials are being lifted, pulled, pushed, or carried.

To prevent such injuries:

1. Use tools to loosen stuck windows. Don't attempt to do it by hand, unless you are standing on a firm support and can use both hands.

2. Follow the ten rules for safe lifting. Among these are:

Size up the load. If it seems more than you can easily handle yourself, get help.

Keep a straight back, and lift by straightening your legs.

In "team lifting" - - where two or more persons work together - - let only one man give the signals, while both or all lift together.

Handling Paint Products Safely

In working with paint products proper precautions should be taken to eliminate health and fire hazards.

Working With Solvents

Solvents sold under various trade names are often used as paint thinners, lacquer solvents, degreasing agents, and paint and varnish removers. Those commonly used by painters include products such as denatured alcohol, turpentine, naphtha, benzine, benzol, mineral spirits, and toluol.

Some of the solvents not so commonly used are carbon bisulphide, carbon tetrachloride and ether.

Exposure which would not harm a strong, healthy individual may cause serious injury to an individual suffering from liver, heart or other illness. Heavy drinkers are particularly susceptible.

Early signs of excessive vapor exposure may be nausea, headache and dizziness, followed by more serious discomfort a few hours later. Liquid solvents may act as skin irritants by removing the natural oils from the skin, leaving the skin rough, reddened and open to dermatitis infections. As with vapor, the extent of the reaction depends upon the susceptibility of the individual.

To assure safe use of solvents, these precautions should be observed:

1. Flammable solvents should never be used where vapors may come in contact with gas or electrical heating units, grinding wheels or any other source of ignition. The fact that there is no source of fire in the immediate vicinity where the solvent is to be used is no guarantee of safety. Solvent vapors are invisible and heavier than air and may travel 30 ft. or more to a source of ignition such as a lighted cigarette or a stove. Do not use any flammable liquid around electric outlets. Especially, do not clean with solvents and steel wool where electric "shorts" may result when contact of the metal wool creates ignition sparks.

2. Avoid working with solvents in large open containers. The solvent should be kept in a bottle or can with a relatively small opening. The container should be kept closed when not in use.

3. Keep windows and doors open as much as possible to provide ventilation and dissipate vapors. Where natural ventilation is inadequate,

artificial ventilation should be provided. Do not use benzol (coal tar derivative) in a closed place under any circumstance. It poisons quietly and painlessly like carbon monoxide by destroying blood cells.

4. Be a "good" workman; avoid spillage. If solvent is accidentally spilled on your clothes, change to clean, dry clothes immediately. If a large solvent spill occurs have someone help you clean up the solvent. Be careful when disposing of solvent-saturated rags. Do not keep rags in your pockets if there is solvent on them. The skin can suffer serious burns resulting in injuries that are painful.

5. If you become nauseated, feel drowsy or dizzy, stop work immediately and get some fresh air. If this feeling persists beyond an hour or two, see a doctor.

6. Wash hands and face frequently with mild soap; follow with application of protective or lubricating cream. Change work clothing frequently. Wear substantial work clothing, including a cap.

7. Do not leave containers of solvent where persons unacquainted with the hazards involved are likely to get to them. Use special care around children. Be sure solvent containers are properly labeled.

8. Eat lunch in a clean, sanitary place away from the place being painted, out of reach of dust and fumes.

Working With Lead

Lead may enter the body and produce toxic symptoms by swallowing, inhaling vapors, dusts, fumes or mists, or by entering through the skin.

When working with paint containing lead, be sure to keep your hands away from your mouth; keep fingernails short and clean. Wash hands carefully before handling food or tobacco. Wear respirator of approved type when burning off paint containing lead, also when spraying or sanding paint containing lead. Be sure adequate ventilation is provided at all times.

Some states in the United States are not required to label paint with accuracy, making it difficult to know which paints contain lead. Treat all exterior paint as lead bearing unless it is clearly stated on the label that it does not contain lead.

Zinc Compounds

Zinc is not poisonous. However, most zinc

paste paints have some lead oxides in them. Thus caution should extend to all paints unless labeled distinctly as being safe and nontoxic.

Acids, Alkalis

Acids used for cleaning, preparation of surfaces, degreasing metal, and other less common uses can only be used when the body is completely protected with goggles, rubber gloves, and adequate clothing. Acids like muriatic, hydrochloric and sulfuric reach their greatest strength when diluted with water. When water and strong acids are mixed together heat is released. Water added to acid may heat so quickly that it turns to steam explosively and reaction could cause dangerous burns. Small quantities of acid should be poured slowly into the water in order to avoid this danger. DO NOT pour water into the acid. Strong chemicals should only be used upon the advice of someone who has authoritative knowledge of their use.

The alkalis are equally dangerous. Some, like trisodium phosphate and sal soda are fairly easy to handle. Strong solutions of these will irritate the skin upon prolonged contact and cause painful skin irritation. Others like lye, caustic soda, and potashes are extremely dangerous and they too, must be used with all precautions which include goggles, rubber gloves and aprons. Caustics, however, are progressively weakened as more water is added to them so that the weaker the solution the less danger from contact. When burns from either acid or alkali are sustained one must immediately wash the area freely with large quantities of clean water and consult a physician at once. A rinse in a solution of ordinary baking soda (sodium bicarbonate) is helpful in case of contact by acid or alkali.

Oxalic acid is especially harmful to the nasal passages and is a toxic poison. It is purchased in the dry form, dissolved, used as a bleach and then usually dries out. This dried material on the surface must never be sanded and allowed to exist in the air as a dust. It should be removed with a cloth moistened with water or alcohol or preferably mineral spirits or turpentine.

Electrical Hazards

Electricity creates danger for the painter. Not only may it ignite his solvents, but it may produce severe shock. Be careful when using water or a water soluble paint around an electric outlet. It is possible to receive a shock from brushes used to apply water mixed paint if bristles come in contact with a hot wire. Aluminum ladders must be handled with extreme care around old and worn wires. A painter with an aluminum ladder must be more careful when working near electric outlets because he and the ladder and the moist ground beneath may form a perfect ground. Terminal boxes are forbidden but often encountered. The best possible way to be safe from injury from electricity is to make sure that the electricity is cut off from its source.

Fire Hazards

A real danger of personal injury exists from fire from blowtorches, acetylene torches, and other kinds of paint removers relying upon heat or open flame. Learn the safety rules for each of these tools. It is regarded as certain that any failure in using these rules correctly will almost certainly cause personal disability or destruction of property. Wall paint materials are flammable, some more than others. Treat them all as though they would burn at any moment. Be extremely careful not to smoke around them or throw matches at them. Keep them in closed containers or containers with small openings. Above all, observe the rules of cleanliness. Keep the floors clean; pick up all dropcloths and wiping cloths. Dispose of them in an approved manner in a safety container or in a pot of water or burn them in a safe place immediately.

Personal Hygiene

Some of the minor injuries usually thought of as petty annoyances can be serious if not taken care of promptly. Small scratches, splinters, blisters, burns, and even bruises should be treated and carefully watched for evidence of infection. Splinters must be removed immediately. Always carry an adequate first aid kit as part of your everyday equipment.

Always wash carefully before each meal, after work and before the use of tobacco. Bathe often; soak in a hot tub whenever possible; use a protective cream on the skin before starting work; and wash in hot water and soap. Use as little solvent to clean the skin as possible. Drink a great deal of milk and water. Make sure the water is fresh and not exposed to paint fumes. Keep down dust as much as possible by using clean dropcloths and wiping cloths. Underclothes should be changed at least once a day and overalls at least once a week. Overall pant legs should have no cuffs to catch on protruding objects or to catch shoe heels to cause tripping. Careful use should be made of the pockets and loops on overalls to prevent dropping of tools from heights and endangering those below.

Shears, knives, screwdrivers, and all sharp instruments should be kept point or edge down in pockets, or sheath. Even sharpened pencils should not be exposed.

Do not perspire heavily and then expose the wet body to cold drafts. Unsightly blackheads in the skin are a sign that washing is not vigorous or often enough. Keep the fingernails clean.

It is necessary that a painter exposed to the hazards and hard work of this trade lead a generally clean, healthy life, with good sleep habits. Management and labor join in advising against the use of alcohol. A man may be able to stand some solvents at work and some alcohol at home, but seldom both. After a period of time the additional load may undermine health.

Unit 13

APPRENTICESHIP

Fundamentals of Apprenticeship

Apprenticeship, in its simplest terms, is training for those occupations commonly known as skilled crafts or trades, that require a wide and diverse range of skills and knowledge, as well as maturity and independence of judgment.

As practiced by modern industry, apprenticeship is a system of training in which the young worker entering industry is given thorough instruction and experience, both on and off the job, in all the practical and theoretical aspects of the work in a skilled trade. Apprenticeship in one form or another has weathered varying social and industrial conditions from antiquity down to modern times. It is still with us, under a voluntary program of cooperation between labor and management; between industry and government; and between the shop and the school.

It is at the local level, that the joint efforts of labor, employers, government, and the schools culminate in the actual employment and training of apprentices. The local Joint Apprenticeship Committee has authority and responsibility for the selection and training of apprentices within its own area.

Effective Apprenticeship Program

An effective apprenticeship program, as recommended by the Federal Committee on Apprenticeship and cooperating State apprenticeship agencies, should contain provisions for the following:

1. The starting age of an apprentice to be not less than 16.

2. A schedule of work processes in which an apprentice is to be given training and experience on the job.

3. Organized instruction designed to provide the apprentice with knowledge in technical subjects related to his trade. (A minimum of 144 hours per year of such instruction is normally considered necessary.)

4. A progressively increasing schedule of wages.

5. Proper supervision of on-the-job training with adequate facilities to train apprentices.

6. Periodic evaluation of apprentice's progress, in job performance and related instruction, and maintenance of appropriate records.

7. Employee-employer cooperation.

8. Recognition for successful completion of the program.

Unit 14

REVIEW OF MATHEMATICS

A general working knowledge of arithmetic is necessary if the painter and decorator is to be able to make correctly the many calculations used in his trade.

Addition

Addition is the combining of two or more numbers. The result obtained is known as the sum or total.

For convenience in adding, numbers are grouped in a column: units under units, tens under tens, and hundreds under hundreds, etc., like this:

```
 Hundreds
  Tens
   Units
  8 7 7
  2 1 9
  4 1 7
  3 9 8
  ─────
1,9 1 1
```

The total is read as one thousand, nine hundred, eleven. The number or digit added in each column from the preceding column is called the amount carried.

Typical examples of problems in addition which will be encountered, by the painter and decorator follow:

1. Four ceilings are to be coated. The first contains 192 sq. ft., the second 345, the third 217 and the fourth 141. Figure the total number of square feet in the four ceilings.

2. In making a checkup, a painter finds he has on hand cans containing white exterior paint as follows: 5 gal.; 5 gal.; 5 gal.; 4 gal.; 2 gal.; and 1 gal. How much white exterior paint does he have altogether?

3. From an itemized estimate were obtained these figures: Paint $77.19; Putty $1.50; Wall-

paper $17.00; Paste $2.25; Labor $170.00. What is the total cost of these items?

4. The areas of floors in a home which are to be varnished are: 314, 155, 249, 299, 177, 104 sq. ft. Figure the total area, in square feet.

Subtraction

Subtraction is the process of finding the difference between two numbers. The larger number is called the MINUEND: the smaller number the SUBTRAHEND. The difference between the minuend and the subtrahend is the REMAINDER.

It is customary to write the larger number first, then place the smaller number beneath it, with the units under units, tens under tens, etc., like this:

```
Minuend . . . . . . . 987
Subtrahend. . . . . . 455
                      ───
Difference . . . . . . 532
```

A problem which is a little more difficult and involves "borrowing" follows:

```
875
578
───
297
```

To work the second problem we begin to work from the units column at the right. 8 cannot be subtracted from 5 as it is greater than 5. Therefore, it will be necessary to borrow 1 ten or ten units from the tens column (7) and add it to the 5 units. (1 from the tens column equals 10 units) 10 units plus 5 units equals 15 units. 15 units minus 8 units equals 7 units. Place this figure under the line in the units column. 1 has already been used from the tens column of the minuend, so we have 6 tens from which 7 tens is to be subtracted. 7 cannot be taken from 6, so it is necessary to borrow 1 hundred or one hundred units from the hundreds column. 100 units equals 10 of the tens column so 6 tens plus 10 tens equals 16 tens. 16 tens is greater than 7 tens so we can subtract the second figure in the subtrahend 7, leaving 9 as the remainder, which is written to the left of the first remainder, under the tens column. 100 units have been used from the hundreds column, so there are left 7 one hundreds instead of 8 one hundreds. 7 one hundreds minus 5 one hundreds leaves 2 one hundreds for the remainder. Write the 2 to the left of the last remainder 9 under the hundreds column, as shown.

Multiplication

Multiplication is the process of finding the product of two numbers. Example: 48 x 5. If you add 48 five times, as 48 + 48 + 48 + 48 + 48, you will find the answer is 240. There is another way to get the answer, 240, called multiplication. The "x" sign is used to indicate the operation, and is read TIMES, as 2 x 4 is read two times four; the result of 2 x 4 = 8. 8 is called the PRODUCT. The two numbers used when multiplying are called the FACTORS of the product. The number which indicates how many times another number should be added is called the MULTIPLIER. The number which is added to itself a certain number of times is called the MULTIPLICAND, for example:

```
Multiplicand . . . . . .   48
Multiplier . . . . . . . .    5
Product . . . . . . . .  240
```

Now let's take a problem that is a little more complicated, like:

```
  367
   23
 1101
  734
 8441
```

3 x 7 = 21. We put 1 under the 3 (units column) and add 2 to the next operation. 3 x 6 = 18. Now add the 2 left from the first multiplication and you have 18 + 2 = 20. Put 0 under the 2 and add 2 to the next operation. 3 x 3 = 9. The sum 9 + 2, which was carried over, equals 11, so put 11 down. Now multiply 367 x 2. First multiply 2 x 7 = 14. Put the 4 under the 0. Notice that when you multiply by hundreds the first number is put in the hundred column of the multiplicand. The same holds true for thousands. Add the 1

to the next operation. 2 x 6 = 12 + 1 = 13. Put the 3 under 1 and carry 1. 2 x 3 = 6 + 1 = 7. Put the 7 to the left of the last number. Draw a line indicating the figures are to be added, then add. The product is 8441.

Division

If you had on hand 18 paint brushes and wished to give each of 3 painters an equal number of these brushes, you could give each painter one brush at a time until all 18 were distributed. A quicker way would be to find out how many threes there are in 18. This operation is called DIVISION and is the process of finding how many times one number is contained in another. The sign ÷ indicates division. (8 ÷ 2 = 4).

The number to be divided is called the DIVIDEND. The number by which the dividend is divided is called the DIVISOR. The result obtained by dividing one number by another is called the QUOTIENT. Where a number is not contained in another number an equal number of times, the amount of the dividend left is called the REMAINDER. Let's solve a typical problem:

The roof of a building to be stained contains 3000 sq. ft. If one gallon of stain will cover 250 sq. ft., how many gallons will be needed to stain the entire roof?

To find out, we will divide 3000 by 250.

```
         12
250 )3000
      250
      500
      500
```

250 is contained in 300 once, so we put down the 250 as shown and subtract this from 300 which leaves 50. Bring 0, the next digit, down from the dividend and you have 500. 250 is contained in 500 twice. Put down 500, subtract and you have 0 left over or no remainder. This indicates 12 gallons of stain will be needed for the 3000 sq. ft. While this problem is a very simple one, it illustrates the procedure.

When the divisor is ONE digit, the operation is called SHORT DIVISION. When the divisor is made up of TWO OR MORE digits, as 250, the operation is called LONG DIVISION.

Problems in division may be checked by multiplying the two factors, as 250 x 12 = 3000.

Fractions

A fraction is one or more parts or portions

of a whole unit. In painting and decorating work, it is frequently necessary for a painter to deal with parts or portions of units, the dimensions or measurements of which are expressed in fractions. Since a part of an inch, a yard, a dollar, a gallon, or any other unit with which the painter is working may be expressed as a fraction, it is often necessary for him to solve problems involving addition, subtraction, multiplication or division of fractions.

In writing fractions, the figure above the line indicates the number of fractional units to be considered and is called the NUMERATOR. The number below the line is the DENOMINATOR, and represents the number of equal parts into which the unit is divided, for example:

$$\text{Numerator} \ldots \ldots \frac{7}{8}$$
$$\text{Denominator} \ldots \ldots$$

This shows the unit was divided into 8 equal parts; 7 of the equal parts are being considered. When a fraction has a value less than a whole unit, it is called a PROPER fraction. 7/8 is an example of a proper fraction. If the value of a fraction is greater than a whole unit, like 9/8, it is called an IMPROPER FRACTION. Both proper and improper fractions are called COMMON FRACTIONS. When a whole number and a fraction are combined, they are called MIXED NUMBERS, like 2 7/8.

CHANGING DENOMINATIONS OF FRACTIONS: Multiplying or dividing both the numerator and denominator of a fraction of the same number does not change its value. For example:

$$\frac{1}{4} \times \frac{4}{4} = \frac{4}{16}$$

$$\frac{4}{16} \div \frac{4}{4} = \frac{1}{4}$$

In the first example, the numerator and denominator of the fraction 1/4, are both multiplied by 4; in the second example the numerator and denominator of the fraction 4/16 are divided by 4.

Addition of Fractions

Fractions must be changed to a common denominator, before they can be added. After the fractions to be added have been changed to a common denominator, the numerators are added and the sum placed over the common denominator.

Problem: Add 3/4, 5/8, 9/16, and 5/32.

Fourths, eighths, and sixteenths can be changed into 32nds, so 32 will be our common denominator. To change given fractions to common denominator:

$$3/4 = \frac{24}{32}$$
$$5/8 = \frac{20}{32}$$
$$9/16 = \frac{18}{32}$$
$$5/32 = \frac{5}{32}$$
$$\frac{67 \text{ (numerators added)}}{32}$$

Changing this to a mixed number gives us 2 3/32.

Subtraction of Fractions

Before fractions can be subtracted, they must be changed to a common denominator. After fractions have been changed to a common denominator, the numerators are subtracted.

Problem: Subtract 19/32 from 63/64.

To get a common denominator, we change the 19/32 into 64ths, giving us 38/64.

$$\frac{63}{64}$$
$$\text{Subtract } \frac{38}{64}$$
$$\text{Difference } \frac{25}{64}$$

Multiplication of Fractions

In multiplying fractions, multiply the numerators for a new numerator and the denominators for a new denominator.

Problem: Multiply 5/8 x 1/2
Multiply the numerators   5 x 1 = 5
Multiply the denominators   8 x 2 = 16
5 is the new numerator, 16 the new denominator, therefore 5/8 x 1/2 = 5/16.

Division of Fractions

In dividing fractions, invert the divisor; then proceed as in multiplication of fractions.
Problem: 7/8 ÷ 1/2
Invert the divisor 1/2 to 2/1
Multiply the fractions 7/8 x 2/1 = 14/8

Problem:

7/8 ÷ 2

2 is a whole number whose denominator is 1, so write it 2/1

Invert the divisor 2/1 to 1/2

Multiply the fractions 7/8 x 1/2 = 7/16

In dividing mixed numbers, change them to improper fractions and proceed as in dividing proper fractions.

Problem:

6 3/4 ÷ 2 1/8

Change to improper fractions 6 3/4 = 27/4

2 1/8 = 17/8

Write problem as 27/4 ÷ 17/8

Invert divisor 17/8 to 8/17

Multiply fractions 27/4 x 8/17 = 216/68, or 3 3/17.

Decimal Fractions

Knowing how to figure in decimal fractions is of considerable importance to painters and decorators, especially those who estimate and determine job costs. It should be remembered too, that it is the decimal system upon which the monetary system of the United States is based.

A common fraction can have any number for a denominator as 1/3, 2/7, 1/18, etc. A DECIMAL fraction must have 10 or a power of 10 (like 10 x 10, 100 x 10, etc.) for the denominator.

In writing decimals, a point (.) called a DECIMAL POINT, is used to indicate the denominator of its equivalent decimal fraction. For example:

1/10 = .1

3/100 = .03

89/1000 = .089

375/10000 = .0375

In writing decimals, the decimal point is placed according to the number of zeros in the denominator, because there are as many decimal places as zeros in the denominator.

```
          decimal point
          tenths
          hundredths
          thousandths
   .      3   7   5
```

.375 would be read 375/1000.

In writing decimals, it is often necessary to add zeros to the numerator, between the deci-

mal point and the numerator to indicate the denominator 375/10000 would be written .0375.

When a number consists of a whole number and a decimal fraction, it is called a MIXED DECIMAL FRACTION. In a mixed decimal fraction the whole number is always written to the LEFT of the decimal point and the fraction part of the number is to the right as 5.125. A decimal point is read AND. 5.125 would be read 5 and 125 thousandths. Or, it might be read 5 point 125.

Adding Decimal Fractions

In adding decimals, the figures to be added are written so the decimal points are under each other like this:

```
    .75
   2.154
   9.0006
  11.435
  -------
  23.3396
```

The decimal point in the sum is placed directly under the decimal point in the figures being added.

Subtracting Decimal Fractions

In subtracting decimals, write the larger number (Minuend) first. Under it place the smaller number (Subtrahend), so the decimal point of one number is directly under the decimal point of the other, the same as in addition.

Problem:

45.875 minus 21.225

```
  45.875  Minuend
  21.225  Subtrahend
  ------
  24.650  Difference
```

The decimal point in the difference is directly under those of the minuend and subtrahend.

Multiplication of Decimals

In multiplying decimals write the numbers including decimals under each other the same as in multiplying whole numbers. Place the decimal point in the proper place in the number, but disregard the decimal point while multiplying.

Problem:

Multiply .675 x .22

```
       .675
        .22
      1350
      1350
     .14850
```

Count the decimal places in the multiplicand (3) and the multiplier (2). Add these figures for the total number of decimal places in the product. 3 + 2 = 5. Starting at the right hand digit 0, in the product, count to the left five places and put in the decimal point as .14850. The number of decimal places in the product is always the sum of those in the multiplier and the multiplicand. If there are not enough figures in the product, zeros are added to the left of the other figures in the product to make the decimal places needed.

Division of Decimals

In the division of decimals, the divisor is changed to a whole number. If the divisor is already a whole number no such change is required. In dealing with common fractions, we learned that the numerator and denominator of a fraction can be multiplied by the same number and not change the value, as:

$$\frac{1 \times 10}{2 \times 10} = \frac{10}{20}$$

The same rule applies when dealing with decimals. To see how this works, let's take the problem:

$$8.25 \div .75$$

To make the divisor .75 a whole number, we multiply it by 100, which gives us 75. Since we multiplied the divisor by 100, we must also multiply the dividend 8.25 by 100. This gives us 825.

The problem when set up ready for division looks like this:

```
           11.  quotient
      75. ) 825.
            75
            75
```

Divide as in regular division.

The decimal point in the quotient is placed over the decimal point in the dividend.

Percentage

Percentage means "by the hundredths."

When a common fraction is used for percent, the denominator must be 100 as:

10/100 = 10%; 8/100 = 8%.

When a decimal fraction is used for percent, two decimal places are used, as .10; .08. When a common fraction is changed to percent, the numerator is divided by the denominator and the division must be carried out two places for the percent or to the hundredths place.

Measures of Capacity and Weight

The standard liquid measures of capacity used by painters and decorators are as follows:

```
    3 Teaspoons (tsp.) - 1 tablespoon (tbsp.)
   16 tbs . . . . . . . . - 1 cup
    1 cup . . . . . . . . - 2 gills (gi.)
    2 cups . . . . . . . - 1 pint (pt.)
    4 gills . . . . . . . - 1 pt.
    4 cups . . . . . . . - 1 quart (qt.)
    2 pts . . . . . . . . - 1 qt.
    4 qts . . . . . . . . - 1 gallon (gal.)
31 1/2 gals . . . . . . . - 1 barrel (bbl.)
    2 bbls . . . . . . . - 1 hogshead (hhd.)
    1 gal . . . . . . . . - 231 cu. in.
7 1/2 gals . . . . . . . - 1 cu. ft.
    1 gal. water . . . . - 8 1/3 lbs.
    1 cu. ft. water . . . - 62 1/2 lbs.
```

Avoirdupois Weight Table

```
   16 ounces (oz.) - 1 pound (lb.)
  100 lbs. - 1 hundredweight (cwt.)
 2000 lbs. - 1 ton (T.)
```

Linear Measure Table

```
   12 inches (in.) - 1 foot (ft.)
    3 ft. - 1 yard (yd.)
```

Square Measure Table

```
  144 square inches (sq. in.) - 1 square foot
  (sq. ft.)
    9 sq. ft. - 1 square yard (sq. yd.)
  100 sq. ft. - 1 painter's square
```

Finding Areas of Surfaces

In order to estimate the amount of material needed to cover a surface, a painter must be able to determine the areas of surfaces. Of primary importance are rules for computing the areas of rectangles, triangles, and circles.

RECTANGLE: A rectangle is a right-angled parallelogram (a four-sided figure with the opposite sides parallel, and therefore equal).

To find the area of a rectangle, the length is multiplied by the width. The area of a rectangle 12 ft. long and 6 ft. wide would be 72 square feet.

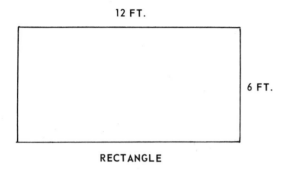

12 FT.

6 FT.

RECTANGLE

TRIANGLE: The area of a triangle equals one-half of the base times the altitude.

One-half of 12 (base) is 6 ft. 6 x 6 (altitude = 36 square feet; the area of the triangle shown.

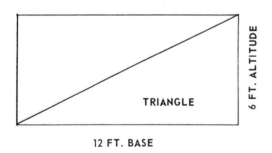

TRIANGLE

6 FT. ALTITUDE

12 FT. BASE

CIRCLE: A circle is a closed curve in which all points are an equal distance from the center.

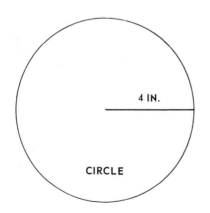

4 IN.

CIRCLE

A straight line drawn from the center of a circle to any point in the circumference (line around outside) is called the radius of the circle. The area of a circle equals the radius squared (multiplied by itself, like 4 x 4) times 3.1416, called Pi and represented by the Greek letter π.

To find the area of a circle which has a radius of 4 inches, we first square the 4, which gives us 16; then multiply 16 by 3.1416 which gives us 50.2656 square inches, as the area of the circle which has a radius of 4 inches (8 in. diameter).

CYLINDER: To find the lateral area of a cylinder, the circumference of the base is multi-

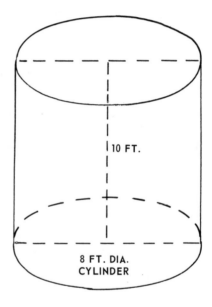

10 FT.

8 FT. DIA.
CYLINDER

plied by the altitude. Let's assume that the cylinder is 8 ft. in diameter and 10 ft. high.

We find the circumference of the circle or

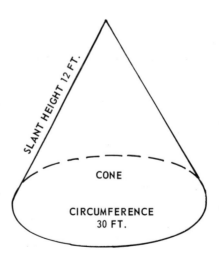

SLANT HEIGHT 12 FT.

CONE

CIRCUMFERENCE
30 FT.

base, by multiplying the diameter 8 x 3.1416, which gives us 25.1328. Multiplying the circumference 25.1328, by the altitude 10, would give us 251.328, which is the lateral surface area of the cylinder.

The top and bottom areas are determined by following the procedure described for finding the area of a circle.

CONE: To find the lateral area of a cone (solid whose bottom is a circle and whose sides taper evenly to a point) the circumference of the base is multiplied by one-half the slant height.

For example: If the circumference is 30, we would multiply 30 by one-half the slant height of 12 or 6, which would give us 180, as the area of the lateral area of the cone.

Unit 15

HOW TO READ BLUEPRINTS

There are many good reasons why the apprentice printer should learn how to read blueprints. He must be able to visualize how a building will look when completed; to determine the size, shape and location of the parts to be painted and decorated, and the amount of staging necessary to complete the job. He must be able to determine the amount of paint and wallpaper required.

Blueprint "Language"

Whether the plans are for a large hotel or a small cottage, the same "language" is used. On an architectural drawing some lines are thicker than others, some are broken, others are solid. Variations in thickness and character have definite meaning.

Specifications accompanying the blueprints, usually supplied in the form of a typewritten sheet specify kinds and grades of painting materials to be used. Standards of workmanship and a time limit for completion of the work are also included in the specifications.

Drawings (plates) 1 to 15 inclusive that follow, which are used through courtesy of Practical Builder Magazine, Chicago, will acquaint the apprentice with various types of lines, sym-

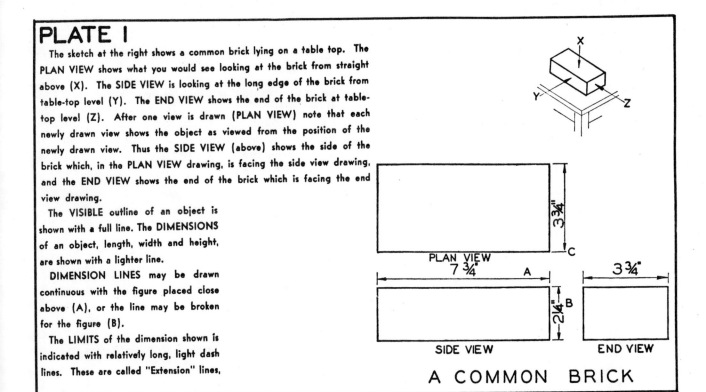

PLATE I

The sketch at the right shows a common brick lying on a table top. The PLAN VIEW shows what you would see looking at the brick from straight above (X). The SIDE VIEW is looking at the long edge of the brick from table-top level (Y). The END VIEW shows the end of the brick at table-top level (Z). After one view is drawn (PLAN VIEW) note that each newly drawn view shows the object as viewed from the position of the newly drawn view. Thus the SIDE VIEW (above) shows the side of the brick which, in the PLAN VIEW drawing, is facing the side view drawing, and the END VIEW shows the end of the brick which is facing the end view drawing.

The VISIBLE outline of an object is shown with a full line. The DIMENSIONS of an object, length, width and height, are shown with a lighter line.

DIMENSION LINES may be drawn continuous with the figure placed close above (A), or the line may be broken for the figure (B).

The LIMITS of the dimension shown is indicated with relatively long, light dash lines. These are called "Extension" lines.

PLAN VIEW
7 3/4"   A
3 3/4"   C

SIDE VIEW
2 1/4"   B

END VIEW
3 3/4"

A COMMON BRICK

239

bols, indications, views, and other information which is standard architectural drafting practice. Basic in its beginning, concerning itself with simple lines and views, the series develops into more complex detailing. Each plate should be studied and digested thoroughly so

painter a better understanding of construction drawings as applied to residential construction.

Such a series, even if confined only to residential construction, could continue almost indefinitely, using the limitless source found in variety of plan layout, types of construction,

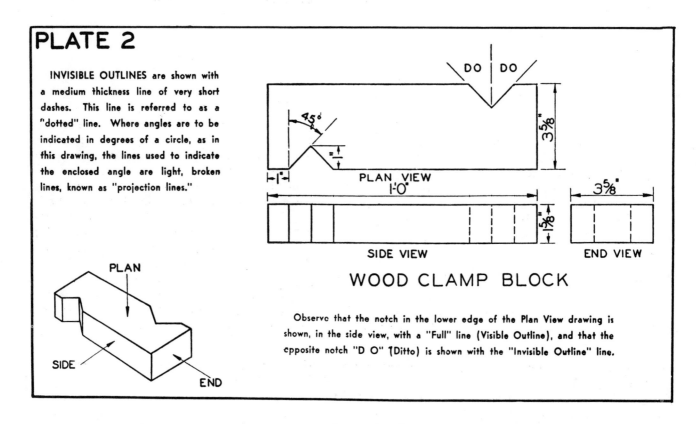

PLATE 2

INVISIBLE OUTLINES are shown with a medium thickness line of very short dashes. This line is referred to as a "dotted" line. Where angles are to be indicated in degrees of a circle, as in this drawing, the lines used to indicate the enclosed angle are light, broken lines, known as "projection lines."

PLAN VIEW
1'-0"

SIDE VIEW   END VIEW

WOOD CLAMP BLOCK

Observe that the notch in the lower edge of the Plan View drawing is shown, in the side view, with a "Full" line (Visible Outline), and that the opposite notch "D O" (Ditto) is shown with the "Invisible Outline" line.

that subsequent plates will be more easily understood. It is important for the apprentice painter to be able to visualize, from a set of blueprints, just how the building will look both outside and inside when completed.

The following plates are intended to give the

selection of materials and methods of fabrication. However, this series will touch on the basic fundamentals of the subject and a thorough understanding of these fundamentals should qualify the reader to interpret most any type of residential drawing that may be encountered.

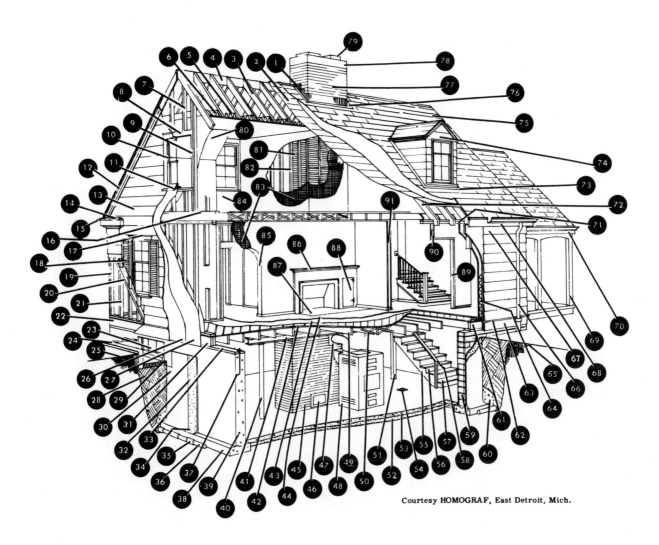

Courtesy HOMOGRAF, East Detroit, Mich.

1. FLASHING
2. ROOF BOARDS
3. RAFTERS
4. RIDGE BOARD
5. CEILING JOISTS
6. CEILING INSULATION
7. GABLE STUDS
8. WINDOW HEADER
9. ROUGH WINDOW OPENING
10. WINDOW SASH
11. WINDOW SILL
12. GABLE RAKE MOLDING
13. BEVEL SIDING
14. CORNICE RETURN
15. GUTTER
16. FLOOR PLATE
17. DRIP CAP MOLDING
18. SHUTTERS
19. CORNER STUDS
20. DIAGONAL BRACING
21. WALL STUDS
22. JOIST TRIMMER
23. BASEMENT SASH

24. WINDOW AREA-WAY
25. GRADE LINE
26. BUILDING PAPER
27. SHEATHING
28. BACKFILL
29. AGGREGATE FILL
30. WATERPROOFING
31. JOIST HEADER
32. CEMENT PLASTER
33. BOND PLATE
34. CEMENT COVE
35. TARPAPER JOINT COVER
36. DRAIN TILE
37. ANCHOR BOLTS
38. CONCRETE FOOTING
39. CONCRETE FOUNDATION WALL
40. PIPE COLUMN
41. STEEL BEAM
42. WOOD SUB-FLOOR
43. FLOORING FELT
44. FINISH FLOORING
45. MASONRY CHIMNEY
46. ASH PIT CLEANOUT

47. THIMBLE
48. FURNACE
49. FLOOR JOISTS
50. BRIDGING
51. POST OR COLUMN
52. AGGREGATE FILL
53. CONCRETE FLOOR SLAB
54. FLOOR DRAIN
55. STAIR STRINGER
56. STAIR RISER
57. STAIR TREAD
58. STAIR RAIL
59. CEMENT BLOCK FOUNDATION WALL
60. AGGREGATE FILL
61. JOIST TRIMMER
62. DRIP CAP
63. WEATHER BOARD
64. WALL INSULATION
65. EARTH
66. CONDUCTOR
67. FRIEZE BOARD
68. FACIA OR CORNICE BOARD

69. PORCH POST
70. PORCH FRIEZE BOARD
71. TOP PLATES
72. RAFTERS
73. FLASHING
74. DORMER
75. SHINGLES
76. FLASHING
77. MASONRY CHIMNEY
78. CEMENT CAP
79. CHIMNEY POT OR FLUE LINING
80. ANGLED CEILING
81. MASONRY
82. FURRING STRIPS
83. LATH
84. PLASTER
85. PLASTER ARCH
86. MANTLE
87. HEARTH
88. WOOD BOX
89. CASED OPENING
90. HEADER
91. PARTITION

HOUSE PARTS DICTIONARY. A careful study of this drawing will enable the apprentice painter to become familiar with terms used in describing various parts of a frame dwelling, including the foundation.

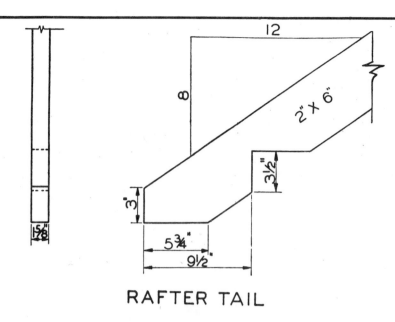

RAFTER TAIL

PLATE 3

It is often-times unnecessary to show the entire length of a structural member, or the full height wall, etc. But this drawing shows only the rafter "Tail." Where drawings are "broken" for short distances, the "break" is like this.

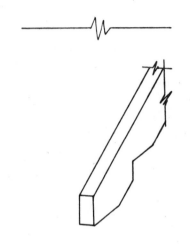

When all essential information can be shown in two views, or even in one view if that is possible, rather than in three, only the necessary views are drawn. The conventional way of showing the "pitch" of the roof is to indicate, as in the drawing above, the number of inches that the roof slope rises in each 12 inches of the horizontal "run" of the rafter. This roof will have an 8" to 12" pitch.

PLATE 4

This is the first assembly drawing; showing a completed structure made up of several parts. Complicated assembly drawings are further explained by making separate drawings of their parts, called "parts drawings" or "detail drawings."

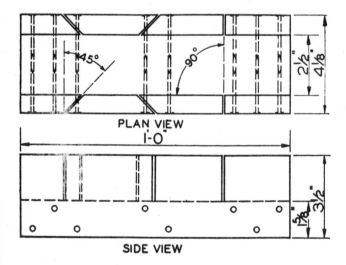

PLAN VIEW

SIDE VIEW

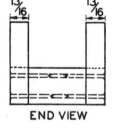

END VIEW

SMALL MITRE BOX

Note that the location of the nails—for greatest strength and rigidity—is indicated in this drawing. Well done drawings are thoroughly "dimensioned" with unmistakable figures and fractions. Construction drawings should be "drawn to scale" but also they should be completely dimensioned; the mechanic should not be compelled to scale drawings for dimension information. "Scaling" blueprints is time-consuming and inaccurate.

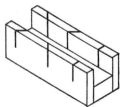

PLATE 5

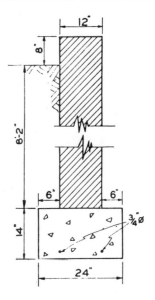

It is often necessary to give more complete information than can be given in drawings of the outside surfaces, in order to reveal "what is inside."

In such cases we "cut through" the wall, or the floor construction, or whatever it may be, and show in our drawing the necessary "inside information."

Such a drawing is called a section.

In making section drawings, materials are distinctly indicated by varying the lining or "texturing" of the "cut" materials, each variation representing or symbolizing the materials which have been "cut".

Many ways of lining or texturing "cut" materials have become generally accepted as meaning certain materials, such as masonry, concrete, etc., and are called "Symbols."

There are "symbols" in all of the building trades, and it is wise to learn those in such trades as general contract work, plumbing and heating, and electric work as applied to building.

Symbols for the warm air heating and the air conditioning field are in the process of development.

Below are examples of some of the symbols used on section drawings in the general contract construction field.

ROUGH WOOD

FINISHED WOOD

CONCRETE

METAL

BRICK MASONRY

EARTH

PLATE 6

Whereas "Symbols" (Plate 5) are used to indicate and identify materials and items of construction, they differ from "conventions."

"Conventions," as used in making construction drawings, are generally-accepted short-cut and simplified drawings showing and explaining various elements of construction, such as doors, windows, types of wall construction, types of columns, etc.

For example, a double hung window in a frame wall is shown in plan drawings by the simple "convention" of two lines drawn across the wall to indicate the width of the sash, and two lines drawn parallel with the wall between the first two lines. (Upper Right.)

An alternate convention sometimes used for double hung windows in a frame wall suggests the weight boxes and projecting window sill. (Right.) Some typical conventions are illustrated below

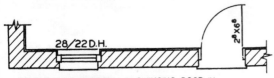

30/24 D.H.

30/24 D.H.

32/22 D.H.

DOUBLE HUNG WINDOW & IN-SWINGING DOOR IN EXTERIOR BRICK VENEER WALL

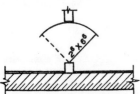

28/22 D.H.

DOUBLE HUNG WINDOW & IN-SWINGING DOOR IN EXTERIOR MASONRY WALL

JUNCTURE OF FRAME PARTITION WITH FACE BRICK WALL BACKED UP WITH COMMON BRICK. ALSO DOUBLE-ACTING DOOR.

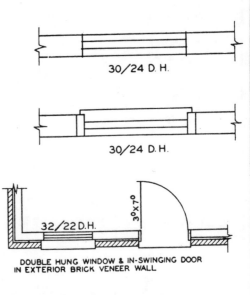

BRICKED-IN OPENING IN BRICK MASONRY WALL ALSO FLUE WITH FLUE LINING.

243

PLATE 7

The purpose of a "set of plans" which includes both drawings and specifications, is to give full and complete information to the builder and his men as to what to build.

Since the mechanics depend principally upon the drawings for their information, the drawings should be thoroughly "dimensioned," and anything not fully explained in the general drawings should be "detailed."

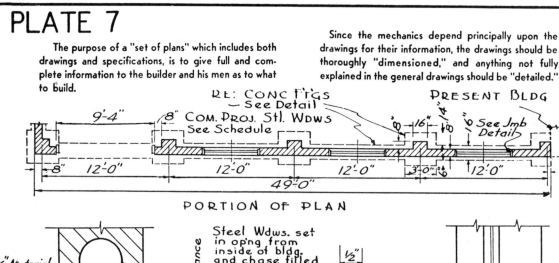

RE: CONC FT'GS
— See Detail

8" COM. PROJ. STL. WDWS
See Schedule

PRESENT BLDG

See Jmb Detail

9'-4"

8" | 12'-0" | 12'-0" | 12'-0" | 3'-0" | 12'-0" | 4"

49'-0"

PORTION OF PLAN

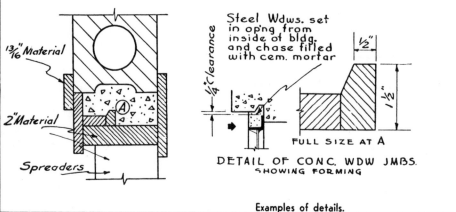

13/16" Material

2" Material

Spreaders

Steel Wdws. set in op'ng from inside of bldg. and chase filled with cem. mortar

1/4" Clearance

1/2"

1/2"

FULL SIZE AT A

DETAIL OF CONC. WDW JMBS.
SHOWING FORMING

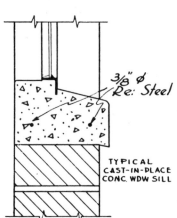

3/8" Ø
Re: Steel

TYPICAL
CAST-IN-PLACE
CONC. WDW SILL

Examples of details.

PLATE 8

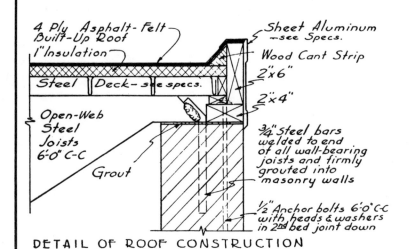

4 Ply Asphalt-Felt
Built-Up Roof

1" Insulation

Steel — Deck—see specs.

Open-Web
Steel
Joists
6'-0" C-C

Grout

Sheet Aluminum
—see Specs.

Wood Cant Strip

2"x6"

2"x4"

3/4" steel bars welded to end of all wall-bearing joists and firmly grouted into masonry walls

1/2" Anchor bolts 6'-0" C-C with heads & washers in 2nd bed joint down

DETAIL OF ROOF CONSTRUCTION

Drawings are advantageously supplemented by notes.

There are many situations wherein a quickly lettered note will clarify possible questions; particularly questions as to the exact kind of material indicated in the drawing.

For example, the 4-ply asphalt-felt built-up roof noted in the drawing to the left might be a tarred felt and coal tar pitch roof insofar as the drawing only would indicate, and the sheet metal flashing and facia combined, as indicated in the drawing, could be copper, stainless steel, galvanized iron, or other metal.

Generous notes on drawings save a lot of time thumbing through the specifications, — and they help to avoid mistakes.

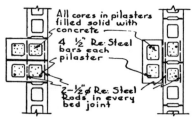

All cores in pilasters filled solid with concrete

4 1/2" Re: Steel bars each pilaster

2-1/2" Ø Re: Steel Rods in every bed joint

SKETCH OF REINFORCED PILASTERS
Not drawn to scale

There are various practices in building construction which have become more or less "standardized," and many construction draftsmen do not deem it necessary to "detail" such "standardized" construction.

"2 x 4 studs, 16" O.C."—"Joists 2 x 10, 16" O.C."—"8" Com. Brick" —"8" x 8" Flue"—these and similar notations represent about all the "detailing" there is to be found covering such items in many "Plans."

There should be more detailing. Detail drawings remove doubts, permit closer "figuring," and save time and expense on the job.

How to Read Blueprints

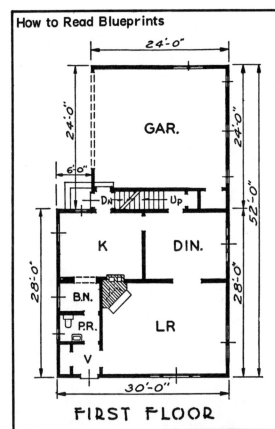

FIRST FLOOR

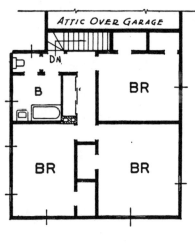

SECOND FLOOR

The type and arrangement of the house, its appearance, and the extent of the plumbing, heating and electric facilities, etc., are intended to meet the needs and the wishes of the family that is to own and live in the house. The drawings and specifications, in most cases, accurately describe the structure which the builder is asked to build for a fixed sum of money. There should be no deviations from the working drawings.

Thoroughly detailed drawings and completely informative specifications of the "plan," enable the contractor to "figure" with confidence, and to perform the work in the manner intended by the architect and owner.

PLATE 9

The floor plans show the over-all size and plan form of the building, and the arrangement of the rooms. The approximate location of doors and windows, fireplaces, chimneys, cabinets, and the like is indicated also, but these locations are shown exactly in framing details.

PLATE 10

Because of the difference in thickness of the various side-wall sheathings, it is a usual practice to show measurements for framing from the "framing line"; i. e., from the line of the outer edge of the studding.

Note the reinforcement of the first floor joists which "carry" the partitions parallel with the joists, and the trimming surrounding the chimney and fireplace.

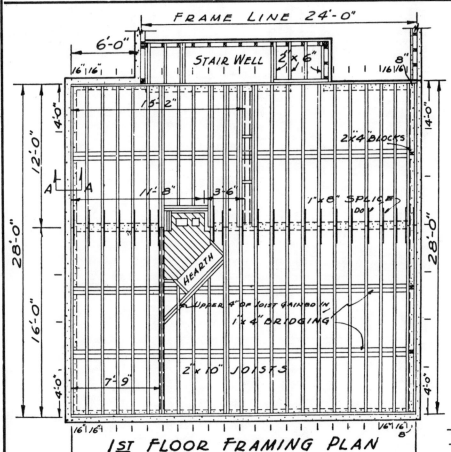

1ST FLOOR FRAMING PLAN

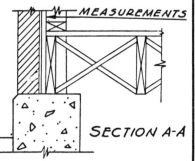

SECTION A-A

PLATE II

The many drawings which comprise a "set" are coordinated in every respect so that related drawings, no matter where they appear in the sequence, thoroughly explain the work to be done by the various trades employed on the job.

Drawings should not show discrepancies between one another, however, it is always wise to study and check them to see that no serious conflict exists before "figuring" the job or starting construction.

Each trade should carefully "plot" its runs of ducts, steam and water lines, electrical conduit, plumbing supplies and drains on the plans to make certain that terminals as designated in the plan can be reached without undue cutting of structural members or weakening of the structure.

As the plans for this house develop, it will be noted that the framing is ORDERLY, that the studs are set directly over, and in vertical alignment with the floor joists; that second floor studs are directly over those of the first floor.

This greatly facilitates the work of all trades and makes a sounder structure which is less subject to racking, twisting, sagging, etc.

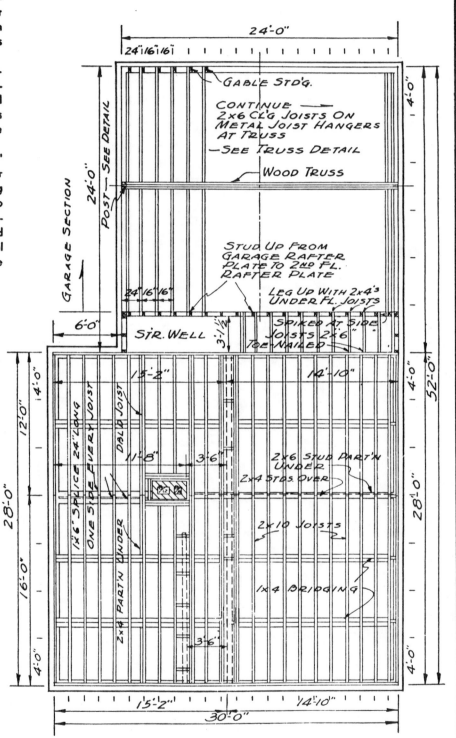

2ND FLOOR FRAMING PLAN

ELEVATIONS:
TOP OF BEARING PLATE FOR 2ND FLOOR JOISTS   108'-5 11/16"
  "   "   "   "   " GARAGE SECTION   107'-7 1/4"

How to Read Blueprints

Because building trades mechanics find it more convenient to "work from the blueprints" rather than from the specifications, generous notes and dimensioning are shown. These should be analyzed and understood as they interpret the "hidden" conditions that cannot be shown with complete clearness, on the drawing.

PLATE 12

Since the basic principle of sound structural design is to provide UN-YIELDING support for concentrated loads, this plan is divided into two general areas by a partition-foundation wall which provides stable support for the first and second floor joists, the ceiling joists (second floor) and for the roof thrust bracing.

It is most important that the building be constructed in strict accordance with the working drawings; that no deviations are made for fear of weakening the structure and complicating the constuction of related or adjoining sections, and complicating the installation of plumbing, electrical wiring, heating, etc.

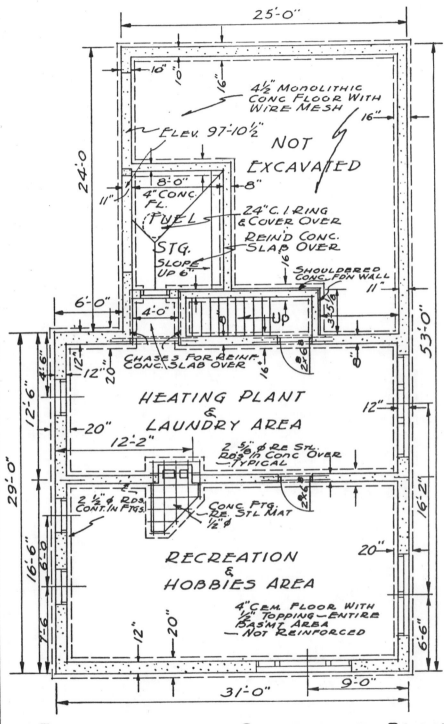

FOUNDATION & BASEMENT PLAN

ELEVATIONS:
TOP OF CONC. FOUNDATION: 99'-2⅜"
"   "   FOOTING, GARAGE SECTION: 94'-9"

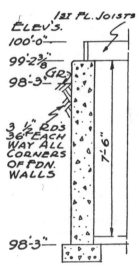

TYPICAL SEC.
FOUND'N WALLS

247

Note the electric symbols for architectural plans listed under, "Key of Symbols", and the way in which they are employed in making drawings. While it is unnecessary for the builder to know what every symbol means, it is necessary that he knows the more common ones and that he has a good knowledge of the manner in whch a wiring system is indicated on working drawings.

A house which is inadequately wired is not only inconvenient, but may become a fire hazard. Strict compliance with working drawings is necessary to prevent future trouble and by studying these drawings, the builder can gain knowledge that will be applicable to many residential wiring jobs.

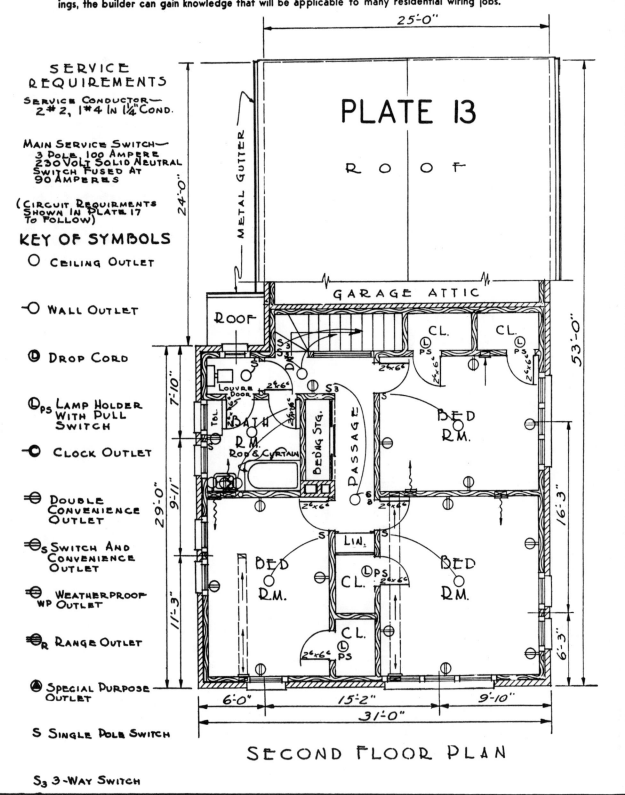

SERVICE REQUIREMENTS

SERVICE CONDUCTOR—
2 #2, 1 #4 IN 1¼" COND.

MAIN SERVICE SWITCH—
3 POLE, 100 AMPERE
230 VOLT SOLID NEUTRAL
SWITCH FUSED AT
90 AMPERES

(CIRCUIT REQUIRMENTS
SHOWN IN PLATE 17
TO FOLLOW)

KEY OF SYMBOLS

○ CEILING OUTLET

−○ WALL OUTLET

Ⓛ DROP CORD

ⓁPS LAMP HOLDER WITH PULL SWITCH

−◑ CLOCK OUTLET

⊜ DOUBLE CONVENIENCE OUTLET

⊜S SWITCH AND CONVENIENCE OUTLET

⊜ WEATHERPROOF WP OUTLET

⊜R RANGE OUTLET

⬤ SPECIAL PURPOSE OUTLET

S SINGLE POLE SWITCH

S₃ 3-WAY SWITCH

PLATE 13

R O O F

GARAGE ATTIC

SECOND FLOOR PLAN

248

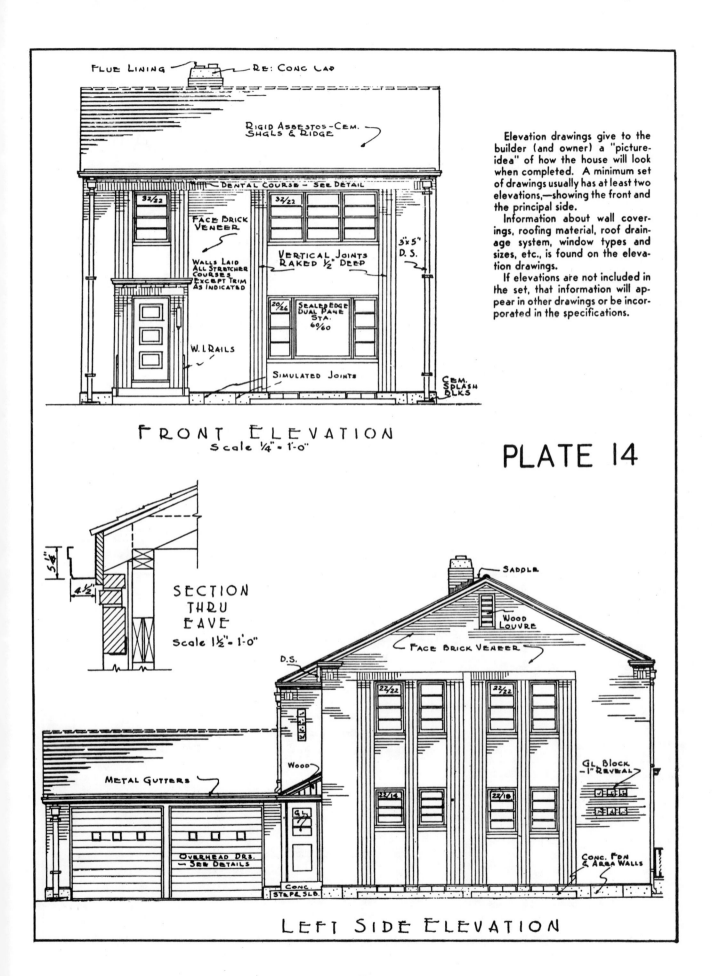

FLUE LINING ——— RE: CONC CAP

RIGID ASBESTOS-CEM.
SHGLS & RIDGE

DENTAL COURSE — SEE DETAIL

32/22

32/22

FACE BRICK
VENEER

3"x5"
D.S.

VERTICAL JOINTS
RAKED ½" DEEP

WALLS LAID
ALL STRETCHER
COURSES
EXCEPT TRIM
AS INDICATED

20/26 SEALED EDGE
DUAL PANE
STA.
60/60

W. I. RAILS

SIMULATED JOINTS

CEM.
SPLASH
BLKS

FRONT ELEVATION
Scale ¼" = 1'-0"

Elevation drawings give to the builder (and owner) a "picture-idea" of how the house will look when completed. A minimum set of drawings usually has at least two elevations,—showing the front and the principal side.

Information about wall coverings, roofing material, roof drainage system, window types and sizes, etc., is found on the elevation drawings.

If elevations are not included in the set, that information will appear in other drawings or be incorporated in the specifications.

PLATE 14

5'4"

4½"

SECTION
THRU
EAVE
Scale 1½" = 1'-0"

SADDLE

WOOD
LOUVRE

FACE BRICK VENEER

D.S.

22/22

22/22

METAL GUTTERS

GL. BLOCK
-1" REVEAL

WOOD

22/14

22/18

GL.

CONC. FDN
& AREA WALLS

OVERHEAD DRS.
— SEE DETAILS

CONC.
STEPS SLB.

LEFT SIDE ELEVATION

These "Cross Section Drawings" are typical of those found on most well prepared working drawings. The principal reasons for this type of drawing is to illustrate the component parts and their relation to one another; their sizes and placement.

Plate 10 of this series discussed "Leveling" and the employment of elevations or heights of the various structural elements, above or below a given reference point.

Note on these drawings that distances between "levels" are quickly and accurately found by subtracting any one elevation from another. For example, the height from the top of the 2nd floor joist to the top of the rafter plate is, by subtraction, 117 ft. 9 in., less 109 ft. 3-5/16 in. =8 ft. 5-11/16 in. This height is made up of an 8 ft. stud, a 2 x 4 sole plate and a double 2 x 4 rafter or top plate and a 13/16 in. thick sub floor.

Likewise, the level of the top of the footings is found to be 6 ft. 10-5/8 in. below the finished grade line, by subtracting 91 ft. 4-3/8 in. from 98 ft. 3 in.

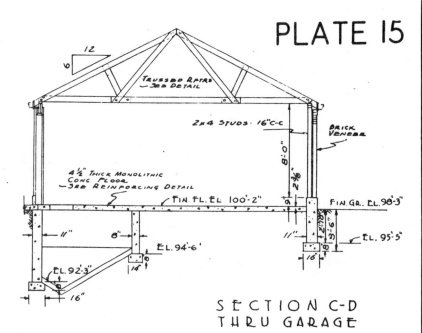

SECTION C-D
THRU GARAGE

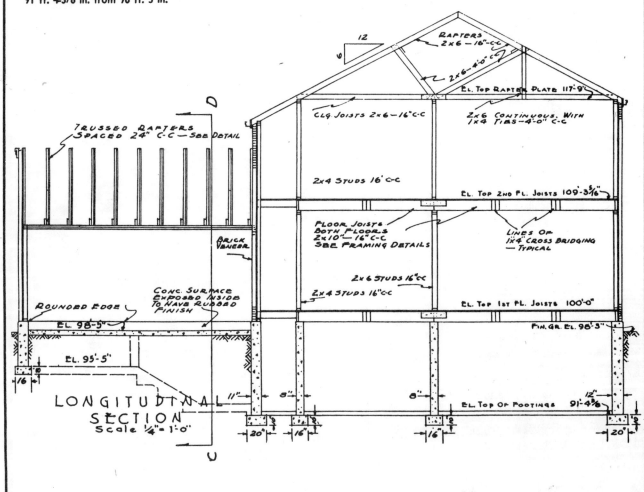

LONGITUDINAL
SECTION
Scale ¼"=1'-0"

Unit 16

ESTIMATING COST, MATERIALS

The average journeyman painter is not often asked to make out estimates, but most foremen are expected to be able to figure job costs. A knowledge of the elements that constitute costs will not only provide better relations between employer and employee, but will also be of considerable value to the painter who decides to enter the contracting business.

Many painting contractors fail to make a success of their businesses simply because they do not know how to estimate. Some are careless and guess at prices; others are not familiar with the elements that must be considered in figuring costs and quoting prices.

Estimating Essentials

To estimate a job properly four main factors must be considered: Cost of materials, Cost of labor, General overhead, and Profit expected.

Estimating Materials

To determine how much paint or finishing material will be needed for a job it is first necessary to determine the number of square feet in the surface to be painted or finished. The drawings and explanatory notes, Fig. 16-1, show how this can be done, for both the outside of a building and the rooms inside the building.

The conversion of this data into gallons of paint is done by dividing the total area of each type of surface, wood shingles, clapboard, plaster, concrete, etc. - - by the number of square feet each gallon of paint will cover. Information on coverage may be obtained from paint manufacturers, and by keeping a careful record of coverage obtained with products used on various jobs.

The unit on which the estimator usually bases his prices is the square (100 square feet).

Figuring Roof Areas

To figure the area of a roof, first figure it as if the roof were flat. If the foundation is 40 ft.

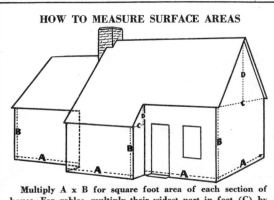

HOW TO MEASURE SURFACE AREAS

Multiply A x B for square foot area of each section of house. For gables, multiply their widest part in feet (C) by half the height (D). Add together all these square foot figures to obtain the total area to be painted. For trim, figure one gallon of paint for each 300 feet of usual width trim.

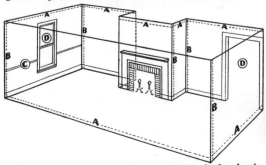

Multiply the sum of the (A) measurements in feet by the height of room in feet (B) to get the square foot area of the wall surfaces. For the ceiling multiply length by width. From the total deduct the square foot areas of doors and windows (D). For chair rail (C), baseboard, window frames and similar trim, measure the number of running feet and allow about one pint of paint per hundred feet.

Fig. 16-1. How to measure areas to determine number of square feet in surfaces to be painted.

by 50 ft., the area of the roof, if it were flat, would be 2,000 sq. ft.

Next, we must determine the pitch (slant) of the roof, or height to the gable. Roofs are usually, one-quarter pitch, one-third pitch, or one-half pitch. By this we mean that the height of the gable is one-fourth, one-third, or, one-half the width of the house. See Fig. 16-2.

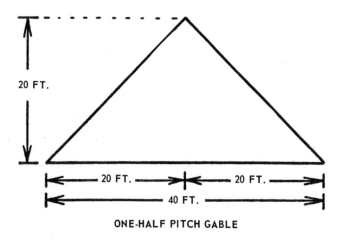

ONE-HALF PITCH GABLE

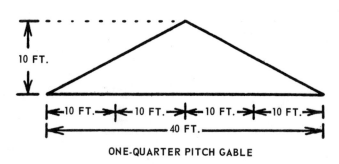

ONE-QUARTER PITCH GABLE

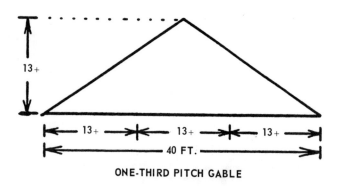

ONE-THIRD PITCH GABLE

Fig. 16-2. Height of gable in one-half pitch roof is one-half the width of the house; in one-quarter pitch roof the gable height would be one-fourth of house width; in one-third pitch roof, one-third.

If the 2,000 sq. ft. flat roof has a roof with one-fourth pitch, you would add to this flat roof area one-fourth of 2,000 or 500, making a total of 2,500 sq. ft. For a one-third pitch roof one-third of 2,000 would be added, and for a one-half pitch roof, one-half of 2,000. When a competitive estimate is made on large work, the area must be calculated more exactly by the use of geometry.

Estimating Labor Costs

Labor is usually the largest item in a painting contract, so it obviously must receive careful attention. By keeping accurate records, the estimator or contractor may determine from past experience, the approximate time required to apply materials to units or squares of various surfaces, and use the constant or average figure thus obtained, to determine the cost of labor required for an entire job.

While it is possible to estimate fairly accurately the time required for painting straight, ordinary work, estimating the time needed to paint windows, fancy trim, lattice work, and various cut-up surface is more difficult. Such estimating calls for careful study, experience, and special attention to details.

The Price Guide, issued by the Painting and Decorating Contractors of America, is a valuable reference for many types of estimating, and it is recommended that the apprentice become thoroughly familiar with its use.

Estimating Overhead

General overhead includes all costs that cannot be charged to a specific job, or piece of work. Such costs would include: Pay or time spent in making estimates (including jobs not obtained); office rent; telephone; light; fuel; depreciation on truck, ladders, and scaffolding; office equipment; insurance; taxes; Association dues; losses from bad debts; donations to charities; advertising expense, etc.

Keeping of accurate records over a period of time and using figures based on actual experience, is the best guide as to what percentage to include for overhead expense.

Profit

Profit is covered last but it is by no means of least importance.

Percentage of profit to be included when preparing price estimates is for the head of the business to determine. This should be based somewhat on quality of work done, experience, decorating ideas furnished, and the rates charged by competitors that do work of comparable quality.

The net profit on a job is the amount of money left after all expenses - - Cost of materials, and labor, plus overhead, have been deducted from the gross amount received from the job.

Two Kinds of Estimates

There are two types of estimates which a painting contractor should prepare. One is a careful estimate he makes for his own information in quoting his potential customer a figure. The other is a less detailed estimate which he makes out for presentation to this prospect. Needless to say, it is important for him to carefully file copies of both estimates. The estimate he makes for himself supplies a valuable record when the contract is signed, and additional information is added regarding the work done.

The copy of the estimate which is presented to the prospect is his protection against "extras" which some customers might try to wedge in without paying the extra amount which is justified.

Making Estimates from Blueprints

In estimating from blueprints and plans the entire job must be visualized. The blueprints indicate dimensions such as room sizes, ceiling heights, locations of windows, doors, etc. Specifications accompanying the plans give details of millwork, information on wall surfaces, areas to be tiled, kind of wood to be used on floors, quality of finishing materials required, number of coats, areas to be painted, varnished, etc.

Heights of jobs to be done should be carefully noted. The height of a job may have considerable bearing on the price. For example, there may be a small louver in a gable which requires two coats of paint. The operation is small but a forty foot ladder may be required to reach the louver. Two men will be needed to handle the ladders.

A contractor who is making an estimate cannot afford to overlook a single detail.

Wallpaper Estimating

Every paperhanger should be able to figure how many rolls of paper are needed for a room, the quantity of paste and other supplies required, and to estimate accurately the time needed to do a papering job. He should also be able to estimate accurately the time required to do the necessary preparatory work.

The single roll, which is considered the basic unit of wallpaper, contains 36 sq. ft. Paper is usually sold in bolts containing double or triple rolls, however, because there is less waste in units of larger size. Common widths of wallpaper are 18 and 30 in. A few papers come in 20 in. widths. A single roll of 18 in. paper is 24 ft. long; a double roll is 48 ft. long. A bolt of 18 in. paper contains two single rolls, a bolt of 20 in. paper two single rolls, and a bolt of 30 in. paper contains three single rolls. Foreign papers vary in length and width and in quantity contained in the rolls.

Figuring Quantity of Paper Needed

There are two principal ways of figuring amounts of paper needed for a room - - the strip method, and the square footage method. There are a number of factors which must be taken into consideration in estimating the number of rolls needed such as waste due to allowance for cutting, sizes of doors and window openings, etc.

Strip Method

In estimating by the strip method it is necessary to determine actual number of strips needed. Knowing how many strips can be cut from each roll or bolt of paper, it is easy to figure how many bolts will be required for job.

First, measure the distance around the room and deduct the width of the openings. Then, divide by the width of the paper, to determine the number of strips needed. Add enough strips to allow for space over and under openings.

When the number of strips has been determined, multiply this figure by length per strip (including waste and amount needed for matching of pattern). If 18 in. paper is being used, divide overall length of paper needed by 48 (length of paper in a double roll 18 in. wide) to determine the number of double rolls required.

Since wallpaper cannot be figured to the very inch, most dealers advise purchasing more than the actual amount figured and will take back unused undamaged full rolls.

Figuring Square Footage

The quantity of paper needed for a room may also be figured by determining the square footage of the area to be covered, and dividing this by the number of square feet in a single roll of paper. Allowance must, of course, be made for window and door openings, waste and matching of patterns.

Ceiling Estimating

The amount of paper needed for a ceiling can be figured by using either the strip or square footage method.

Border paper is sold by the running yard, so the amount of border needed may be determined by simply measuring the distance around the room.

Estimating Time Required

Exclusive of preparation of the surface,

paperhanging is considered a piecework proposition; that is, it is paid for at a certain rate per roll.

The time needed to do a paperhanging job naturally varies with the kind of surface to be papered, the shape of the room, number of openings, and the kind and quality of paper or covering to be hung. For the contractor, efficiency and skill of the paperhanger are also important factors.

In the preparation of the walls, the time required to size and sand must be estimated. Sizing a wall should not take as long as painting.

Since the quantity of paper needed for a particular job can be figured accurately, a price per roll can be established by figuring the amount of paper a workman can hang in a certain time, making allowance for paste, size, depreciation of tools, overhead and profit.

Once the price per roll is determined, it is an easy matter to figure the total cost of a paperhanging job. You simply multiply the number of rolls needed for the job, by the price per roll. Preparatory work is best figured by estimating the time required or it can be added to the per roll price.

Acknowledgments

This book contains material obtained from many different sources. The publishers wish to record here, their deep appreciation of the splendid cooperation of the individuals and organizations which have made this book possible.

Special credit is due:

Acme Paints, Inc.
Aluminum Company of America
American Ladder Institute
Arkansas Soft Pine Bureau
Baker Brush Company
John Berg Mfg. Company
Breinig Brothers, Inc.
Samuel Cabot, Inc.
California Redwood Association
California State, Dept. of Education
California State, Dept. of Industrial Relations
Chicago Bronze & Color Works
De Vilbiss Company
Douglas Fir Plywood Association
Dow Chemical Company
E. I. du Pont de Nemours & Company, Inc.
Forest Products Laboratory
General Electric Company, Lamp Div.
The Glidden Company
Goodyear, Chemical Div.
Gray Company, Inc.
Hardwood Plywood Institute
Hom-O-Graf Company
Insulation Board Institute
Jewel Paint & Varnish Company
Johnson's Wax
Keystone Paint & Varnish Corporation
Adolph Koretz Company
Luminall Paints
Maas and Waldstein Company
Maple Flooring Manufacturers' Association
The Martin-Senour Company
Minwax Company, Inc.
Monsanto Chemical Company
Benjamin Moore & Company

Munsell Color Company, Inc.
National Lead Company
National Oak Flooring Manufacturers' Assn.
National Paint, Varnish & Lacquer Assn., Inc.
National Safety Council
Northern Pine Manufacturers' Assn.
Norton Company
O'Brien Corporation
Patent Scaffolding Company, Inc.
Philippine Mahogany Assn., Inc.
Pittsburgh Plate Glass Company
Ponderosa Pine Woodwork
Portland Cement Association
Practical Builder
Pratt & Lambert, Inc.
Ransburg Electro-Coating, Inc.
Red Cedar Shingle Bureau
Red Devil Tools
Safway Steel Products, Inc.
Sasgen Derrick Company
Shellac Information Bureau
The Sherwin-Williams Company
Superior Paint & Varnish Corp.
Truscon Laboratories
U. S. Dept. of Agriculture
U. S. Dept. of Commerce
U. S. Plywood Corporation
Valspar Corporation
L. R. Van Allen Company
Wallpaper Institute
George E. Watson Company
West Coast Lumbermen's Association
Western Pine Association
Westinghouse Electric Corp., Lamp Div.
Wooster Brush Company

DICTIONARY OF TERMS

ABRASION RESISTANCE: Resistance to mechanical wear.

ABRASIVE: A substance used for the wearing away of a surface by rubbing. Examples of abrasives are: powdered pumice, rottenstone, silica, sandpaper, garnet paper, steel wool.

ABRASIVE COATINGS: In closed coating of paper no adhesive is exposed as surface of paper is completely covered with abrasive. In open coating, surface of backing paper is covered with regulated amount of abrasive, exposing the adhesive. Space between the abrasive grains reduces loading and filling when sanding gummy or soft materials.

ABSORB: To swallow up or suck in, like wood absorbing a finishing material.

ACCELERATE: To quicken or hasten the natural progress of certain actions or events.

ACETIC ACID: A compound, which in the pure state is a colorless, pungent, biting liquid. Vinegar contains 4 to 12 percent of acetic acid.

ACETONE: A water-white volatile solvent with ether-like odor. Acetone is made by destructive distillation of hardwood, fermentation of butyl alcohol, and from petroleum sources. Used extensively in making paint removers.

ACHROMATIC: Colorless; without color.

ACID NUMBER: A designation on the amount of free acid in oils, flats, waxes and resins, expressed as the number of milligrams of potassium hydroxide required to neutralize one gram of the material being tested.

ACOUSTIC PAINT: Paint which absorbs or deadens sound.

ACRYLIC RESINS: Synthetic resins of excellent color and clarity used in both emulsion and solvent-based paints.

ACTIVATOR: A catalyst, curing agent or co-reactant, as for an epoxy resin.

ADHESION: Bonding strength; the attraction of a coating to the substrate, or of one coat of paint to another.

ADSORPTION: The process of attraction to a surface; the attachment of foreign molecules on the surface of a substance.

ADVANCING COLORS: Colors that give an illusion of being closer to the observer. Warm colors in which red-orange predominates are advancing colors.

AGRICULTURAL VARNISHES: Varnishes designed to protect and beautify farm implements and machinery.

AIR DRY: To dry a coating at ordinary room conditions.

AIRLESS SPRAYING: Spraying without atomizing air, using hydraulic pressure.

ALCOHOL: A flammable solvent miscible with water. The alcohols commonly used in painting are ethyl alcohol as a shellac solvent, and methyl alcohol or wood alcohol in paint removers.

ALCOHOL RESISTING: Showing no damage when in contact with alcohol.

ALIPHATIC: A term to describe a major class of organic compounds, many of which are useful as solvents.

ALIZARIN: Pigment which is bright red with blue undertone, made by complicated chemical process.

ALIZARIN LAKE: A red pigment made from the organic coal tar dyestuff, alizarin. Its color is dark bluish-red. Some purple pigments are also marketed under this name.

ALKALI: Caustic or basic substance which release hydroxyl ions in aqueous medium. Lye is the most common alkali.

ALKYD: A synthetic resin, made usually with phthalic anhydride, glycerol and fatty acids from vegetable oils.

ALLIGATORING: Condition of paint film in which surface is cracked and develops an appearance somewhat similar to skin on back of an alligator.

ALUMINUM LEAF: Aluminum hammered into very thin sheets.

ALUMINUM OXIDE: Hard and sharp abrasive made by fusing mineral Bauxite at high temperature.

ALUMINUM PAINT: Mixture of finely divided aluminum particles in flake form combined with vehicle.

ALUMINUM SILICATE: White extender pigment made from China clay, feldspar, etc. which provides very little color or opacity.

AMBIENT TEMPERATURE: Room temperature or the temperature of the surroundings.

AMERICAN GALLON: 231 cubic inches.

AMERICAN PROCESS ZINC OXIDE: Zinc oxide pigment made directly from zinc ores. Sometimes called "direct" process.

AMERICAN VERMILLION: Chrome orange pigment.

AMINE ADDUCT: Amine curing agent combined with a portion of the resin.

AMINES: Organic substituted ammonia; organic compounds having an NH_2 group.

AMYL ACETATE (BANANA OIL): Solvent for nitrocellulose, formed by esterification of acetic acid with amyl alcohol.

ANALOGOUS HARMONY (Related Harmony): Colors which are related by containing one color in common.

ANCHOR PATTERN: Profile, surface roughness.

ANHYDROUS: Free from moisture.

ANILINE COLORS: Coal-tar derivates precipitated on base which is colorless.

ANTI-CORROSIVE PAINT: Metal paint designed to inhibit corrosion. Applied directly to the metal.

ANTI-FLOODING AGENT: A synthetic organic product used to reduce floating and flooding of iron blues, carbon blacks, chrome greens, etc.

ANTI-FOULING PAINT: A special coating for ship bottoms. It contains poison like copper or mercury, formulated to effect the release of the poison at a controlled rate, to prevent attachment and growth of marine organisms such as barnacles and algae.

ANTIMONY OXIDE: Pure white pigment which provides about same hiding power as lithopone.

ANTIQUING: Furniture finishing technique intended to give appearance of age or wear.

ANTI-SKINNING AGENT: A synthetic organic product, used to prevent forming of surface skin in packaged varnishes and paints.

APPLICATOR: One who applies; tool for applying.

APPRENTICE PAINTER: One engaged in learning the painting trade who is covered by a written agreement with an employer, association of employers or other responsible agency. Such an agreement provides for a certain number of years of reasonably continuous employment and for participation in an approved program of training in skills and related technical and general subjects.

AQUEOUS: Containing water.

AROMATIC: Derived from or belonging to a major class of organic compounds, many of which are useful as solvents.

ASBESTINE: Natural fibrous magnesium silica which is pure white in color. It is used as an extender pigment in paints.

ASPHALT: Black solid bitumen found naturally. Also the residue from distillation of petroleum.

ASPHALT CUT BACK: Asphalt plus thinner; asphalt solution; asphalt coating formed by dissolving asphalt.

ASPHALT EMULSION: Asphalt dispersion; not a solution; a water emulsion of asphalt.

"BACK PRIMED:" When a coat of paint is applied to the back of woodwork and exterior siding to prevent moisture from entering the wood and causing the grain to swell it is said to be "back primed."

BAKELITE: A registered trademark identifying phenolic products useful in varnish manufacture.

BAKING JAPAN: An enamel to which the artificial heat of an oven is usually applied in order to attain the maximum hardness or toughness of film.

BAKING FINISHES: Baking at elevated temperatures improves certain types of coatings used on metal articles, such as automobiles and refrigerators, etc. Baking may be done in an oven, under infrared lamps, or by induction heating according to the demands of shape, space, and other requirements. The article that is coated must, of course, be able to withstand the temperature required for the proper baking of the finish.

BARIUM SULPHATE (BARYTES): Extender pigment made from mineral, barite. Unaffected by acids, alkalies.

BATAVIA: Batavia dammar. See dammer.

BEESWAX: Wax produced by honey bee.

"BENNY:" Slang for benzine.

BENZENE: Sometimes called "Benzol." Often confused with "Benzine" due to similarity in pronunciation. Benzene is a very powerful aromatic solvent for many materials. Its use is restricted, however, due to its toxicity and also due to the fact that it is a fire hazard.

BENZINE (VARNISH MAKERS' AND PAINTERS' NAPHTHA - VM&P): Petroleum product used by painters as thinning solvent and diluent. Highly flammable.

BENZOL: See benzene.

BINDER: The nonvolatile portion of a paint which serves to bind or cement the pigment particles together. Oils, varnishes and proteins are examples of binders. See vehicle.

BITING: Solvent in topcoat dissolves or bites into coat below. If lacquer solvent is too biting, dried lacquer surface may be rough or provide "orange peel" effect.

BITUMEN: Originally asphalt. Now any mineral hydrocarbon, but usually black pitchy material.

BLAST ANGLE: Angle of nozzle with reference to surface; also angle of particle propelled from wheel with reference to surface.

BLANC FIXE: Artificially prepared barium sulphate. An extender pigment.

BLAST CLEANING: Cleaning with propelled abrasives.

BLEACHING: Restoring discolored or stained wood to its normal color or making it lighter by using bleaching agents.

BLEEDING STAIN: Stain which works up or "bleeds" through succeeding coats of finishing materials.

BLENDING: Mixing one color with another so the colors mix or merge gradually.

BLISTERING: Formation of bubbles on surface of paint or varnish film, generally caused by moisture behind the film.

BLOOM (Varnish): Clouded appearance on varnished surface.

BLOWTORCH: A gasoline torch used in burning off paint film. Should be used only by experienced painters. It is a dangerous fire hazard when used by amateurs.

BLOWN OIL: A vegetable or fish oil which has been thickened (bodied) by air blown through it.

BLUE LEAD: A basic sulphate of lead containing small amounts of lead sulphide and carbon that impart a bluish-gray color. Used primarily for its rust-preventive value.

BLUSHING: A lacquer finish is said to "blush" when it takes on white or grayish cast during drying period. Blushing is usually caused by the precipitation or separating of a portion of the solid content of the material, causing an opaque appearance.

BODY: Thickness of a fluid. (Becoming obsolete.) More suitable words are "consistency" or "viscosity."

BODY COAT: Intermediate coat of paint between priming and finishing coats.

BOILED OIL: Drying oil treated with driers to shorten the drying time.

BOILING POINT: Temperature at which a liquid boils. Water boils at 100 deg. C or 212 deg. F.

BONDERIZING: A five-step proprietary custom process for phosphatizing.

BONDING: Adhesion.

BONE BLACK: Pigment made from calcined animal bones. Dark in color, but does not have a strong tinting strength like lampblack.

"BOX THE PAINT:" After the paint has been thoroughly mixed by stirring, boxing consists of pouring it back and forth from one pail to another. This insures the most uniform consistency.

BRIDGING: Forming a skin over a depression.

BRILLIANT COLOR: Very bright.

BRITTLE: Easily broken; not tough.

BRONZING LIQUID: A vehicle especially formulated for use as a binder for aluminum or gold bronze powder.

BRUSHABILITY: The ability or ease with which a paint can be brushed.

BRUSH HAND: A painter whose ability lies in his skill in applying material.

BUBBLING: A term used to describe the appearance of bubbles on the surface while a coating is being applied.

BUFFING COMPOUND: Soft abrasive in stick form, bonded with wax.

BULKING VALUE (Pigment): Bulking value of a pigment is its ability to add volume to a paint.

BURNED OR FIERY FINISH: Wood finish in which hard portion of grain stands out in relief; produced by using blowtorch and stiff-bristled brush.

BURNING IN: Repairing a finish by melting stick shellac into the damaged places, by using a heated knife blade or iron.

BURNT SIENNA: Sienna that has been roasted. Reddish brown in color.

BURNT UMBER: Umber that has been roasted. Dark brown in color.

BUTT JOINT (Wallpaper): Joint made by trimming both selvedges and butting the edges together. This is used in highest type of work.

BUTYL ACETATE: A lacquer solvent made from butyl alcohol by reaction with acetic acid.

BUTYL ALCOHOL: Obtained from corn by fermentation; an alcohol of higher boiling range than wood alcohol or grain alcohol.

CADMIUM LITHOPONE: A series of yellows and reds that are permanent to light and resistant to alkalies.

CADMIUM RED: Non-fading red pigment made from cadmium and selenium metals. It is heat and alkali resistant.

CADMIUM YELLOW: Pigment prepared by precipitation from acid solution of soluble cadmium salt with hydrogen sulphide gas. Fast to alkalies but not to acids.

CAKING: Hard settling of pigment from paint.

CALCIMINE: Inexpensive paint composed mostly of whiting or chalk, glue and water. Sometimes written Kalsomine.

CALCINED: Heated to high temperature in absence of air.

CALCIUM CARBONATE (Whiting): Earth product obtained from deposits of chalk, dolomite, etc. Used as extender pigment.

CALCIUM DRIERS: Used widely in combination with other metal driers to convert paint to hard films.

CALCIUM SULPHATE: White inert pigment which provides very little color or opacity.

CALENDERED PAPERS: Wallpapers with hard finish.

CANDELILLA WAX: Wax obtained from small shrub grown in Texas and Mexico; softer than Carnauba wax.

CARBON BLACK: Jet black, non-bleeding pigment, made by burning natural gas in insufficient supply of air.

CARBON TETRACHLORIDE: A non-flammable liquid with good solvent properties.

CARNAUBA WAX: A hard wax obtained from species of palm grown mostly in Brazil.

CASEIN: The protein of milk and the principal constituent of cheese. Casein is used extensively in the manufacture of water paints.

CAST: Inclination of one color to look like another. For example, sulphur is yellow with a greenish "cast."

CASTOR OIL: Oil obtained from the castor bean. Nondrying. May be converted to a drying oil by chemical treatment.

CATALYST: A substance which by its presence accelerates velocity of reaction between substances.

CAULKING COMPOUND: A semidrying or slow-drying plastic material used to seal joints or fill crevices around windows, chimneys, etc. Usually made in two grades; the gun type for application by use of a special gun; and the knife type for use with a putty knife.

CAVITATION: Undercutting, crevice forming; may be caused by fluids at high velocities and by flashing from liquid to gaseous state.

CELLULOSE: An inert substance, the chief component of the cell walls of plants. Nitrocellulose, used extensively in making lacquer, is prepared from cellulose (cotton linters) by treatment with chemicals.

CELLULOSE ACETATE: A binder made by chemical reaction of acetic acid on cellulose (cotton linters).

CELLULOSE NITRATE: A binder made by chemical reaction of nitric acid on cellulose (cotton linters). Also known as nitrocellulose and pyroxylin.

CEMENT BASE PAINT: A paint composed of Portland cement, lime, pigment and other modifying ingredients. Sold as dry powder. Mixed with water for application.

CENTIPOISE: A metric unit of viscosity.

CERESIN: A hydrocarbon wax which possesses considerable flexibility.

CHALK: A form of natural calcium carbonate. See whiting.

CHALKING: The decomposition of a paint film into a loose powder on the surface. Mild chalking, accompanied by satisfactory color retention in tinted paint, is considered a desirable characteristic. Heavy chalking which washes off to leave an unprotected surface, is highly undesirable. Before recoating a heavily chalked surface, all of the chalk should be removed. This is usually accomplished by vigorous brushing.

CHECKING: The formation of short narrow cracks in the surface of a paint film. These cracks may assume many patterns, but the usual ones resemble the print of a bird's foot or small squares.

CHEMICALLY ACTIVE (Pigment): Pigments which react with oil of vehicle to form soaps which influence toughness of film, increase durability, etc. Also, pigments such as red lead which react with acids formed at metal surface to prevent rust.

CHEMICALLY PURE (C.P.): Of the highest grade but not necessarily 100 percent pure.

CHINA CLAY (ALUMINUM SILICATE): Inert pigment which consists mostly of hydrated aluminum silicate. Imparts to paint quality of easy brushing.

CHINAWOOD OIL: See tung oil.

CHINESE BLUE: A form of iron blue.

CHINESE RED: Chrome orange deep.

CHIPPING: (1) Cleaning steel using special hammers. (2) Type of paint failure.

CHROMA: Color purity or intensity: Term is used to differentiate pure, intense colors from colors that are grayed.

CHROME GREEN: Mixture of chrome yellow and Prussian blue. One of industry's most important green pigments.

CHROME ORANGE: An orange pigment composed principally of basic lead chromate.

CHROME YELLOW: Important inorganic yellow pigment made by mixing solutions of lead acetate and potassium bichromate. Highly corrosion-inhibiting.

CHROMIUM OXIDE: See chromium oxide green.

CHROMIUM OXIDE GREEN: Green pigment which is extremely permanent in color and has good resistance to both alkali and heat.

CHRONOMETER: An instrument used to indicate the color of light liquids and oils.

CITRONELLA OIL: An oil with a peculiar odor, obtained from a species of grass grown in Asia.

CLEANER: (1) Detergent, alkali, acid or other cleaning material; usually water or steam borne. (2) Solvent for cleaning paint equipment.

CLEAN SURFACE: One free of contamination.

CLOSE-GRAIN WOODS: Woods such as birch, maple, etc. where the fibers are fine and are held closely together are called close-grain woods.

COAGULATE: To change from a liquid into a dense mass; solidify; curdle.

COAL-TAR EPOXY PAINT: Paint in which binder or vehicle is combination of coal tar with epoxy resin.

COAL-TAR PITCH: Refined, common pitch obtained as distillation residue from coal tar.

COAL-TAR SOLVENT: Derived from the distillation of coal tar. Four main products for the paint industry are benzene, toluene, xylene and solvent naphtha.

COAL-TAR URETHANE PAINT: Paint in which binder or vehicle is combination of coal tar with polyurethane resin.

"COATING IN:" Applying a coat of paint.

COATINGS: Surface coverings; paints; barriers.

COAT OF PAINT: One layer of dry paint, resulting from a single wet application. Single layer of paint spread at one time and allowed to harden.

COBALT BLUE: Blue pigment, stable in color. Made by heating mixture of cobalt oxide and aluminum hydrate.

COBALT DRIER: Powerful drier which is soluble in all drying oils. Known as surface dryer.

COBWEBBING: Permature drying causing a spider web effect.

COHESION: Property of holding a film together.

COLD-CHECKING: Checking caused by low temperature.

COLD COLOR: A bluish or greenish color; a color not suggestive of warmth.

COLD WATER PAINT: The paint in which the binder or vehicle portion is composed of casein, glue or a similar material dissolved in water. Usually employed on concrete, masonry or plaster surfaces.

COLLOIDAL SUSPENSION: A substance divided into fine particles which remains in permanent suspension in a liquid.

COLOR: A property of visible phenomena (fact that may be scientifically described) in which certain impressions or effects are formed on the retina of the eye by the light of different wave lengths. Color may be divided into three principal parts, hue, tint and shade.

COLOR-IN-JAPAN: A paste formed by mixing a color pigment with Japan. Used principally for tinting.

COLOR-IN-OIL: A paste formed by mixing a color pigment in linseed or other vegetable oil. Used principally for tinting.

COLOR MAN: The term applies to the individual--either the journeyman or contractor-- who is an expert in tinting and matching colors.

COLOR PIGMENTS: Pigments such as blue, red, etc. which absorb a portion of the light which falls upon them and reflect or return to the eye certain groups of light bands which enable us to recognize various colors.

COLOR RETENTION: When a paint product exposed to the elements shows no signs of changing color it is said to have good color retention.

COLORING STRENGTH (Pigments): Relative strength or ability of pigments to color base material which is white or light in color.

COLORS-IN-JAPAN: Pigment colors ground and mixed with Japan drier.

COMPATIBLE: Paint pigments are compatible when they are capable of being used together without harmful chemical reactions.

CONCRETE, Testing For Alkaline Material In: Concrete may be tested for evidence of alkali by applying a few drops of a 1 percent solution of phenolphthalein in alcohol to scattered spots on floor which have been dampened with water. If masonry is alkaline, drops turn red or purple. Another method is to dampen several pieces of red litmus paper and apply them at random over concrete floor. If litmus paper turns blue, alkali is present and neutralizing agent is essential before painting. To remove alkali, wash surface with a 10 percent solution of muriatic acid and water. Rinse floor with clean water to remove acid and lime and allow one to four days for thorough drying.

CONDENSATE: A product obtained by cooling vapors of a substance being distilled.

CONGO GUM: A gum resin obtained from the Congo region of Africa.

CONSISTENCY: The fluidity or viscosity of a liquid or paste; resistance of a product to flow.

CONVERTER: That which causes change to different state; catalyst; curing agent; promoter.

COOL COLORS: Hues or colors in which blue predominates. The term "cool" is used because of the association with ice, water and sky.

COPALS: Group of resinous substances exuding from various tropical trees. Copal is collected from living trees and is also dug from the ground as a fossil. Some of copal resins are amber, congo, kauri, manila, Pontianak, West India gum, and zanzibar.

COPOLYMERIZATION: Interaction of two or more different molecules to form a new compound having higher molecular weight and different physical properties.

CORROSION: Decay; oxidation; deterioration due to interaction with environment; eaten away by degrees.

COUMARONE-INDENE RESINS: Resins derived as by-products in making coke from coal.

COVERAGE: Amount of surface a given quantity of paint will cover; also, how well paint conceals surface being painted.

CRACKING: Splitting; disintegration of paint by breaks through film.

CRACKLE FINISH: A finish in which alligatoring is produced, allowing the undercoat to show through the cracks. Cracking is produced by rapid drying of topcoat over slow drying undercoat.

CRATERING: Formation of holes or deep depressions in paint film.

CRAWLING: Varnish defect in which poor adhesion of varnish to surface in some spots causes it to crawl or gather up into globules instead of covering the surface.

CRAZING: Minute, interlacing cracks on the surface of a finish.

CREOSOTE OIL: Distillate from coal tar which is heavier than water, used largely as a wood preservative.

CREOSOTE STAIN: Creosote made mostly from wood and coal tars is mixed with linseed oil, drier and thinned with benzine or kerosene.

CROSSLINKING: A particular method by which chemicals unite to form films.

CROSS-SPRAY: Spraying first in one direction and second at right angles.

CRYPTOMETER: An instrument used to measure the opacity of paint.

CRYSTALLIZING LACQUER: Novelty finish which crystallizes forming unusual crystal and floral patterns, as it dries.

CURING: Setting up; hardening.

CURING AGENT: Hardener; promoter.

CURTAINING: Sagging.

CUT: Dispersion of a certain number of pounds of shellac or resin per gallon of volatile liquid. A 4 lb. cut of shellac contains 4 lbs. of dry shellac and 1 gal. of alcohol.

"CUT IN THE SASH:" Painting the window sash. This is ordinarily done with a brush, often called a sash tool, which permits the painter to get a clean edge.

CYANIC: Containing blue, or pertaining to blue color.

DAMMAR: A natural resin used extensively in the preparation of varnishes and lacquers. Usually classified according to the place from which it is shipped to market--Singapore dammar, Batavia dammar, etc.

DEAD FLAT: Having no gloss at all.

DELCALCOMANIA: Paint films in the form of pictures or other decorations which can be transferred from a temporary paper mounting to other surfaces.

DECORATIVE PAINTING: Architectural painting; aesthetic painting.

DEEP (Color): Intense or strong color with no apparent presence of black.

DEGREASER: Chemical solution (compound) for grease removal.

DEHYDRATED CASTOR OIL: A drying oil prepared from castor oil.

DENATURED ALCOHOL: Grain or ethyl alcohol made unsuitable for beverage purposes by adding compounds of a poisonous nature.

DESTRUCTIVE DISTILLATION: Distilling a product at a temperature so high that products obtained are of different chemical composition than existed in the original material.

DILUENT (LACQUER): Volatile portion of vehicle not capable by itself of dissolving nitrocellulose.

DIP COATING: Process of finishing article by immersing it in finishing material.

DIPENTENE: Solvent made by destructive distillation of pine stumps; is stronger than turpentine.

DISCOLORATION: Color change.

DISTEMPER: A water paint in which the vehicle protein is usually casein, egg white, glue, etc. The term, used principally in Great Britain to designate water type paints, is practically obsolete in the United States.

DISTILLATE: A condensed product produced by cooling vapors of a material heated sufficiently to drive off part of the material in the form of vapor.

DOMINANT COLOR: Color that predominates, or is outstanding.

DRAGON'S BLOOD: A red gum exuded from the fruit of a species of trees grown in the Malay peninsula. The color is not permanent.

DRIERS: Compounds of certain metals which hasten the drying action of oils when added to paints or varnishes. Some driers are in dry form--others, in paste form. Most of them are solutions of metallic soaps in oils and volatile solvents. They are known as driers, oil driers, Japan driers, liquid driers and Japans. The metallic soaps most commonly used are those of lead, manganese and cobalt.

Dictionary of Terms

DRIFT: (Overspray) Spray loss.

DROP BLACK: See bone black.

DROP CLOTH: A large piece of fabric used by a painter while painting a room to protect furniture, rugs and other articles from paint damage.

DRY SPRAY: Overspray or bounce back; sand finish due to spray particle being partially dried before reaching the surface.

DRY TO HANDLE: Time interval between application and ability to pick up without damage. A film of paint is "dry to handle" when it is hardened sufficiently so that it may be handled without being damaged.

DRY TO RECOAT: Time interval between application and ability to receive next coat satisfactorily.

DRY TO TOUCH: Time interval between application and tack-free time. A film of paint is "dry to touch" when it is hardened sufficiently so that it may be touched lightly without any of it adhering to the fingers.

DRYING: Act of changing from liquid to solid state by evaporation of volatile thinners and by oxidation of oils.

DRYING OIL: An oil which hardens in air.

DRYING OILS: Oils which are converted to solids when exposed to the oxygen in the air. Linseed oil, tung oil and perilla oil are the three principal vegetable oils of the drying class. Menhaden, or fish oil, is the only animal oil of the drying class suited for use by the paint industry. See semi-drying oils.

DRYING TIME: Time interval between application and final cure.

DULL: Term applied to colors that have a neutral or grayed quality.

DULL RUBBING: Act of rubbing a dried film of finishing material to a dull finish, usually with abrasive paper, pumice stone, steel wool and oil or water.

DUPLEX PAPER: Wallpaper which consists of two separate papers pasted together; used to create a highly embossed effect.

DUST FREE: A film of paint is "dust free" when dust no longer adheres to it.

DUTCH METAL: Thin leaves of bright brass which are used for overlaying in the same manner in which gold leaf is applied.

DYE: A material used for dyeing or staining.

EARTH PIGMENT: Pigments which occur as deposits in earth and are removed by mining. Such pigments as a whole are permanent in color, non-bleeding and are not readily changed by heat, light, moisture and alkalies.

EDGING: Striping.

EFFLORESCENCE: A deposit of water soluble salts on the surface of masonry or plaster caused by the dissolving of salts present in the masonry, migration of the solution to the surface and deposition of the salts when the water evaporates.

EGG SHELL LUSTER: Finish that closely resembles the luster of an egg shell.

ELASTIC: Ability to return to the original volume or shape after distorting force has been removed.

ELECTROSTATIC SPRAYING AND DIPPING: By this method the article to be sprayed is attached to one pole of a high voltage electrostatic field. The mist from the spray gun is given an opposite charge and thereby becomes attracted to the article. The mist travels around corners with the result that the article is coated more uniformly on all sides and with very little overspray.

The same principle applies to articles which have been dipped in paint, but this time it is used in reverse for the purpose of removing excess paint. The "tears" and "beads" which collect at the bottom of the dipped article are repelled and fly off, leaving the article free from them.

EMBOSSED PAPERS: Wallpaper run through rollers with raised areas, to provide a light relief effect.

EMERY: Slow-cutting, short-lived abrasive.

EMULSIFYING AGENTS: Substances of chemical nature that intimately mix and disperse dissimilar materials ordinarily immiscible, such as oil and water, to produce a stable emulsion.

A substance which when added to a liquid permits suspension of fine particles or globules in the liquid.

EMULSION: A preparation in which minute particles of one liquid, such as oil, are suspended in another, such as water.

EMULSION PAINT: A paint made by emulsifying the film-forming portion in a volatile liquid, usually water.

ENAMEL: Type of paint made by grinding or mixing pigments with varnishes or lacquers.

ENGLISH CHALK: Chalk obtained from the cliffs of England.

EPOXY ADDUCT: Epoxy resin having all of the required amine incorporated but requiring additional epoxy resin for curing.

EPOXY AMINE: Amine-cured epoxy resin.

EPOXY ESTER: Epoxy-modified oil; single package epoxy.

EPOXY RESINS: Resins obtained by condensation reaction between phenols and epichlorohydrin.

EROSION: Wearing away of paint films; heavy chalking tends to accelerate erosion.

ESSENTIAL OILS: Oils which have an odor, such as cedar oil, camphor oil, etc.

ESTER: Organic compound formed from an alcohol and an organic acid by eliminating water.

ESTER GUM: Resin produced synthetically by rosin reacting with glycerine.

ETCH: Surface attack by chemical means.

ETHYL ACETATE: Rapid evaporating solvent made from ethyl alcohol and acetic acid.

ETHYL ALCOHOL: Alcohol produced by the distillation of fermented grain or from petroleum sources.

ETHYL LACTATE: A solvent made by a reaction between ethyl alcohol and lactic acid.

EVAPORATION RATE: Rate of solvent release.

EXTENDER PIGMENTS: Pigments which provide very little hiding power but are useful in stabilizing suspension, improving flow, lowering gloss, and providing other desirable qualities.

FADEOMETER: Device for measuring color retention or fade resistance.

FADING: Reduction in brightness of color.

FALSE BODY: Thixotropic.

FAT PAINT: Too much oil.

FATTY ACID: Acid which is present in oils or fats in combination with glycerine.

FEATHERING: A term used to describe the sanding or rubbing down of a surface to a feathery edge - - where coating material gradually becomes thinner around the edge until it finally disappears.

"FEEL:" The painter's term for the working qualities of a paint.

FERROUS: Pertaining to, or derived from iron.

FERROUS SULPHATE: A product commonly known as copperas.

FILLER: Inert material used to fill or level porous surfaces, like open-pore woods such as oak, walnut.

FILM BUILD: Dry thickness characteristics per coat.

FILM FORMER: Substance which forms skin or membrane when dried from liquid state.

FILM INTEGRITY: Degree of continuity of film.

FILM THICKNESS GAUGE: Device for measuring film thickness above substrates; dry or wet film thickness gauges are available.

FILMOGENS: Film-forming materials such as linseed oil and varnish resins.

FINISH COAT: Last coat applied in a paint or wood-finishing job.

FIRE RETARDANT PAINT: Paint containing substance which slows down rate of combustion of flammable material or renders material incapable of supporting flame.

FISH OIL: Only animal oil used to any extent in paint industry. Extracted from fish such as sardine, menhaden and pilchard.

FIXATIVE: A protective coating applied to drawings in crayons, charcoal, etc., usually by spraying, to prevent colors from rubbing off.

FLAG: End of hog brush bristle which divides into two or more branches like a tree. Flagging provides brush with ability to hold paint.

FLAKING: Detachment of small pieces of paint film.

FLASH POINT: Degree of temperature at which a flammable liquid starts to emit flammable gases.

FLAT FINISH: Dull finish, no gloss.

FLATTING AGENT: An ingredient - - usually a metallic soap, such as calcium, aluminum or zinc stearate - - used in lacquers and varnishes to reduce the gloss or to give a "rubbed" appearance.

FLATTENING OIL: A varnish-like composition, made of thickened oil dissolved in a thinner, used to reduce paste paint to a flat paint.

FLAT MILL: A kind of grinding mill used to grind paint pigments. The mill consists of two stones, a lower stone which revolves and an upper stone which is stationary.

FLAT VARNISH: Varnish which dries with reduced gloss, made by adding such materials as silica, wax, metallic soaps to the varnish.

FLAT WALL PAINT: A type of interior paint which is designed to produce a flat or lusterless finish.

FLINT PAPER: Abrasive paper which is grayish-white in color. Inexpensive but has short working life.

FLOATING: Separation of pigment colors on surface.

FLOCK FINISH: Finish obtained by spraying or sifting flock (short fibers of wool, silk, rayon) onto a surface to which the flock fibers will adhere.

FLOCOATING: Process of finishing by flowing finishing material on article by means of hose, allowing excess to drain into tank.

FLOODING: See floating.

FLOOR VARNISH: A varnish made specifically for application to floors.

FLOWING VARNISH: A varnish which has been designed to produce a smooth lustrous surface without rubbing or polishing.

FLUORESCENT PAINT: Luminous paint which glows only during activation by ultraviolet or "black" light.

"FOOTS:" Settlings in vegetable oils.

FORM LACQUER: Thin lacquer or varnish used to coat concrete forms to prevent concrete from adhering to the forms.

FOSSIL RESIN: Any of the natural or earth type resins, such as kauri and the Congo copals, which derive their characteristics through aging in the ground.

FRENCH POLISHING: High-grade wood finish obtained by applying shellac or French varnish with a cloth pad, and linseed oil as a lubricant to prevent the pad from sticking.

FRENCH PROCESS ZINC OXIDE: Zinc oxide

pigment made from metallic zinc. Sometimes called "indirect" process. See American process zinc oxide.

FROTHING: Foaming.

FUGITIVE COLORS: Colors which are not permanent; subject to fading.

FUNGICIDE: A substance poisonous to fungi; retards or prevents fungi growth.

FUSEL OIL: Oily liquid produced in small quantities when ethyl alcohol is produced by fermentation of grain.

GALVANIZED IRON: Sheet metal coated by dipping in hot zinc.

GARNET PAPER: Abrasive which is reddish in color, hard and sharp; comes from same source as semi-precious jewel by that name. More expensive than flint paper but lasts longer.

GAS CHECKING: Fine checking; wrinkling, frosting under certain drying conditions; said to be caused by rapid oxygen absorption or by impurities in the air.

GEL: A jelly-like substance.

"GHOSTING:" A coating with a skippy appearance.

GILDING: Process of obtaining a finish by using metal leaf (metal hammered into very thin sheets).

GILSONITE: A black, coal-like substance obtained from mines and used in the manufacture of black asphaltum varnish.

GLAZING: (Puttying)--setting glass. A process of applying transparent or translucent coatings over a painted surface to produce blended effects.

GLOSS: A term used to indicate the shine, luster or sheen of a dried film.

GLOSS OIL: A varnish composed primarily of limed rosin and petroleum thinner.

GLOSS RETENTION: Ability to retain original sheen.

GLYCERINE (GLYCEROL): A type of alcohol which is sweet tasting, clear, almost colorless and odorless. Glycerine is used extensively in the production of alkyd resins and ester gum.

GOLD PAINT: Mixture of bronze powder and bronzing liquid.

GRAIN ALCOHOL: Ethyl alcohol made from grain by distillation.

GRAINNESS: Roughness of a protective film resembling grains of sand.

GRAINING: Simulating the grain of wood by using paint.

GRAIN RAISING: Causing short fibers on surface of bare wood to stand up by applying water. Liquids that do not raise the grain are known as non-grain-raising.

GRAPHITE: Black pigment consisting mostly of carbon obtained from natural deposits, or produced from coke in electric furnace.

GRAYISH: Lacking in intensity of color.

GREEN LAKE: Mixture of Prussian blue and yellow lake, sold under various trade names.

GRIND GAUGE: (Hegeman)--Proprietary instrument for measuring smoothness of liquid paint.

GROUND COAT: The coating material which is applied before the graining colors or glazing coat.

GROUND PAPER: Wallpaper coated with an overall background color.

GUM: A natural mucilaginous vegetable secretion that hardens but, unlike a resin, is water-soluble.

GUM ARABIC: The dry gummy exudation of Acacia Senegal. This white powdered resin is sometimes used in cold water paint and in show card colors.

GUM TURPENTINE: Oleoresinous material obtained from living pine trees. Gum turpentine,

when distilled, provides gum rosin, and gum spirits of turpentine.

GYPSUM: A common mineral composed of hydrous calcium sulphate. Gypsum, when heated, forms plaster-of-Paris. Fabricated gypsum products used in building include wallboards, plasterboards, etc.

HAIR LINES: Very narrow cracks in a paint or varnish film.

HAMMERED EFFECT FINISH: So called because of its resemblance to hammered metal. Produced by incorporating an aluminum powder in vehicle which controls leafing and non-leafing effect to create unique designs.

HAND PRINTS: Wallpapers printed by hand, usually with the silk-screen process.

HANSA YELLOW: A family of organic yellow pigments.

HARD OIL FINISH: A varnish giving the effect of a rubbed-in-oil finish but producing a hard surface. The term has gradually been extended to cover all sorts of interior architectural varnishes with a moderate luster.

HARDENER: Curing agent; promoter; catalyst.

HEAVY BODIED OIL: A high viscosity oil.

HIDING POWER: Capacity of a paint to hide or obscure the surface on which it is applied; degree of opacity of a pigment or paint.

HIGH BOILING SOLVENT: A solvent with an initial boiling point above 302 deg. F. (150 deg. C.).

HIGH BUILD: Producing thick dry films per coat.

HIGHLIGHTING: Making certain parts of finished project appear lighter than other parts.

HOLIDAYS: Areas of a surface missed by the painter.

HONEYCOMBING: Lack of vertical film integrity; formation of cell structure; voids.

HOT LACQUER PROCESS: Process where heat is used instead of volatile thinner to reduce the consistency of lacquer. Hot lacquer can be applied with a higher percentage of solids than room-temperature lacquer.

HOUSE PAINT, OUTSIDE: Paint designed for use on the exterior of buildings, fences and other surfaces exposed to the weather.

HUE: A general term used to distinguish one color from another, like a red hue, yellow hue, etc.

HUMIDITY: Amount of water vapor in the air.

HYDRAULIC SPRAYING: (See Airless) - Spraying by hydraulic pressure.

HYDROCARBON: Compound consisting of hydrogen and carbon.

HYDROCARBON RESINS: Obtained by catalytic polymerization of petroleum fractions.

HYDROPHILIC: Having an affinity for water; capable of uniting with or dissolving in water.

HYDROPHOBIC: Having antagonism for water; not capable of uniting or mixing with water.

HYDROUS: Containing water.

HYGROSCOPIC: Tendency to absorb water.

IMPASTO: Thick application of pigment to canvas or other surface, which makes the painting stand out in bold relief.

IMPERIAL GALLON: Unit of volume measure used in Great Britain and Canada. It contains 277.42 cubic inches and weighs 10 pounds; compared with U.S. gallon of 231 cubic inches and 8.33 pounds in weight.

INDIAN RED: Red pigment made artifically by calcining copperas. Has excellent permanency, is non-bleeding, alkali and acid-fast.

INDUCTION BAKING: Using heat induced by electrostatic and electromagnetic means for baking of finishes.

INERT: Chemically inactive.

INERT PIGMENT: A nonreactive pigment, filler.

INFRARED: Invisible part of spectrum between

radio waves and red portion of visible spectrum.

INHIBITIVE PIGMENT: One which retards corrosion process.

INHIBITOR: An agent added to retard corrosion.

INORGANIC: Composed of matter other than vegetable or animal.

INORGANIC COLORS: Chemical colors obtained by combining two or more inorganic chemicals.

INSULATING VARNISH: A varnish especially designed for the electrical insulation of wires, coils and electrical appliances.

INTENSE COLOR: A strong, vivid color.

INTERCOAT CONTAMINATION: Presence of foreign matter between successive coats.

INTERMEDIATE COAT: Middle coat; guide coat.

INTUMESCE: To form a voluminous char on ignition; foaming or swelling when exposed to flame.

IODINE NUMBER: A means of identifying and specifying qualities of oils, resins and waxes, based on fact that different qualities of these products will absorb different quantities of iodine.

IONIZATION: Breaking up of molecules into two or more oppositely charged ions. An ion is one of electrified particles into which molecules are divided by the use of water and other solvents.

IRON BLUE: Blue pigment which depends on iron content to provide blue color.

IRON DRIERS: Driers with high tinting strength which limits use to colored finishes.

IRON OXIDE: Iron oxide is available in three forms; red, brown and yellow. It is sold under a variety of names, such as Red Oxide, Jeweler's Rouge, Venetian Red, Ferric Oxide, Indian Red, Red Ochre, Mineral Rouge, Spanish Oxide, Turkey Red, etc.

IVORY BLACK: A high grade bone black pigment. Its name is accounted for by the fact that it was formerly made by charring or burning ivory.

JAPAN COLOR: Colored paste made by grinding high-quality colors in hard drying varnish.

JAPAN DRIER: Varnish gum with a large proportion of metallic (lead, cobalt, manganese, etc.) salts added to hasten drying. It is used in paints, varnishes, enamels.

JAPANESE LACQUER: Varnish made from sap of tree which grows in Japan. Lacquer becomes very hard and black as it dries.

JOURNEYMAN PAINTER: One who has had at least three year's experience and schooling as an apprentice.

JUXTAPOSITION OF COLORS: Placing colors side by side, or close together. Complementary colors such as blue and orange in juxtaposition accentuate each other.

KAOLIN: Inert pigment which tends to impart easy brushing properties to paint products in which it is used.

KAURI GUM: A fossil copal found in New Zealand.

KAURI REDUCTION: Test for solvent power of petroleum solvents.

KEROSENE: A distillate obtained in petroleum refining which evaporates slowly.

KETONES: Organic solvents containing CO grouping; commonly used ketones are acetone (dimethyl ketone); MEK (methyl ethyl ketone); and MIBK (methyl isobutyl ketone).

KETTLE BODIED OIL: Oil which has been held at an elevated temperature until the oil has thickened.

KILN DRYING: Drying of wood, paint, varnish or lacquer in room or compartment with heat, and humidity regulated.

LAC: A natural resin secreted by certain insects which live on the sap of trees in India and other Oriental countries. Marketed in various forms; seed lac, button lac, shellac.

LACQUER: Finishing material that dries by the evaporation of the thinner or solvent. There are many different types of lacquers, the most important being that based on cellulose nitrate. Besides the cellulosic compound, lacquers contain resins, plasticizers, solvents and diluents.

LAITANCE: Milky white deposit on new concrete; efflorescence.

LAKE PIGMENT: Pigment made by putting an organic dye on a base of fine particles of inert or translucent pigment.

LAMPBLACK: Pigment made by burning coal tar distillates without sufficient air. Not quite true black.

LAPPED JOINT (Wallpaper): Joint made by trimming one selvedge and overlapping the other.

LATEX: Rubber-like; a common binder for emulsion (water) paints. There are natural and synthetic latexes.

LEAD CARBONATE, BASIC: A type of white lead pigment.

LEAD DRIER: Almost water-white drier which works on body of paint film. Various combinations of lead, cobalt and other driers are used in formulating many modern finishes.

LEAD OXIDE: Compound in several combinations of lead and oxygen, e.g., litharge and red lead.

LEAD SULPHATE, BASIC: A type of white lead.

LEADED ZINC OXIDE: White pigment made by combining lead sulphate and zinc oxide.

LEAFING: The overlapping arrangement of aluminum or gold bronze powders in a paint, similar to that of fallen leaves. Good leafing is important in producing a metallic appearance and is caused by using treated or coated pigments along with suitable bronzing liquids.

LEVELING: The formation of a smooth film on either a horizontal or vertical surface, independent of the method of application. A film which has good leveling characteristics is usually free of brush marks or orange peel effects.

LIFTING: Softening of undercoat by solvents used in coats which follow. Usually caused by not allowing sufficient time for undercoat to harden before applying additional coats.

LINING PAPER: Wallpaper without a ground (overall background color), used mostly for wall conditioning.

LINOLEUM AND OILCLOTH VARNISHES: Special highly flexible and elastic varnishes.

LINSEED OIL: Vegetable oil obtained by crushing seed of flax plant. Drying properties accentuated by heating oil to 130 to 200 deg. C. to form what is known as "boiled" linseed oil. Metallic salts or driers are added to increase rate of drying.

LIQUID DRIERS: Solution of driers in paint thinners.

LIQUID WOOD FILLER: Varnishes of low viscosity, usually containing extending pigment, for use as a first coating on open-grain woods. Its purpose is to afford a non-absorbent surface for succeeding coats of varnish. It is frequently colored so as to stain and fill in one operation.

LITHARGE: Lead monoxide of brownish color used as a source of lead for driers and for red lead.

LITHOL RED: Pigment which is bright red with bluish cast. Does not bleed in oils but tends to bleed when washed with soap and water.

LITHOPONE: White pigment made from barium sulphide and zinc sulphate.

LIVERING: Formation of curds or gelling. Coagulation of varnish finishing material into a viscous, rubber-like mass. Trouble is usually caused by chemical reaction of two or more products.

LONG-OIL VARNISH: Varnish with a large percentage of oil to gum resin--usually more than 25 gallons of oil to 100 pounds of resin. Long-oil varnish is more elastic, and more durable than short-oil varnish. Spar varnish is a typical example of long-oil varnish.

MADDER: Coloring matter originally derived from the pulverized root of a plant cultivated in Europe and Asia Minor. Now largely made synthetically.

MADDER LAKE: Transparent red pigment made by precipitating extract from madder root upon metallac salt base. Has excellent value in weak tints.

MAGNESIUM SILICATE: White extender pigment which adds "fluffiness" to products in which it is used. Provides very little opacity.

MAINTENANCE PAINTING: (1) Repair painting; any painting after the initial paint job; in a broader sense it includes painting of items installed on maintenance. (2) All painting except that done solely for aesthetics.

MALEIC RESINS: Resins based on reaction between maleic anhydride or maleic acid with glycerine and rosins.

MANDREL TEST: A physical bending test for adhesion and flexibility.

MANGANESE DRIER: Compound of manganese. Classified as "through" drier as it acts on both top and body of film.

MANILA RESINS: Natural resin, obtained by tapping Agathis alba trees. Alcohol soluble.

MARBLEIZING: Finishing process used to make surface being treated look like marble.

MARINE VARNISHES: Varnishes especially designed to resist long immersion in salt or fresh water and exposure to marine atmosphere.

MASKING TAPE: Adhesive coated paper tape used to mask or protect parts of surface not to be finished.

MASS TONE: Base covering.

MASTIC: A heavy bodied coating of high build.

MEDIUM VALUE (Color): Color midway between a dark color and a light color.

MELTING POINT: Temperature at which a crystalline solid changes to a liquid.

METAL PRIMER: First coating applied in finishing metal.

METALLIC SOAP: A compound of metal and organic acid. Metallic soaps are used as driers, fungicides, suspending agents, flatting agents.

METHYL ACETATE: A liquid (water white) used as a lacquer solvent.

METHYL ALCOHOL: Poisonous alcohol obtained by destructive distillation of wood.

METHYL ETHYL KETONE (MEK): A strong solvent.

METHYL ISOBUTYL KETONE (MIBK): A strong solvent.

MICA PIGMENT: Extender pigment made from silicates of aluminum and potassium which are split into very thin plates or sheets. Used as reinforcing pigment since it tends to reduce checking and cracking.

MIL: Unit of thickness, 1/1000 inch.

MILAGE: Coverage rate; square feet per gallon at a given thickness.

MILDEW: Whitish or spotted discoloration caused by parasitic fungi.

MILDEWCIDE: Substance poisonous to mildew; prevents or retards growth of mildew.

MILL SCALE: Oxide layer formed on steel by hot rolling.

MILL WHITE: White paint used to augment illumination on interior wall surface of in- dustrial plants, office and school buildings. The vehicle is usually of the varnish type.

MILORI BLUE: An iron blue pigment.

MINERAL BLACK: A natural black pigment based on graphite.

MINERAL OIL: Oil obtained from petroleum by distillation or other process.

MINERAL SPIRITS: Petroleum product which has about the same evaporation rate as gum turpentine.

MISCIBLE: Capable of being mixed. Examples: lacquer thinner is miscible with lacquer; water and alcohol are miscible.

MISSES: Holidays; skips; voids.

MOBILITY: The degree to which a material flows.

MOISTURE: Finely divided particles of water.

MOISTURE CONTENT OF WOOD: The amount of water contained in wood; usually expressed as a percentage of the weight of oven-dry wood.

MOISTURE VAPOR TRANSMISSION (MVT): Moisture vapor transmission rate through a membrane.

MONOCHROMATIC HARMONY: Color harmony formed by using shades and tints of a single color.

MOPPING: Swabbing, as with roofing asphalt.

MUD-CRACKING: Irregular cracking, as in a dried mud puddle.

MULTI-COLOR SPRAYING: Spraying a surface with two or more different colors at one time from one gun. The multiple colors exist separately within the material and when sprayed create an interlacing color network with each color retaining its individuality.

MURIATIC ACID: A dilute form of hydrochloric acid.

NAPHTHA: A product obtained between gasoline and benzine, in refining petroleum.

NATURAL RESINS: Essentially the result of exudation of trees. Divided into two large classes--dammars and copals. Resins are usually named after the locality in which they are found or the port of shipment.

NAVAL STORES: A group of products derived from the pine tree such as turpentine, rosin and pine oil.

NEOPRENE: A rubber-like film former; a type of elastomer based on polymers of 2-chloro-butadiene-1, 3.

NITROCELLULOSE: See cellulose nitrate.

NON-DRYING OILS: Oils which are unable to take up oxygen from the air and change from a liquid to a solid state. Mineral oils are non-drying oils.

NON-GRAIN-RAISING STAIN (NGR Stain): Wood stain which does not raise the grain of the wood. Made by dissolving dyes such as used in making water stains in special solvent, instead of water.

NONTOXIC: Not poisonous.

NON-VOLATILE: Portion of a product which does not evaporate at ordinary temperature.

NOZZLE: Orifice; sandblast nozzle; spray gun nozzle.

OATMEAL PAPER: Wallpaper made by sprinkling sawdust over adhesive surface.

OCHRE: Earth pigment, yellow in color.

OIL ABSORPTION: A measure of the ability of pigments to absorb oil.

OIL COLORS: Colors ground to form of paste, in linseed oil.

OIL LENGTH: Oil length in varnish is measured by the oil in gallons per hundred pounds of resin. A long-oil varnish is tougher than a short-oil varnish. Rubbing varnish is a typical short-oil varnish and spar varnish is a typical long-oil varnish.

OIL SOLUBLE: Capable of being dissolved in oil.

OIL STAIN (PENETRATING): Wood stain consisting of oil-soluble dyes and solvents such as turpentine, naphtha, benzol, etc. Penetrates into pores of wood; has tendency to bleed.

OITICICA OIL: Drying oil obtained from nut of oiticica tree.

OLEORESINOUS VARNISH: Varnish composed of resin or gum dissolved in a drying oil which hardens as it combines with oxygen from the air.

OPACITY: Hiding power.

OPAQUE: Impervious to light; not transparent.

OPEN-GRAIN WOODS: Woods of loose, open formation with minute openings between the fibers, such as oak and walnut, are called "open-grain" woods.

ORANGE MINERAL: Red lead prepared by roasting basic carbonate white lead. Used mainly in printing ink for its characteristic color.

ORANGE PEEL: Spray painting defect, in which the lacquer coat does not level down to a smooth surface but remains rough, like the peeling of an orange.

ORGANIC: Compounds produced by plants and animals.

ORGANOSOL: Film former containing resin plasticizer and solvent; colloidal dispersion of a resin in plasticizer containing more than 5 percent volatile content.

ORIFICE: Opening; hole.

OVERCOAT: Second coat; topcoat.

OVERLAP: Portion (width) of fresh paint covered by next layer.

OVERSPRAY: Sprayed paint which did not hit target; waste.

OXALIC ACID: Type of wood bleach.

OXIDIZE: To unite with oxygen.

PAINT: An adhesive coating which is applied as a thin film to various surfaces for decoration, protection, aid to morale, safety, sanitation, illumination, fire-retarding and other purposes.

PAINT COATING: Paint in position on a surface.

PAINT GAUGE: An instrument used to measure the thickness of paint coatings.

PAINT HEATER: Device for lowering viscosity of paint by heating.

PAINT PROJECT: Single paint job.

PAINT REMOVER: A mixture of active solvents used to remove paint and varnish coatings.

PAINT SYSTEM: The complete number and type of coats comprising a paint job. In a broader sense, surface preparation, pretreatments, dry film thickness, and manner of application are included in the definition of a paint system.

PARRAFFIN OIL: Light gravity mineral oil used as a lubricant in wood finishing.

PARA RED: Pigment which is coal tar product. Brilliant, opaque, non-fading, but has tendency to bleed.

PASS: (Spray) Motion of the spray gun in one direction only.

PASSIVATION: Act of making inert or unreactive.

PASTE WOOD FILLER: A compound supplied in the form of a stiff paste for filling the open-grain of hardwoods, such as oak, walnut and mahogany.

PEARL LACQUER: Lacquer into which has been suspended guanine crystals - - multi-faceted crystals found in skin attached to scales of sardine herring that thrive in cold water.

PEELING: Detachment of a paint film in relatively large pieces. Paint applied to a damp, or greasy, surface usually "peels." Sometimes it is due to moisture back of the painted surface.

PENETRATING STAIN: Stain made by dissolving oil-soluble dyes in oil or alcohol.

PENTAERYTHRITOL RESINS: Resin made by reacting pentaerythritol, a high alcohol, with rosin.

PERILLA OIL: Drying oil obtained from seeds of brush called Perilla Ocymoide, grown largely in China and Japan.

PERMEABILITY: Quality or state of being permeable.

pH: A measure of alkalinity, acidity or neutrality in acqueous (watery) solutions.

PHENOL-ALDEHYDE RESINS: Resins produced from phenols and formaldehyde.

PHENOLIC RESIN: Resin based essentially on reaction between phenol and formaldehyde.

PHENOLIC-RESIN PRIMER-SEALER: Finish well suited for fir and other softwoods, which penetrates into pores of wood, dries, and equalizes density of hard and soft grains.

PHOSPHATIZE: Form a thin inert phosphate coating on surface usually by treatment with H_3PO_4 (phosphoric acid).

PHOSPHORESCENT PAINT: Luminous paint which emits light after the white light has been turned off. No phosphorus is used.

PHTHALIC ANHYDRIDE: A white crystalline material used in making synthetic resins.

PHTHALOCYANINE BLUE: Organic blue pigment developed synthetically. Outstanding in fade resistance.

PHTHALOCYANINE GREEN: Complex copper compound pigment with bluish-green cast.

PICKLING: A dipping process for cleaning steel and other metals; the pickling agent is usually an acid.

"PICK UP SAGS:" When a too-heavy coating of paint has been applied and starts to sag, or run down the surface, the painter brushes up through the sagging paint to level it off.

PIGMENT: Material in the form of fine powders insoluble in oils, varnishes, lacquers, thinners and the like. Used to impart color, opacity, certain consistency characteristics and other effects.

PIGMENT GRIND: Dispersion of pigment in a liquid vehicle.

PIGMENT OIL STAIN (Wiping Stain): Consists of finely ground insoluble color pigments, such as used in paints, in solution with linseed oil, varnish, mineral spirits, etc. according to formula being used.

PIGMENT VOLUME CONCENTRATION (PVC): Percent by volume occupied by pigment in dried film.

PIN-HOLING: Formation of small holes through the entire thickness of coating; see cratering.

PIN STRIPES: Fine stripes.

PITCH: A black or dark viscous substance obtained as a residue in distilling tar, oil from bones, etc. It also occurs in natural form, as asphalt.

PLASTER OF PARIS: A white powdery substance formed by calcining (heating) gypsum. When mixed with water it forms a paste which soon sets. Originally brought from a suburb of Paris.

PLASTICIZER: An agent added to certain plastics and protective coatings to impart flexibility, softness, or otherwise modify the properties.

PLASTISOL: Film former containing resin and plasticizer with no solvents.

POLE-GUN: Spray gun equipped with an extension tube.

"POLISHING:" Said of wall paints where shiny spots or surfaces have resulted from washing or wiping.

POLYAMIDE: Product used in making dripless paint. See thixotropic paint.

POLYCHROME FINISH: Finish obtained by blending together a number of colors.

POLYMERIC: Composed of repeating chemical units. All plastics and polymers are polymeric.

POLYVINYL ACETATE (PVA): A synthetic resin used extensively in emulsion (water) paints; produced by the polymerization of vinyl acetate.

POLYVINYL CHLORIDE (PVC): A synthetic resin used in solvent type coatings and fluid bed coatings, produced by the polymerization of vinyl chloride; PVC is also used in emulsion (water) paints.

POT LIFE: Time interval after mixing during which liquid material is usable with no difficulty.

POWDER STAINS: Stains in form of powder which are mixed with solvents to produce wood stains.

PRECIPITATE: A substance separated from a solution in concrete state (solid form) by chemical action or by application of heat or cold.

PRIMARY COLOR: A color which cannot be obtained by mixing other colors.

"PRIME IN THE SPOTS:" Apply a priming coat to those spots that have been scraped, wire brushed, shellacked, have had the old paint burned off or consist of newly patched plaster.

PRIMER: Paint applied next to surface of material being painted. First coat in painting operation.

"PRINT FREE:" Paint sufficiently dry so that no imprint is left when something is pressed against it.

PROFILE: Surface contour as viewed from edge.

PROOF (SPIRIT): Indication of percentages of water and grain alcohol; a mixture which is 100 proof would be 50 percent water, 50 percent alcohol by volume. A mixture which is 120 proof would contain 60 percent alcohol.

PRUSSIAN BLUE (Ferric Ferrocyanide): Pigment which is deep in color and has great strength. Not affected by acids; easily affected by alkali.

PUFFING AGENT: A synthetic organic product used to produce increased viscosity in varnishes and paints.

PUMICE STONE: A stone of volcanic origin, which is pulverized to produce a soft abrasive used extensively in rubbing finishing coats of fine wood finishes.

PUTTY: A dough-like mixture of pigment and oil (usually whiting and linseed oil--sometimes mixed with white lead). Used to set glass in window frames, fill nail holes and cracks.

"PUTTY COAT:" Final smooth coat of plaster.

PYROXYLIN: See cellulose nitrate.

QUICK DRYING: A material with a relatively short drying time.

"RAW:" Raw linseed oil.

RAW OIL: Oil as received from the press or separated from the solvent in the solvent extraction process.

RAW SIENNA: See Sienna.

RECOAT TIME: Time interval required between application of successive coats.

RED LABEL GOODS: Flammable or explosive materials with flash points below 80 deg. F. (26.7 deg. C.).

RED LEAD: A compound formed by roasting lead or litharge. It is used extensively in paints for protecting iron and steel against corrosion.

REDUCER: Volatile ingredients used to thin or reduce viscosity of a finishing material.

REFINED SHELLAC: A grade of orange or white shellac from which the wax has been removed.

REFLECTANCE: Degree of light reflection.

REFRACTIVE INDEX: Ratio of velocity of light in a certain medium compared with its velocity in air under same conditions.

RELATIVE HUMIDITY: Indication in terms of percentage of amount of water vapor in a given volume of air at a given temperature, compared to total amount of water vapor the air could hold at the given temperature.

REMOVERS: Compositions designed to soften old varnish or paint coats so that they may be easily removed by scraping or washing.

RESIN HARDNESS: Method of indicating hardness of resins. Usually from No. 1 (hardest) to No. 6.

RESINS: Normally transparent or translucent semi-solid or solid substances of either vegetable or synthetic origin which when heated are soluble in drying oils and solvents. Once dissolved they remain in solution.

RETARDERS (Lacquer): Slow drying solvents or extenders added to lacquer to delay drying of the lacquer.

"RIDE THE BRUSH:" To bear down on the brush to the extent that the paint is applied with the sides of the bristles instead of the flat ends. This shortens the life of the brush.

ROLLER COATING: Process of finishing an article by means of hard rubber or steel rollers.

ROSIN: A resin obtained from pine trees containing principally isomers of abietic acid. Wood rosin is obtained from stump or dead wood, using steam distillation. Gum rosin is obtained from the living tree.

ROTTENSTONE: A siliceous (contains silica) limestone which when finely pulverized, is used in wood finishing. It has negligible cutting action but is fine for polishing. Rottenstone is also known as tripoli.

RUBBING OIL: Neutral, medium-heavy mineral oil used as a lubricant for pumice stone in rubbing varnish, also lacquer.

RUBBING VARNISH: A hard-drying varnish which may be rubbed with an abrasive and water or oil to a uniform leveled surface.

RUNS: Also known as "sags." Irregularities of a surface due to uneven flow.

RUST: Rusting of metal is generally explained as oxidizing process where oxygen from air combines with iron to form a metallic oxide; water combines with oxide to form rust.

RUST-INHIBITIVE WASHES: Solutions which etch the metal and form a dull gray coating of uniformly fine texture, thus producing rust-inhibitive surface receptive to priming coat.

SAFFLOWER OIL: Oil from seed of thistle-like plant grown mostly in Egypt and India.

SAGS: See runs.

SALT: Substance that results from reaction between acid and base.

SALT SPRAY: A salt fog test environment.

SANDBLAST: Blast cleaning using sand as an abrasive.

"SAND DOWN:" Remove the gloss of an old finish and smooth it prior to refinishing.

"SAND FINISH:" Rough finish plaster wall.

SANDING SEALER: A lacquer used as a seal coat over a filler. Generally given some filling action by adding inert substances.

SAPONIFY: To convert an oil or a fat into soap by action of an alkali. When linseed oil paint comes in contact with a surface that contains strong alkali and water, like new concrete floor, the oil is saponified and loses its bonding qualities.

SAPONIFICATION NUMBER: Number of milligrams of potassium hydroxide needed to neutralize the acid in one gram of substance after it has been saponified.

SATIN FINISH: Term used in describing dried film of paint or other finishing material which does not have a full luster, but a dull luster like that of satin.

SCALING: Finish condition in which pieces of the dried finishing material come off, exposing the surface below.

SCARLET LAKE: Pigment made by precipitation of aniline color upon base of alumina hydrate and barium sulphate.

SEALER: A liquid coating composition, usually transparent, such as varnish, that also contains pigment for sealing porous surfaces, such as plaster, preparatory to application of the finish coats. Wood floor sealer is a thin varnish.

SECONDARY COLORS: Colors made by combining primary colors. For example, the secondary color orange, is obtained by mixing red and yellow.

SELF-CLEANING: Term used to describe paint in which rate of chalking is controlled so dirt on surface will be washed away with accumulated chalk.

SELF PRIMING: Use of same paint for primer and for subsequent coats. The paint may be thinned differently for the different coats.

SELVEDGES: Edges of wallpaper without printing.

SEMI-DRYING OILS: Oils which "dry" to a soft, tacky film. Principal semi-drying oil used in the paint industry is soybean oil.

SEMI-GLOSS: Sheen on dry finish which is about half way between dead flat finish and full gloss.

SERRATED: Notched, or toothed on the edge.

SETTING UP: Initial drying of coating to point where it is no longer able to flow.

SETTLING: Caking; sediment.

SHADE: Degree of color obtained by adding black to a color or hue.

SHADING LACQUER: Transparent colored lacquer used in shading. Applied with a spray gun.

"SHADOWING:" When preceding coats show through the last coat, the finish is said to be "shadowing."

SHARP LUSTER: A very high gloss.

SHELF LIFE: Maximum interval in which a material may be stored in usable condition.

SHELLAC: Resinous material commonly known as flake shellac; secreted by insect. Shellac is obtainable in two forms--orange and bleached.

SHEPHERD VIOLET TONER: A complex manganese phosphate pigment having extreme acid resistance and light fastness.

SHIP BOTTOM PAINT: Special product designed to prevent corrosion and fouling with marine life on the bottom of ships.

"SHOP PRIMED OR SHOP COATED:" Said of a prefabricated article that has been primed at the factory.

"SHORT:" When paint is "short," it is usually due to the absence of easy brushing liquids. A "short" paint, therefore, does not have uniform appearance.

SHORT-OIL VARNISH: One made with a relatively low proportion of oil to resin. See long oil varnish.

SHOT BLASTING: Blast cleaning using steel shot as the abrasive.

SHRINKAGE: Decrease in volume on drying.

SIENNA: A pigment obtained from the earth, which is brownish yellow when raw; orange red or reddish brown when burnt.

SILEX: A form of silica used extensively in making paste wood fillers; it is chemically inert and does not absorb moisture or shrink.

SILICA: An inert pigment made from quartz rock, which is highly resistant to acids, alkalis, heat and light.

SILICATE OF SODA (Water-glass): White powdery substance, soluble in water; dries to hard, transparent film when exposed to air.

SILICON CARBIDE: Abrasive crystals are shiny black; very hard and brittle. Made by fusing silica sand and coke in electric furnace.

SILICONE RESINS (SILICONES): Resins derived from silica. Have exceptional resistance to heat and corrosive chemicals, good electrical properties. Silicone resins are used as vehicles for high temperature paints and enamels; also for up-grading alkyd enamels.

SILK SCREEN FINISHING: Process of finishing where paint is forced through open meshes of a fabric screen. Parts of the screen are blocked off and do not print, thus producing the design.

SILKING: A surface defect characterized by parallel hair-like striations in coated films.

SILT: Particles so fine that they are scarcely visible to the naked eye, unless finishing material is placed in glass tube and placed before proper light.

SILVER LEAF: Thin leaf made of silver, used mostly for lettering on glass. Aluminum leaf is used where silver color is required on wood or metal surfaces as silver would tarnish.

SINGAPORE DAMMAR: A dammar found in the Malay states and adjacent islands. Exported from Singapore.

SINGLE ROLL: A single roll of American-made wallpaper is a roll containing 36 square feet of paper. Wallpaper usually comes in bolts which contain two or three single rolls.

SIZE: Solution of gelatin-type material, such as resin, glue or starch, used to fill or seal pores of surface and prevent absorption of finishing materials.

SKIN: A tough layer or skin formed on the surface of a paint or varnish in the container. Caused by exposure to air.

"SKIPPY:" Said of paint that causes the brush to skip on the surface, leaving some spots uncoated and others too thickly coated. This condition can be caused by lack of sufficient vehicle, to permit easy, uniform application or by liquids that "pull."

SKIPS: Uncoated spots on finished surface.

SLATE FLOUR: Filler used to considerable extent in asphalt mixtures in roofing mastics, etc.

"SLIP UNDER THE BRUSH:" When coating materials are easy to apply, this is sometimes said of them.

SLOW DRYING: Requiring 24 hours or longer before recoating.

SMALT: Deep blue pigment prepared by fusing together potash, silica and oxide of cobalt, and reducing to powder the glass thus formed. Smalt is sometimes applied to freshly coated surfaces to provide unusual decorating effect.

SOLID: Nonvolatile portion of paint.

SOLIDS VOLUME: Percentage of total volume occupied by nonvolatiles.

SOLUBILITY: Quality or state of being soluble or dissolved.

SOLVENT: A liquid capable of dissolving a material is said to be a solvent for the material.

SOLVENT BALANCE: Ratio of amounts of different solvents in a mixture of solvents.

SOLVENT RELEASE: Ability to permit solvents to evaporate.

SOYBEAN OIL: Oil made from seed of soybean, a leguminous annual plant.

SPACKLING COMPOUND: Kind of plaster which is used to fill surface irregularities and cracks in plaster. This compound when mixed with paste paint makes what is known as Swedish putty.

SPALLING: The cracking, breaking or splintering of materials, usually due to heat.

SPAR VARNISH: A very durable varnish designed for severe service on exterior surfaces. Such a varnish must be resistant to rain, sunlight and heat. Named from its suitability for the spars of ships.

SPATTER FINISH: Finish which provides a spattered or spackled effect.

SPECIFIC GRAVITY: The weight of a given volume of a liquid compared with the same volume of water at the same temperature.

SPECTRAL COLORS: Band of colors produced when ray of sunshine is bent by glass prism.

SPECULAR GLOSS: Mirror-like reflectance.

SPIRIT STAIN: A stain made by dissolving a dye in an alcohol.

SPIRIT VARNISH: A varnish made by dissolving a resin in a solvent. It dries primarily by evaporation rather than by oxidation.

SPOT REPAIR: Preventive maintenance; repainting of small areas.

SPRAY HEAD: Combination of needle, tip, and air cap.

SPRAY PATTERN: Configuration of spray, gun held steady.

SPREADING RATE: Amount of area a given volume of coating material can be spread over by spraying, brushing or other method of application. Spreading rate is generally indicated by square feet covered per gallon.

SQUEEGEE: Rigid bar applicator.

STAIN WAX: (Penetrating): Wood finish which produces color of penetrating stain with luster of wax.

STAIN (WOOD): Finish for wood containing a dye or pigment. Stain sinks into fibers of wood to a certain extent while paint and lacquer ordinarily do not penetrate wood.

STAND OIL: Heat-thickened vegetable oil (or combination of vegetable oils, such as linseed and tung).

STARCH COATING: Protective coating for surfaces coated with flat paint, also wallpapers made with colors that do not smear when wet. Starch coating is made by soaking ordinary laundry starch in small quantity of cold water to break up lumps. Boiled water is then poured on to cook starch and make it transparent. Mix to consistency of cream, let cool, and apply with large paint or calcimine brush. Coating should be stippled while still wet, to remove brush marks. It may be removed by using water and sponge.

STEAM CLEAN: A cleaning process using live steam.

STEAM DISTILLED WOOD TURPENTINE: Turpentine made from pine tree stumps by treating shredded chips with live steam to produce a distillate which is fractionated (separated) to yield turpentine, pine oil, and solid residue (rosin).

STEEL WOOL: Steel in fine strands. Comes in grades 3, 2, 1, 0, 2-0, 3-0 and 4-0 (finest).

STENCILING: Placing a design on a wall or other surface by applying the finish through a template cut out of thin, flat paper or metal.

STICK SHELLAC: Shellac which comes in solid stick form. Used extensively for furniture patching.

STIPPLE FINISH: Finish obtained by tapping surface with stipple brush, before paint is dry.

STRAIN: To filter.

"STRETCH:" The width of the area on which a painter will normally apply paint across a ceiling or down a side wall.

STRIKING IN: Materials used in finishing are said to "strike in" when they soften undercoats and sink into them.

"STRIP:" Complete removal of an old finish with paint removers.

STRIPING: Edge painting prior to priming.

STROKE: (Spray) A single pass in one direction.

STYRENE-BUTADIENE RESIN: Synthetic rubber resin; liquid styrene and butadiene gas are copolymerized to form chemical-resistant product with excellent film-forming properties.

SUBLIMATE: A solid substance which, when heated, passes into vapor state and, when cooled, returns to the solid state without passing through liquid state.

SUBSTRATE: Surface to be painted.

SUCTION SPOTTING: Spotting of paint job caused by oil in new coat being absorbed by spots or porous areas of surface.

SUNDAYS: Place skipped when applying finishing materials to a surface.

SURFACE DRYING: Drying of a finishing material on top while the bottom remains more or less soft.

SURFACE TENSION: Property of finishing material which causes it to try to shrink.

SURFACER: A paint used to smooth the surface before finish coats are applied.

SURGE CHAMBER: (Airless spray) A device to eliminate uneven fluid flow.

SWEDISH PUTTY: See Spackling compound.

SYNTHETIC RESIN: An artificial resin or plastic produced by systematic exploitation of chemical reaction of organic substances.

TACKINESS: Stickiness. When a painting material dries out, gels or sets up, it loses tackiness, or stickiness.

TACK RAG: Cloth impregnated with varnish used in wood finishing to remove abrasive dust from surface of wood, before applying finishing materials.

TALC: A hydrous magnesium aluminum silicate used as an extender in paints. Helps make paint smooth. It is also known as talcum powder and soapstone.

TALL OIL: A blend of resin and oil acids obtained as a by-product from the sulfate process for making paper.

TAPE TEST: A particular type of adhesion test.

TAR: A thick brown or black liquid with a characteristic odor--a residue from the distillation of wood, peat, coal, shale or other vegetable or mineral material.

TEMPERA: A water-thinned or water-emulsion paint.

TENSILE STRENGTH: Resistance to elongation; the greatest longitudinal stress a substance can bear without rupture or remaining permanently elongated.

TERTIARY COLORS: Colors made by combining colors on color wheel that are adjacent, like red and orange.

TEST PATTERN: Spray pattern used in adjusting spray gun.

TEXTURE PAINT: One which may be manipulated by brush, trowel or other tool to give various patterns.

THERMOPLASTIC: Material which can be repeatedly softened by heat and formed to new shape, without chemical change.

THERMOSETTING: Material which undergoes irreversible chemical reaction when heated and molded. Once formed, it cannot be reheated and reshaped.

THINNERS: Volatile liquids used to lower or otherwise regulate the consistency of paint and varnish.

THIXOTROPIC PAINT: Property exhibited by some paint of becoming fluid when shaken, or disturbed. After cessation of mechanical disturbance, such as stirring or putting brush into paint, rigidity develops again.

"THROUGH DRYING:" Uniform drying of the entire paint film.

THUMBNAIL PROOF: Checking hardness of a finish by pressing thumbnail against it.

TIFFANY FINISH: A multi-color, blended finish, used mostly for wall decoration.

TINCTURE: A dilute extract of a chemical or drug.

TINGE: Slight trace of color.

TINT: A light value of a color--one made by adding white to the color.

TITANIUM: A metal which is the basis for the pigment, titanium dioxide.

TITANIUM CALCIUM: Paint pigment made by combining titanium dioxide of rutile type and calcium sulphate.

TITANIUM DIOXIDE: White pigment used extensively in paint making. Comes in two forms, rutile and anatase. It is chemically inactive and is not affected by dilute acids, heat or light.

TOLUIDINE RED: Brilliant non-bleeding red pigment made from coal tar product.

TOLUOL (TOLUENE): Lacquer diluent made normally by coal tar distillation.

TONE: A graduation of color, either a hue, a tint, or a shade; as a gray tone.

TONER: A color modifier.

"TOO MUCH DRAG:" Refers to paint that has excessive "pull" or "drag" in its application.

TOOTH: Roughened or absorbent quality of a surface which affects adhesion and application of a coating.

TOUCH-UP PAINTING: Spot repair painting usually conducted a few months after initial painting.

TOXIC: Poisonous.

TRAFFIC PAINT: A paint--usually white, red or yellow--used to designate traffic lanes, safety zones and intersections.

TRIAD COLOR HARMONY: Harmony obtained by using colors from three equidistant points of the color wheel. Red, yellow and blue make up a triad.

TRIM ENAMEL PAINT: Surface coating differing from ordinary house paint by faster drying, by having more gloss and showing fewer brush marks. Used mostly on trim, shutters, screens.

TRUE COMPLEMENT COLOR HARMONY: Two colors directly across the color wheel from each other are true complements. Examples are red and green, and orange and blue.

TUMBLING: Method of finishing or polishing by using a tumbling barrel. Articles to be finished and finishing material are put into barrel which is turned or tumbled.

TUNG OIL: Oil obtained from seeds of fruit of tung tree.

TURPENTINE: Colorless, volatile liquid having a characteristic odor and taste. Obtained by distillation of the oleoresinous secretions found in living and dead pine trees.

"TURPS:" Slang for turpentine.

TUSCAN RED: A red pigment consisting of a combination of iron oxides and a lake.

TWO-COAT SYSTEM: Two-coat paint application for initial painting.

TWO-COMPONENT GUN: One having two separate fluid sources leading to spray head.

ULTRAMARINE BLUE: Blue pigment made by heating a mixture of China clay, sodium carbonate, carbon and sulphur. It is not affected by alkalies, but is easily affected by acids.

ULTRA-VIOLET LIGHT: Light of short wave length which is invisible but has active chemical effect on finishing materials.

UMBER: A pigment obtained from the earth, which when raw is brown in color; when burnt it has a reddish hue. The color of umber is due to oxides of iron and of manganese.

UNDERCOAT: Second coat in three-coat work, or first coat in repainting.

UNDERTONE: A color covered up by other colors but when viewed by transmitted light,

Dictionary of Terms

shows through the other colors modifying the effect.

UNGROUNDED PAPER: Wallpaper without a basic background color.

UNSAPONIFIABLE MATTER: Substance in resins and fats which does not unite with caustic alkali to form a soap.

UREA-FORMALDEHYDE RESIN: Product obtained by chemical reaction between urea and formaldehyde in presence of catalyst.

UREA-MELAMINE RESINS: Melamine-formaldehyde resins which produce tough finish that approaches porcelain.

URETHANE RESINS: A particular group of film formers; isocyanate resins.

U.S.P: Letters affixed to name of material to indicate that it conforms in grade to specifications of United States Pharmacopoeia and that it is approved for use in medicinal preparations. The material does not necessarily have to be chemically pure.

VACATIONS: The uncoated portion of a finished object. Also known as "skips" and "holidays."

VALUE: Term used to distinguish dark colors from light ones. Dark values are known as shades; light values as tints.

VAN DYKE BROWN: A brown pigment which consists of decomposed vegetable matter that has almost approached the coal state. It is weak in hiding power compared to umber and sienna.

VARNISH: A liquid composition which is converted to a translucent or transparent solid film after application in a thin layer.

VARNISH (CLEAR): Varnish which is transparent and contains no pigment.

VARNISH-STAIN: Interior varnish tinted with pigments or dyes.

VEGETABLE OILS: Oils obtained from the seeds or nuts of vegetable growth. Includes linseed, soybean, perilla, tung, castor, etc.

VEHICLE: Liquid portion of paint. See binder.

VENETIAN RED: Pigment with brick-red color, made synthetically by calcining copperas and whiting.

VENTURI: A tube having a restriction to promote a velocity increase.

VERMILLION: Sulphide of mercury used as a pigment.

VERTICAL PATTERN: A spray pattern whose longest dimension is vertical.

VINYL RESIN: Resin or polymer produced by reaction between acetylene and acetic acid in presence of mercuric catalyst.

VISCOSITY: Internal friction of a fluid which influences its rate of flow or exhibits resistance to change of form.

VM&P NAPHTHA: Varnish and paint manufacturers naphtha; an aliphatic solvent.

VOLATILE: Said of a liquid that evaporates.

WALLBOARD: Term refers to such boards as pressed cellulose fibers, plasterboard, cement-asbestos board, plywood, used in place of plaster in interior surfaces.

WALL SIZE: Solution such as glue, starch, casein, shellac, varnish or lacquer, used to seal or fill pores of wall surface to stop suction, counteract chemicals or stains and prepare surface for paint, paper or fabric.

WARM COLORS: Colors in which red-orange predominates. This term is applied not only because of the association with fire, heat and sunshine, but because they are actually warmer than cool colors.

WARMING COLORS: Any color except green may be "warmed" by adding red. Green is warmed by adding yellow.

WASH COAT: A very thin coat of finishing material, usually shellac.

WASH PRIMER: A thin inhibiting paint usually chromate pigmented with a polyvinyl butyrate binder.

WASHING: Rapid dissolution or emulsification of a paint film when wet with water.

WATER BLASTING: Blast cleaning using high velocity water.

WATER PAINT: Paint in which water is used as thinner.

WATER SPOTTING: Spotty changes in the color or gloss of a paint film. May be caused by various factors, such as emulsification or the solution of water soluble components.

WATER STAIN: Stain soluble in and mixed with water.

WATER-THINNED PAINT: A paint whose thinner is mainly water. The binder may be a material that (1) requires water for setting, e.g., Portland cement; (2) which is soluble in water, e.g., casein; (3) which is emulsifiable in water, e.g., flat wall paint binders.

WATER WHITE: Transparent and colorless like water.

WAVE LENGTH (Color term): Computed distance between vibrations of light that produce visible color sensation on eye. In visible spectrum, red-orange has longest wave length; violet the shortest. Wave lengths are measured in millimicrons. Wave lengths shorter than violet are called ultraviolet; wave lengths longer than red-orange are called infrared.

WAX: Substance derived from vegetable, animal and mineral matter used in painting industry mostly for making polishes.

WEATHEROMETER: A testing device intended to simulate atmospheric weathering.

"WET EDGE TIME:" The length of time before a "stretch" of paint sets up without showing lap marks when the painter applies the next "stretch."

WET FILM GAUGE: Device for measuring wet film thickness.

WHITE LEAD (Basic Carbonate): Basic carbonate white lead is a compound of lead, carbon dioxide and water. Lead is melted and cast into disks or "buckles," which are about six inches in diameter. The buckles are placed in porcelain pots each containing dilute acetic acid. The pots are covered with boards and layers of tanbark. Heat and carbonic acid generated by fermentation of the tanbark, with the acid vapors, combine to transform the lead into basic carbonate white lead.

WHITE LEAD (CARTER PROCESS): In the Carter process melted lead is blown into fine granules by a jet of air or superheated steam. The powdered lead is placed in revolving drums, or cylinders and subjected to the action of air and carbon dioxide gas from burning coal.

WHITE LEAD (Basic sulphate): White pigment obtained from lead sulphide ore by a process of fuming or burning.

WHITEWASH: One of oldest paints. Principal ingredient is lime paste. Whitewash formula: Casein 5 lb., Trisodium phosphate 3 lb., Lime paste 8 gal. Eight gallons of stiff lime paste are obtained by slaking 25 lb. of quicklime in 10 gal. of water. Casein should be soaked in 2 gal. of hot water until softened. Trisodium phosphate dissolved in 1 gal. of water is added to casein mixture and casein allowed to dissolve. This solution should be mixed with lime paste and 3 gal. of water.

WHITING: Calcium carbonate, limestone, or chalk in pigment form. Used extensively for making putty and as an extender in paints.

WIPING STAIN: See Pigment oil stain.

WIRE BRUSH: A hand cleaning tool comprised of bundles of wires; also the act of cleaning a surface with a wire brush, including power brushes.

WIRE EDGE JOINT (Wallpaper): Joint made by trimming both selvedges and lapping one edge slightly over the other.

WITHERING: Withering or loss of gloss is often caused by varnishing open-pore woods without filling pores, use of improper undercoating, and applying topcoat before undercoat has dried.

WOOD ALCOHOL: Poisonous alcohol obtained by destructive distillation of wood.

WRINKLE FINISH: A varnish or enamel film which exhibits fine wrinkles or ridges. Used extensively as a novelty finish.

XANTHIC: Containing yellow, or pertaining to yellow color.

XYLOL (XYLENE): Coal tar distillate used in the paint industry as a solvent, as a solvent ingredient, and as a process material in synthetic enamel.

YELLOWING: Development of yellow color or cast, in whites, on aging.

ZINC: Ore obtained from mines; used extensively as paint pigment.

ZINC CHROMATE (Zinc Yellow): Metal priming pigment with important rust-inhibitive properties.

ZINC DRIERS: Do not function well when used alone but have many properties which are important when used with other driers.

ZINC DUST: Finely divided zinc metal, gray in color. Used primarily in metal primers.

ZINC (LEADED): Basic lead sulphate united with zinc oxide.

ZINC OXIDE: A compound of zinc used as a white pigment in many types of paint.

ZINC SULPHIDE: Compound of zinc used as white pigment in paints. See lithopone.

INDEX

Index